Pimp My LUNCH

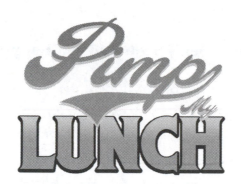

Also by Jerry Scott and Jim Borgman

Zits: Sketchbook 1
Growth Spurt: Zits Sketchbook 2
Don't Roll Your Eyes at Me, Young Man!: Zits Sketchbook 3
Are We an "Us"?: Zits Sketchbook 4
Zits Unzipped: Zits Sketchbook 5
Busted!: Zits Sketchbook 6
Road Trip: Zits Sketchbook 7
Teenage Tales: Zits Sketchbook No. 8
Thrashed: Zits Sketchbook No. 9

Treasuries
Humongous Zits
Big Honkin' Zits
Zits: Supersized
Random Zits

Pimp My LUNCH

Zits® Sketchbook No. 10

by JERRY SCOTT and JIMBORGMAN"

**Andrews McMeel
Publishing**

Kansas City

Zits® is syndicated internationally by King Features Syndicate, Inc. For information, write King Features Syndicate, Inc., 888 Seventh Avenue, New York, New York 10019.

07 08 09 BBG 10 9 8 7 6 5

ISBN-13: 978-0-7407-5443-2
ISBN-10: 0-7407-5443-2

Library of Congress Control Number: 2005925657

Zits® may be viewed online at
www.kingfeatures.com.

www.andrewsmcmeel.com

To Waldo and Mulder. Good dogs.

—J.B. & J.S.

Zits

by JERRY SCOTT and JIM BORGMAN

CURFEW: 11 PM

NO UNSUPERVISED PARTIES

LIMITED TIME ON THE INTERNET

NO R-RATED MOVIES

NO RIDING IN CARS DRIVEN BY ANYONE UNDER 25

SCOTT and BORGMAN

WE DON'T WANT YOU TO THINK OF THESE SUMMER RULES AS RESTRICTIONS, BUT AS SAFE BOUNDARIES, JEREMY.

I'LL KEEP THAT IN MIND.

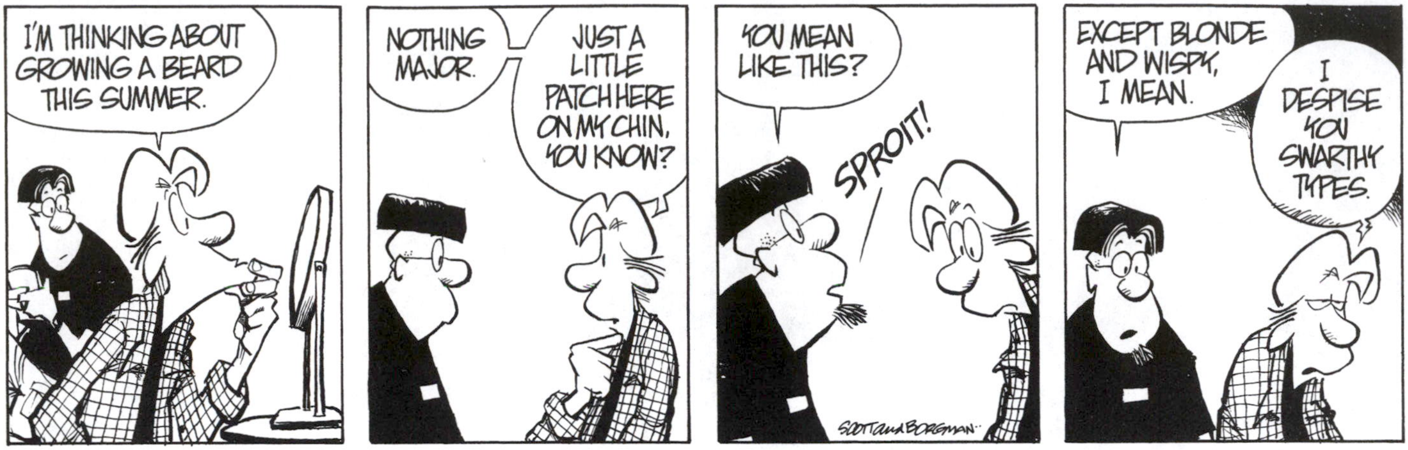
I'M THINKING ABOUT GROWING A BEARD THIS SUMMER.
NOTHING MAJOR.
JUST A LITTLE PATCH HERE ON MY CHIN, YOU KNOW?
YOU MEAN LIKE THIS?
SPROIT!
SCOTT and BORGMAN
EXCEPT BLONDE AND WISPY, I MEAN.
I DESPISE YOU SWARTHY TYPES.

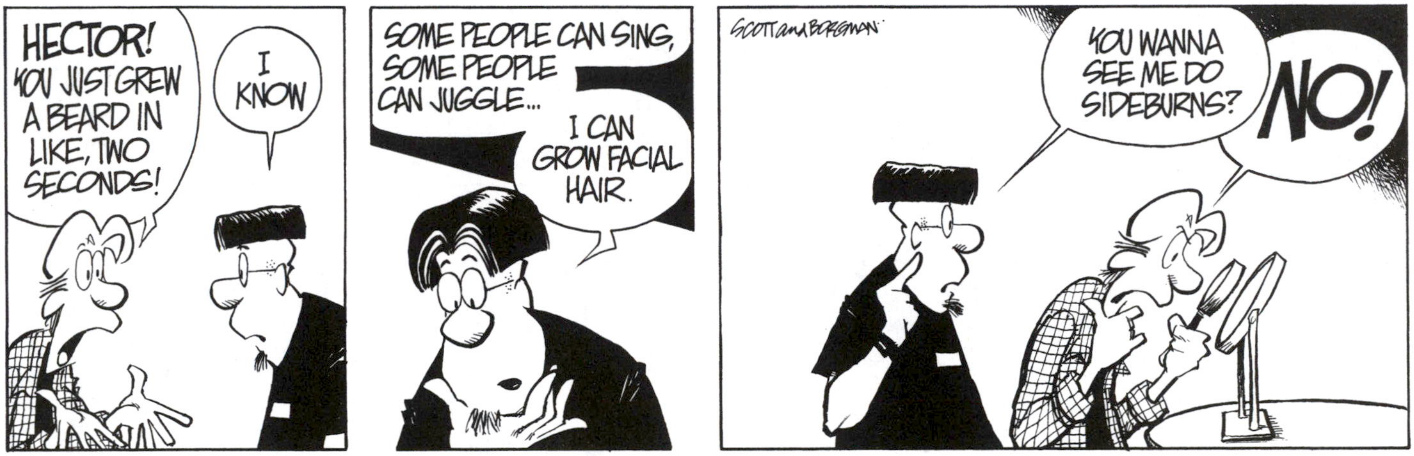
HECTOR! YOU JUST GREW A BEARD IN LIKE, TWO SECONDS!
I KNOW
SOME PEOPLE CAN SING, SOME PEOPLE CAN JUGGLE...
I CAN GROW FACIAL HAIR.
SCOTT and BORGMAN
YOU WANNA SEE ME DO SIDEBURNS?
NO!

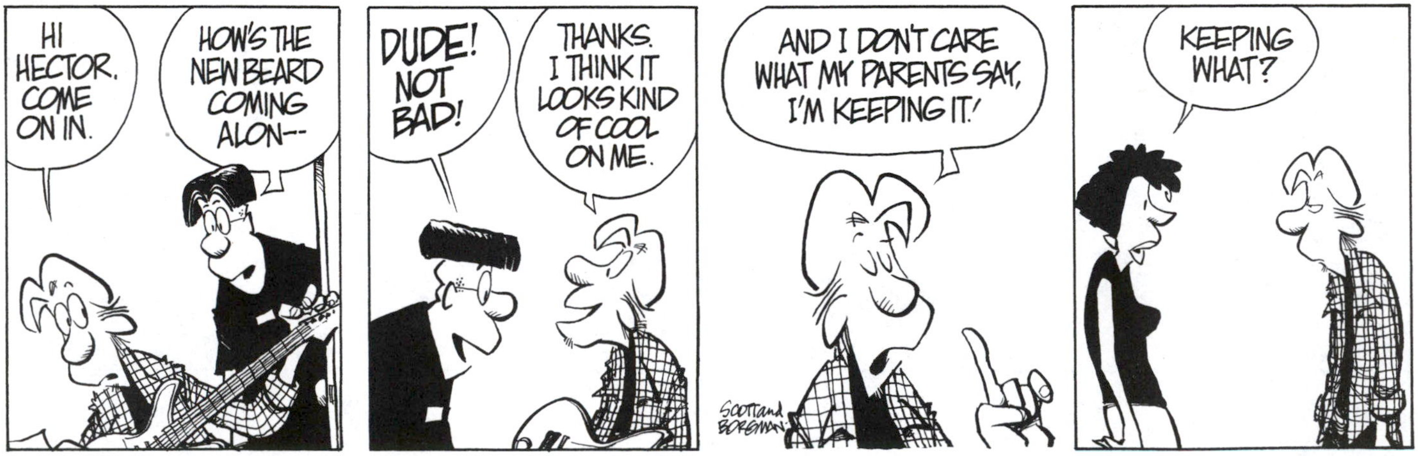
HI HECTOR. COME ON IN.
HOW'S THE NEW BEARD COMING ALON--
DUDE! NOT BAD!
THANKS. I THINK IT LOOKS KIND OF COOL ON ME.
AND I DON'T CARE WHAT MY PARENTS SAY, I'M KEEPING IT!
SCOTT and BORGMAN
KEEPING WHAT?

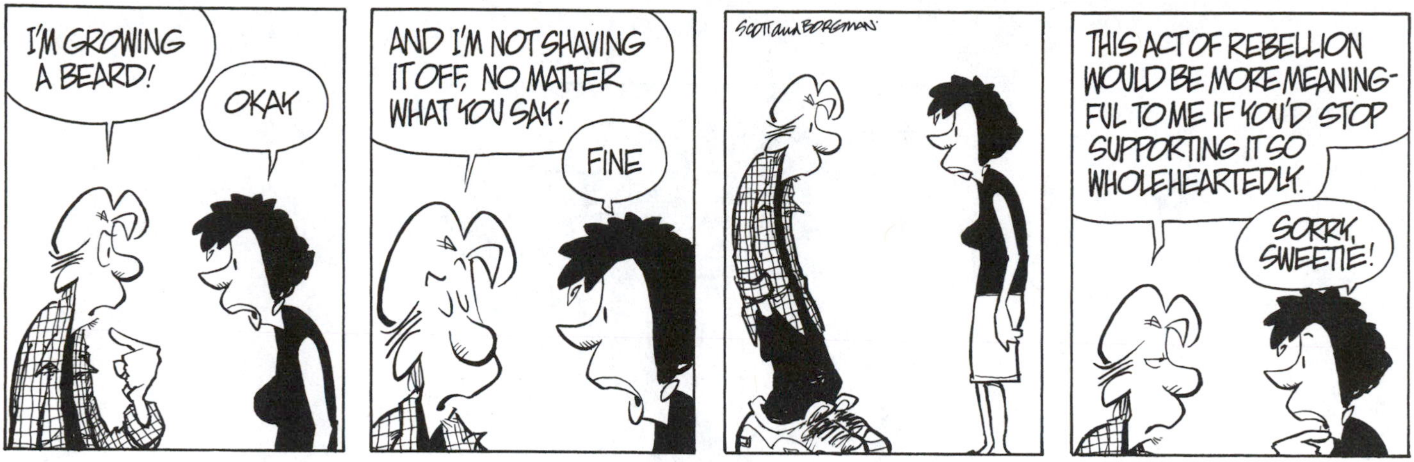
I'M GROWING A BEARD!
OKAY
AND I'M NOT SHAVING IT OFF, NO MATTER WHAT YOU SAY!
FINE
SCOTT and BORGMAN
THIS ACT OF REBELLION WOULD BE MORE MEANINGFUL TO ME IF YOU'D STOP SUPPORTING IT SO WHOLEHEARTEDLY.
SORRY, SWEETIE!

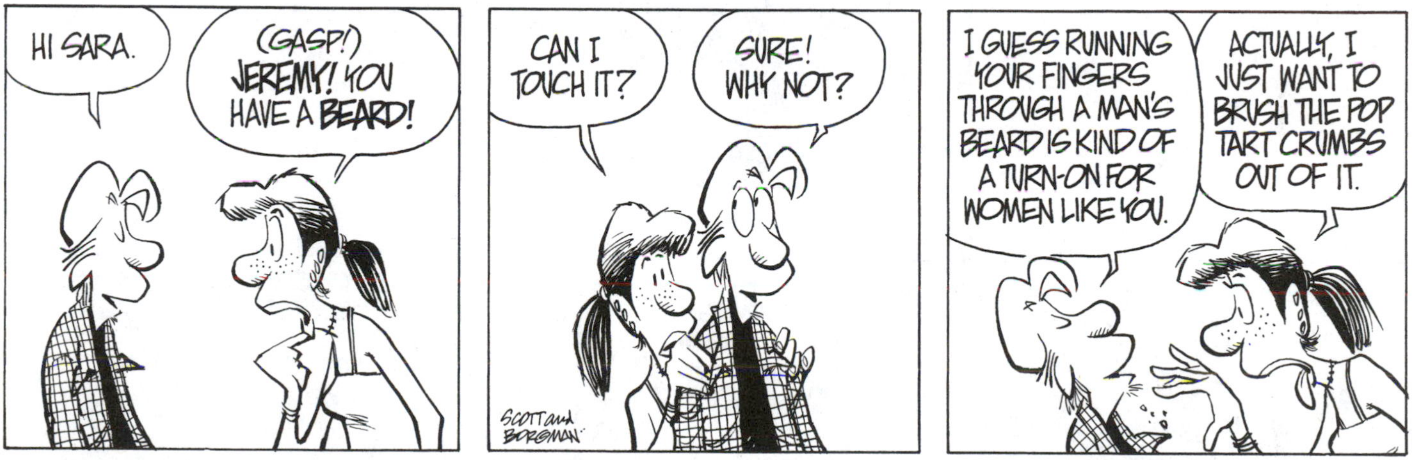
HI SARA.
(GASP!) JEREMY! YOU HAVE A BEARD!
CAN I TOUCH IT?
SURE! WHY NOT?
SCOTT and BORGMAN
I GUESS RUNNING YOUR FINGERS THROUGH A MAN'S BEARD IS KIND OF A TURN-ON FOR WOMEN LIKE YOU.
ACTUALLY, I JUST WANT TO BRUSH THE POP TART CRUMBS OUT OF IT.

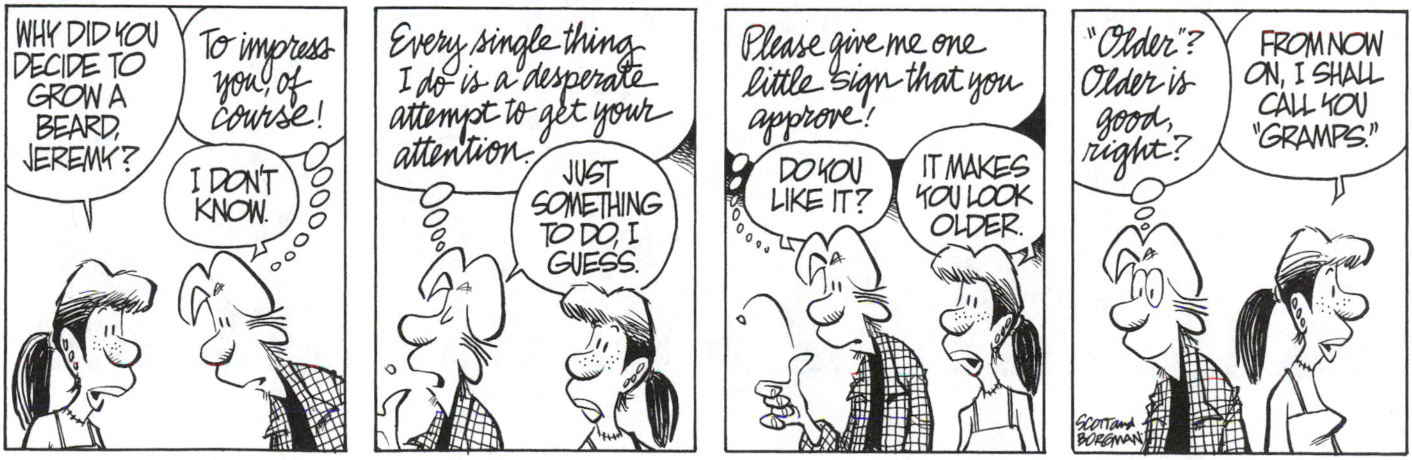
WHY DID YOU DECIDE TO GROW A BEARD, JEREMY?
To impress you, of course!
I DON'T KNOW.
Every single thing I do is a desperate attempt to get your attention.
JUST SOMETHING TO DO, I GUESS.
Please give me one little sign that you approve!
DO YOU LIKE IT?
IT MAKES YOU LOOK OLDER.
"Older"? Older is good, right?
FROM NOW ON, I SHALL CALL YOU "GRAMPS."
SCOTT and BORGMAN

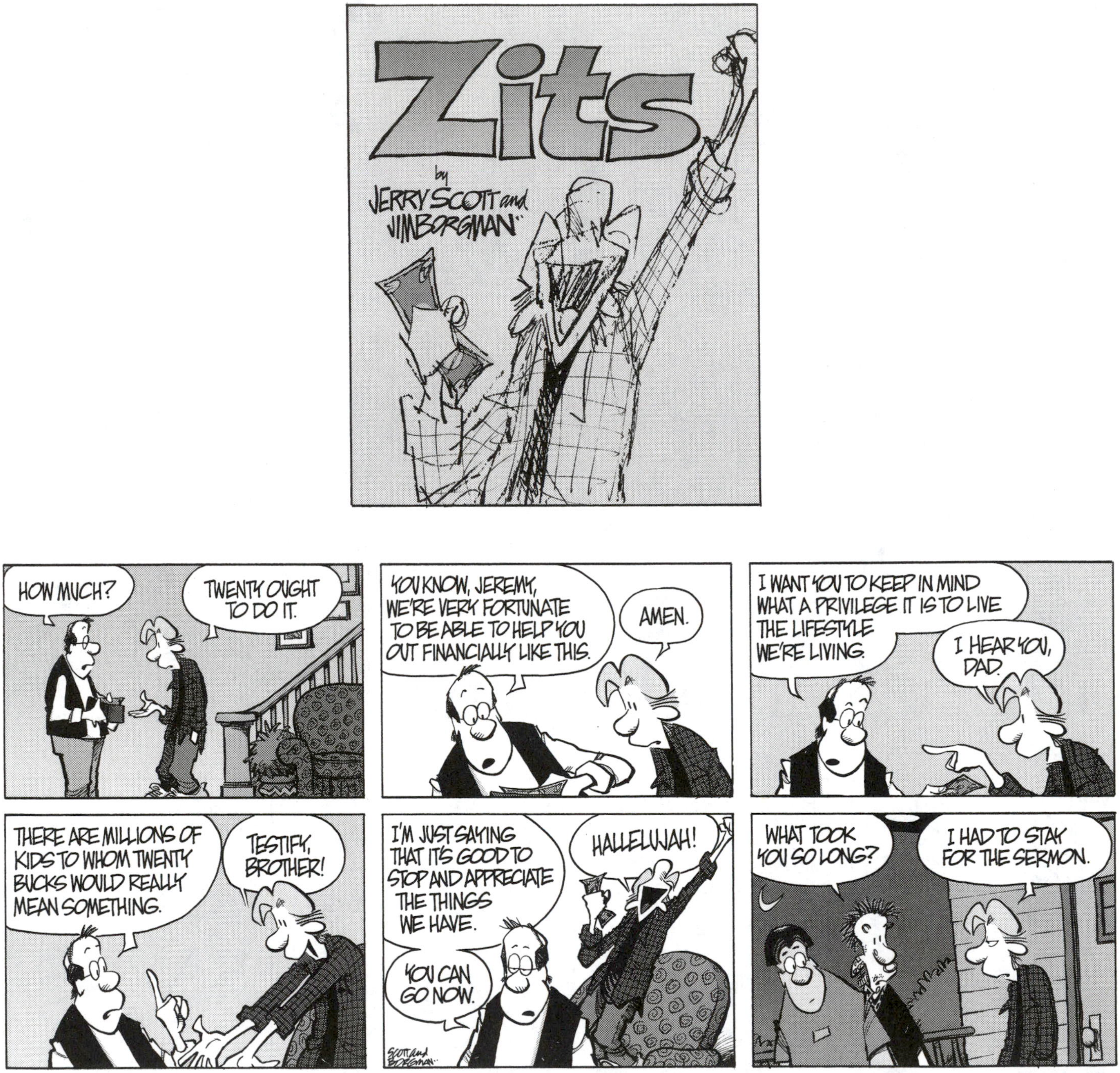
Zits
by
JERRY SCOTT and
JIM BORGMAN
HOW MUCH?
TWENTY OUGHT TO DO IT.
YOU KNOW, JEREMY, WE'RE VERY FORTUNATE TO BE ABLE TO HELP YOU OUT FINANCIALLY LIKE THIS.
AMEN.
I WANT YOU TO KEEP IN MIND WHAT A PRIVILEGE IT IS TO LIVE THE LIFESTYLE WE'RE LIVING.
I HEAR YOU, DAD.
THERE ARE MILLIONS OF KIDS TO WHOM TWENTY BUCKS WOULD REALLY MEAN SOMETHING.
TESTIFY, BROTHER!
I'M JUST SAYING THAT IT'S GOOD TO STOP AND APPRECIATE THE THINGS WE HAVE.
HALLELUJAH!
YOU CAN GO NOW.
SCOTT and BORGMAN
WHAT TOOK YOU SO LONG?
I HAD TO STAY FOR THE SERMON.

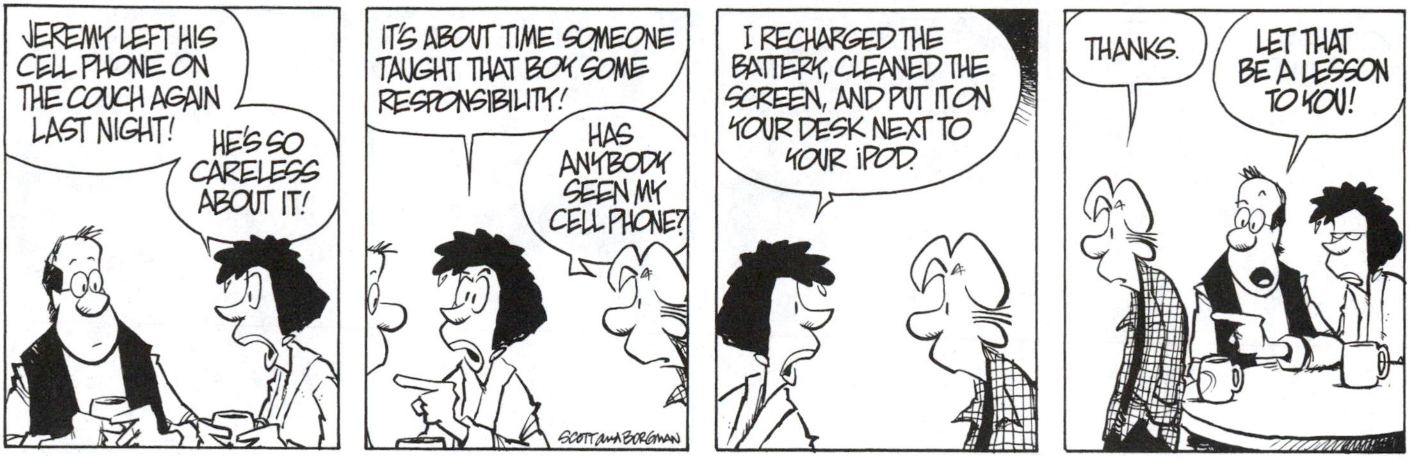
JEREMY LEFT HIS CELL PHONE ON THE COUCH AGAIN LAST NIGHT!
HE'S SO CARELESS ABOUT IT!
IT'S ABOUT TIME SOMEONE TAUGHT THAT BOY SOME RESPONSIBILITY!
HAS ANYBODY SEEN MY CELL PHONE?
SCOTT and BORGMAN
I RECHARGED THE BATTERY, CLEANED THE SCREEN, AND PUT IT ON YOUR DESK NEXT TO YOUR iPOD.
THANKS.
LET THAT BE A LESSON TO YOU!

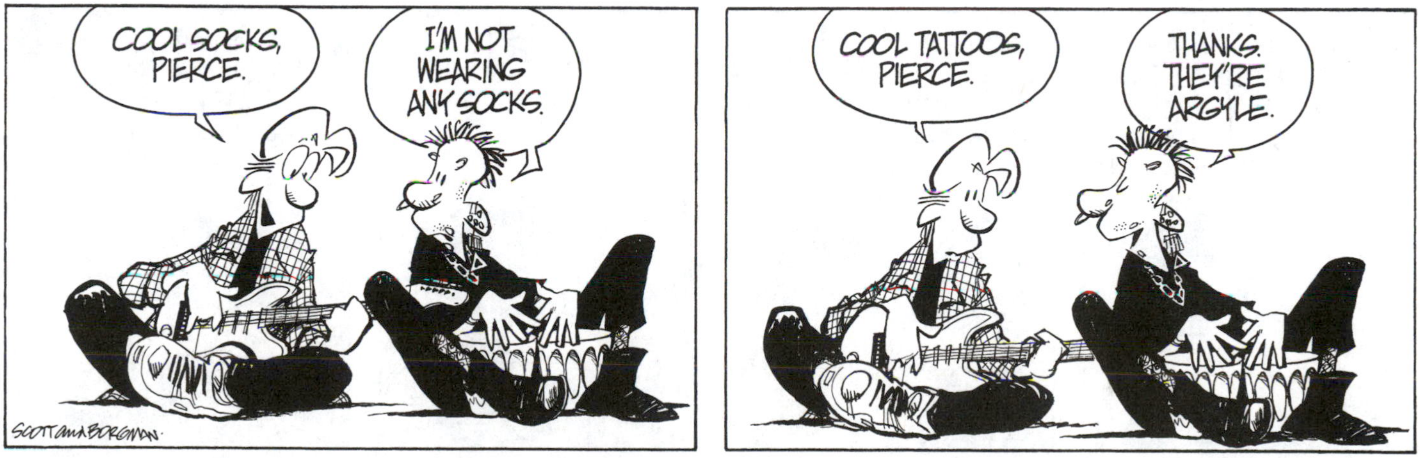
COOL SOCKS, PIERCE.
I'M NOT WEARING ANY SOCKS.
SCOTT and BORGMAN
COOL TATTOOS, PIERCE.
THANKS. THEY'RE ARGYLE.

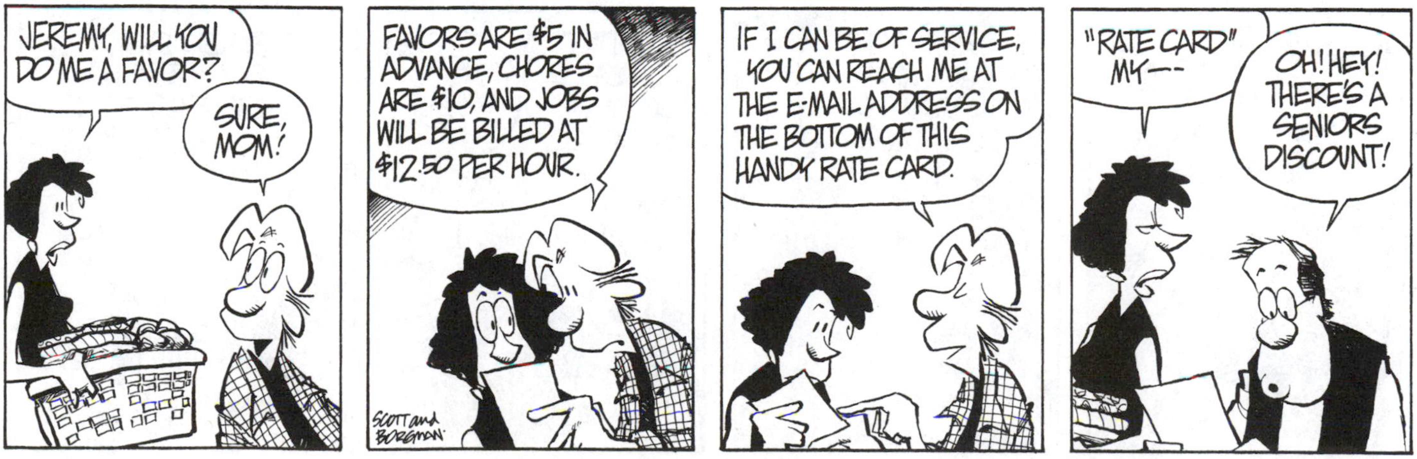
JEREMY, WILL YOU DO ME A FAVOR?
SURE, MOM!
FAVORS ARE $5 IN ADVANCE, CHORES ARE $10, AND JOBS WILL BE BILLED AT $12.50 PER HOUR.
SCOTT and BORGMAN
IF I CAN BE OF SERVICE, YOU CAN REACH ME AT THE E-MAIL ADDRESS ON THE BOTTOM OF THIS HANDY RATE CARD.
"RATE CARD" MY--
OH! HEY! THERE'S A SENIORS DISCOUNT!

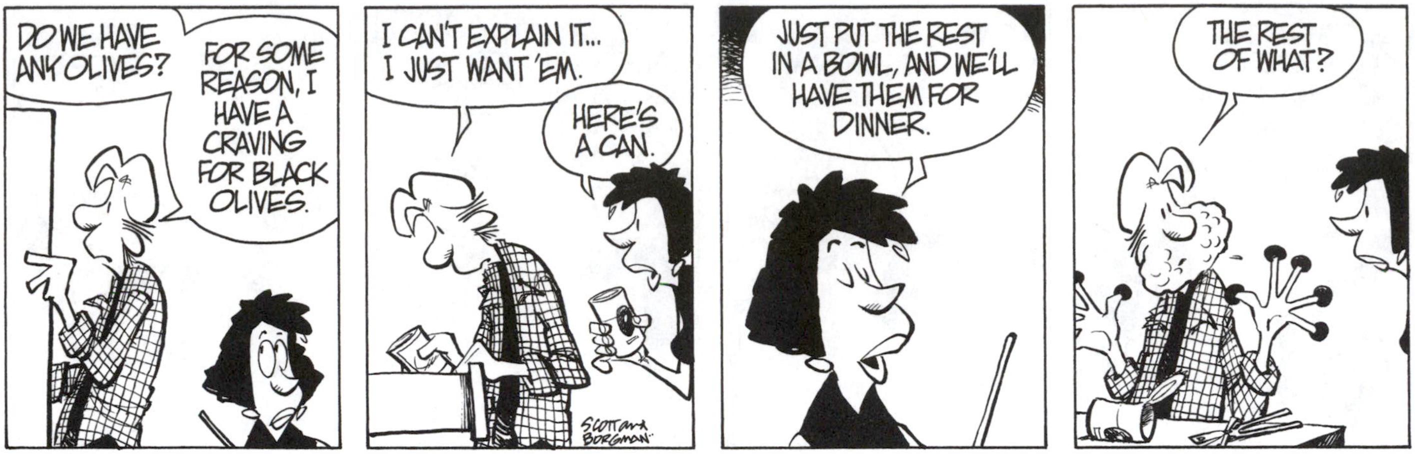
DO WE HAVE ANY OLIVES?
FOR SOME REASON, I HAVE A CRAVING FOR BLACK OLIVES.
I CAN'T EXPLAIN IT... I JUST WANT 'EM.
HERE'S A CAN.
JUST PUT THE REST IN A BOWL, AND WE'LL HAVE THEM FOR DINNER.
THE REST OF WHAT?

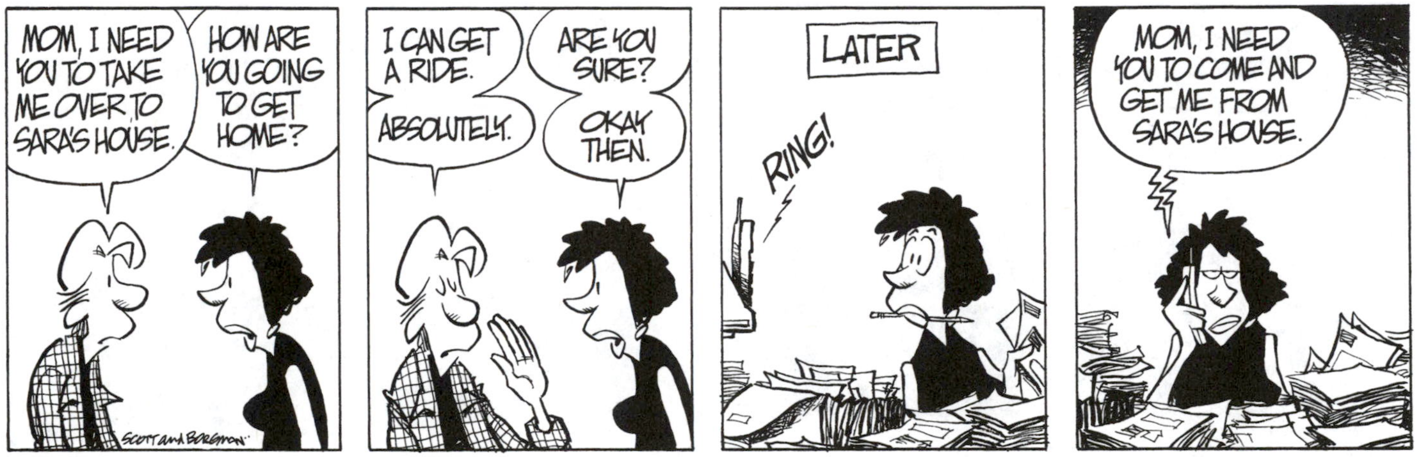
MOM, I NEED YOU TO TAKE ME OVER TO SARA'S HOUSE.
HOW ARE YOU GOING TO GET HOME?
I CAN GET A RIDE.
ARE YOU SURE?
ABSOLUTELY.
OKAY THEN.
LATER
RING!
MOM, I NEED YOU TO COME AND GET ME FROM SARA'S HOUSE.

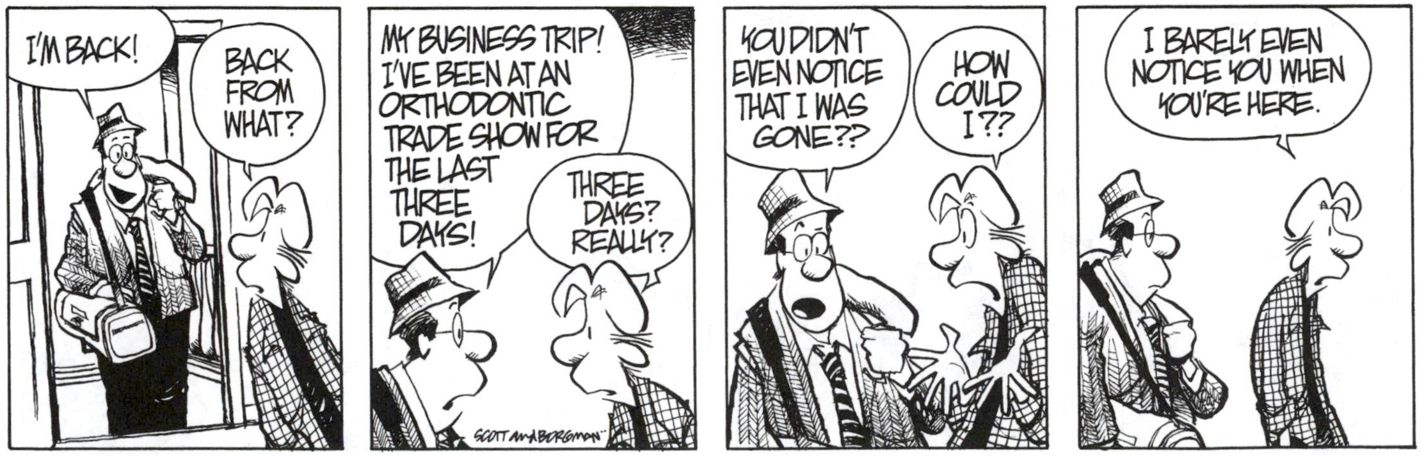
I'M BACK!
BACK FROM WHAT?
MY BUSINESS TRIP! I'VE BEEN AT AN ORTHODONTIC TRADE SHOW FOR THE LAST THREE DAYS!
THREE DAYS? REALLY?
YOU DIDN'T EVEN NOTICE THAT I WAS GONE??
HOW COULD I??
I BARELY EVEN NOTICE YOU WHEN YOU'RE HERE.

Zits
by JERRY SCOTT and JIM BORGMAN

SCOTT and BORGMAN
THAT'S THE LAST TIME I TRY TO INTEREST YOU AND YOUR FRIENDS IN A YAHTZEE TOURNAMENT!
COULD YOU PUT THAT IN WRITING?

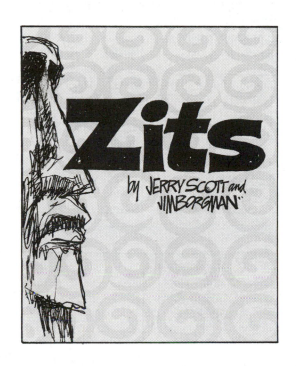

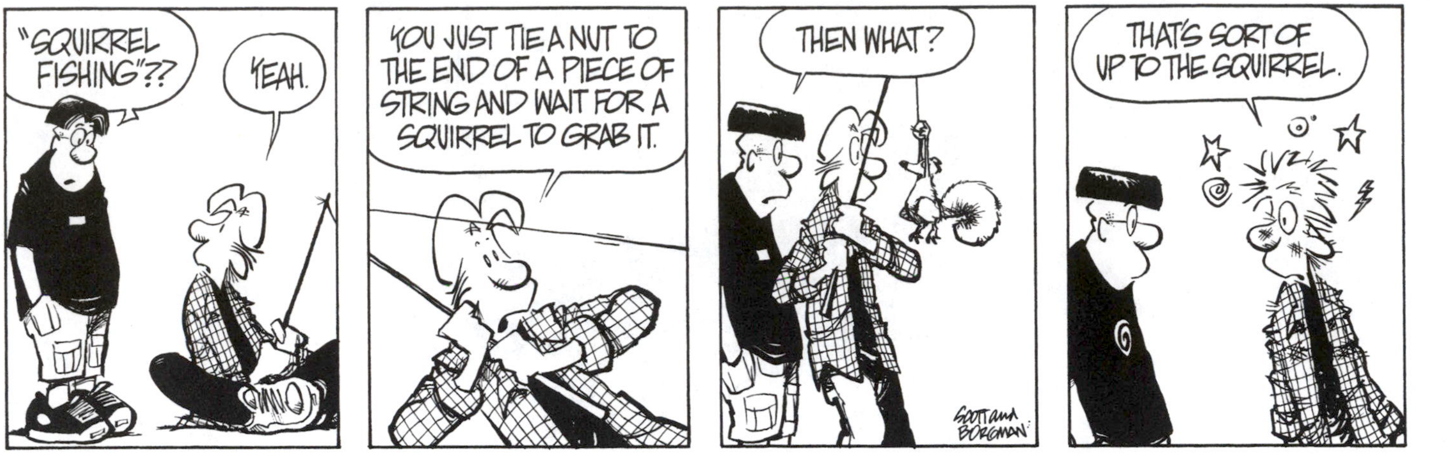
"SQUIRREL FISHING"??
YEAH.
YOU JUST TIE A NUT TO THE END OF A PIECE OF STRING AND WAIT FOR A SQUIRREL TO GRAB IT.
THEN WHAT?
THAT'S SORT OF UP TO THE SQUIRREL.
SCOTT AND BORGMAN

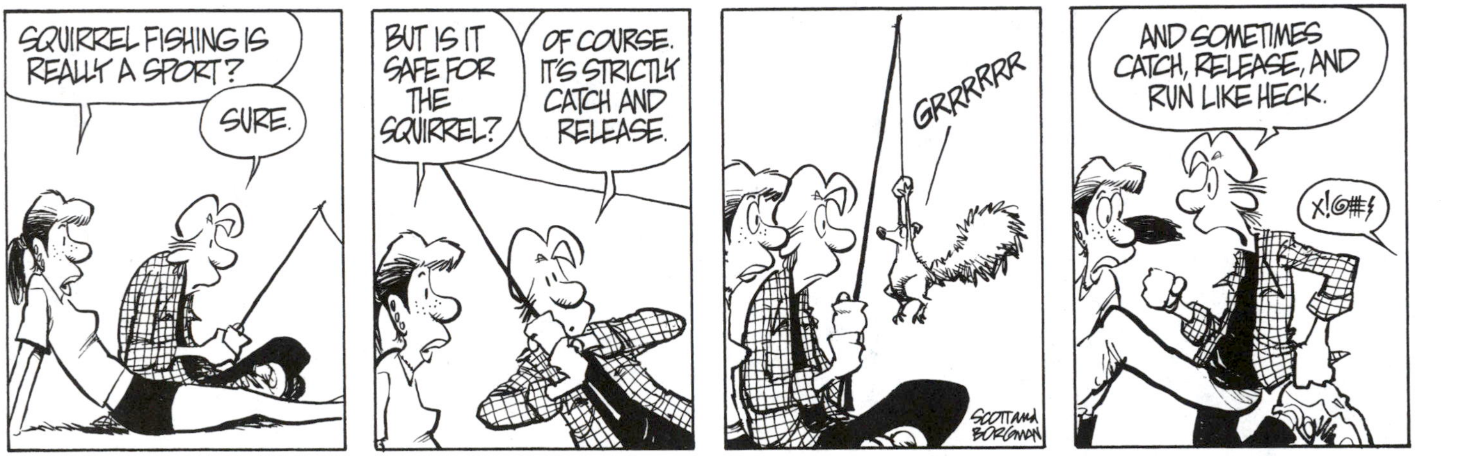
SQUIRREL FISHING IS REALLY A SPORT?
SURE.
BUT IS IT SAFE FOR THE SQUIRREL?
OF COURSE. IT'S STRICTLY CATCH AND RELEASE.
GRRRRRR
SCOTT AND BORGMAN
AND SOMETIMES CATCH, RELEASE, AND RUN LIKE HECK.

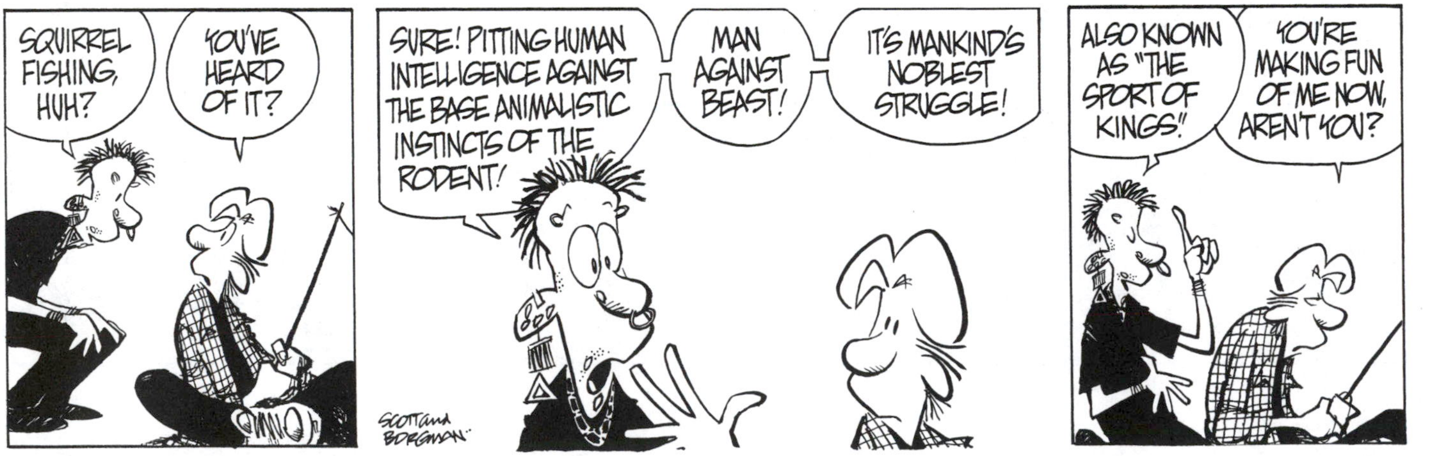
SQUIRREL FISHING, HUH?
YOU'VE HEARD OF IT?
SURE! PITTING HUMAN INTELLIGENCE AGAINST THE BASE ANIMALISTIC INSTINCTS OF THE RODENT!
MAN AGAINST BEAST!
IT'S MANKIND'S NOBLEST STRUGGLE!
SCOTT AND BORGMAN
ALSO KNOWN AS "THE SPORT OF KINGS."
YOU'RE MAKING FUN OF ME NOW, AREN'T YOU?

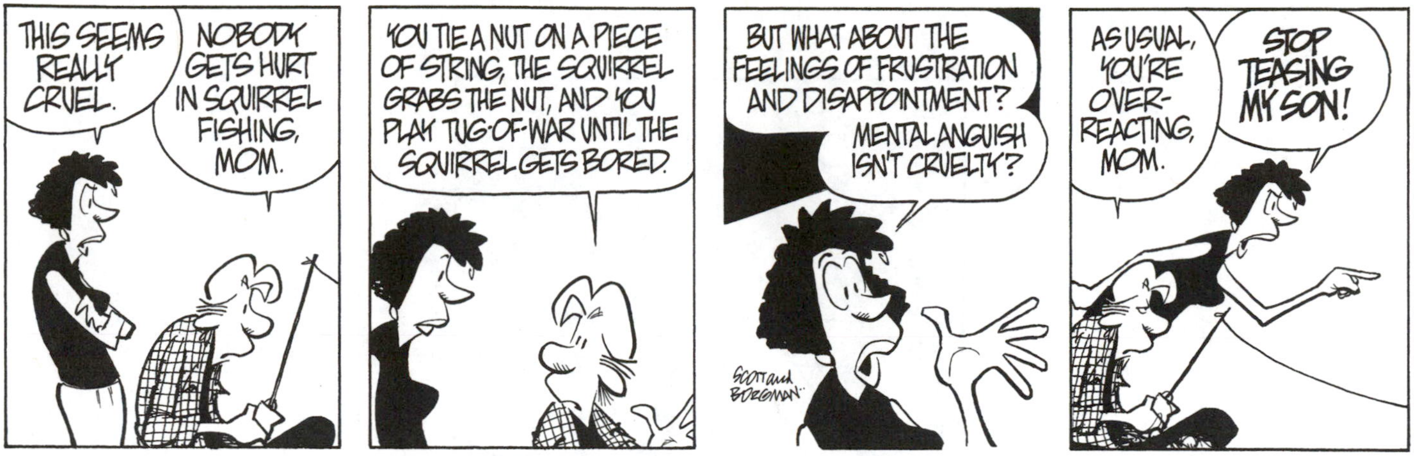
THIS SEEMS REALLY CRUEL.
NOBODY GETS HURT IN SQUIRREL FISHING, MOM.
YOU TIE A NUT ON A PIECE OF STRING, THE SQUIRREL GRABS THE NUT, AND YOU PLAY TUG-OF-WAR UNTIL THE SQUIRREL GETS BORED.
BUT WHAT ABOUT THE FEELINGS OF FRUSTRATION AND DISAPPOINTMENT?
MENTAL ANGUISH ISN'T CRUELTY?
SCOTT and BORGMAN
AS USUAL, YOU'RE OVER-REACTING, MOM.
STOP TEASING MY SON!

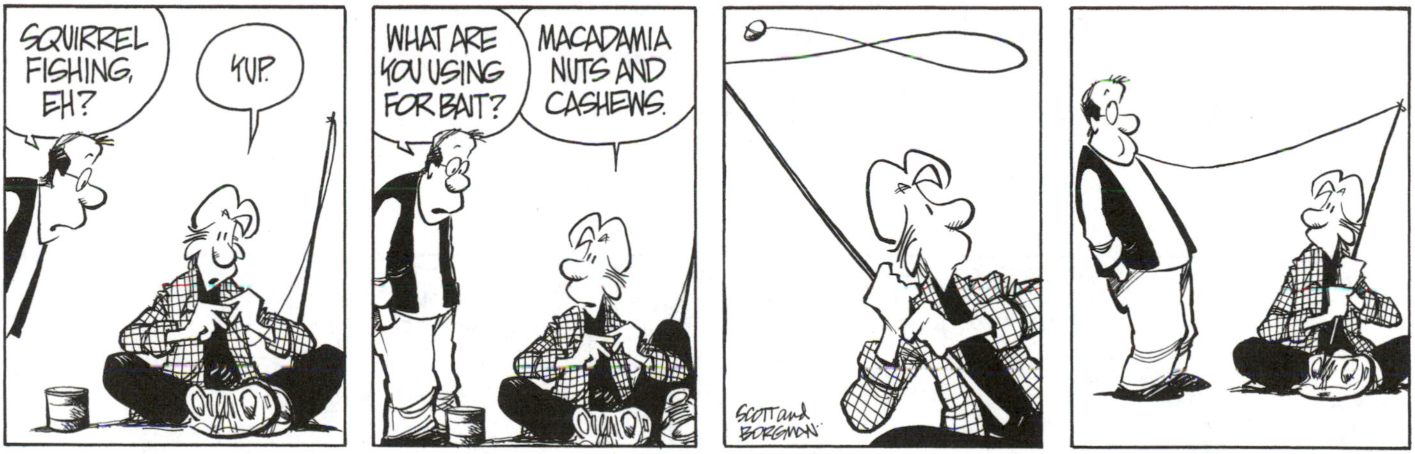
SQUIRREL FISHING, EH?
YUP.
WHAT ARE YOU USING FOR BAIT?
MACADAMIA NUTS AND CASHEWS.
SCOTT and BORGMAN

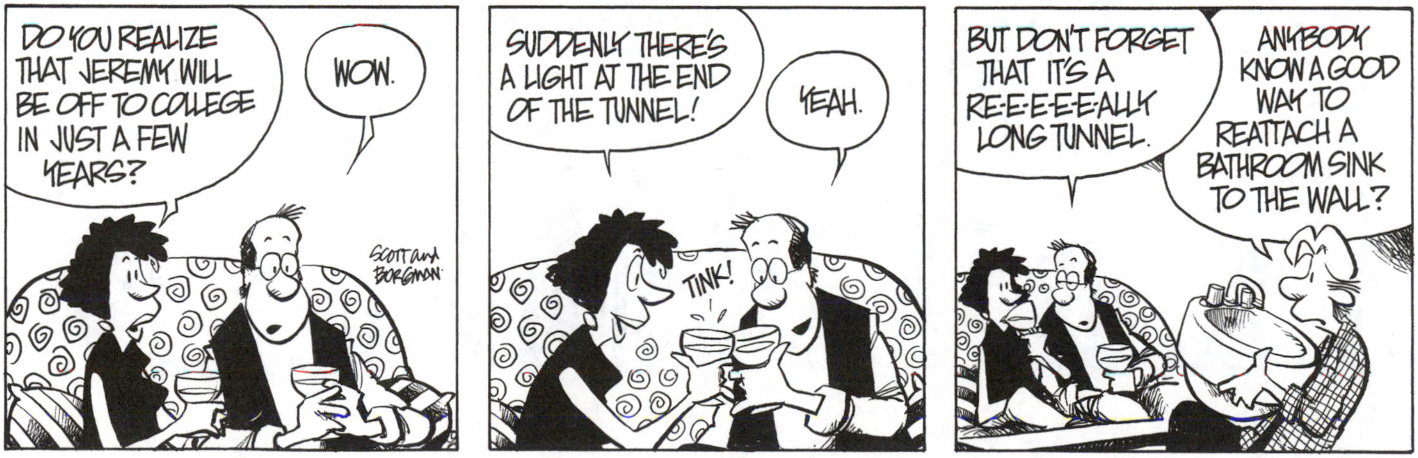
DO YOU REALIZE THAT JEREMY WILL BE OFF TO COLLEGE IN JUST A FEW YEARS?
WOW.
SCOTT and BORGMAN
SUDDENLY THERE'S A LIGHT AT THE END OF THE TUNNEL!
YEAH.
TINK!
BUT DON'T FORGET THAT IT'S A RE-E-E-E-E-ALLY LONG TUNNEL.
ANYBODY KNOW A GOOD WAY TO REATTACH A BATHROOM SINK TO THE WALL?

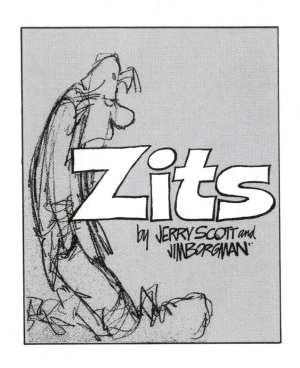

Zits
by JERRY SCOTT and JIM BORGMAN

SOMETIMES I DREAD COMING HOME.

JUST ONCE I'D LIKE TO GO TO MY ROOM WITHOUT GOING THROUGH AN INTERROGATION.

"HOW WAS YOUR DAY?" "WHAT DID YOU DO?" "ARE YOU HUNGRY?!" "WHO DID YOU SEE?" "WHERE DID YOU GO?"

WHY CAN'T THEY UNDERSTAND THAT I JUST WANT TO BE LEFT ALONE?

SLAM!

SCOTT and BORGMAN

AHEM!

LEFT ALONE, NOT IGNORED.

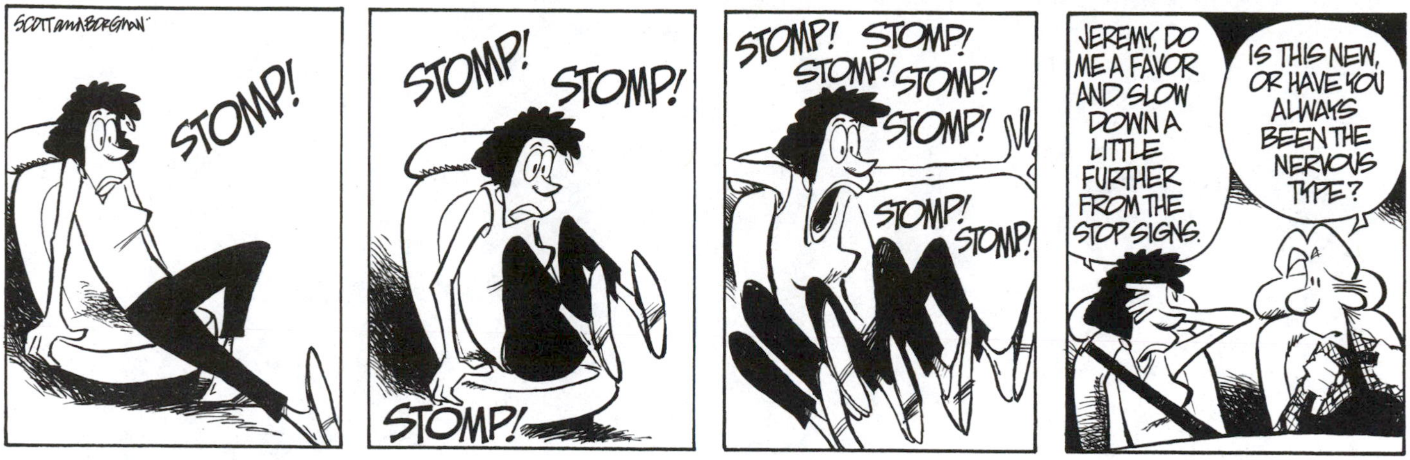
STOMP!
STOMP!
STOMP!
STOMP!
STOMP! STOMP!
STOMP! STOMP!
STOMP!
STOMP!
STOMP!
JEREMY, DO ME A FAVOR AND SLOW DOWN A LITTLE FURTHER FROM THE STOP SIGNS.
IS THIS NEW, OR HAVE YOU ALWAYS BEEN THE NERVOUS TYPE?

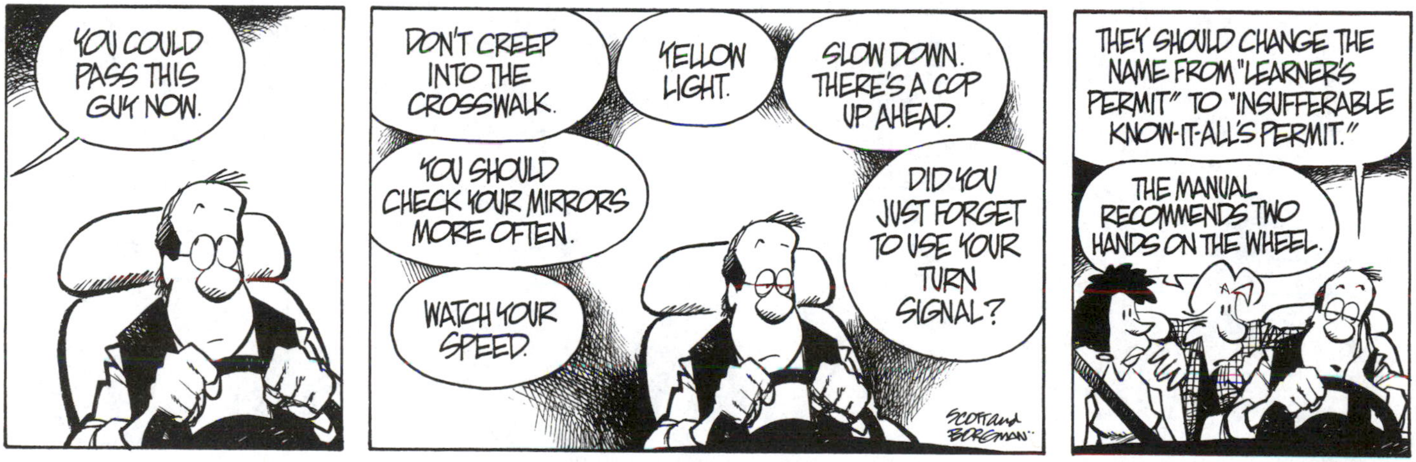
YOU COULD PASS THIS GUY NOW.
DON'T CREEP INTO THE CROSSWALK.
YELLOW LIGHT.
SLOW DOWN. THERE'S A COP UP AHEAD.
YOU SHOULD CHECK YOUR MIRRORS MORE OFTEN.
WATCH YOUR SPEED.
DID YOU JUST FORGET TO USE YOUR TURN SIGNAL?
THEY SHOULD CHANGE THE NAME FROM "LEARNER'S PERMIT" TO "INSUFFERABLE KNOW-IT-ALL'S PERMIT."
THE MANUAL RECOMMENDS TWO HANDS ON THE WHEEL.

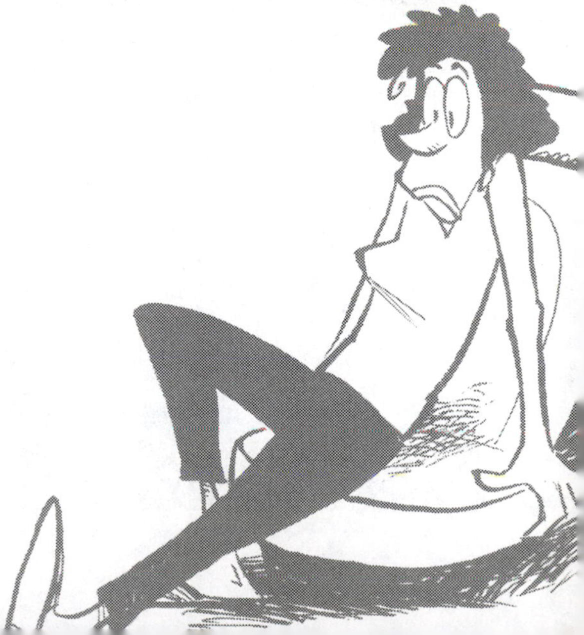

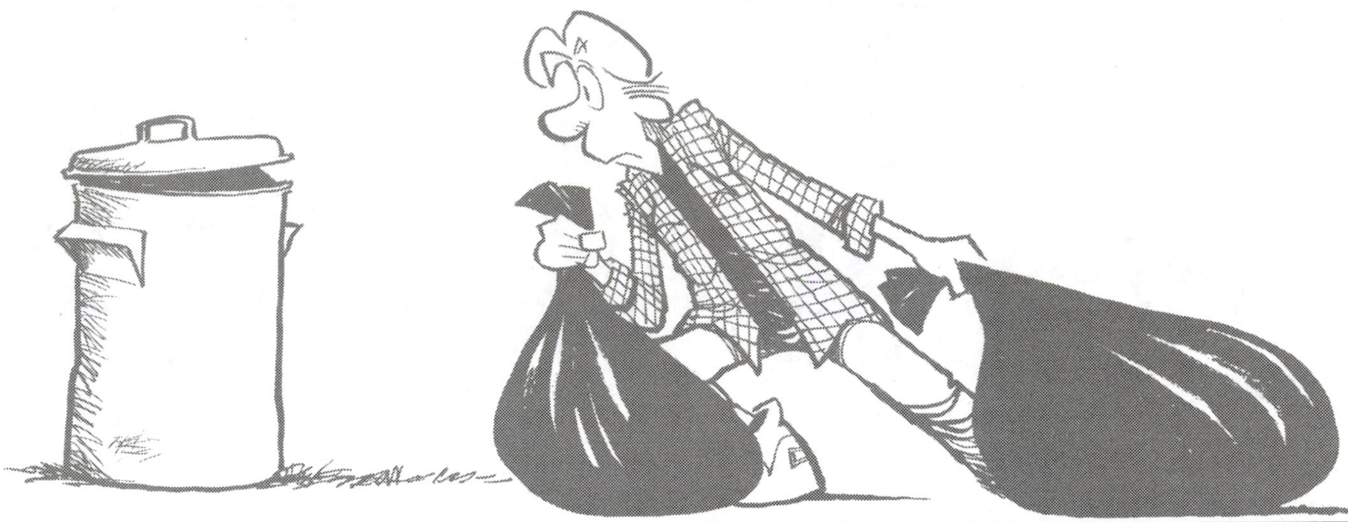

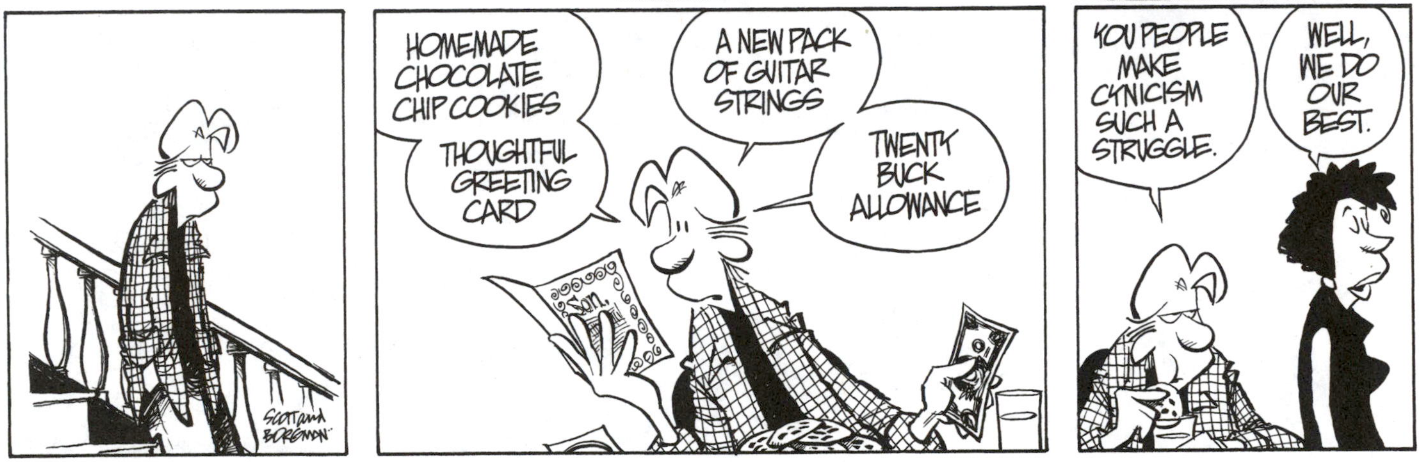
HOMEMADE CHOCOLATE CHIP COOKIES
THOUGHTFUL GREETING CARD
A NEW PACK OF GUITAR STRINGS
TWENTY BUCK ALLOWANCE
Son,
YOU PEOPLE MAKE CYNICISM SUCH A STRUGGLE.
WELL, WE DO OUR BEST.

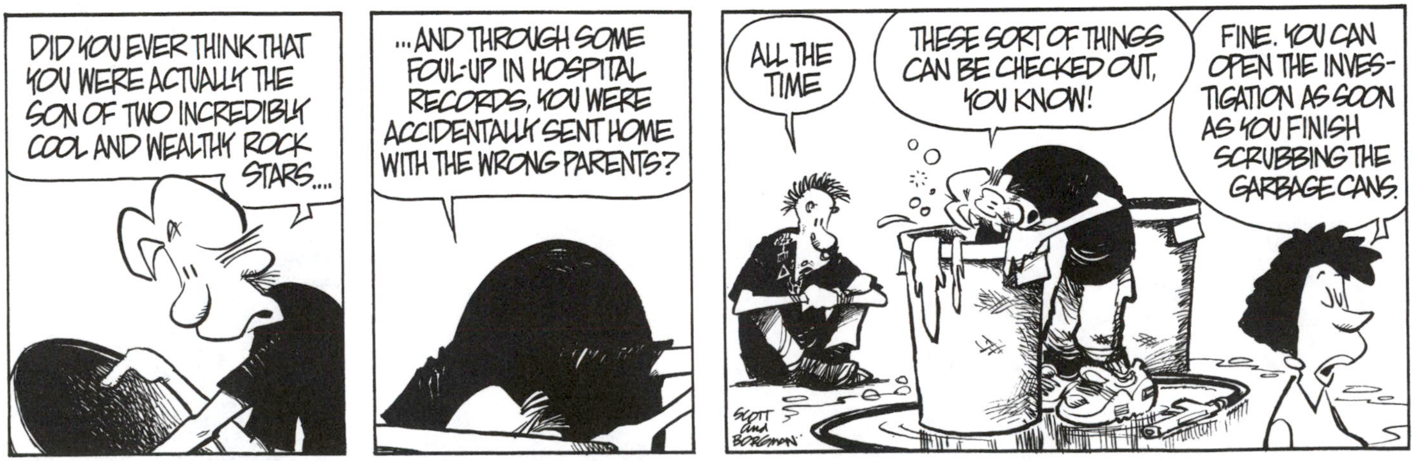
DID YOU EVER THINK THAT YOU WERE ACTUALLY THE SON OF TWO INCREDIBLY COOL AND WEALTHY ROCK STARS....
...AND THROUGH SOME FOUL-UP IN HOSPITAL RECORDS, YOU WERE ACCIDENTALLY SENT HOME WITH THE WRONG PARENTS?
ALL THE TIME
THESE SORT OF THINGS CAN BE CHECKED OUT, YOU KNOW!
FINE. YOU CAN OPEN THE INVESTIGATION AS SOON AS YOU FINISH SCRUBBING THE GARBAGE CANS.

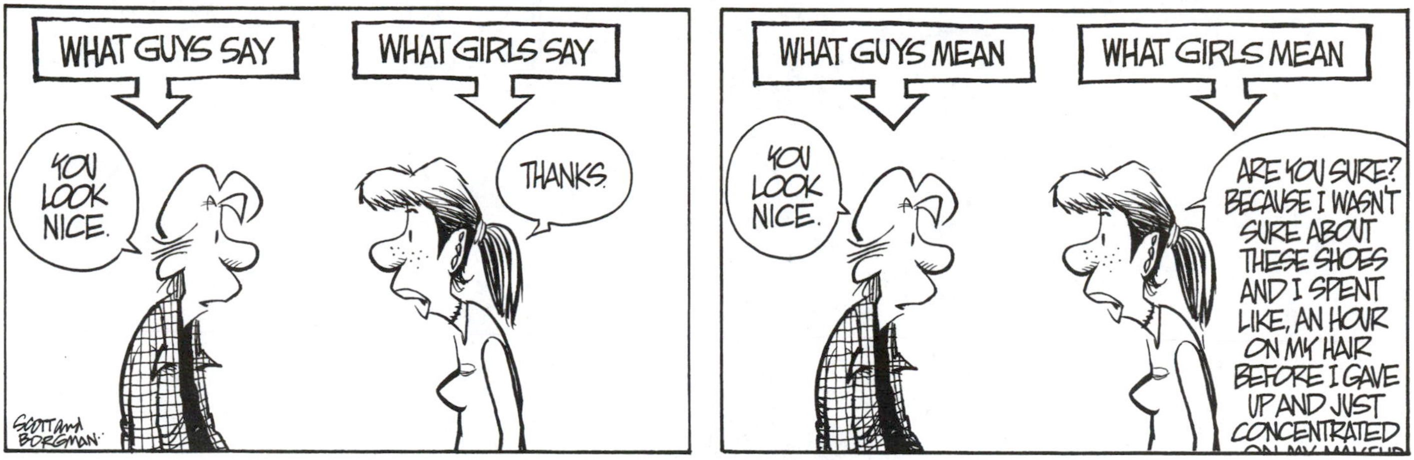
WHAT GUYS SAY
WHAT GIRLS SAY
YOU LOOK NICE.
THANKS.
WHAT GUYS MEAN
WHAT GIRLS MEAN
YOU LOOK NICE.
ARE YOU SURE? BECAUSE I WASN'T SURE ABOUT THESE SHOES AND I SPENT LIKE, AN HOUR ON MY HAIR BEFORE I GAVE UP AND JUST CONCENTRATED

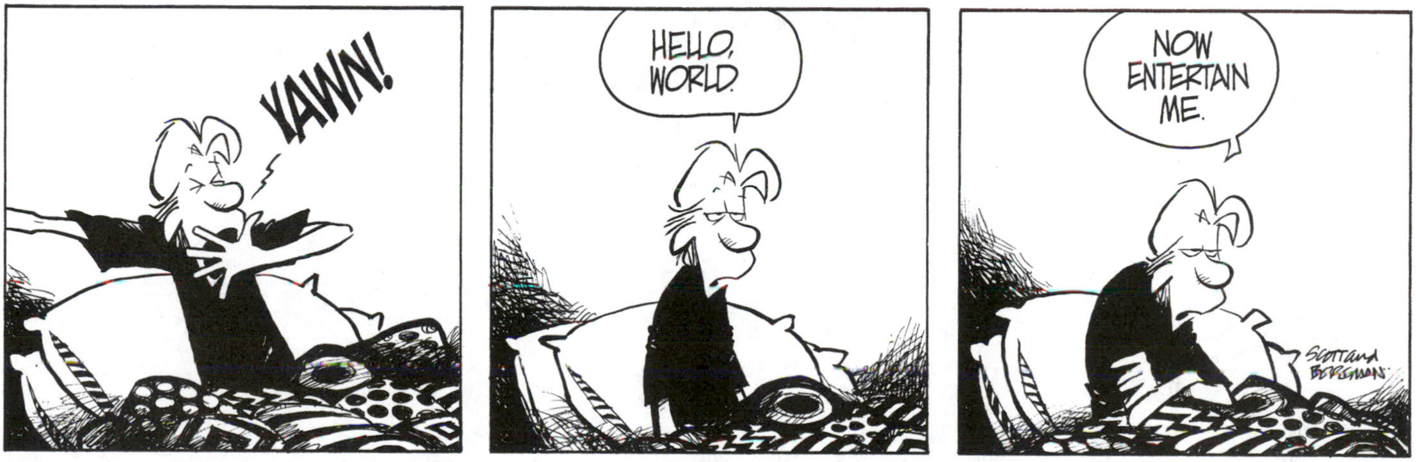
YAWN!
HELLO, WORLD.
NOW ENTERTAIN ME.

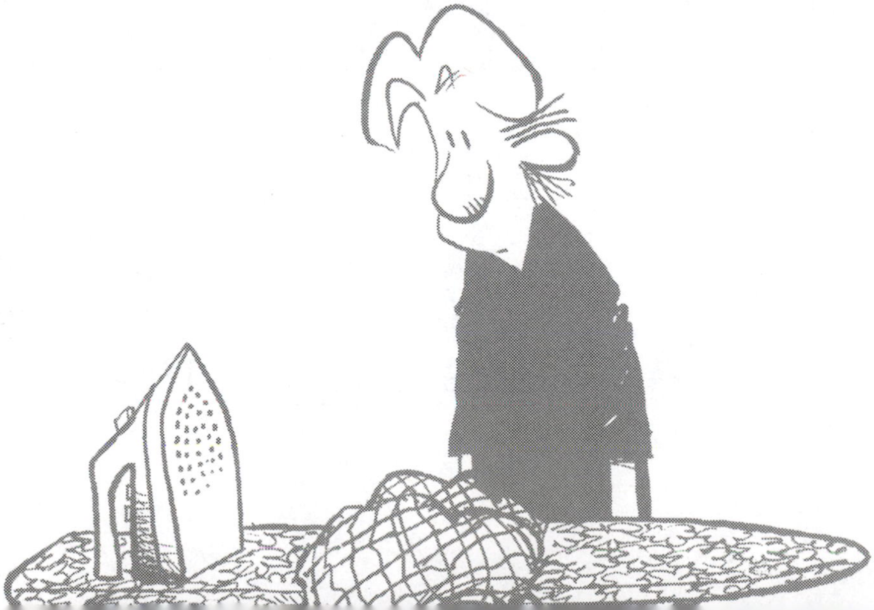

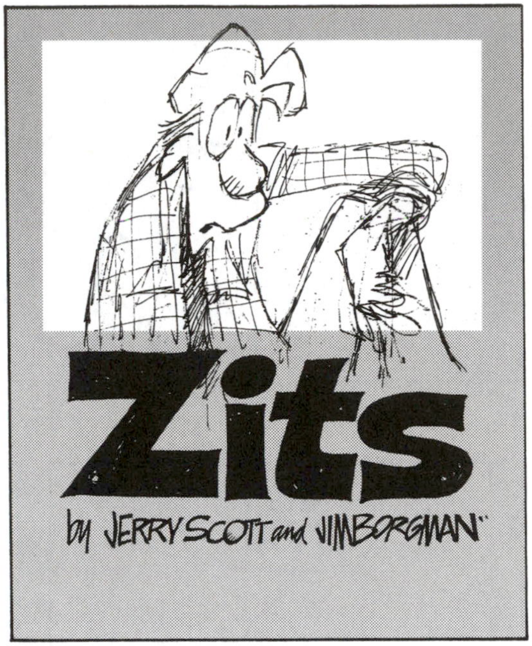
Zits
by JERRY SCOTT and JIM BORGMAN

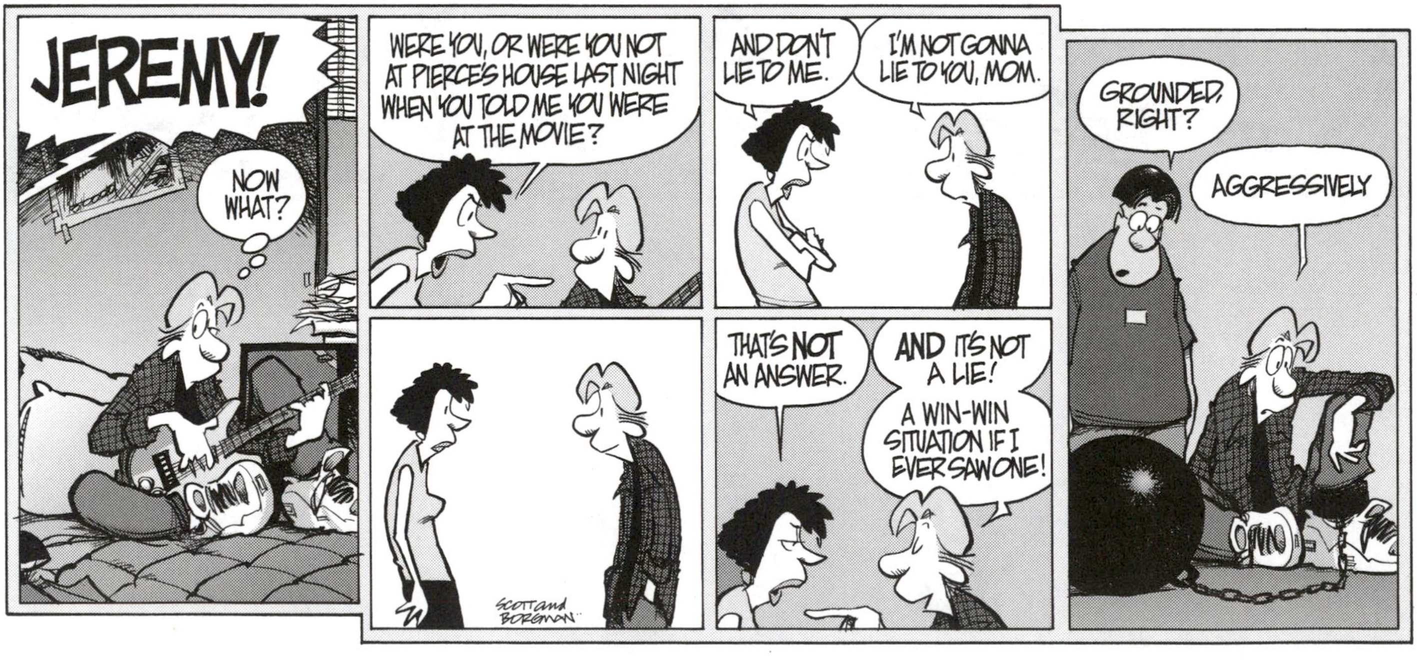
JEREMY!
NOW WHAT?
WERE YOU, OR WERE YOU NOT AT PIERCE'S HOUSE LAST NIGHT WHEN YOU TOLD ME YOU WERE AT THE MOVIE?
AND DON'T LIE TO ME.
I'M NOT GONNA LIE TO YOU, MOM.
SCOTT and BORGMAN
THAT'S NOT AN ANSWER.
AND IT'S NOT A LIE!
A WIN-WIN SITUATION IF I EVER SAW ONE!
GROUNDED, RIGHT?
AGGRESSIVELY

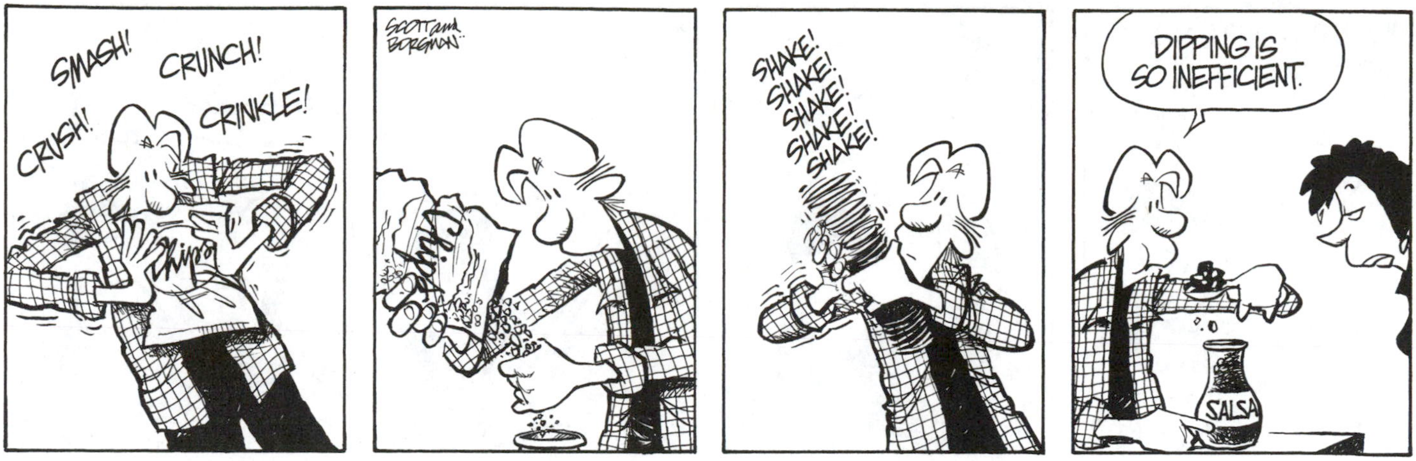
SMASH!
CRUNCH!
CRUSH!
CRINKLE!
Chips
SCOTT and BORGMAN
Chips
SHAKE! SHAKE! SHAKE! SHAKE! SHAKE!
DIPPING IS SO INEFFICIENT.
SALSA

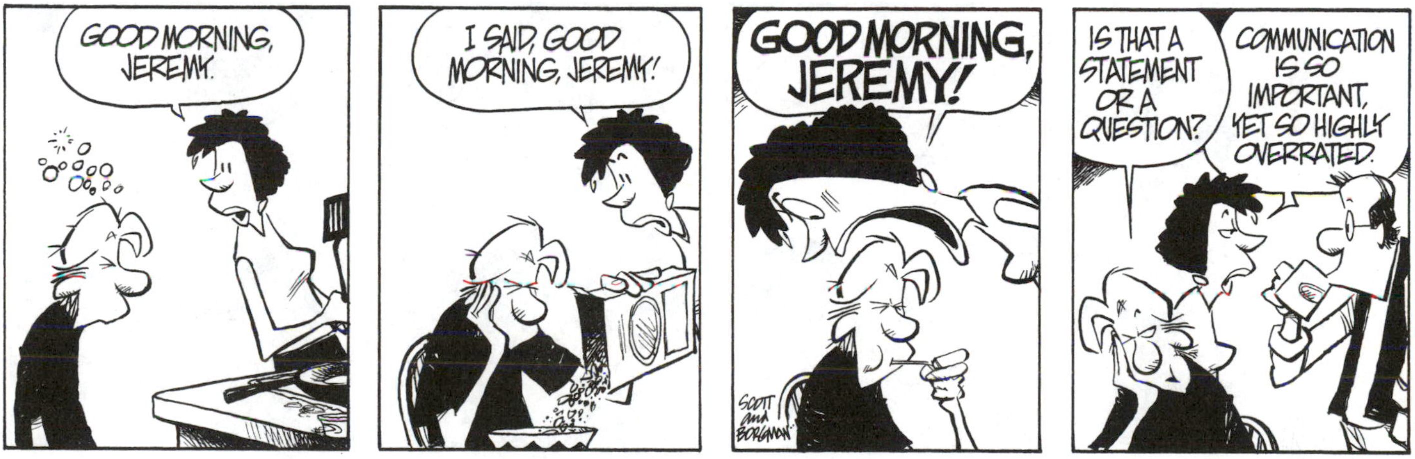
GOOD MORNING, JEREMY.
I SAID, GOOD MORNING, JEREMY!
GOOD MORNING, JEREMY!
SCOTT and BORGMAN
IS THAT A STATEMENT OR A QUESTION?
COMMUNICATION IS SO IMPORTANT, YET SO HIGHLY OVERRATED.

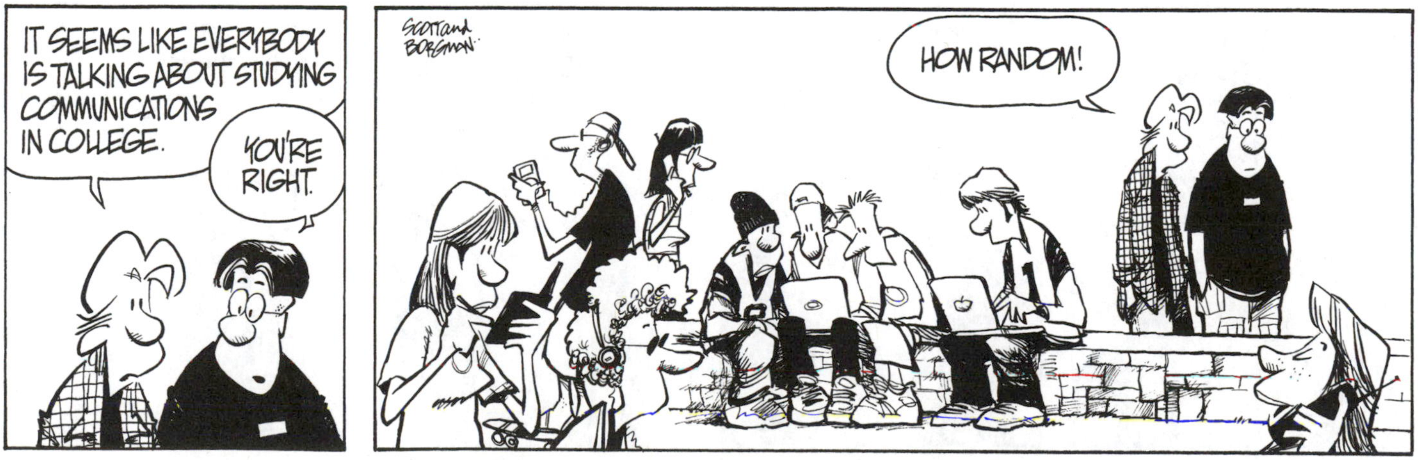
IT SEEMS LIKE EVERYBODY IS TALKING ABOUT STUDYING COMMUNICATIONS IN COLLEGE.
YOU'RE RIGHT.
SCOTT and BORGMAN
HOW RANDOM!

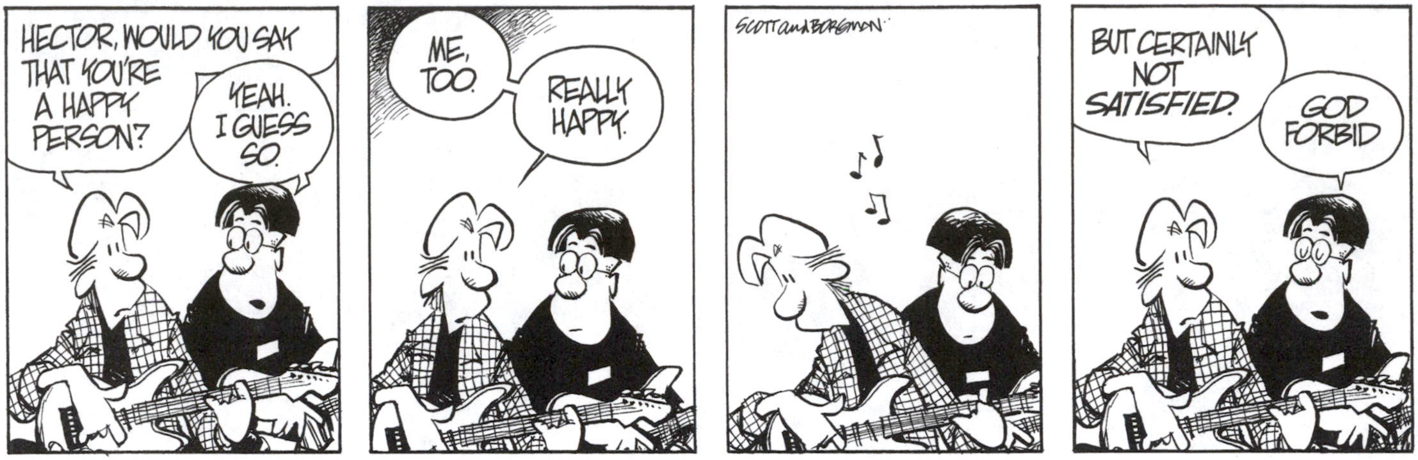
HECTOR, WOULD YOU SAY THAT YOU'RE A HAPPY PERSON?
YEAH. I GUESS SO.
ME, TOO.
REALLY HAPPY.
BUT CERTAINLY NOT SATISFIED.
GOD FORBID

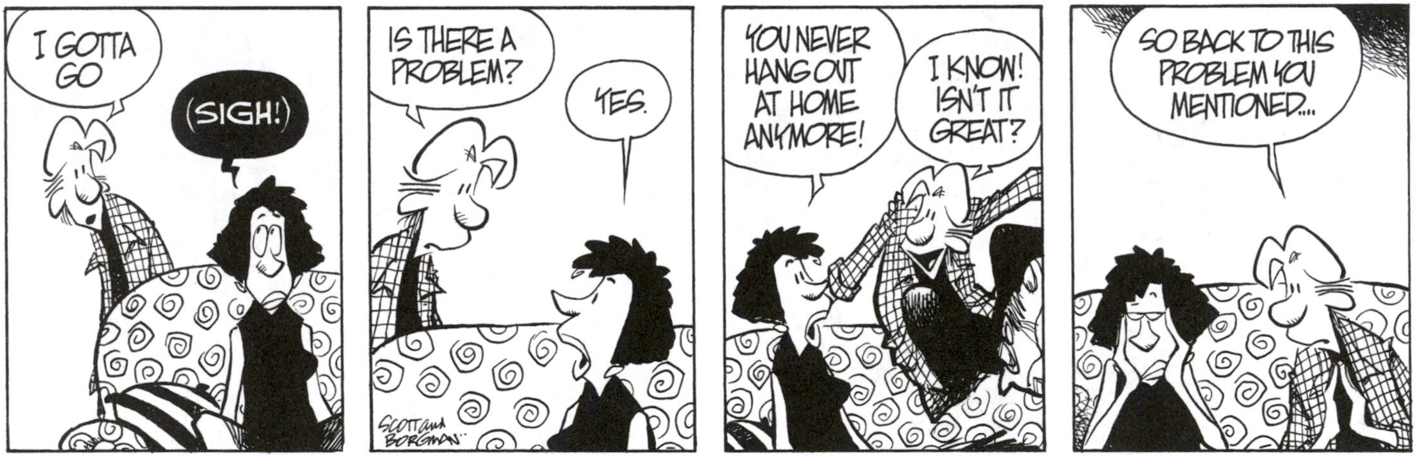
I GOTTA GO
(SIGH!)
IS THERE A PROBLEM?
YES.
YOU NEVER HANG OUT AT HOME ANYMORE!
I KNOW! ISN'T IT GREAT?
SO BACK TO THIS PROBLEM YOU MENTIONED....

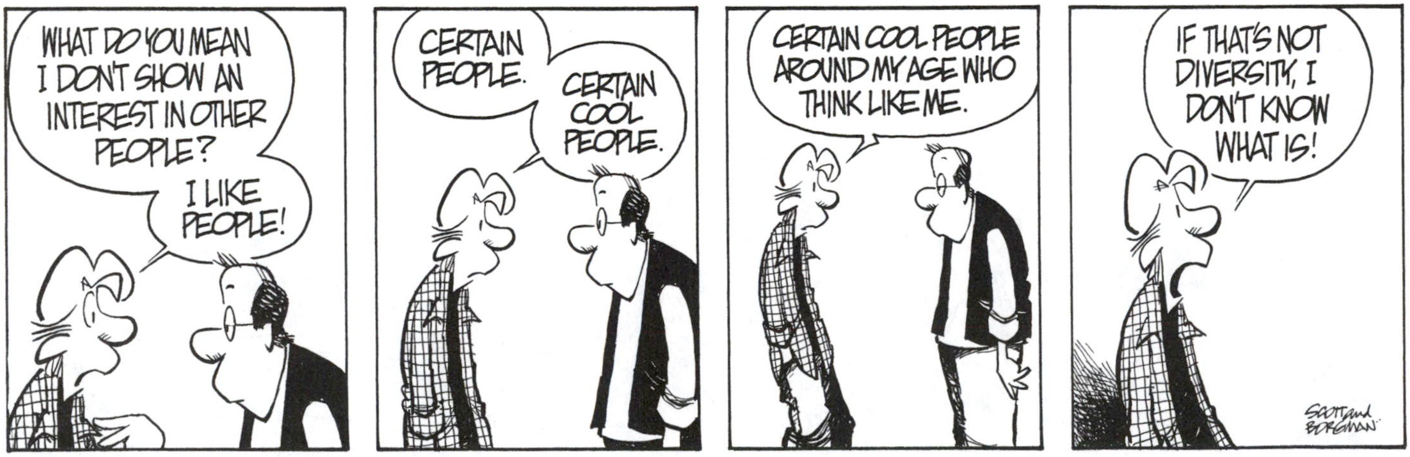
WHAT DO YOU MEAN I DON'T SHOW AN INTEREST IN OTHER PEOPLE?
I LIKE PEOPLE!
CERTAIN PEOPLE.
CERTAIN COOL PEOPLE.
CERTAIN COOL PEOPLE AROUND MY AGE WHO THINK LIKE ME.
IF THAT'S NOT DIVERSITY, I DON'T KNOW WHAT IS!

Zits
by JERRY SCOTT and JIM BORGMAN

OKAY, CALL JEREMY'S CELL PHONE AND TELL HIM THAT WE'RE READY TO GO.
BIP BIP BIP IP IP
BAD BREATH & BEYON
NO ANSWER.
CALL AGAIN.
NO ANSWER.
I'M GETTING A LITTLE WORRIED.
BIP BEEP BIP IP IP
WHERE IS HE??
STILL NO ANSWER.
MAYBE HE'S IN THE MUSIC STORE AND HE CAN'T HEAR IT RINGING.
NO, I HAD HIM SWITCH IT TO "VIBRATE" SO THAT WOULDN'T HAPPEN.
WHAT IS HE... NUMB??
HOW CAN A PERSON NOT FEEL A CELL PHONE VIBRATING IN HIS POCK--
UM...
OH, HI.
YOU'RE LATE.
WHY DIDN'T YOU GUYS CALL?
MASSAGE CHAIR
SCOTT and BORGMAN

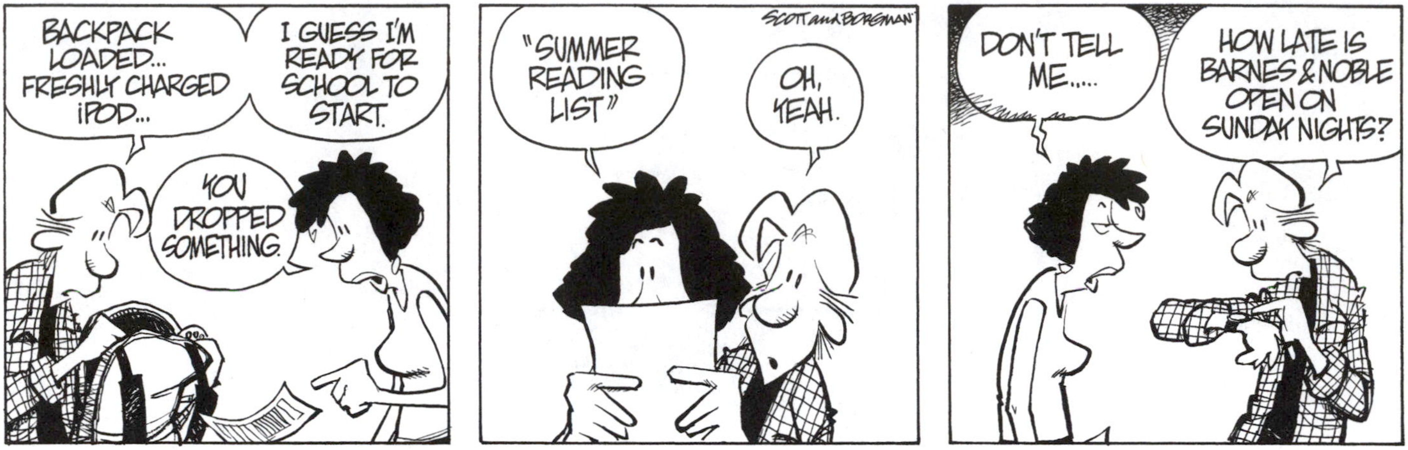
BACKPACK LOADED... FRESHLY CHARGED iPOD...
I GUESS I'M READY FOR SCHOOL TO START.
YOU DROPPED SOMETHING.
SCOTT and BORGMAN
"SUMMER READING LIST"
OH, YEAH.
DON'T TELL ME.....
HOW LATE IS BARNES & NOBLE OPEN ON SUNDAY NIGHTS?

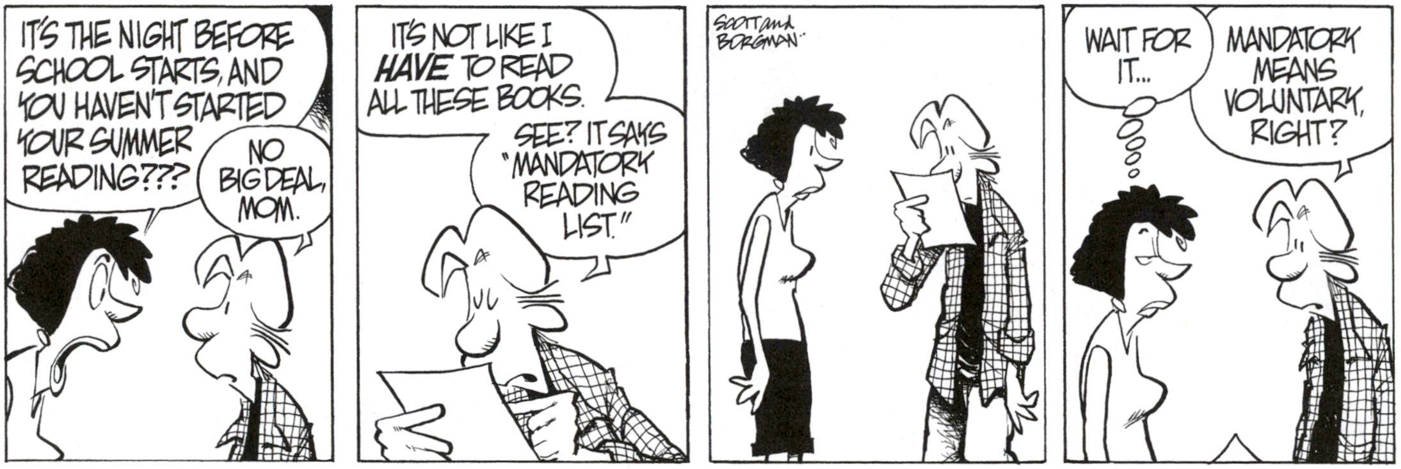
IT'S THE NIGHT BEFORE SCHOOL STARTS, AND YOU HAVEN'T STARTED YOUR SUMMER READING???
NO BIG DEAL, MOM.
IT'S NOT LIKE I HAVE TO READ ALL THESE BOOKS.
SEE? IT SAYS "MANDATORY READING LIST."
SCOTT and BORGMAN
WAIT FOR IT...
MANDATORY MEANS VOLUNTARY, RIGHT?

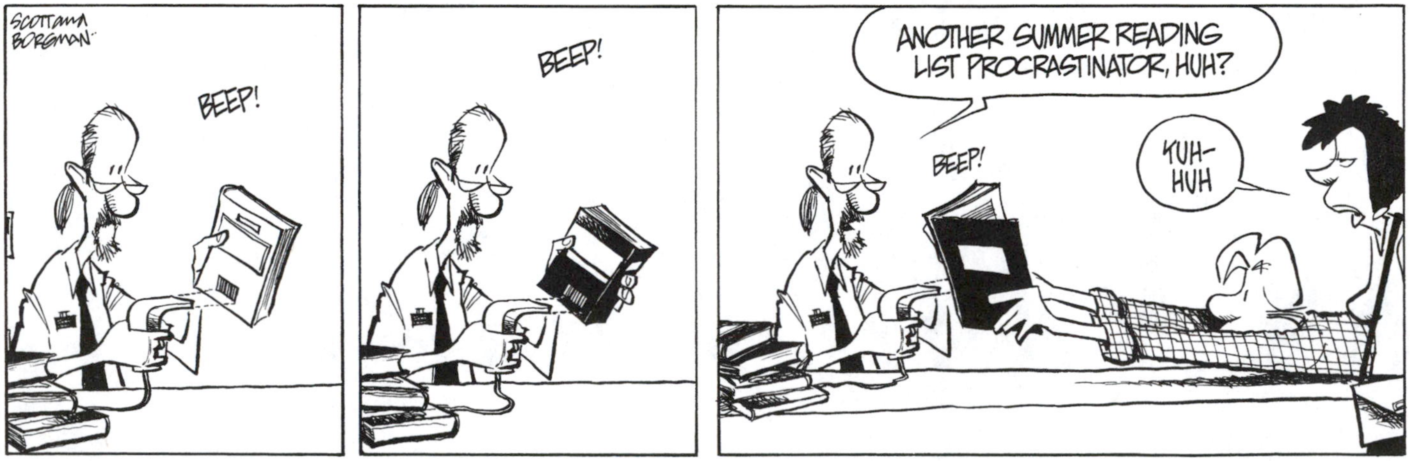
SCOTT and BORGMAN
BEEP!
BEEP!
ANOTHER SUMMER READING LIST PROCRASTINATOR, HUH?
BEEP!
YUH-HUH

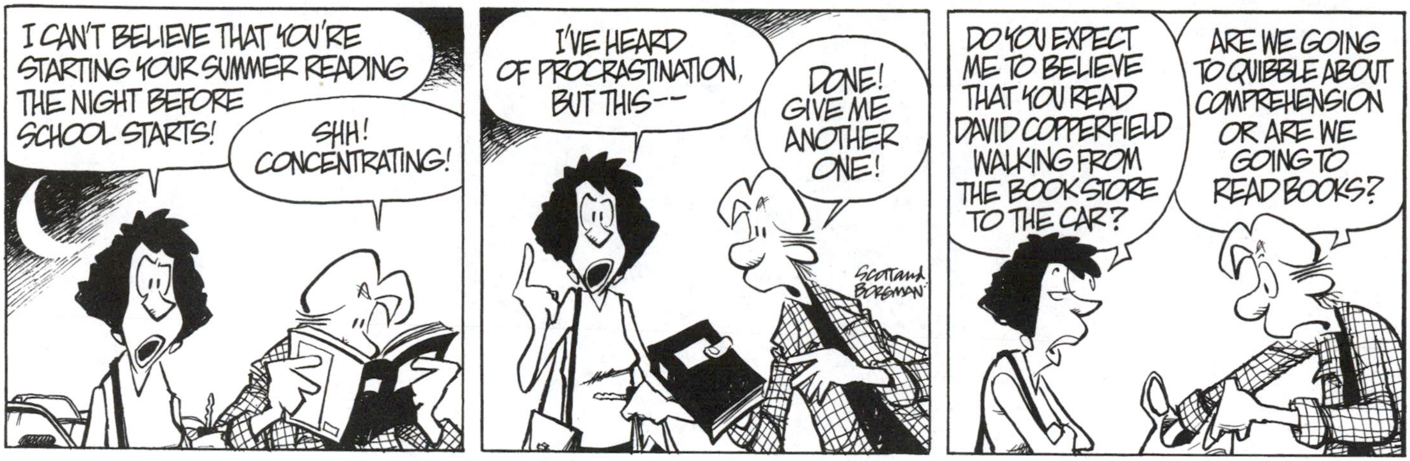
I CAN'T BELIEVE THAT YOU'RE STARTING YOUR SUMMER READING THE NIGHT BEFORE SCHOOL STARTS!
SHH! CONCENTRATING!
I'VE HEARD OF PROCRASTINATION, BUT THIS--
DONE! GIVE ME ANOTHER ONE!
SCOTT and BORGMAN
DO YOU EXPECT ME TO BELIEVE THAT YOU READ DAVID COPPERFIELD WALKING FROM THE BOOK STORE TO THE CAR?
ARE WE GOING TO QUIBBLE ABOUT COMPREHENSION OR ARE WE GOING TO READ BOOKS?

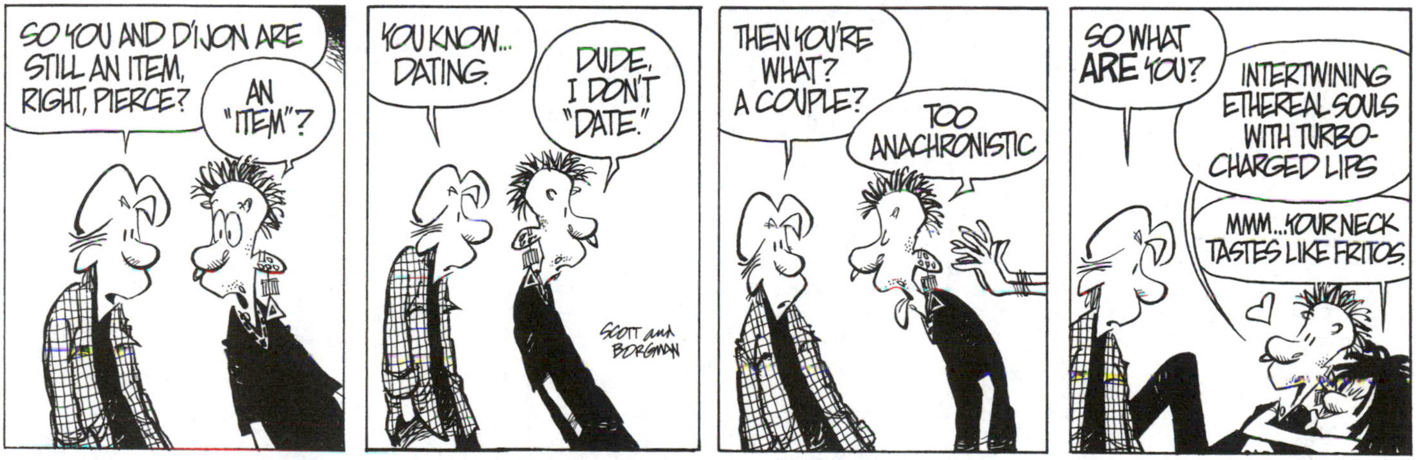
SO YOU AND D'JON ARE STILL AN ITEM, RIGHT, PIERCE?
AN "ITEM"?
YOU KNOW... DATING.
DUDE, I DON'T "DATE."
SCOTT and BORGMAN
THEN YOU'RE WHAT? A COUPLE?
TOO ANACHRONISTIC
SO WHAT ARE YOU?
INTERTWINING ETHEREAL SOULS WITH TURBO-CHARGED LIPS
MMM... YOUR NECK TASTES LIKE FRITOS.

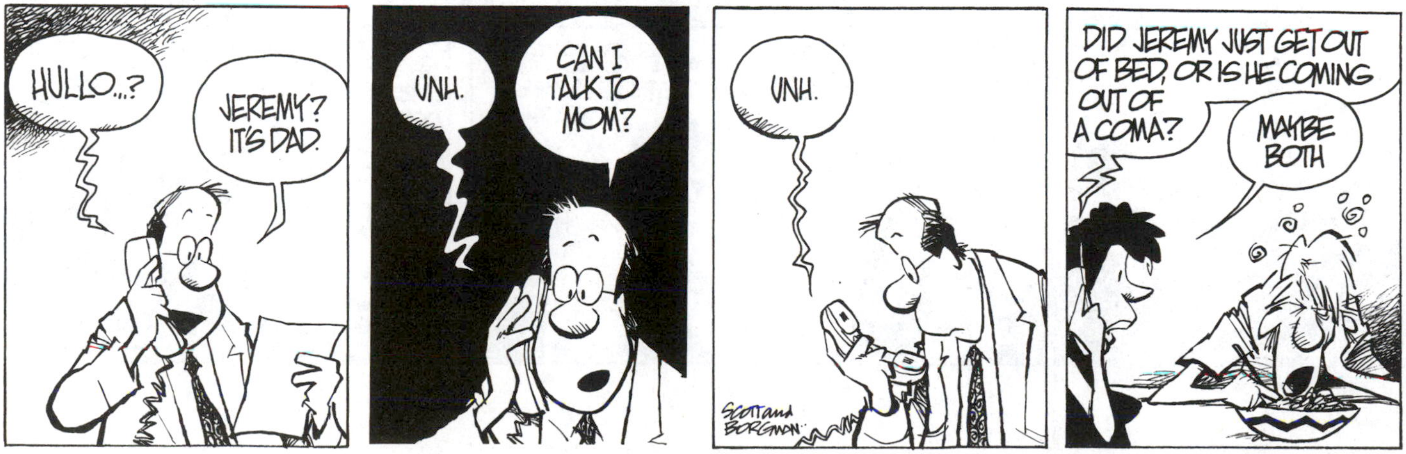
HULLO...?
JEREMY? IT'S DAD.
UNH.
CAN I TALK TO MOM?
UNH.
SCOTT and BORGMAN
DID JEREMY JUST GET OUT OF BED, OR IS HE COMING OUT OF A COMA?
MAYBE BOTH

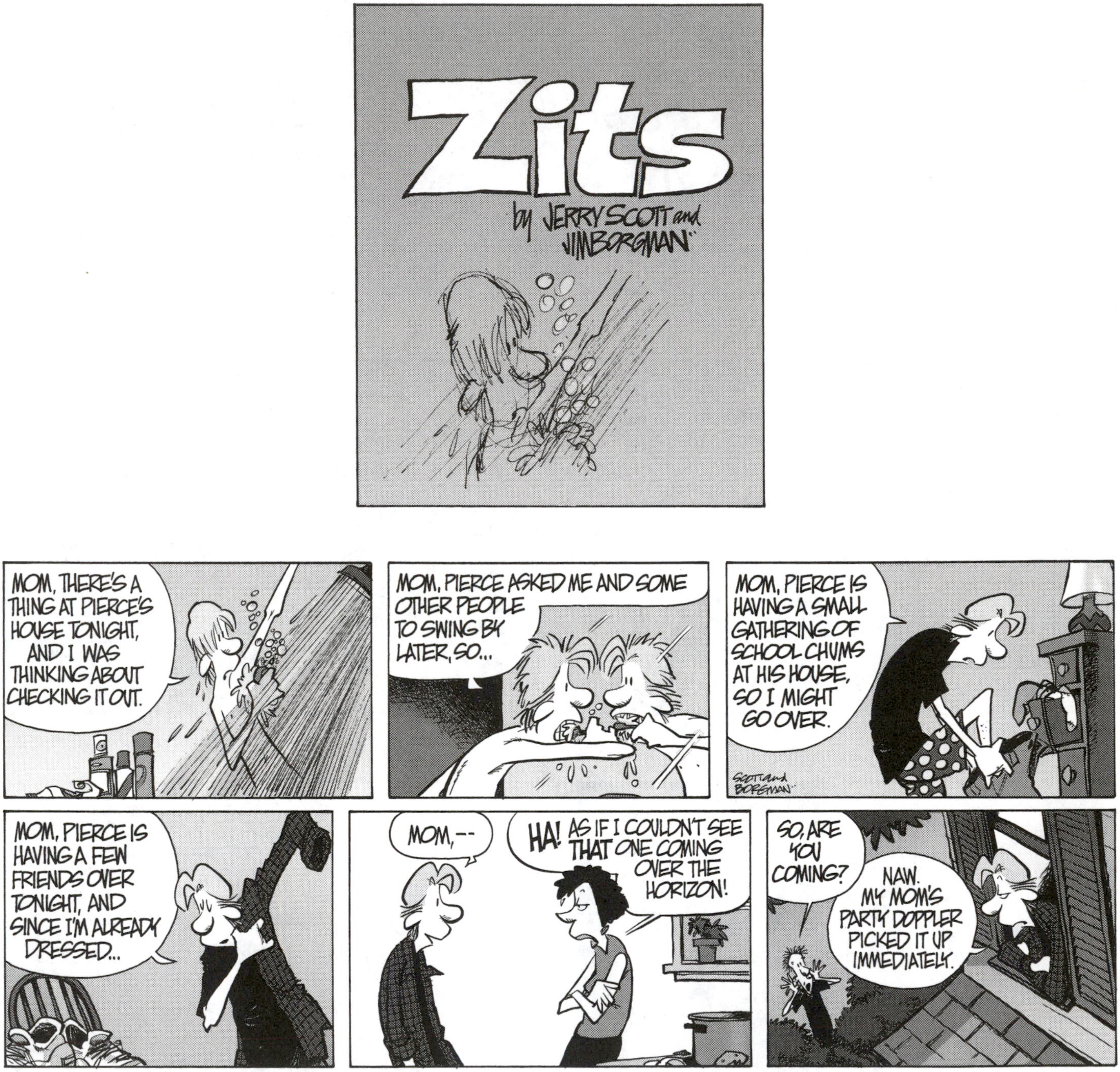
Zits
by JERRY SCOTT and JIM BORGMAN
MOM, THERE'S A THING AT PIERCE'S HOUSE TONIGHT, AND I WAS THINKING ABOUT CHECKING IT OUT.
MOM, PIERCE ASKED ME AND SOME OTHER PEOPLE TO SWING BY LATER, SO...
MOM, PIERCE IS HAVING A SMALL GATHERING OF SCHOOL CHUMS AT HIS HOUSE, SO I MIGHT GO OVER.
SCOTT and BORGMAN
MOM, PIERCE IS HAVING A FEW FRIENDS OVER TONIGHT, AND SINCE I'M ALREADY DRESSED...
MOM, --
HA! AS IF I COULDN'T SEE THAT ONE COMING OVER THE HORIZON!
SO, ARE YOU COMING?
NAW. MY MOM'S PARTY DOPPLER PICKED IT UP IMMEDIATELY.

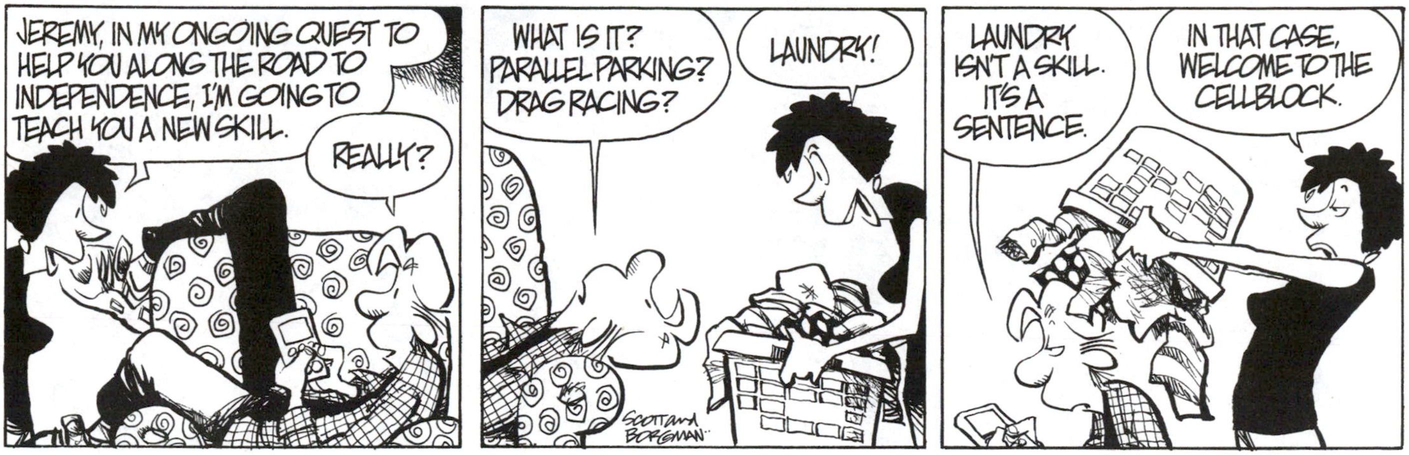
JEREMY, IN MY ONGOING QUEST TO HELP YOU ALONG THE ROAD TO INDEPENDENCE, I'M GOING TO TEACH YOU A NEW SKILL.
REALLY?
WHAT IS IT? PARALLEL PARKING? DRAG RACING?
LAUNDRY!
SCOTT and BORGMAN
LAUNDRY ISN'T A SKILL. IT'S A SENTENCE.
IN THAT CASE, WELCOME TO THE CELLBLOCK.

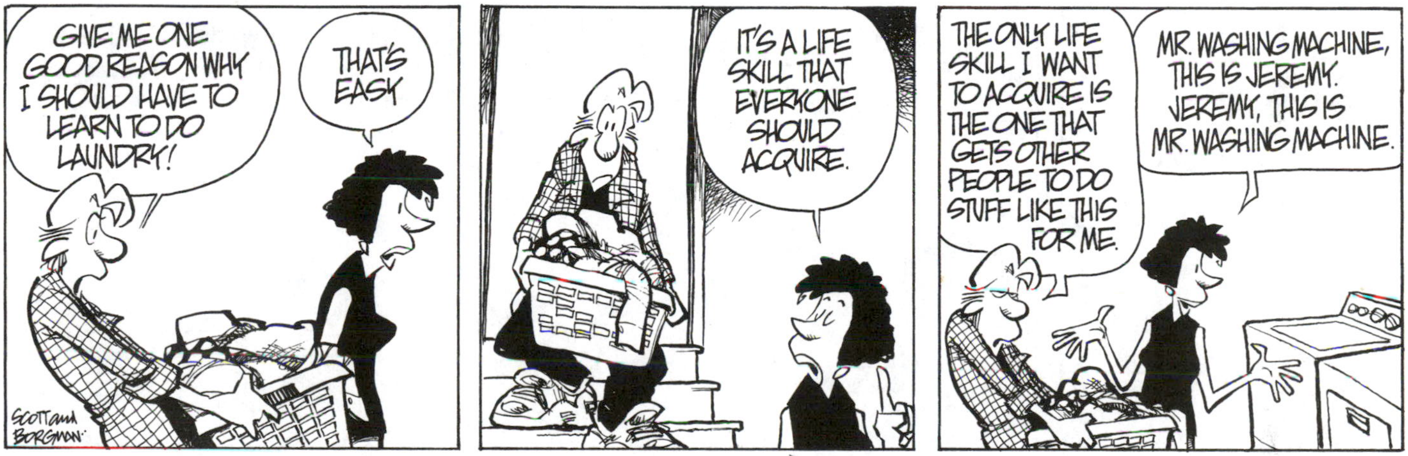
GIVE ME ONE GOOD REASON WHY I SHOULD HAVE TO LEARN TO DO LAUNDRY!
THAT'S EASY
SCOTT and BORGMAN
IT'S A LIFE SKILL THAT EVERYONE SHOULD ACQUIRE.
THE ONLY LIFE SKILL I WANT TO ACQUIRE IS THE ONE THAT GETS OTHER PEOPLE TO DO STUFF LIKE THIS FOR ME.
MR. WASHING MACHINE, THIS IS JEREMY. JEREMY, THIS IS MR. WASHING MACHINE.

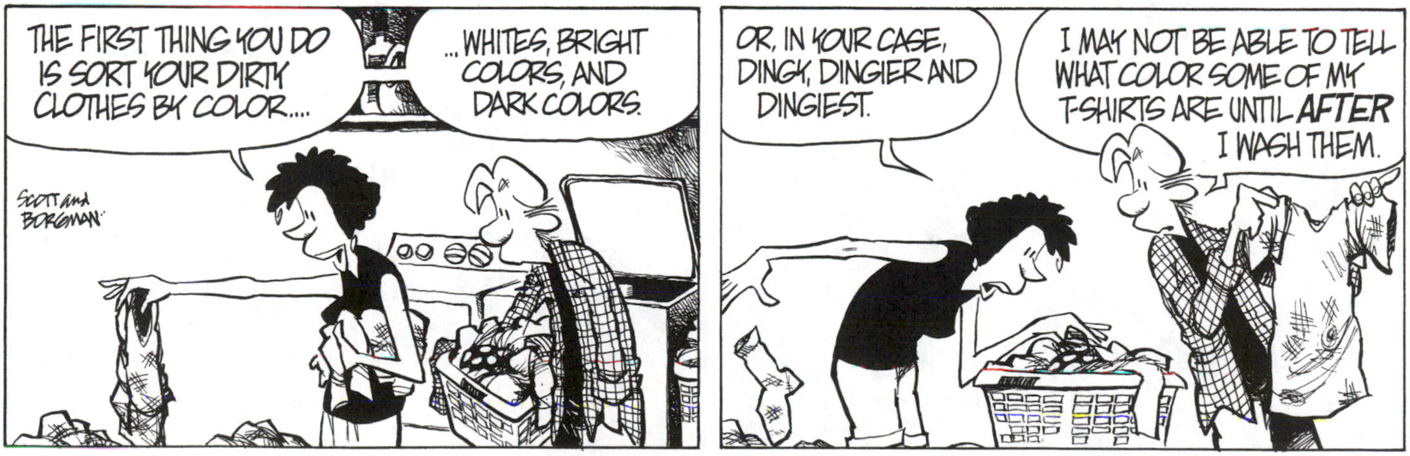
THE FIRST THING YOU DO IS SORT YOUR DIRTY CLOTHES BY COLOR....
...WHITES, BRIGHT COLORS, AND DARK COLORS.
SCOTT and BORGMAN
OR, IN YOUR CASE, DINGY, DINGIER AND DINGIEST.
I MAY NOT BE ABLE TO TELL WHAT COLOR SOME OF MY T-SHIRTS ARE UNTIL AFTER I WASH THEM.

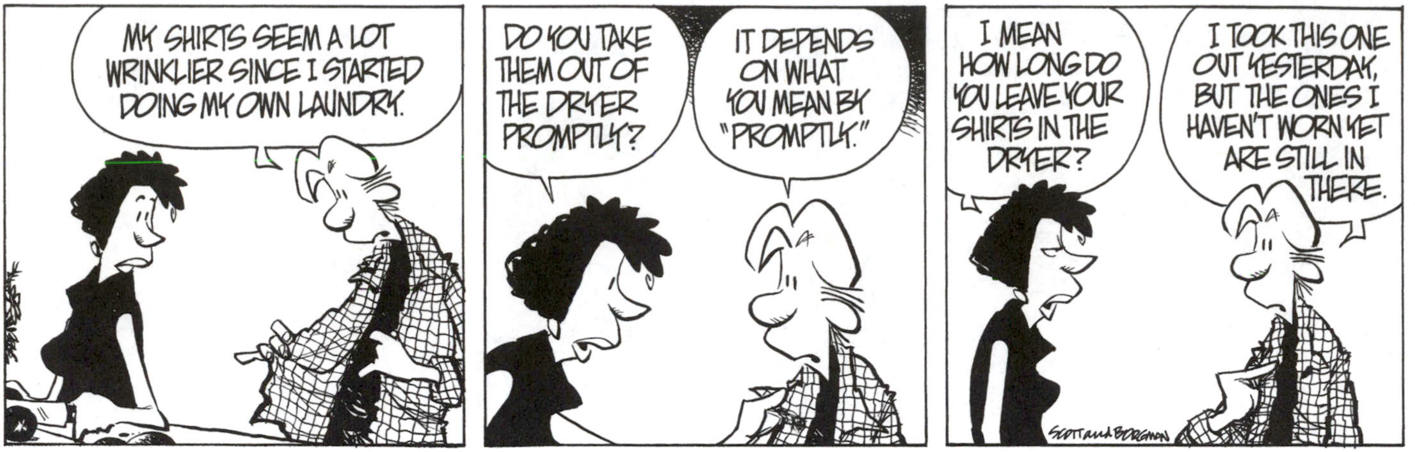
MY SHIRTS SEEM A LOT WRINKLIER SINCE I STARTED DOING MY OWN LAUNDRY.
DO YOU TAKE THEM OUT OF THE DRYER PROMPTLY?
IT DEPENDS ON WHAT YOU MEAN BY "PROMPTLY."
I MEAN HOW LONG DO YOU LEAVE YOUR SHIRTS IN THE DRYER?
I TOOK THIS ONE OUT YESTERDAY, BUT THE ONES I HAVEN'T WORN YET ARE STILL IN THERE.

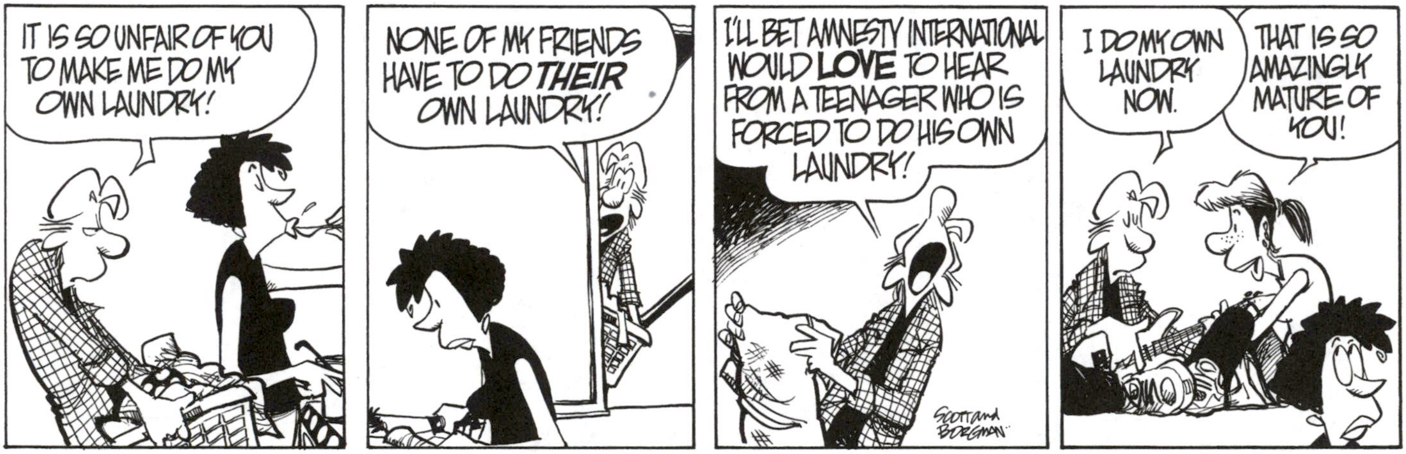
IT IS SO UNFAIR OF YOU TO MAKE ME DO MY OWN LAUNDRY!
NONE OF MY FRIENDS HAVE TO DO THEIR OWN LAUNDRY!
I'LL BET AMNESTY INTERNATIONAL WOULD LOVE TO HEAR FROM A TEENAGER WHO IS FORCED TO DO HIS OWN LAUNDRY!
I DO MY OWN LAUNDRY NOW.
THAT IS SO AMAZINGLY MATURE OF YOU!

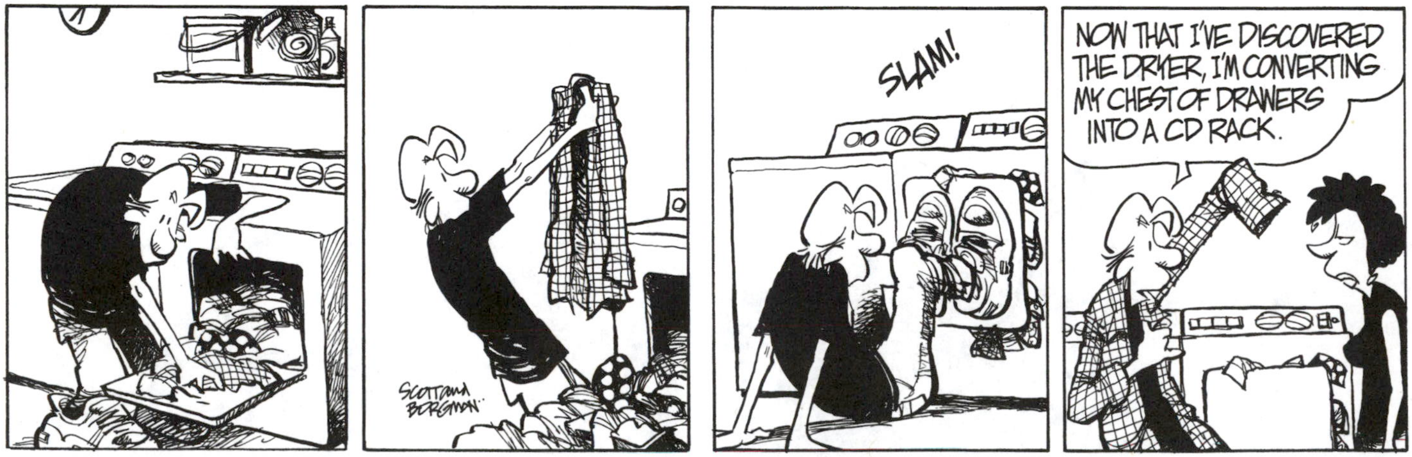
SLAM!
NOW THAT I'VE DISCOVERED THE DRYER, I'M CONVERTING MY CHEST OF DRAWERS INTO A CD RACK.

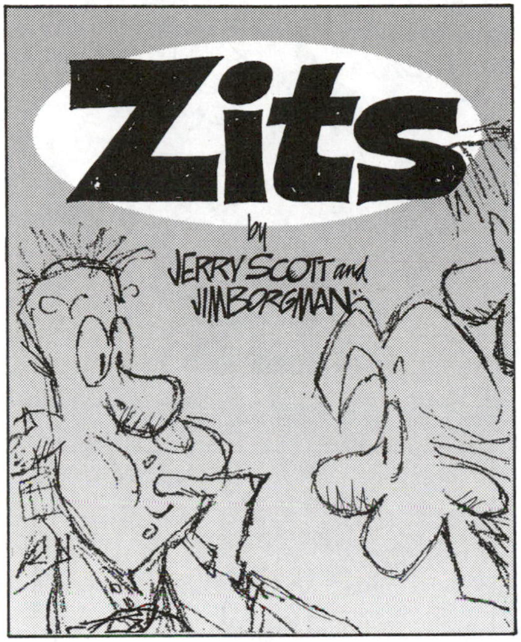
Zits
by
JERRY SCOTT and
JIM BORGMAN

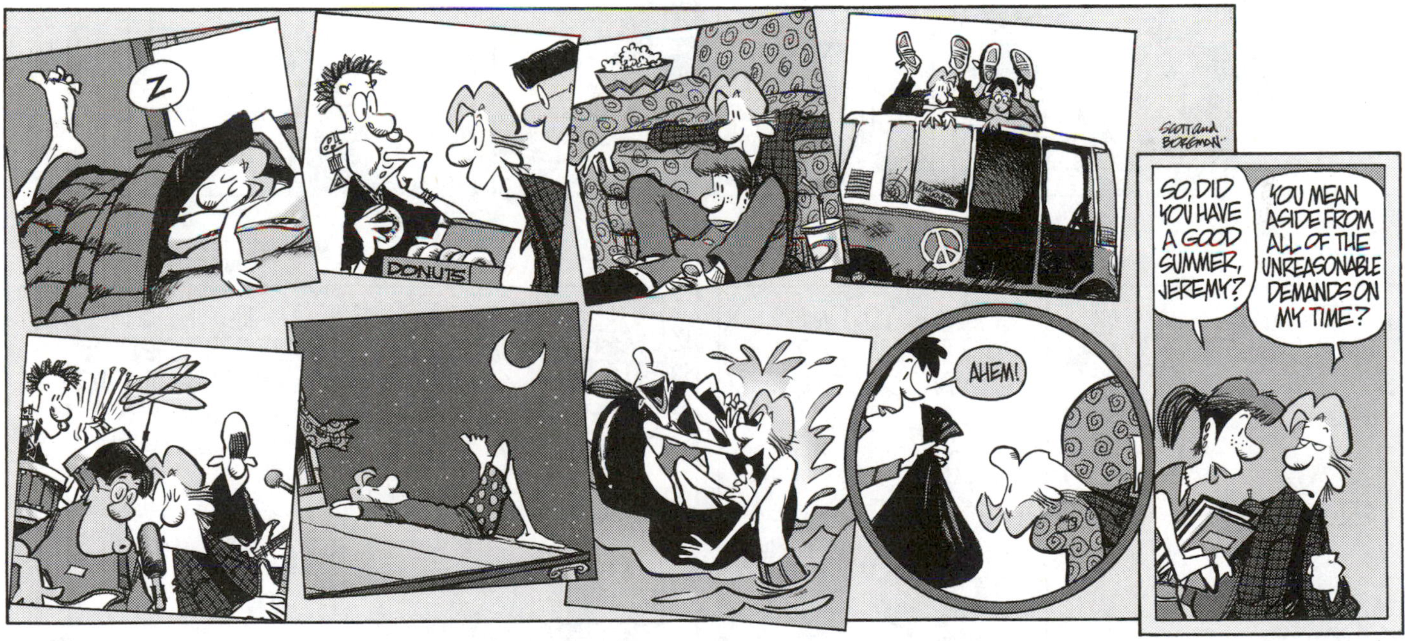
Z
DONUTS
SCOTT and BORGMAN
AHEM!
SO, DID YOU HAVE A GOOD SUMMER, JEREMY?
YOU MEAN ASIDE FROM ALL OF THE UNREASONABLE DEMANDS ON MY TIME?

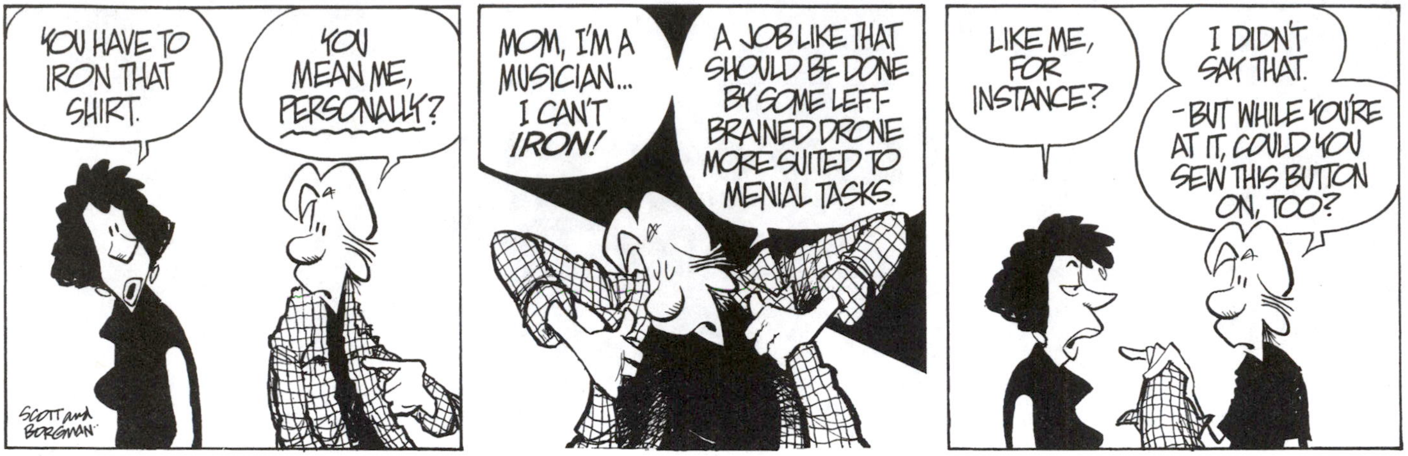
YOU HAVE TO IRON THAT SHIRT.
YOU MEAN ME, PERSONALLY?
SCOTT and BORGMAN
MOM, I'M A MUSICIAN... I CAN'T IRON!
A JOB LIKE THAT SHOULD BE DONE BY SOME LEFT-BRAINED DRONE MORE SUITED TO MENIAL TASKS.
LIKE ME, FOR INSTANCE?
I DIDN'T SAY THAT.
-BUT WHILE YOU'RE AT IT, COULD YOU SEW THIS BUTTON ON, TOO?

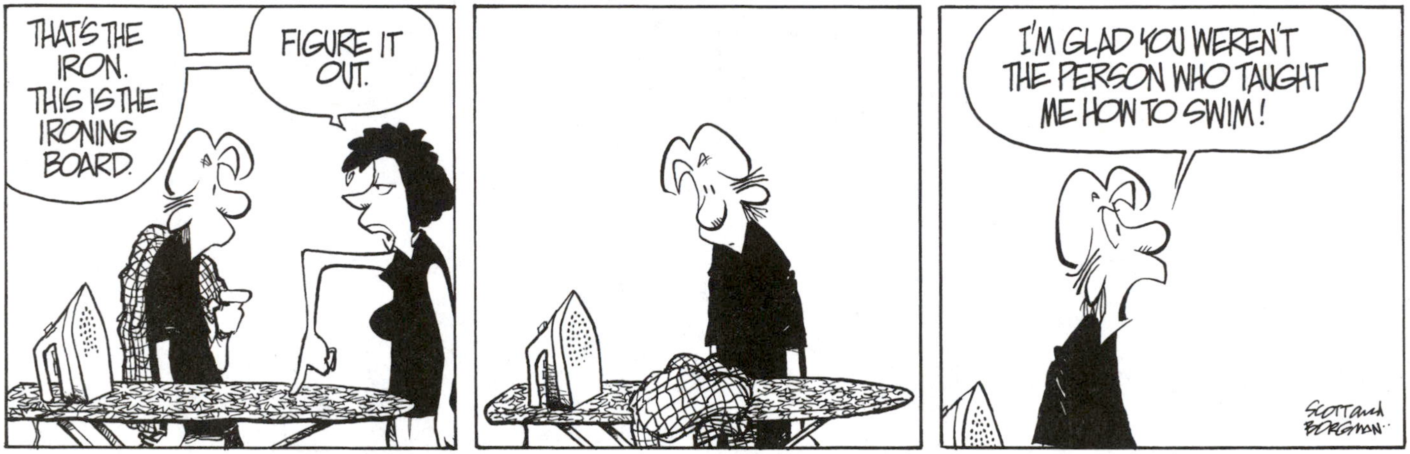
THAT'S THE IRON. THIS IS THE IRONING BOARD.
FIGURE IT OUT.
I'M GLAD YOU WEREN'T THE PERSON WHO TAUGHT ME HOW TO SWIM!
SCOTT and BORGMAN

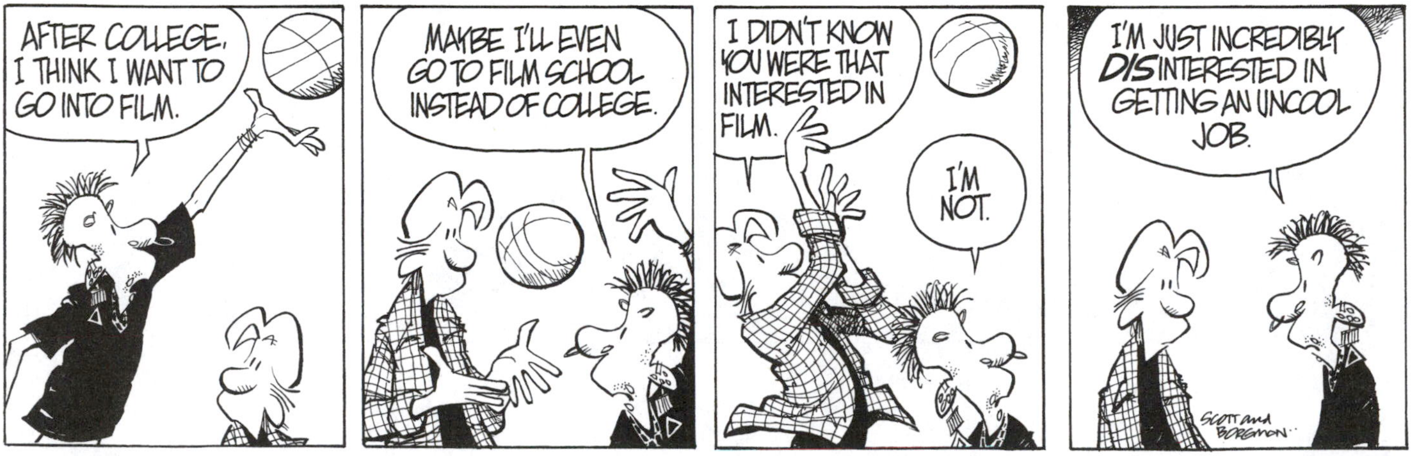
AFTER COLLEGE, I THINK I WANT TO GO INTO FILM.
MAYBE I'LL EVEN GO TO FILM SCHOOL INSTEAD OF COLLEGE.
I DIDN'T KNOW YOU WERE THAT INTERESTED IN FILM.
I'M NOT.
I'M JUST INCREDIBLY DISINTERESTED IN GETTING AN UNCOOL JOB.
SCOTT and BORGMAN

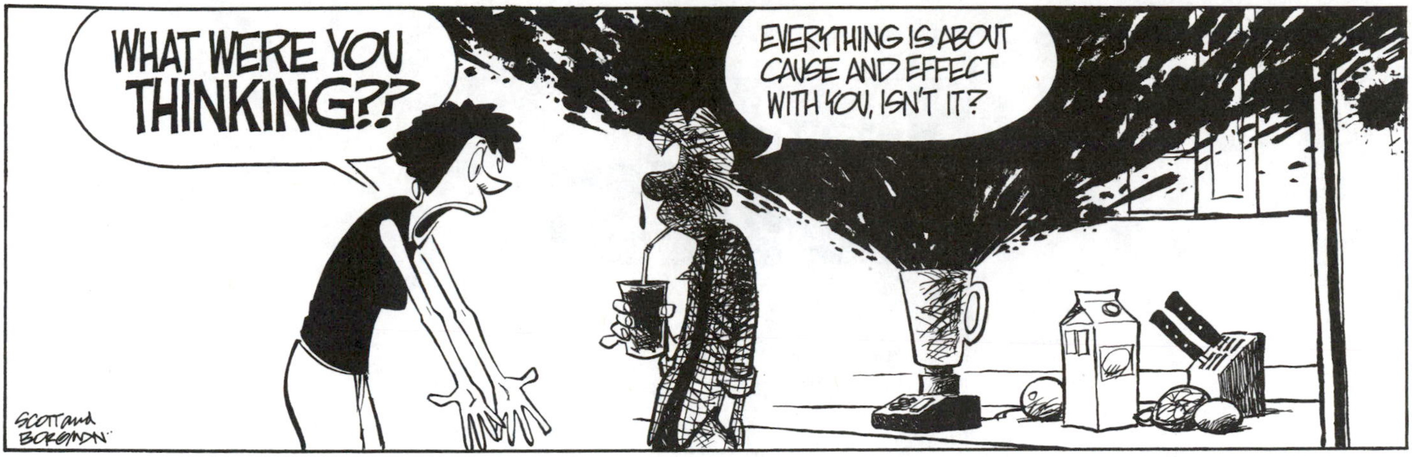
WHAT WERE YOU THINKING??
EVERYTHING IS ABOUT CAUSE AND EFFECT WITH YOU, ISN'T IT?
SCOTT and BORGMAN

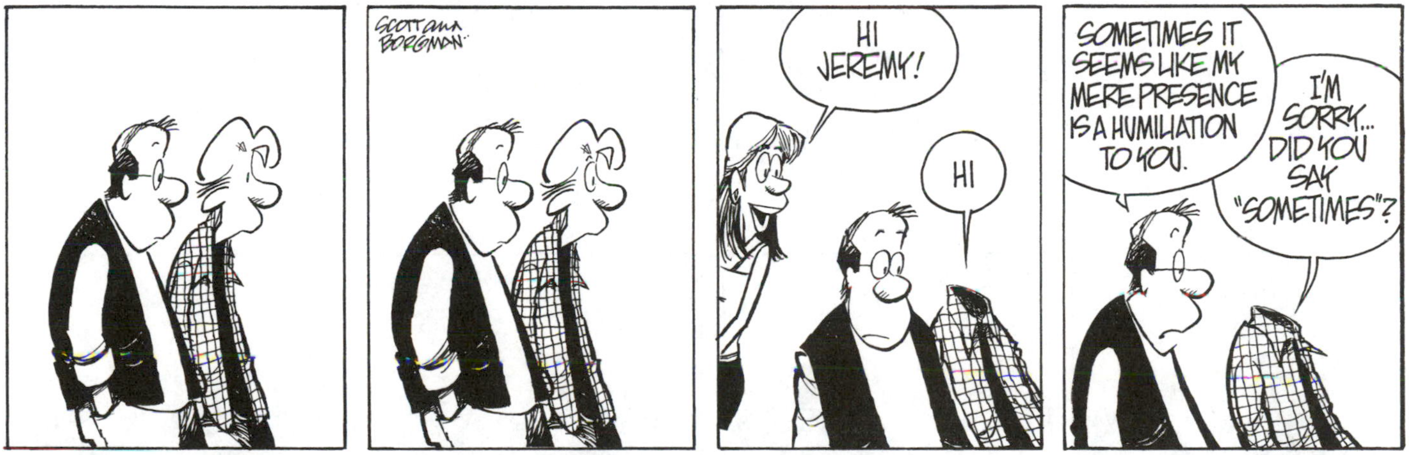
SCOTT and BORGMAN
HI JEREMY!
HI
SOMETIMES IT SEEMS LIKE MY MERE PRESENCE IS A HUMILIATION TO YOU.
I'M SORRY... DID YOU SAY "SOMETIMES"?

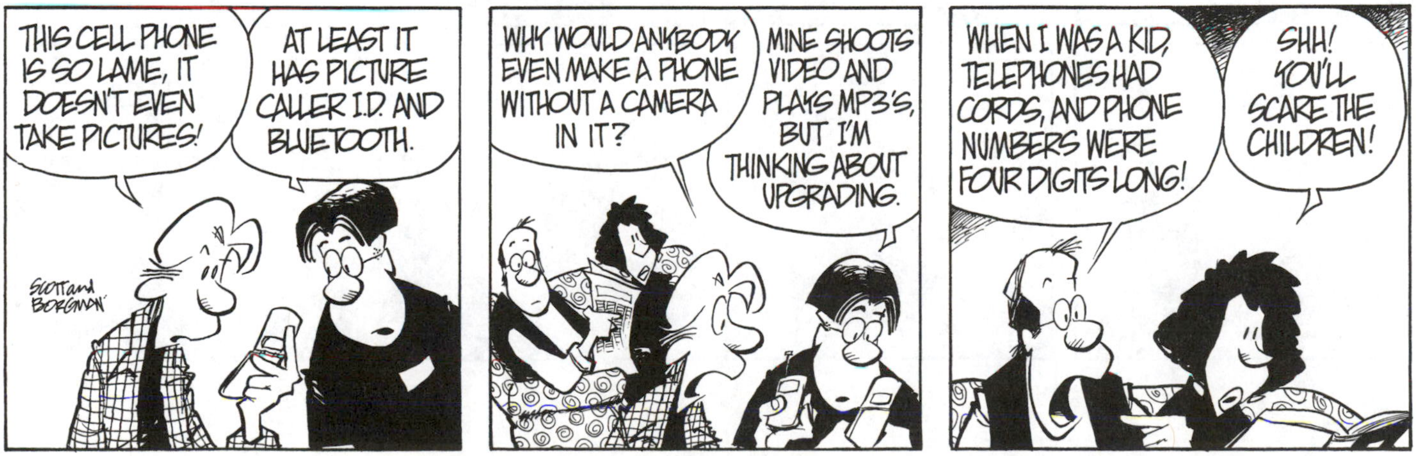
THIS CELL PHONE IS SO LAME, IT DOESN'T EVEN TAKE PICTURES!
AT LEAST IT HAS PICTURE CALLER I.D. AND BLUETOOTH.
SCOTT and BORGMAN
WHY WOULD ANYBODY EVEN MAKE A PHONE WITHOUT A CAMERA IN IT?
MINE SHOOTS VIDEO AND PLAYS MP3'S, BUT I'M THINKING ABOUT UPGRADING.
WHEN I WAS A KID, TELEPHONES HAD CORDS, AND PHONE NUMBERS WERE FOUR DIGITS LONG!
SHH! YOU'LL SCARE THE CHILDREN!

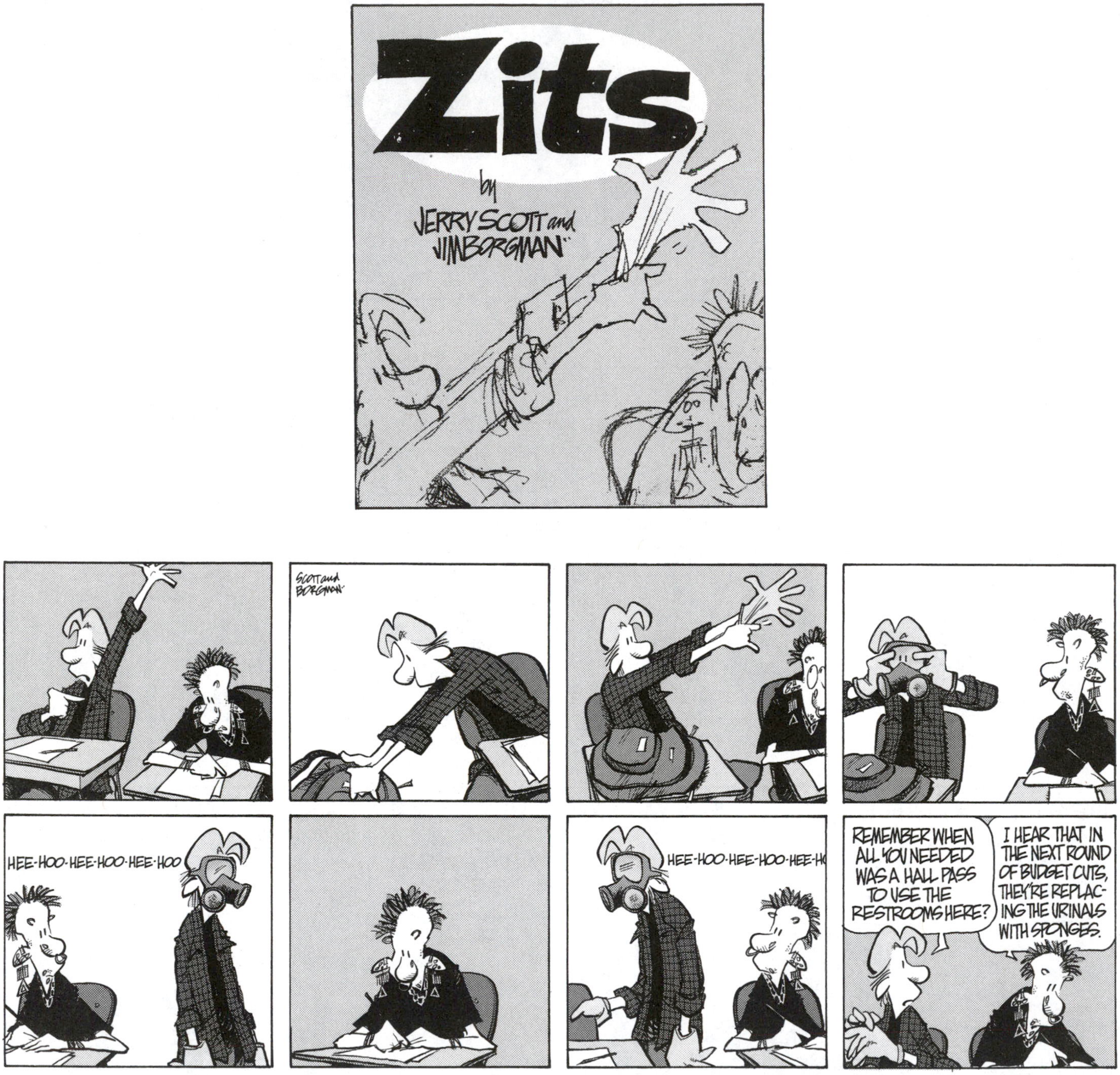
Zits
by
JERRY SCOTT and
JIM BORGMAN
SCOTT and BORGMAN
HEE-HOO-HEE-HOO-HEE-HOO
HEE-HOO-HEE-HOO-HEE-H
REMEMBER WHEN ALL YOU NEEDED WAS A HALL PASS TO USE THE RESTROOMS HERE?
I HEAR THAT IN THE NEXT ROUND OF BUDGET CUTS, THEY'RE REPLACING THE URINALS WITH SPONGES.

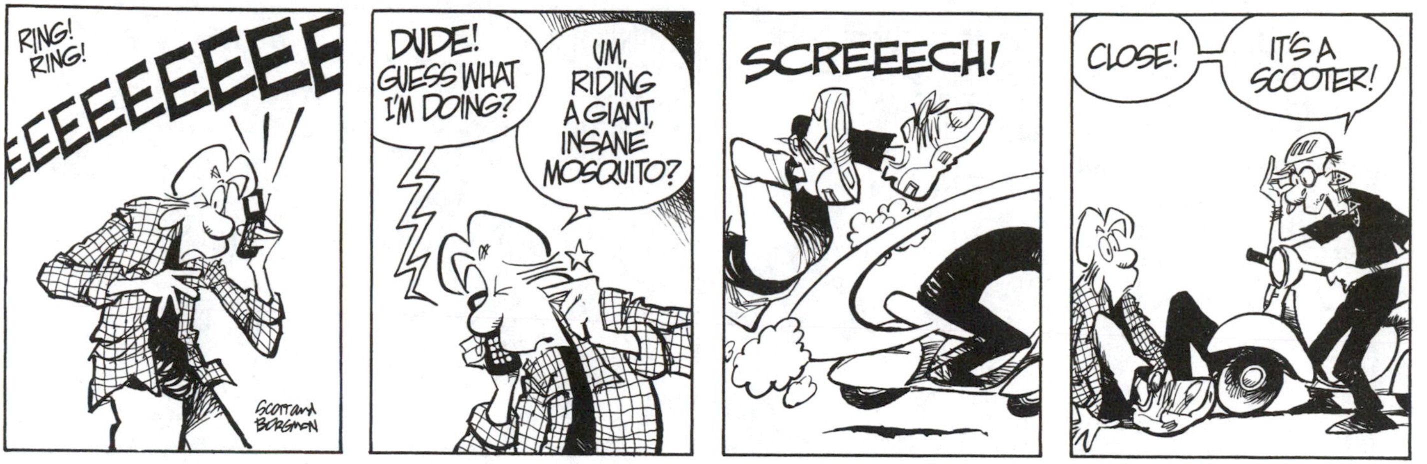
RING! RING!
EEEEEEEEEEE
SCOTT and BORGMAN
DUDE! GUESS WHAT I'M DOING?
UM, RIDING A GIANT, INSANE MOSQUITO?
SCREEECH!
CLOSE!
IT'S A SCOOTER!

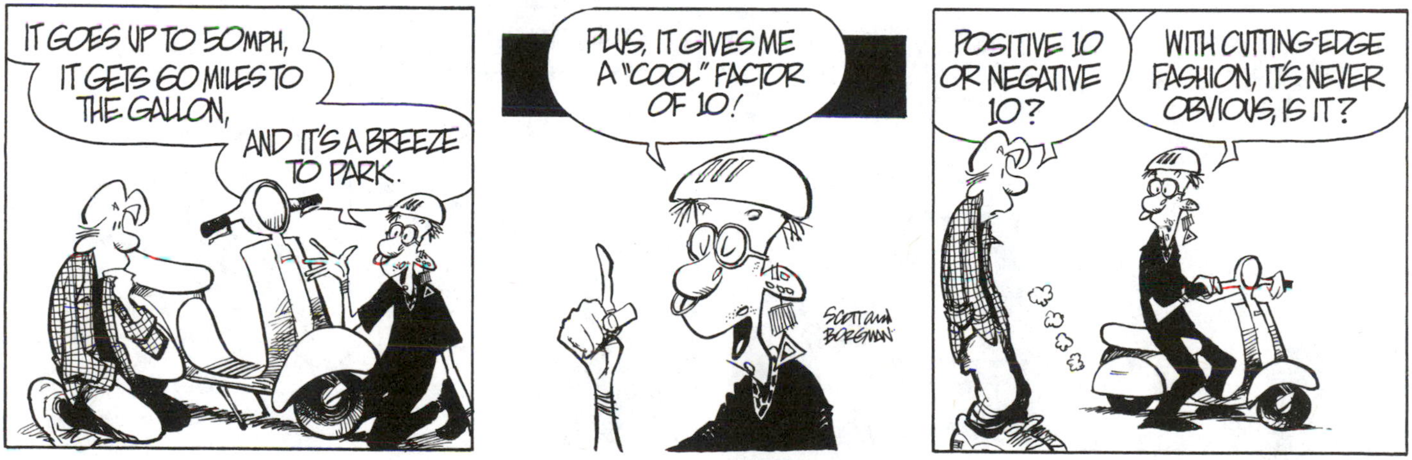
IT GOES UP TO 50MPH, IT GETS 60 MILES TO THE GALLON,
AND IT'S A BREEZE TO PARK.
PLUS, IT GIVES ME A "COOL" FACTOR OF 10!
SCOTT and BORGMAN
POSITIVE 10 OR NEGATIVE 10?
WITH CUTTING-EDGE FASHION, IT'S NEVER OBVIOUS, IS IT?

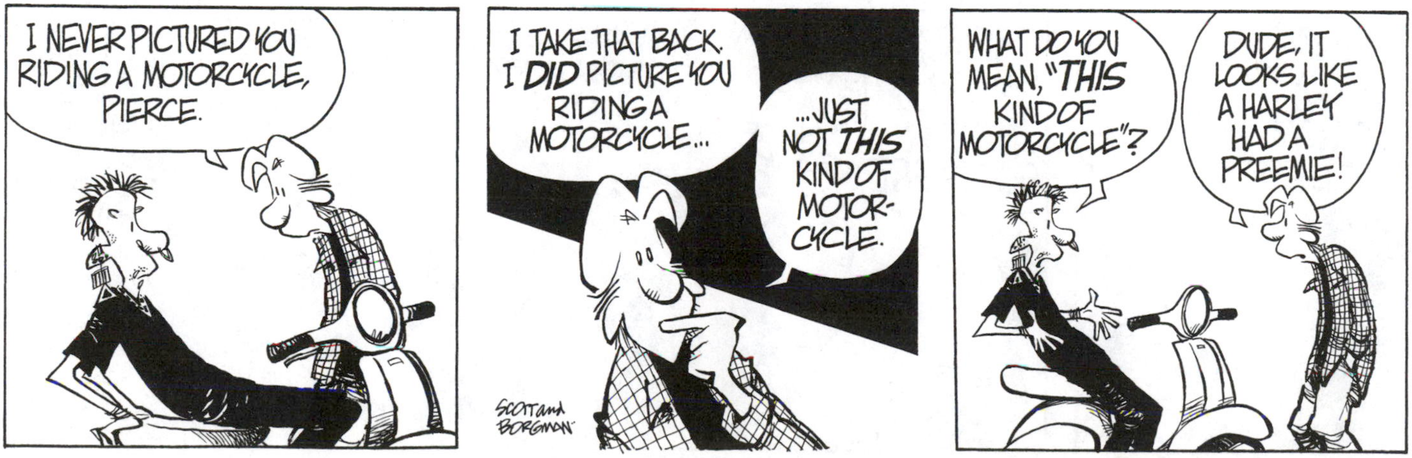
I NEVER PICTURED YOU RIDING A MOTORCYCLE, PIERCE.
I TAKE THAT BACK. I DID PICTURE YOU RIDING A MOTORCYCLE...
...JUST NOT THIS KIND OF MOTOR-CYCLE.
SCOTT and BORGMAN
WHAT DO YOU MEAN, "THIS KIND OF MOTORCYCLE"?
DUDE, IT LOOKS LIKE A HARLEY HAD A PREEMIE!

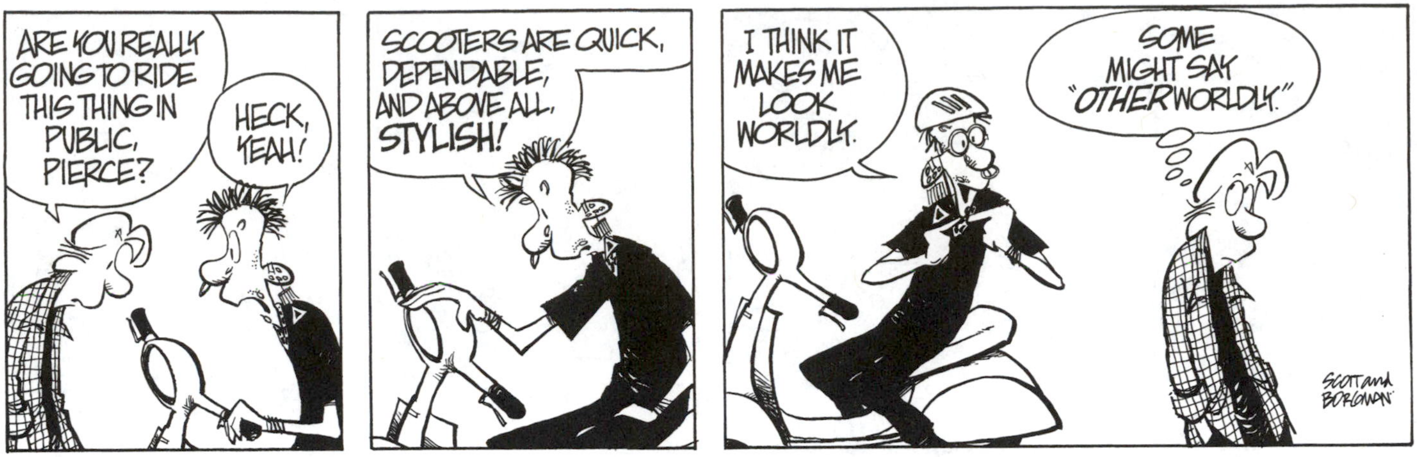
ARE YOU REALLY GOING TO RIDE THIS THING IN PUBLIC, PIERCE?
HECK, YEAH!
SCOOTERS ARE QUICK, DEPENDABLE, AND ABOVE ALL, STYLISH!
I THINK IT MAKES ME LOOK WORLDLY.
SOME MIGHT SAY "OTHERWORLDLY."
SCOTT and BORGMAN

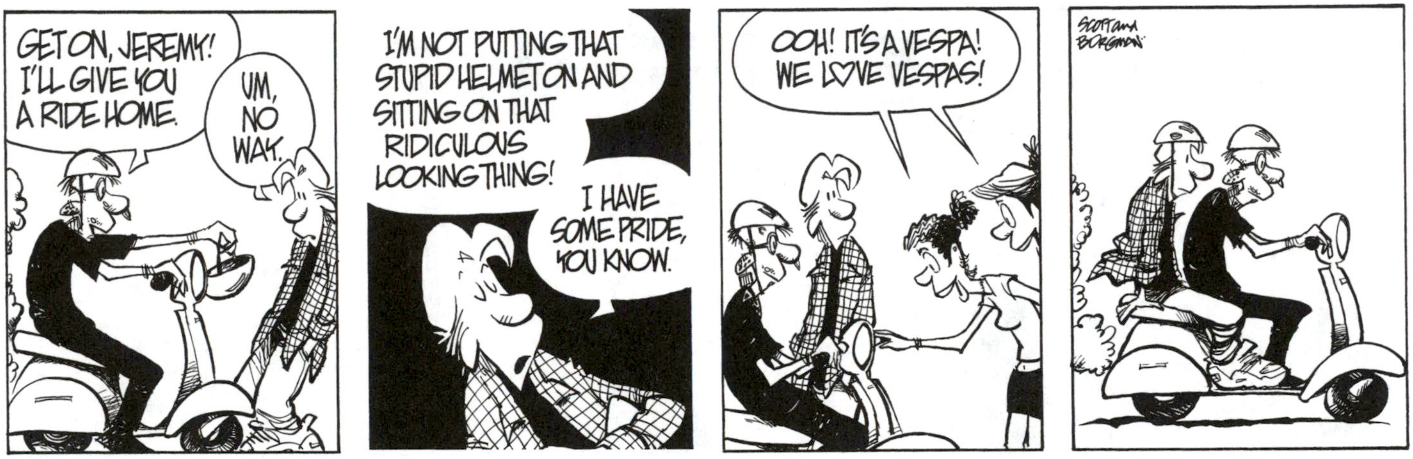
SCOTT and BORGMAN
GET ON, JEREMY! I'LL GIVE YOU A RIDE HOME.
UM, NO WAY.
I'M NOT PUTTING THAT STUPID HELMET ON AND SITTING ON THAT RIDICULOUS LOOKING THING!
I HAVE SOME PRIDE, YOU KNOW.
OOH! IT'S A VESPA! WE LOVE VESPAS!

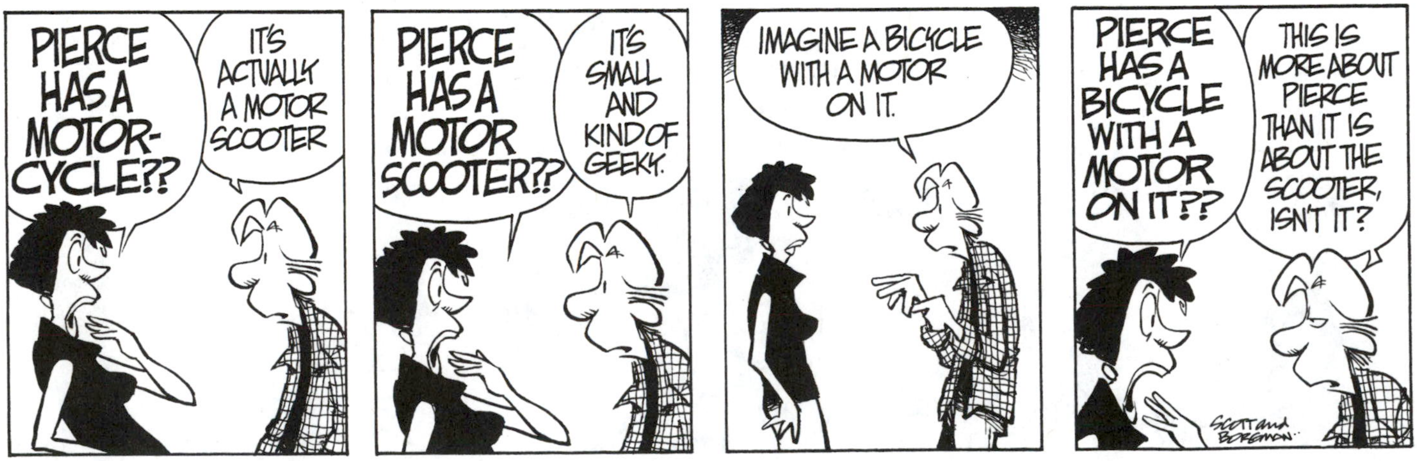
PIERCE HAS A MOTORCYCLE??
IT'S ACTUALLY A MOTOR SCOOTER
PIERCE HAS A MOTOR SCOOTER??
IT'S SMALL AND KIND OF GEEKY.
IMAGINE A BICYCLE WITH A MOTOR ON IT.
PIERCE HAS A BICYCLE WITH A MOTOR ON IT??
THIS IS MORE ABOUT PIERCE THAN IT IS ABOUT THE SCOOTER, ISN'T IT?
SCOTT and BORGMAN

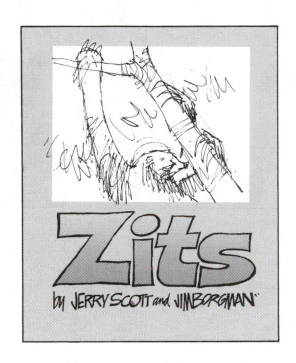

Zits

by JERRY SCOTT and JIM BORGMAN

♪♪♪

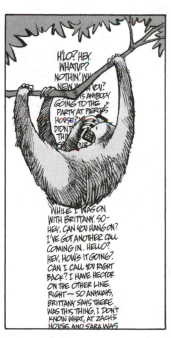

H'LO? HEY. WHATUP? NOTHIN'. WHY? WHO'S NEW WITH YOU? IS ANYBODY GOING TO THE PARTY AT PIERCE'S HOUSE? I DIDN'T THINK SO EITHER—

WHILE I WAS ON WITH BRITTANY. SO— HEY, CAN YOU HANG ON? I'VE GOT ANOTHER CALL COMING IN. HELLO? HEY, HOW'S IT GOING? CAN I CALL YOU RIGHT BACK? I HAVE HECTOR ON THE OTHER LINE. RIGHT—SO ANYWAYS, BRITTANY SAYS THERE WAS THIS THING, I DON'T KNOW WHAT, AT ZACH'S HOUSE AND SARA WAS

SCOTT and BORGMAN

HOW CAN ANYTHING THAT MOVES SO SLOW TALK SO FAST??

IT'S THE NATURE OF THE BEAST.

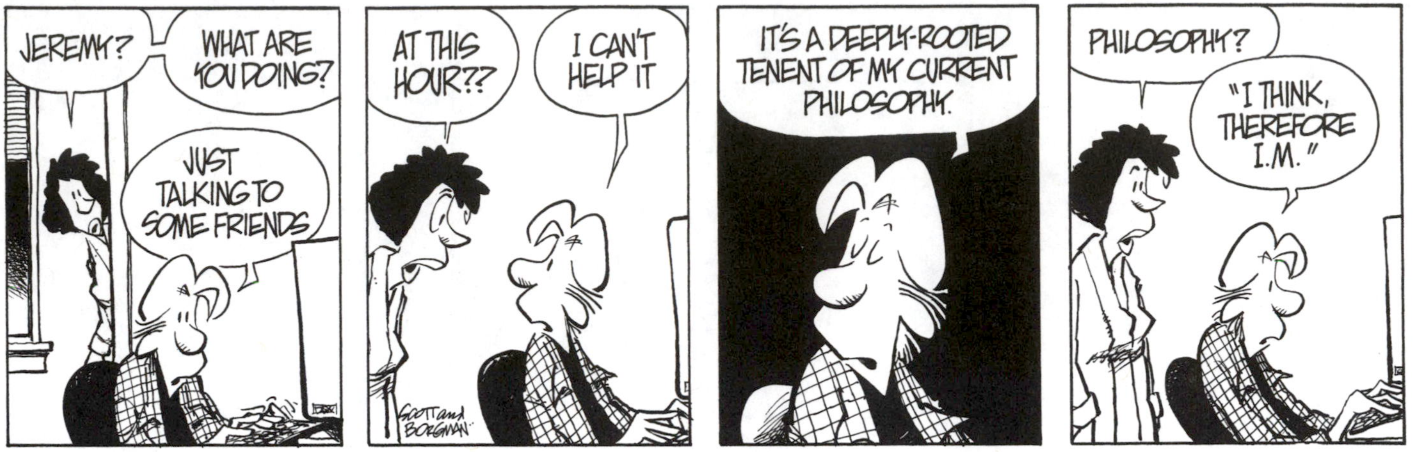
JEREMY?
WHAT ARE YOU DOING?
JUST TALKING TO SOME FRIENDS
AT THIS HOUR??
I CAN'T HELP IT
SCOTT and BORGMAN
IT'S A DEEPLY-ROOTED TENENT OF MY CURRENT PHILOSOPHY.
PHILOSOPHY?
"I THINK, THEREFORE I.M."

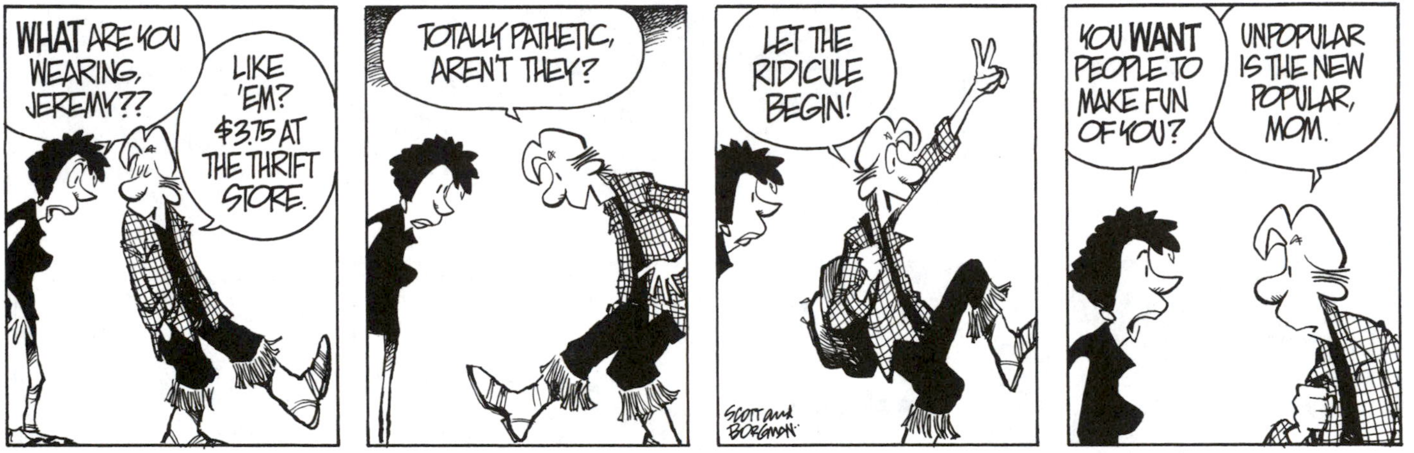
WHAT ARE YOU WEARING, JEREMY??
LIKE 'EM? $3.75 AT THE THRIFT STORE.
TOTALLY PATHETIC, AREN'T THEY?
LET THE RIDICULE BEGIN!
SCOTT and BORGMAN
YOU WANT PEOPLE TO MAKE FUN OF YOU?
UNPOPULAR IS THE NEW POPULAR, MOM.

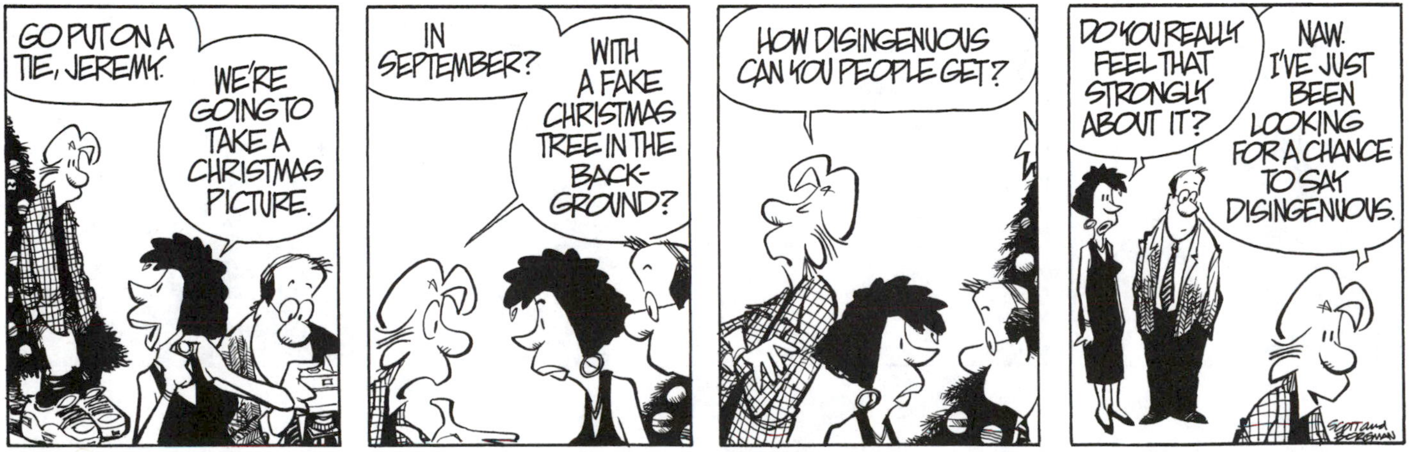
GO PUT ON A TIE, JEREMY.
WE'RE GOING TO TAKE A CHRISTMAS PICTURE.
IN SEPTEMBER?
WITH A FAKE CHRISTMAS TREE IN THE BACK-GROUND?
HOW DISINGENUOUS CAN YOU PEOPLE GET?
DO YOU REALLY FEEL THAT STRONGLY ABOUT IT?
NAW. I'VE JUST BEEN LOOKING FOR A CHANCE TO SAY DISINGENUOUS.
SCOTT and BORGMAN

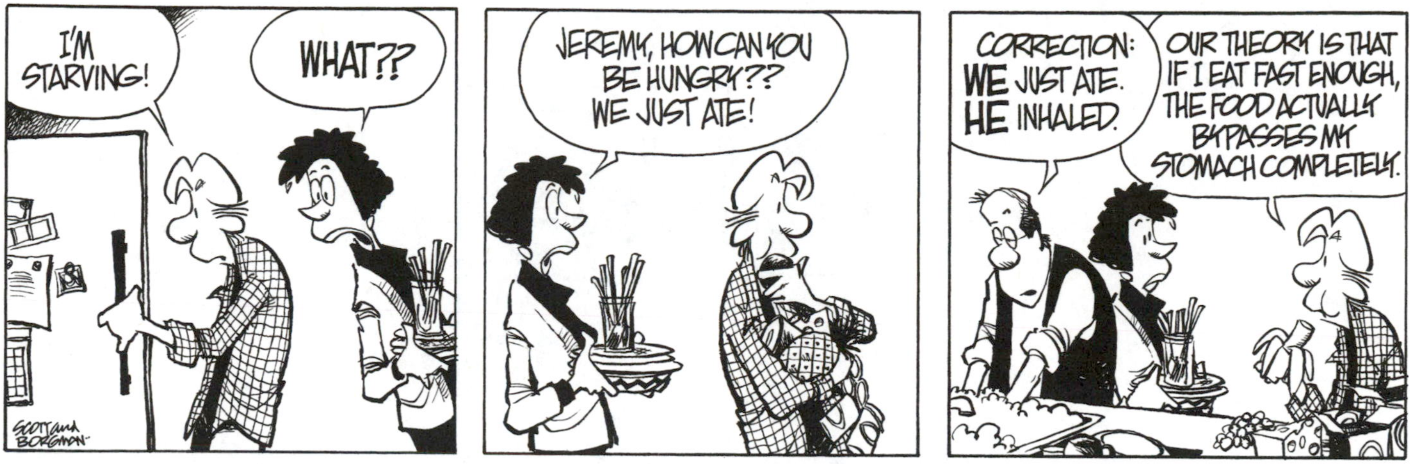
I'M STARVING!
WHAT??
SCOTT and BORGMAN
JEREMY, HOW CAN YOU BE HUNGRY?? WE JUST ATE!
CORRECTION: WE JUST ATE. HE INHALED.
OUR THEORY IS THAT IF I EAT FAST ENOUGH, THE FOOD ACTUALLY BYPASSES MY STOMACH COMPLETELY.

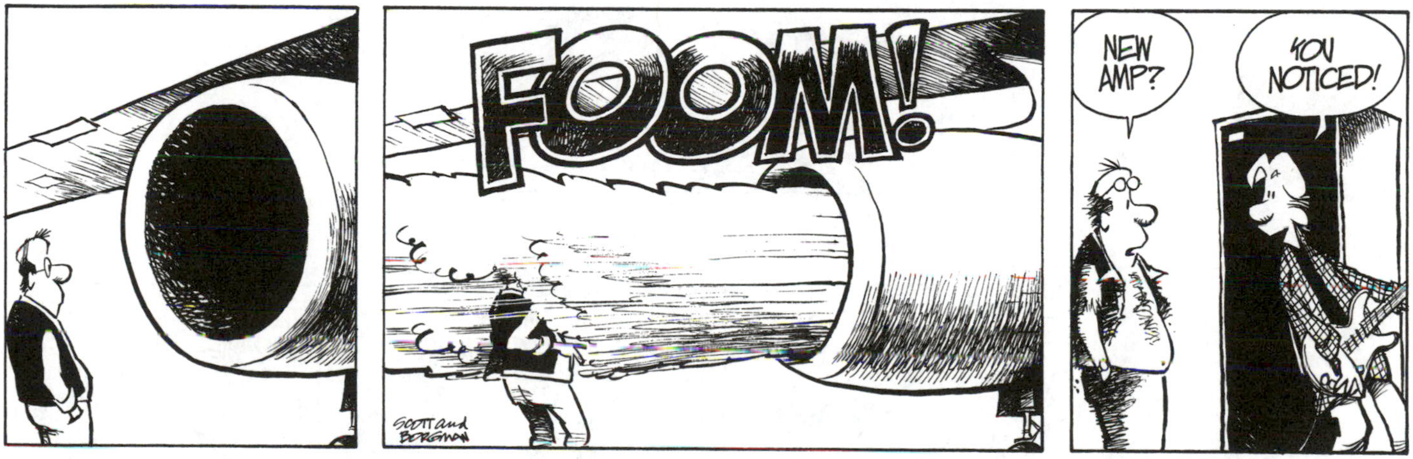
FOOM!
SCOTT and BORGMAN
NEW AMP?
YOU NOTICED!

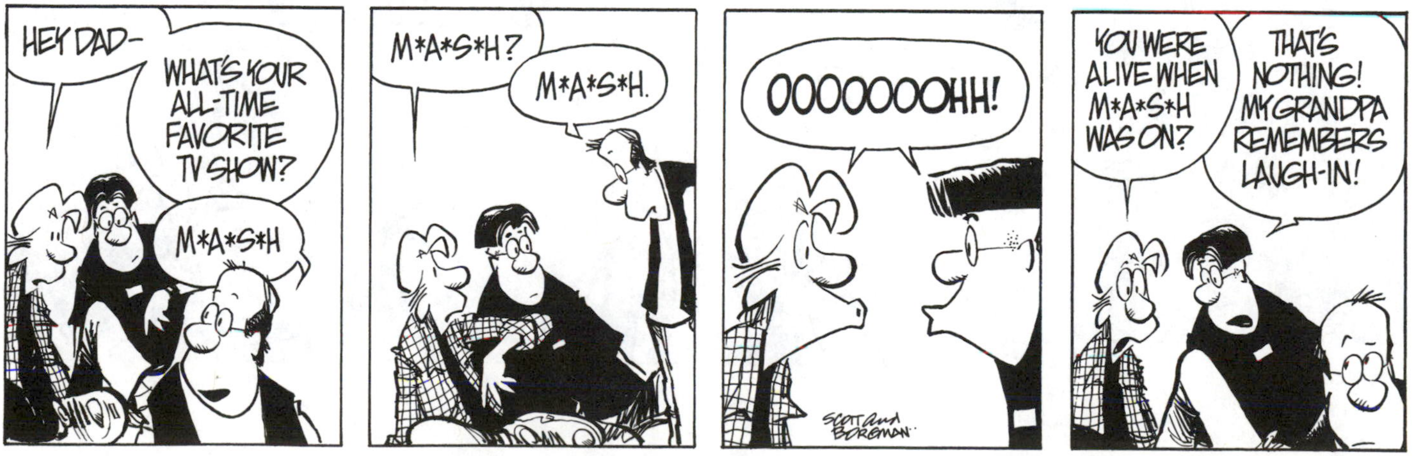
HEY DAD–
WHAT'S YOUR ALL-TIME FAVORITE TV SHOW?
M*A*S*H
M*A*S*H?
M*A*S*H.
OOOOOOOHH!
SCOTT and BORGMAN
YOU WERE ALIVE WHEN M*A*S*H WAS ON?
THAT'S NOTHING! MY GRANDPA REMEMBERS LAUGH-IN!

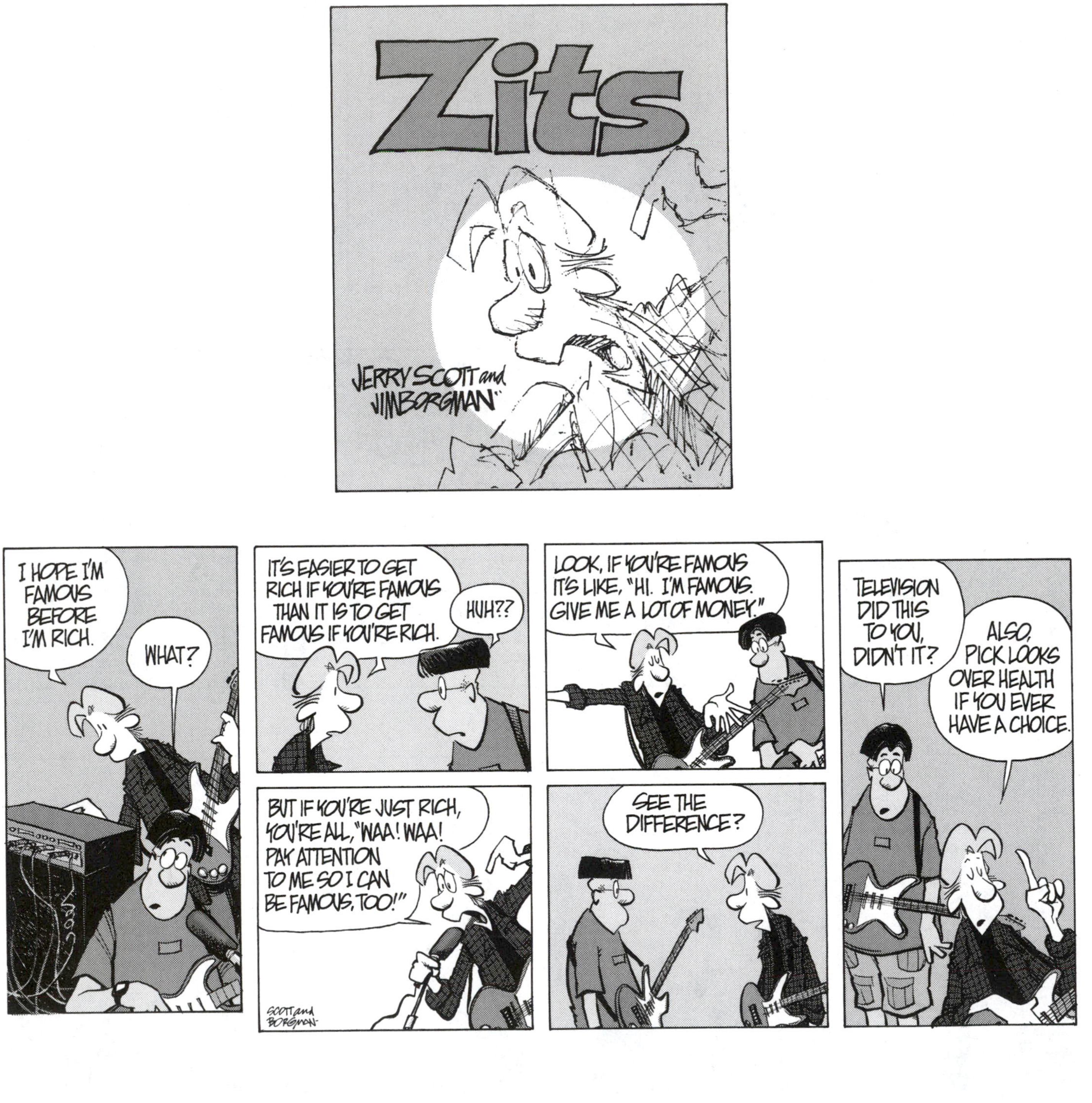
Zits
JERRY SCOTT and JIM BORGMAN
I HOPE I'M FAMOUS BEFORE I'M RICH.
WHAT?
IT'S EASIER TO GET RICH IF YOU'RE FAMOUS THAN IT IS TO GET FAMOUS IF YOU'RE RICH.
HUH??
LOOK, IF YOU'RE FAMOUS IT'S LIKE, "HI. I'M FAMOUS. GIVE ME A LOT OF MONEY."
BUT IF YOU'RE JUST RICH, YOU'RE ALL, "WAA! WAA! PAY ATTENTION TO ME SO I CAN BE FAMOUS, TOO!"
SCOTT and BORGMAN
SEE THE DIFFERENCE?
TELEVISION DID THIS TO YOU, DIDN'T IT?
ALSO, PICK LOOKS OVER HEALTH IF YOU EVER HAVE A CHOICE.

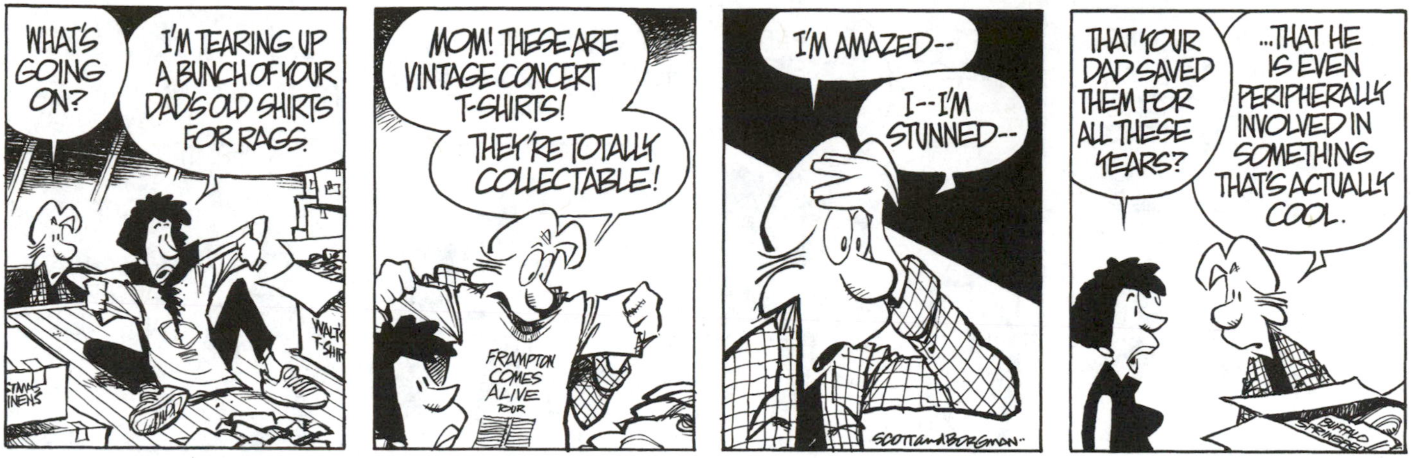
WHAT'S GOING ON?
I'M TEARING UP A BUNCH OF YOUR DAD'S OLD SHIRTS FOR RAGS.
MOM! THESE ARE VINTAGE CONCERT T-SHIRTS!
THEY'RE TOTALLY COLLECTABLE!
FRAMPTON COMES ALIVE TOUR
I'M AMAZED--
I--I'M STUNNED--
SCOTT and BORGMAN
THAT YOUR DAD SAVED THEM FOR ALL THESE YEARS?
...THAT HE IS EVEN PERIPHERALLY INVOLVED IN SOMETHING THAT'S ACTUALLY COOL.

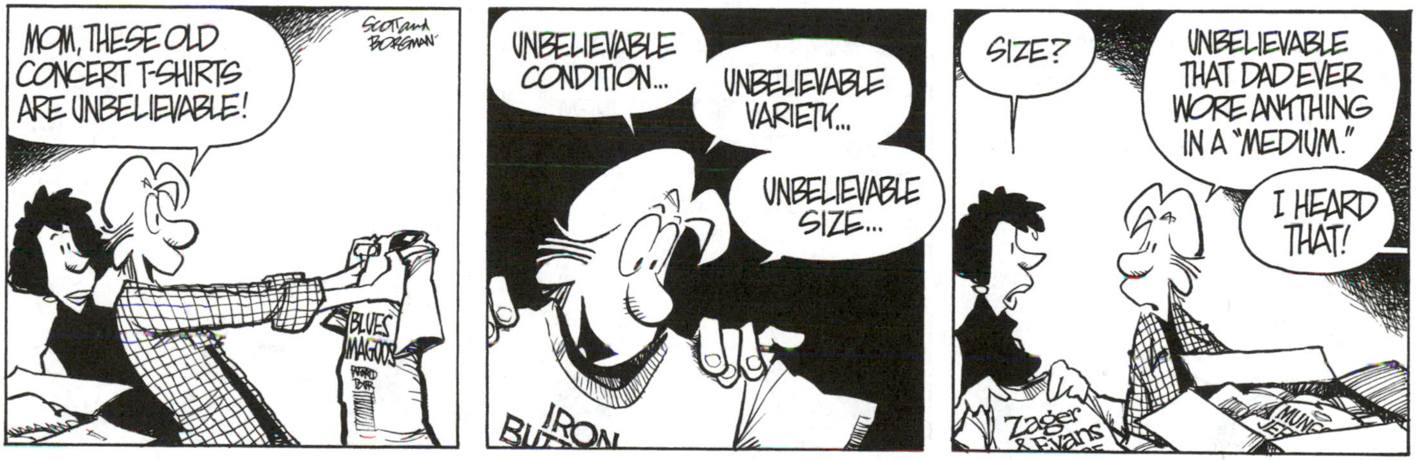
SCOTT and BORGMAN
MOM, THESE OLD CONCERT T-SHIRTS ARE UNBELIEVABLE!
BLUES MAGOOS
UNBELIEVABLE CONDITION...
UNBELIEVABLE VARIETY...
UNBELIEVABLE SIZE...
SIZE?
UNBELIEVABLE THAT DAD EVER WORE ANYTHING IN A "MEDIUM."
I HEARD THAT!
Zager & Evans

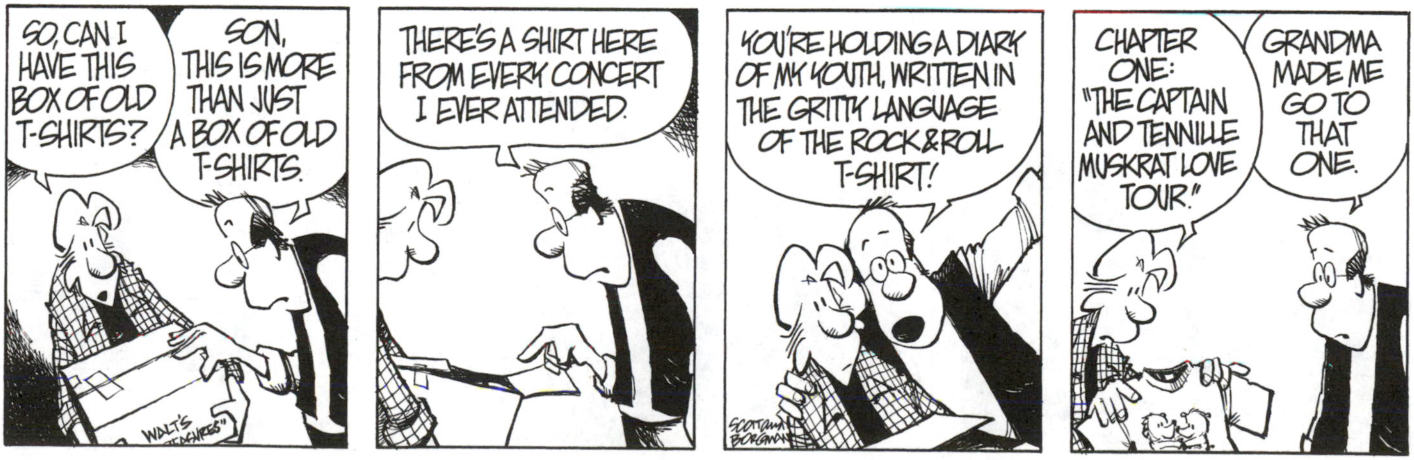
SO, CAN I HAVE THIS BOX OF OLD T-SHIRTS?
SON, THIS IS MORE THAN JUST A BOX OF OLD T-SHIRTS.
THERE'S A SHIRT HERE FROM EVERY CONCERT I EVER ATTENDED.
YOU'RE HOLDING A DIARY OF MY YOUTH, WRITTEN IN THE GRITTY LANGUAGE OF THE ROCK & ROLL T-SHIRT!
SCOTT and BORGMAN
CHAPTER ONE: "THE CAPTAIN AND TENNILLE MUSKRAT LOVE TOUR."
GRANDMA MADE ME GO TO THAT ONE.

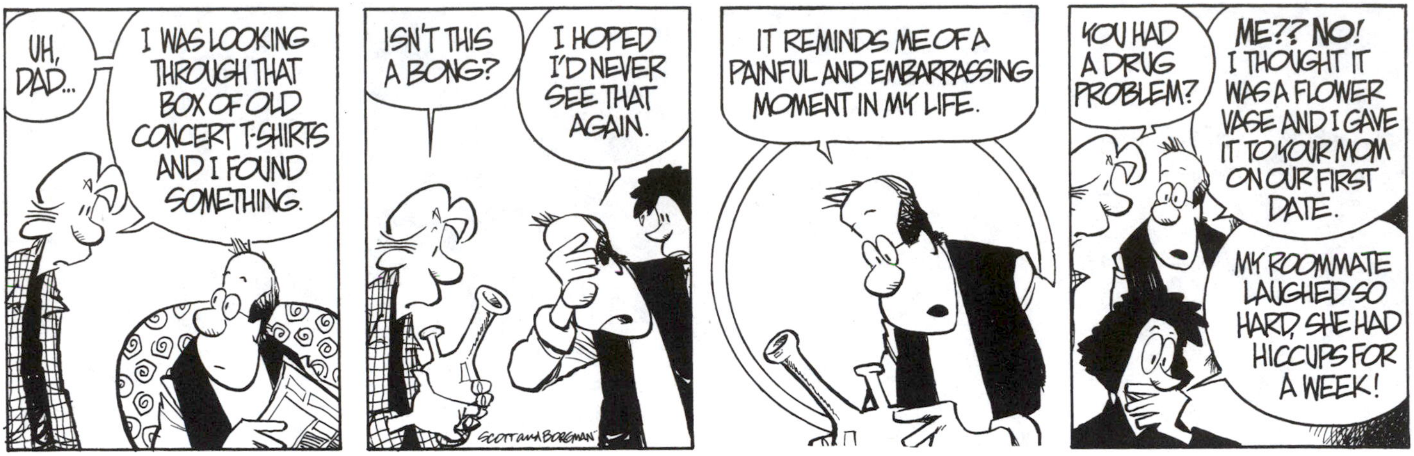
UH, DAD...
I WAS LOOKING THROUGH THAT BOX OF OLD CONCERT T-SHIRTS AND I FOUND SOMETHING.
ISN'T THIS A BONG?
I HOPED I'D NEVER SEE THAT AGAIN.
SCOTT and BORGMAN
IT REMINDS ME OF A PAINFUL AND EMBARRASSING MOMENT IN MY LIFE.
YOU HAD A DRUG PROBLEM?
ME?? NO! I THOUGHT IT WAS A FLOWER VASE AND I GAVE IT TO YOUR MOM ON OUR FIRST DATE.
MY ROOMMATE LAUGHED SO HARD, SHE HAD HICCUPS FOR A WEEK!

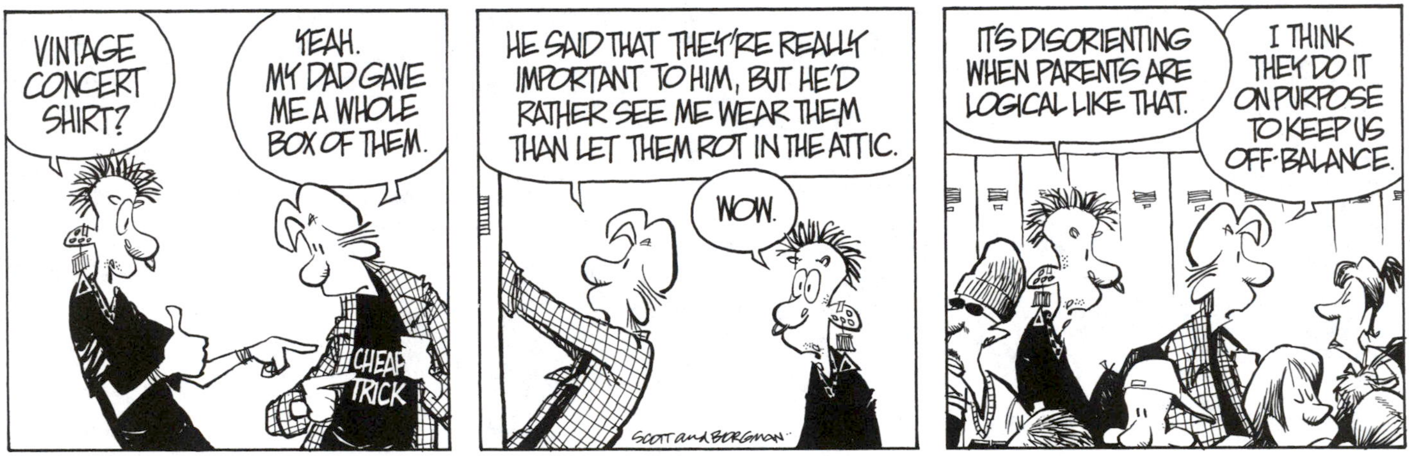
VINTAGE CONCERT SHIRT?
YEAH. MY DAD GAVE ME A WHOLE BOX OF THEM.
CHEAP TRICK
HE SAID THAT THEY'RE REALLY IMPORTANT TO HIM, BUT HE'D RATHER SEE ME WEAR THEM THAN LET THEM ROT IN THE ATTIC.
WOW.
SCOTT and BORGMAN
IT'S DISORIENTING WHEN PARENTS ARE LOGICAL LIKE THAT.
I THINK THEY DO IT ON PURPOSE TO KEEP US OFF-BALANCE.

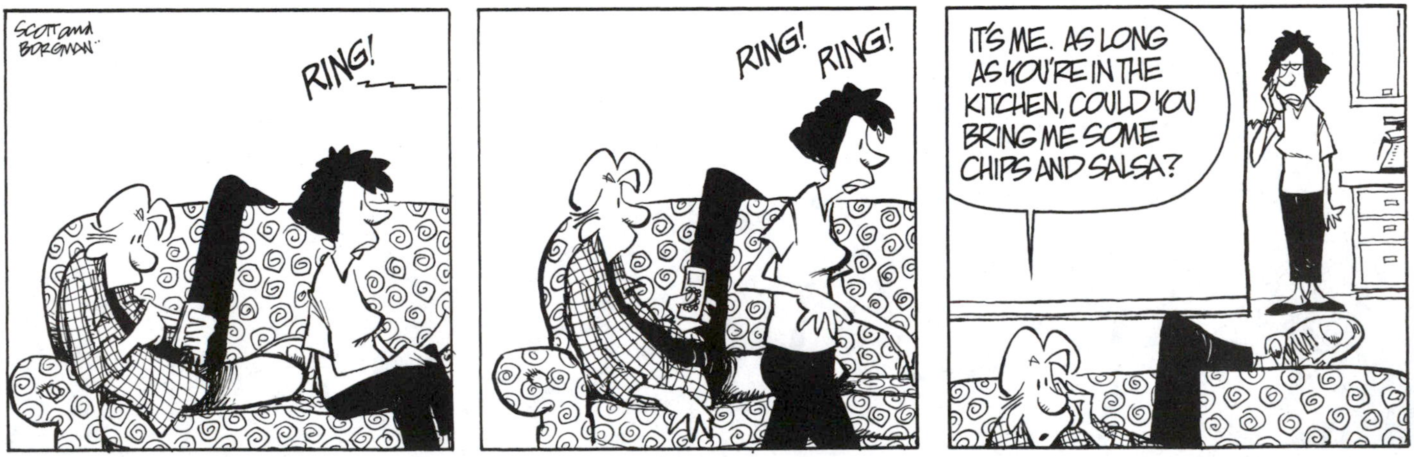
SCOTT and BORGMAN
RING!
RING! RING!
IT'S ME. AS LONG AS YOU'RE IN THE KITCHEN, COULD YOU BRING ME SOME CHIPS AND SALSA?

Zits

by JERRY SCOTT and JIM BORGMAN

DAD! DAD!

DAD? YOU'RE OKAY??

I'M FINE. WHY WOULDN'T I BE?

I SENT YOU A MESSAGE, AND WHEN I DIDN'T HEAR BACK FROM YOU, WELL, NATURALLY I ASSUMED THE WORST!

I'M SO RELIEVED TO SEE THAT YOU'RE NOT DEAD OR LYING AT THE BOTTOM OF AN ABANDONED MINE-SHAFT SOMEWHERE!

SCOTT and BORGMAN

WHICH IS THE ONLY LOGICAL REASON IT WOULD TAKE SOMEBODY SO LONG TO HIT "REPLY"!

NOT EVERYBODY CHECKS THEIR E-MAIL EVERY 15 SECONDS LIKE YOU DO, JEREMY.

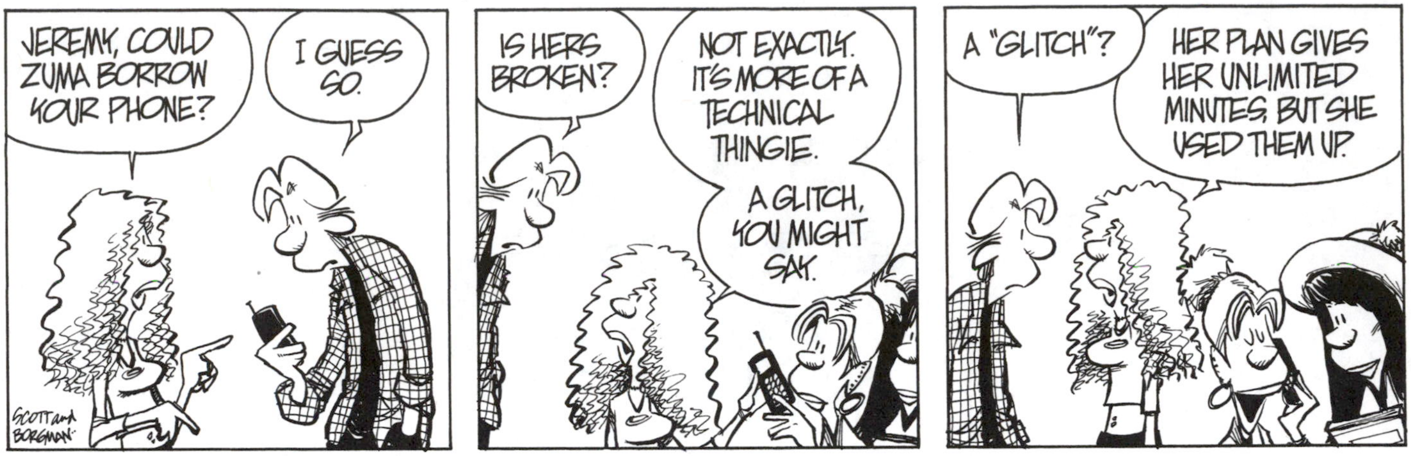
JEREMY, COULD ZUMA BORROW YOUR PHONE?
I GUESS SO.
IS HERS BROKEN?
NOT EXACTLY. IT'S MORE OF A TECHNICAL THINGIE.
A GLITCH, YOU MIGHT SAY.
A "GLITCH"?
HER PLAN GIVES HER UNLIMITED MINUTES, BUT SHE USED THEM UP.

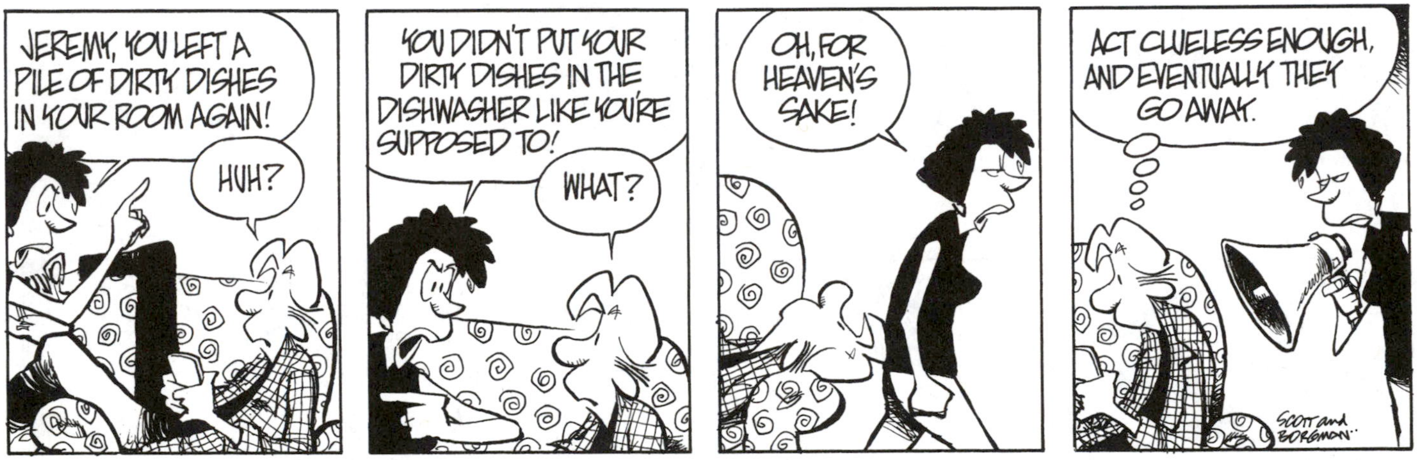
JEREMY, YOU LEFT A PILE OF DIRTY DISHES IN YOUR ROOM AGAIN!
HUH?
YOU DIDN'T PUT YOUR DIRTY DISHES IN THE DISHWASHER LIKE YOU'RE SUPPOSED TO!
WHAT?
OH, FOR HEAVEN'S SAKE!
ACT CLUELESS ENOUGH, AND EVENTUALLY THEY GO AWAY.

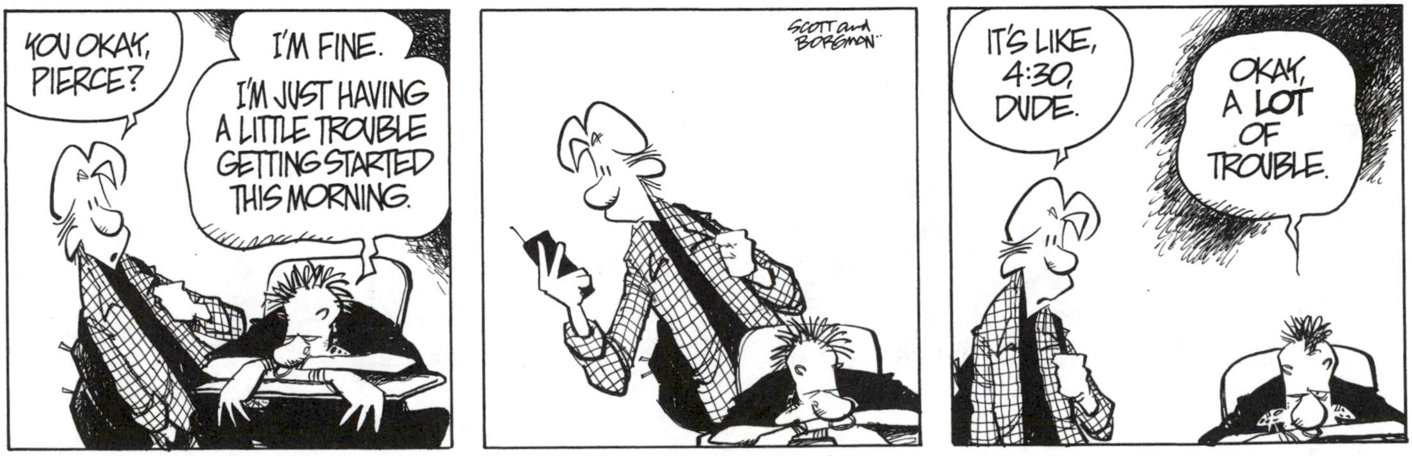
YOU OKAY, PIERCE?
I'M FINE.
I'M JUST HAVING A LITTLE TROUBLE GETTING STARTED THIS MORNING.
IT'S LIKE, 4:30, DUDE.
OKAY, A LOT OF TROUBLE.

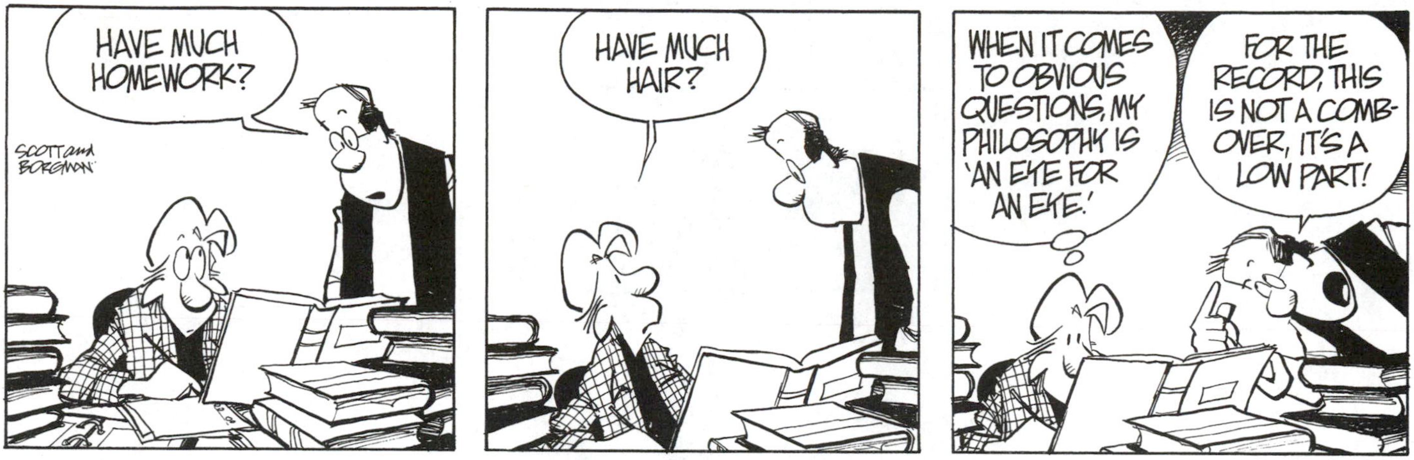
HAVE MUCH HOMEWORK?
HAVE MUCH HAIR?
WHEN IT COMES TO OBVIOUS QUESTIONS, MY PHILOSOPHY IS 'AN EYE FOR AN EYE.'
FOR THE RECORD, THIS IS NOT A COMB-OVER, IT'S A LOW PART!

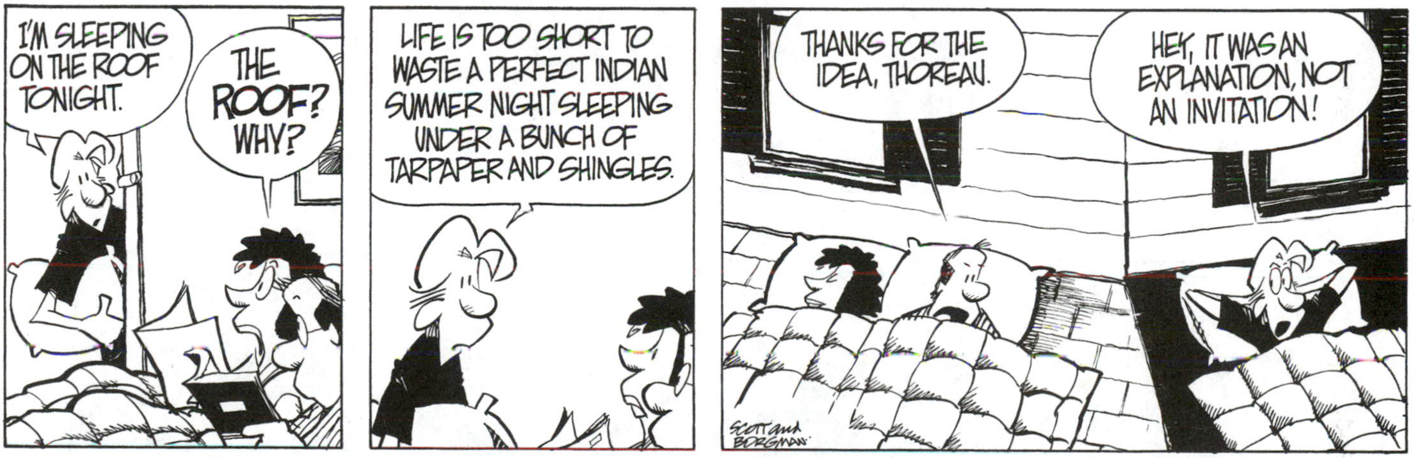
I'M SLEEPING ON THE ROOF TONIGHT.
THE **ROOF**? WHY?
LIFE IS TOO SHORT TO WASTE A PERFECT INDIAN SUMMER NIGHT SLEEPING UNDER A BUNCH OF TARPAPER AND SHINGLES.
THANKS FOR THE IDEA, THOREAU.
HEY, IT WAS AN EXPLANATION, NOT AN INVITATION!

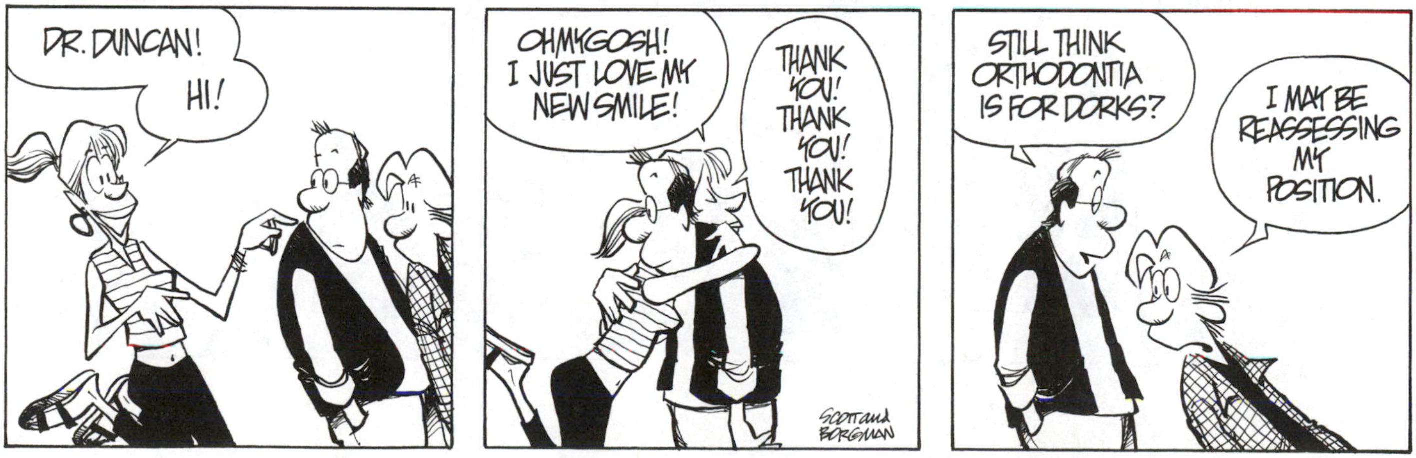
DR. DUNCAN!
HI!
OHMYGOSH! I JUST LOVE MY NEW SMILE!
THANK YOU! THANK YOU! THANK YOU!
STILL THINK ORTHODONTIA IS FOR DORKS?
I MAY BE REASSESSING MY POSITION.

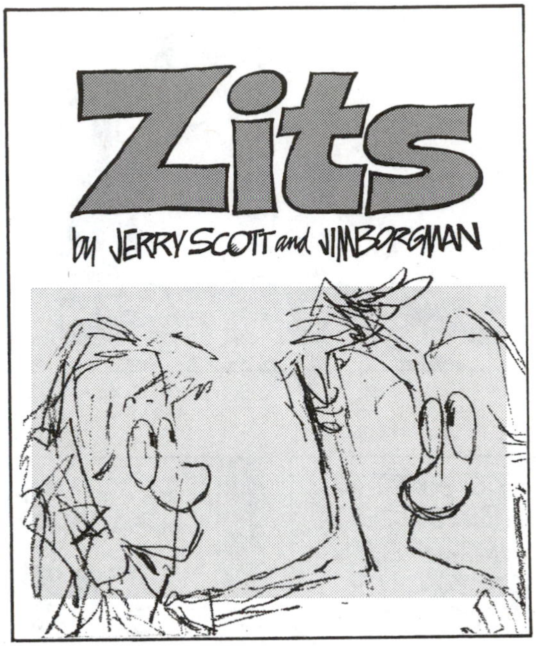
Zits
by JERRY SCOTT and JIM BORGMAN

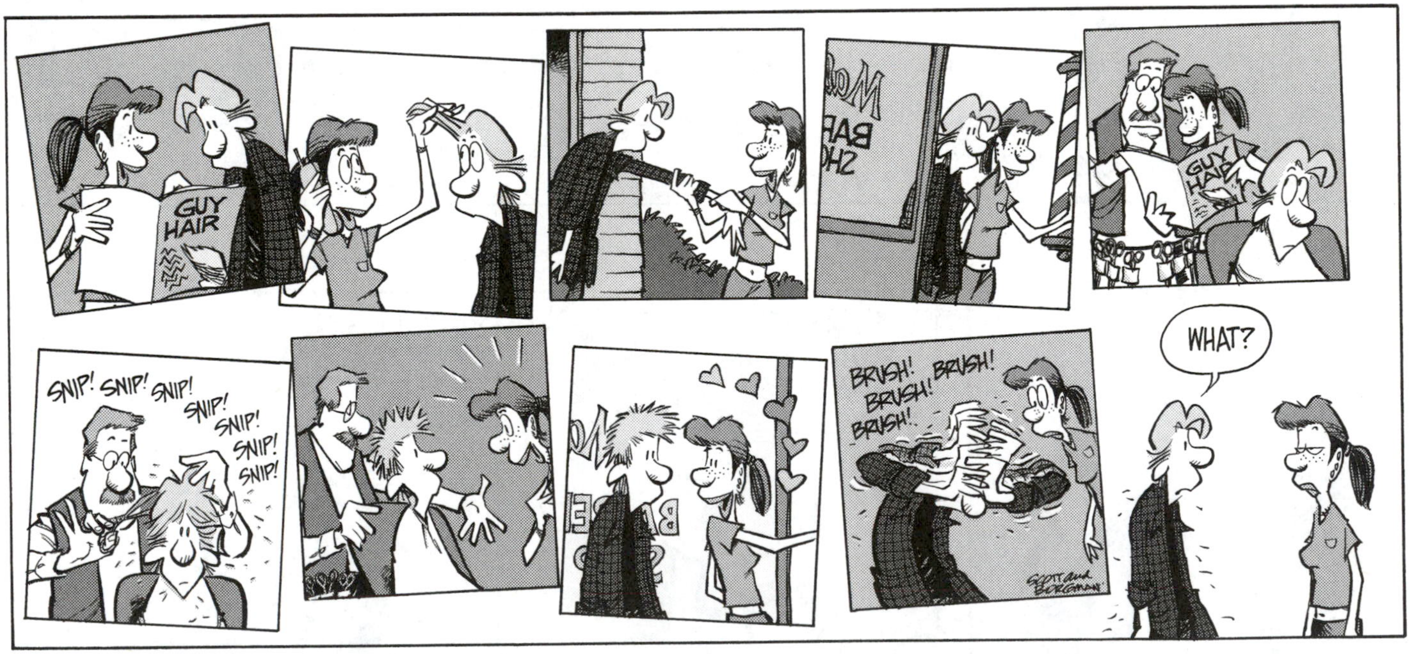
GUY HAIR
SNIP! SNIP! SNIP! SNIP! SNIP! SNIP! SNIP!
BRUSH! BRUSH! BRUSH! BRUSH!
SCOTT and BORGMAN
WHAT?

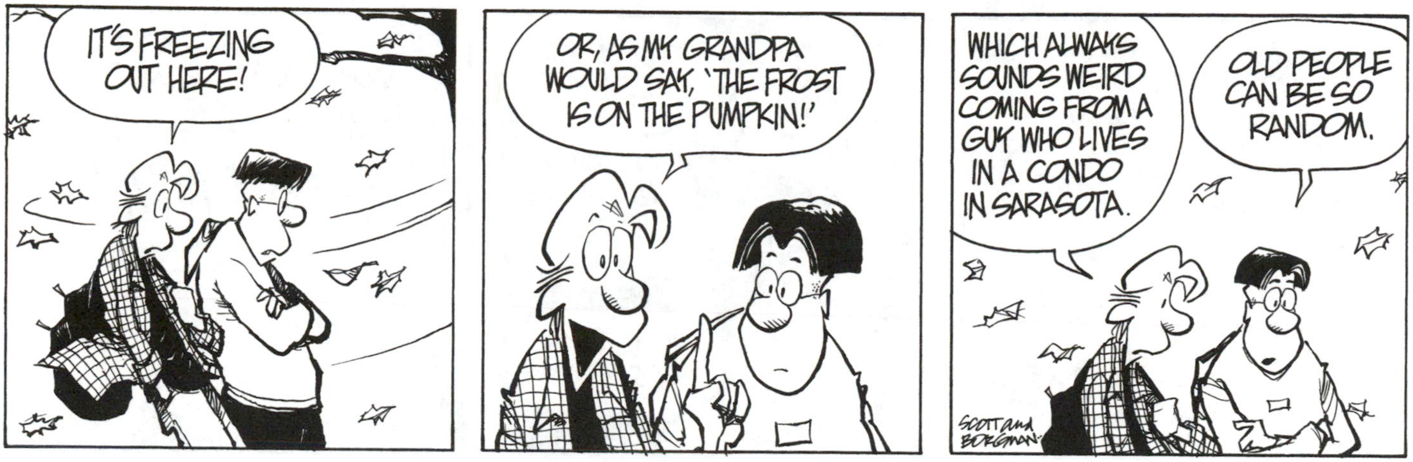
IT'S FREEZING OUT HERE!
OR, AS MY GRANDPA WOULD SAY, 'THE FROST IS ON THE PUMPKIN!'
WHICH ALWAYS SOUNDS WEIRD COMING FROM A GUY WHO LIVES IN A CONDO IN SARASOTA.
OLD PEOPLE CAN BE SO RANDOM.
SCOTT AND BORGMAN

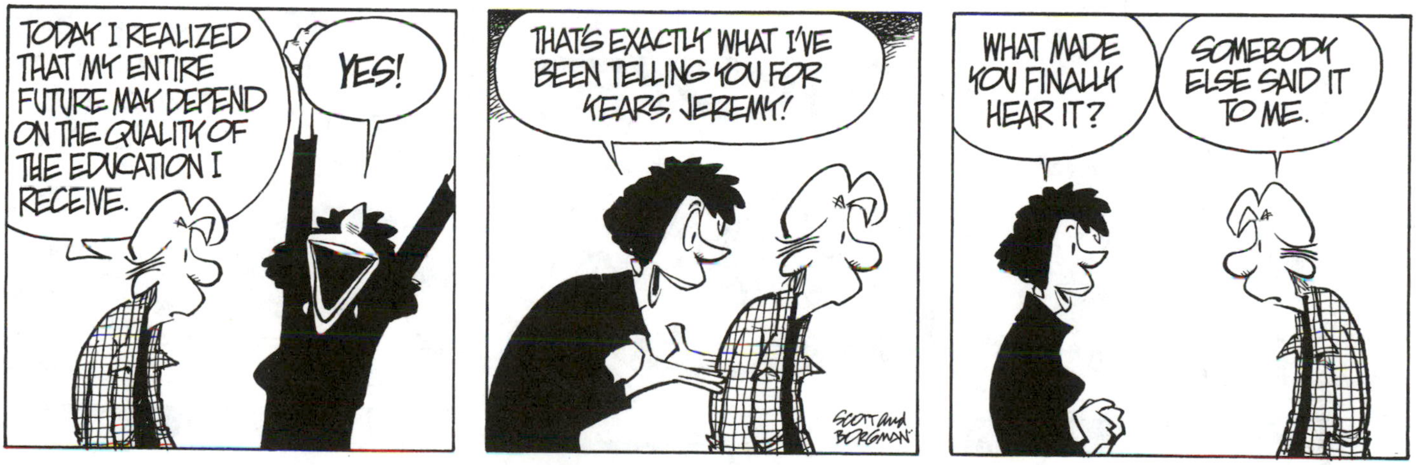
TODAY I REALIZED THAT MY ENTIRE FUTURE MAY DEPEND ON THE QUALITY OF THE EDUCATION I RECEIVE.
YES!
THAT'S EXACTLY WHAT I'VE BEEN TELLING YOU FOR YEARS, JEREMY!
SCOTT AND BORGMAN
WHAT MADE YOU FINALLY HEAR IT?
SOMEBODY ELSE SAID IT TO ME.

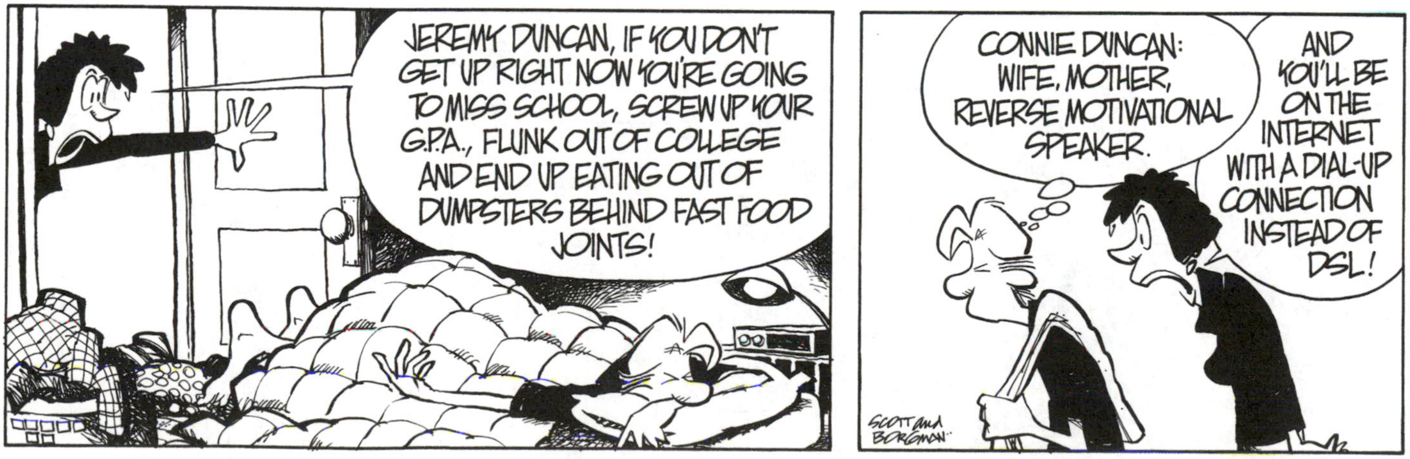
JEREMY DUNCAN, IF YOU DON'T GET UP RIGHT NOW YOU'RE GOING TO MISS SCHOOL, SCREW UP YOUR G.P.A., FLUNK OUT OF COLLEGE AND END UP EATING OUT OF DUMPSTERS BEHIND FAST FOOD JOINTS!
CONNIE DUNCAN: WIFE, MOTHER, REVERSE MOTIVATIONAL SPEAKER.
AND YOU'LL BE ON THE INTERNET WITH A DIAL-UP CONNECTION INSTEAD OF DSL!
SCOTT AND BORGMAN

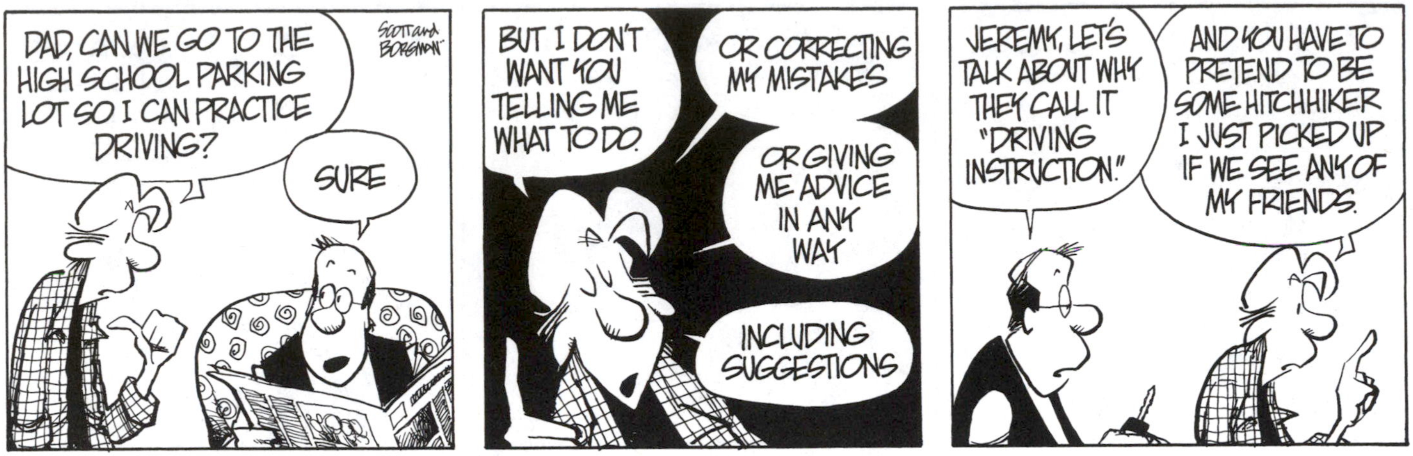
SCOTT AND BORGMAN
DAD, CAN WE GO TO THE HIGH SCHOOL PARKING LOT SO I CAN PRACTICE DRIVING?
SURE
BUT I DON'T WANT YOU TELLING ME WHAT TO DO.
OR CORRECTING MY MISTAKES
OR GIVING ME ADVICE IN ANY WAY
INCLUDING SUGGESTIONS
JEREMY, LET'S TALK ABOUT WHY THEY CALL IT "DRIVING INSTRUCTION."
AND YOU HAVE TO PRETEND TO BE SOME HITCHHIKER I JUST PICKED UP IF WE SEE ANY OF MY FRIENDS.

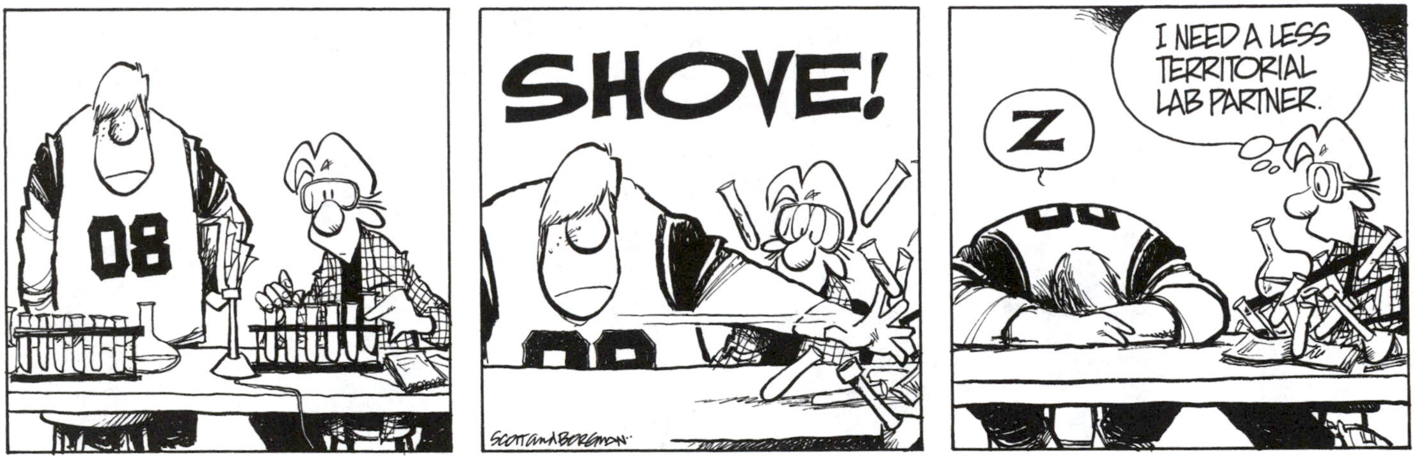
08
SHOVE!
SCOTT AND BORGMAN
Z
I NEED A LESS TERRITORIAL LAB PARTNER.

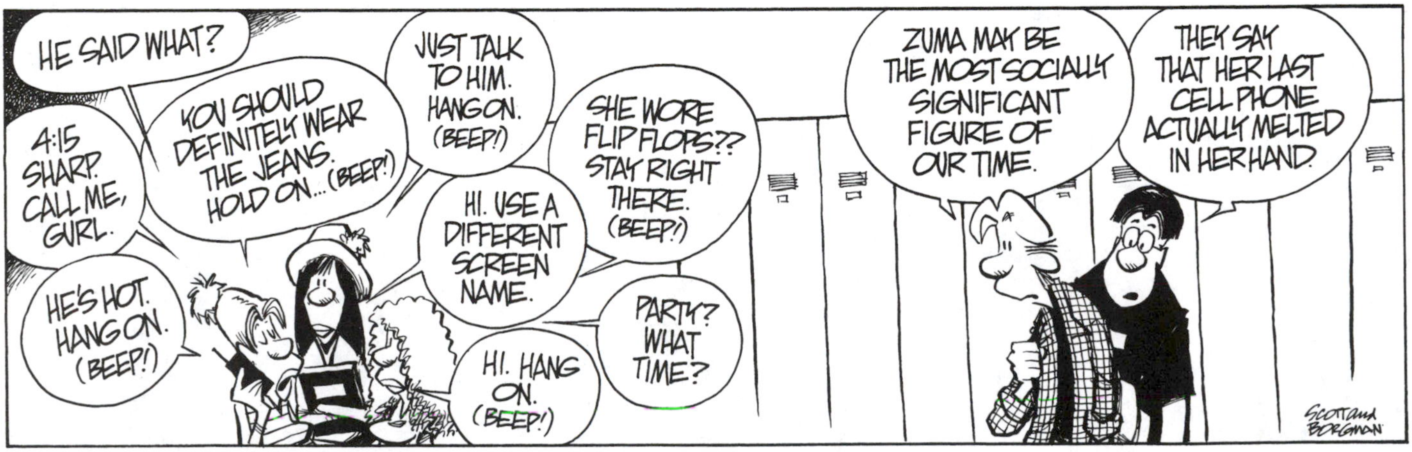
HE SAID WHAT?
4:15 SHARP. CALL ME, GURL.
YOU SHOULD DEFINITELY WEAR THE JEANS. HOLD ON... (BEEP!)
JUST TALK TO HIM. HANG ON. (BEEP!)
SHE WORE FLIP FLOPS?? STAY RIGHT THERE. (BEEP!)
HI. USE A DIFFERENT SCREEN NAME.
HE'S HOT. HANG ON. (BEEP!)
PARTY? WHAT TIME?
HI. HANG ON. (BEEP!)
ZUMA MAY BE THE MOST SOCIALLY SIGNIFICANT FIGURE OF OUR TIME.
THEY SAY THAT HER LAST CELL PHONE ACTUALLY MELTED IN HER HAND.
SCOTT AND BORGMAN

Zits

JERRY SCOTT and JIM BORGMAN"

TEENAGERS TAKE UP TOO MUCH ROOM.

SENDING THE BOY AWAY TO COLLEGE WILL BE A SMALL PRICE TO PAY FOR REGAINING CONTROL OF THE LIVING ROOM.

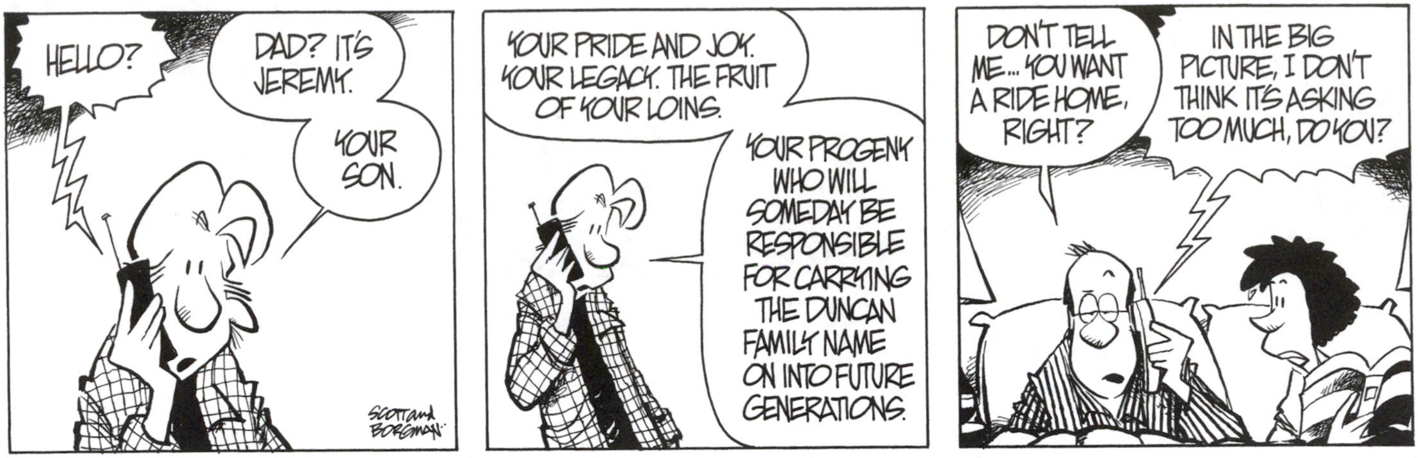
HELLO?
DAD? IT'S JEREMY.
YOUR SON.
SCOTT and BORGMAN
YOUR PRIDE AND JOY. YOUR LEGACY. THE FRUIT OF YOUR LOINS.
YOUR PROGENY WHO WILL SOMEDAY BE RESPONSIBLE FOR CARRYING THE DUNCAN FAMILY NAME ON INTO FUTURE GENERATIONS.
DON'T TELL ME... YOU WANT A RIDE HOME, RIGHT?
IN THE BIG PICTURE, I DON'T THINK IT'S ASKING TOO MUCH, DO YOU?

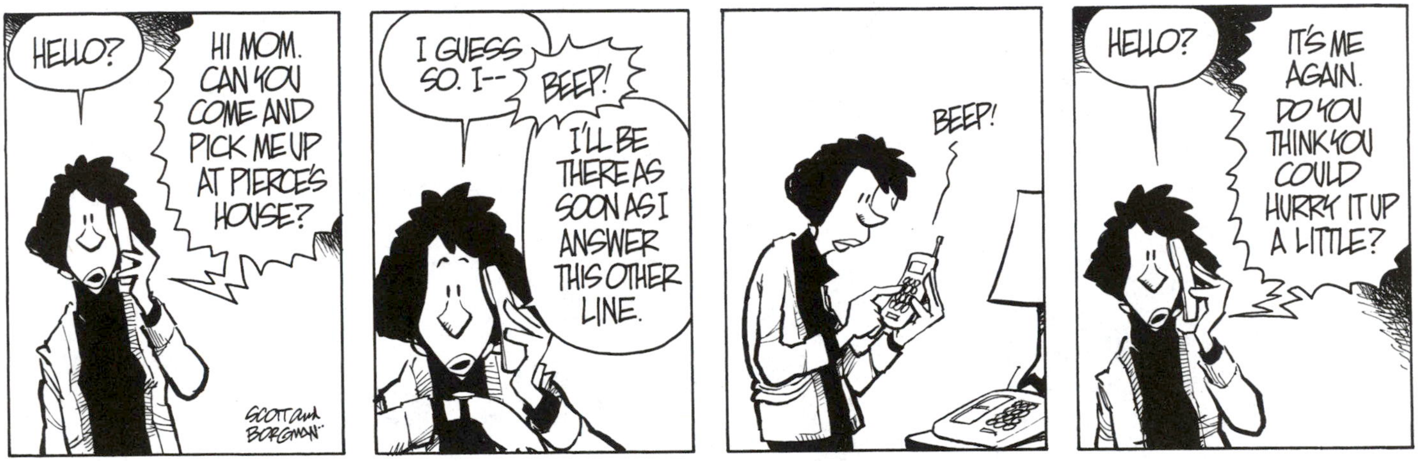
HELLO?
HI MOM. CAN YOU COME AND PICK ME UP AT PIERCE'S HOUSE?
SCOTT and BORGMAN
I GUESS SO. I--
BEEP!
I'LL BE THERE AS SOON AS I ANSWER THIS OTHER LINE.
BEEP!
HELLO?
IT'S ME AGAIN. DO YOU THINK YOU COULD HURRY IT UP A LITTLE?

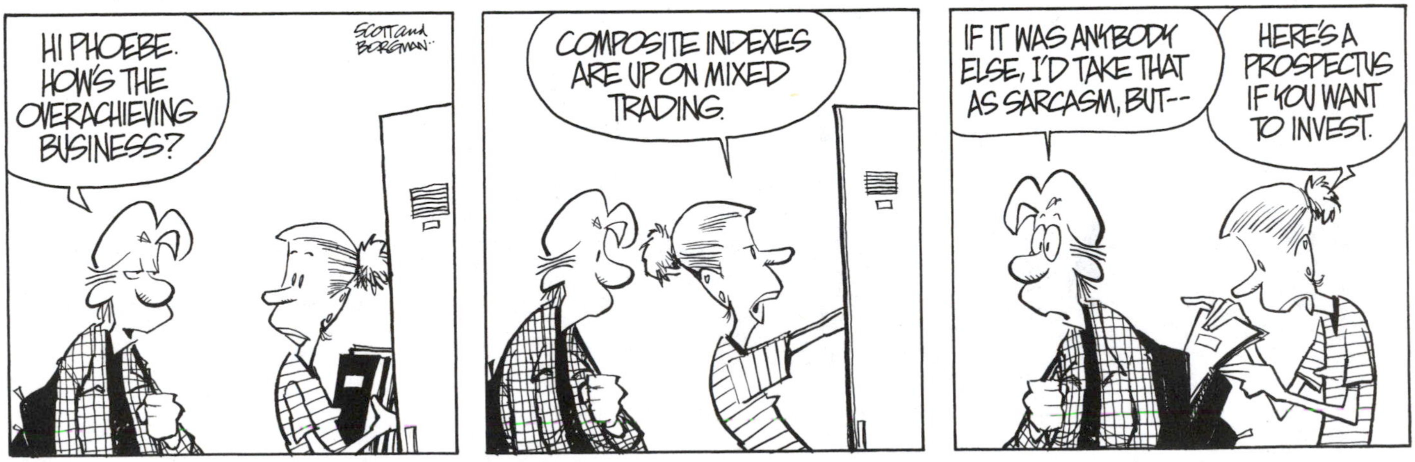
HI PHOEBE. HOW'S THE OVERACHIEVING BUSINESS?
SCOTT and BORGMAN
COMPOSITE INDEXES ARE UP ON MIXED TRADING.
IF IT WAS ANYBODY ELSE, I'D TAKE THAT AS SARCASM, BUT--
HERE'S A PROSPECTUS IF YOU WANT TO INVEST.

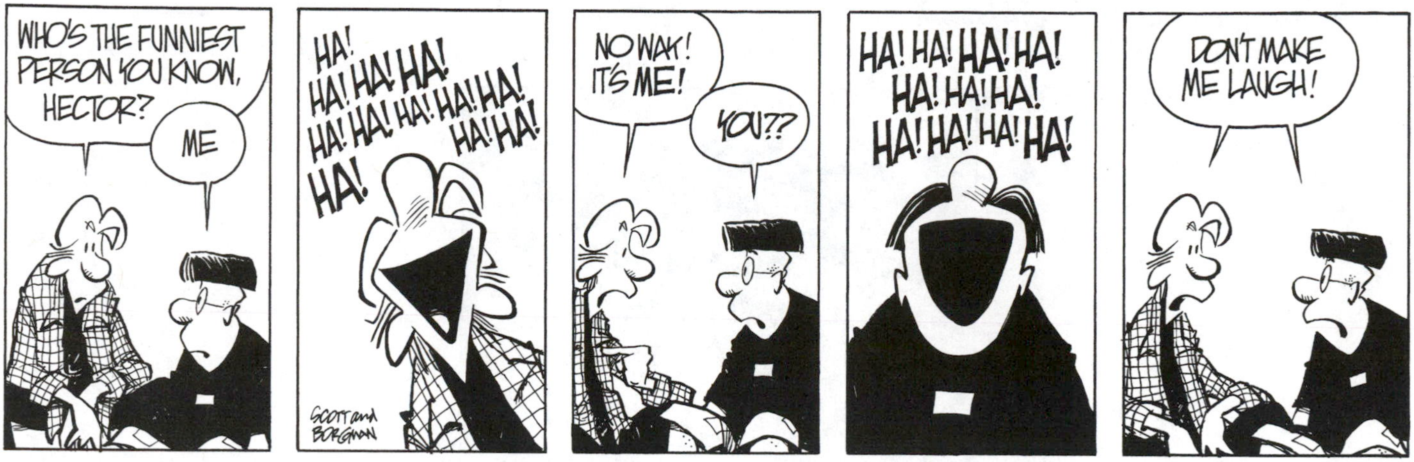
WHO'S THE FUNNIEST PERSON YOU KNOW, HECTOR?
ME
HA! HA! HA! HA! HA! HA! HA! HA! HA! HA! HA! HA!
SCOTT and BORGMAN
NO WAY! IT'S ME!
YOU??
HA! HA! HA! HA! HA! HA! HA! HA! HA! HA! HA!
DON'T MAKE ME LAUGH!

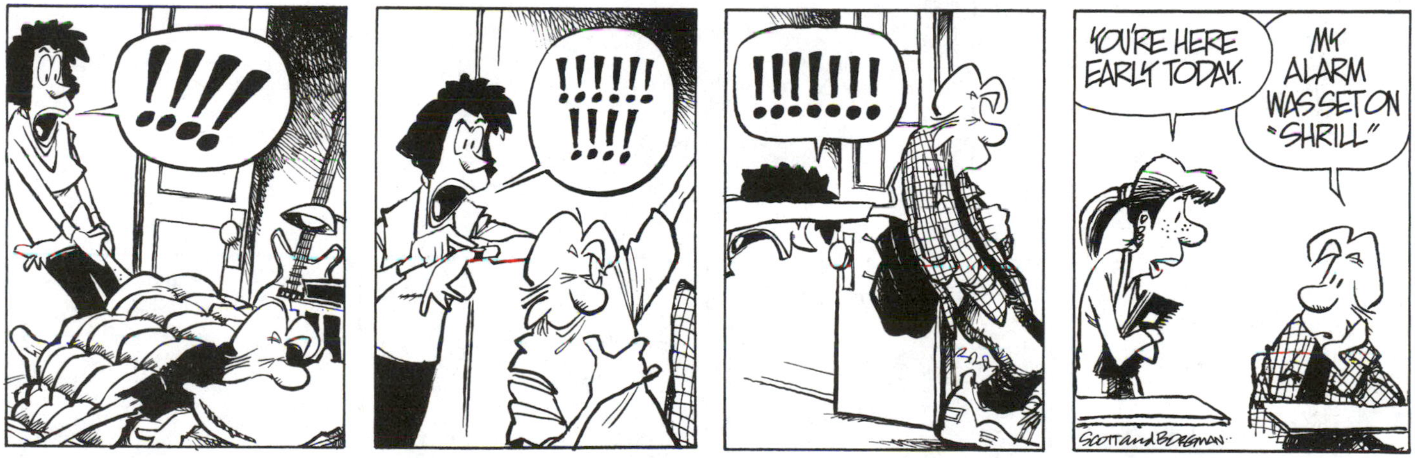
!!!!
!!!!!!
!!!!
!!!!!!!!
YOU'RE HERE EARLY TODAY.
MY ALARM WAS SET ON "SHRILL"
SCOTT and BORGMAN

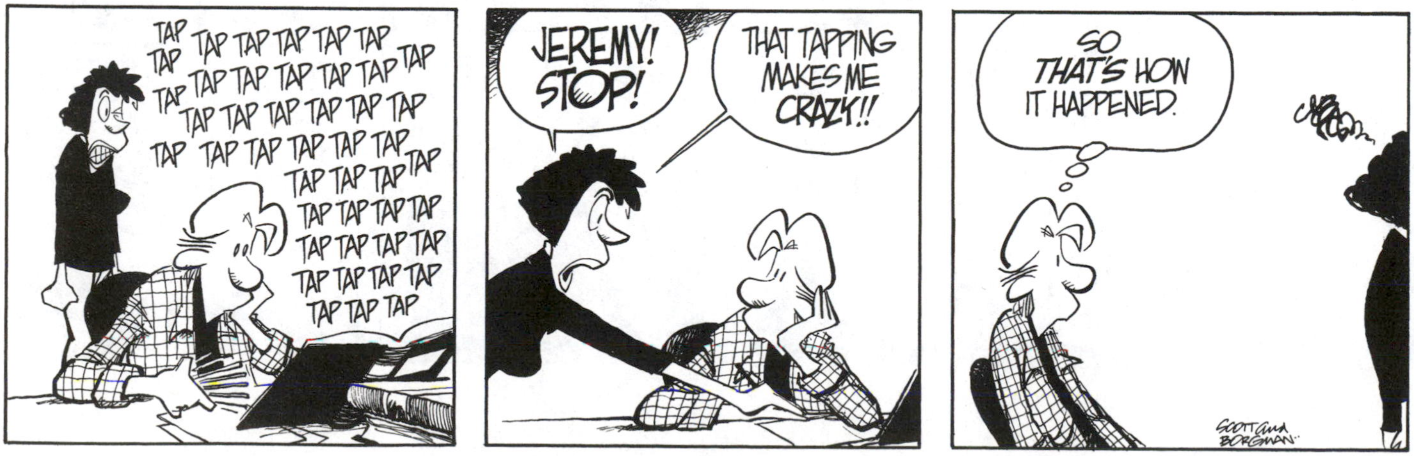
TAP TAP TAP TAP TAP TAP TAP
TAP TAP TAP TAP TAP TAP TAP TAP
TAP TAP TAP TAP TAP TAP TAP TAP
TAP TAP TAP TAP TAP TAP
TAP TAP TAP TAP TAP TAP TAP
TAP TAP TAP TAP
TAP TAP TAP TAP
TAP TAP TAP TAP
TAP TAP TAP TAP
TAP TAP TAP
JEREMY! STOP!
THAT TAPPING MAKES ME CRAZY!!
SO THAT'S HOW IT HAPPENED.
SCOTT and BORGMAN

Zits

JERRY SCOTT and JIM BORGMAN

DUDES!

PIERCE!

YOU'RE LATE, MAN.

WE STARTED WITHOUT YOU.

NO PROBLEM. I'LL GET IN ON THE NEXT HAND-- WHOA!

WHAT?

YOU'RE KEEPING THOSE TWO, RIGHT?

SCOTT AND BORGMAN

I DON'T KNOW. I --

HE'LL TAKE THREE CARDS.

ARE YOU SURE?

TRUST ME.

NOW BET!

BET EVERYTHING!

RAISE! RAISE!

I DIDN'T REALIZE THAT YOU KNEW SO MUCH ABOUT POKER, PIERCE.

POKER?? OH-IS THAT WHAT YOU GUYS ARE PLAYING?

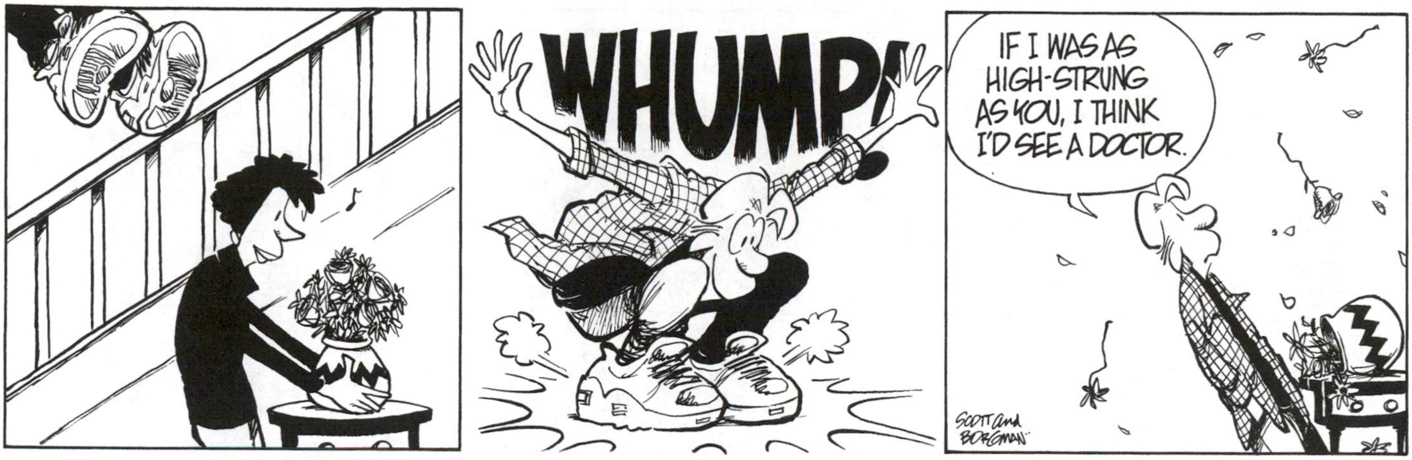
WHUMP!
IF I WAS AS HIGH-STRUNG AS YOU, I THINK I'D SEE A DOCTOR.
SCOTT and BORGMAN

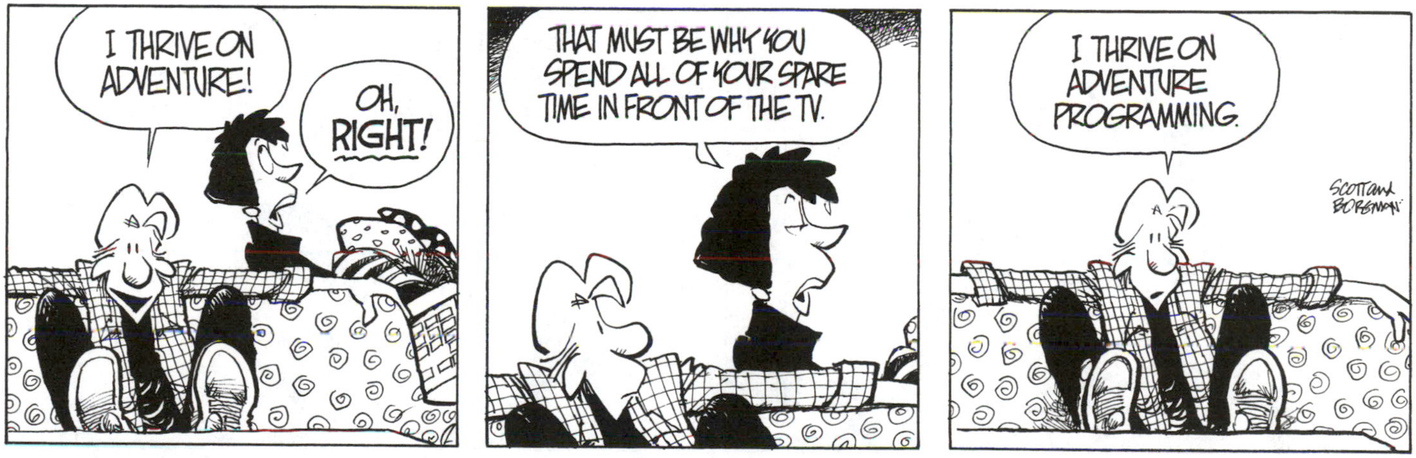
I THRIVE ON ADVENTURE!
OH, RIGHT!
THAT MUST BE WHY YOU SPEND ALL OF YOUR SPARE TIME IN FRONT OF THE TV.
I THRIVE ON ADVENTURE PROGRAMMING.
SCOTT and BORGMAN

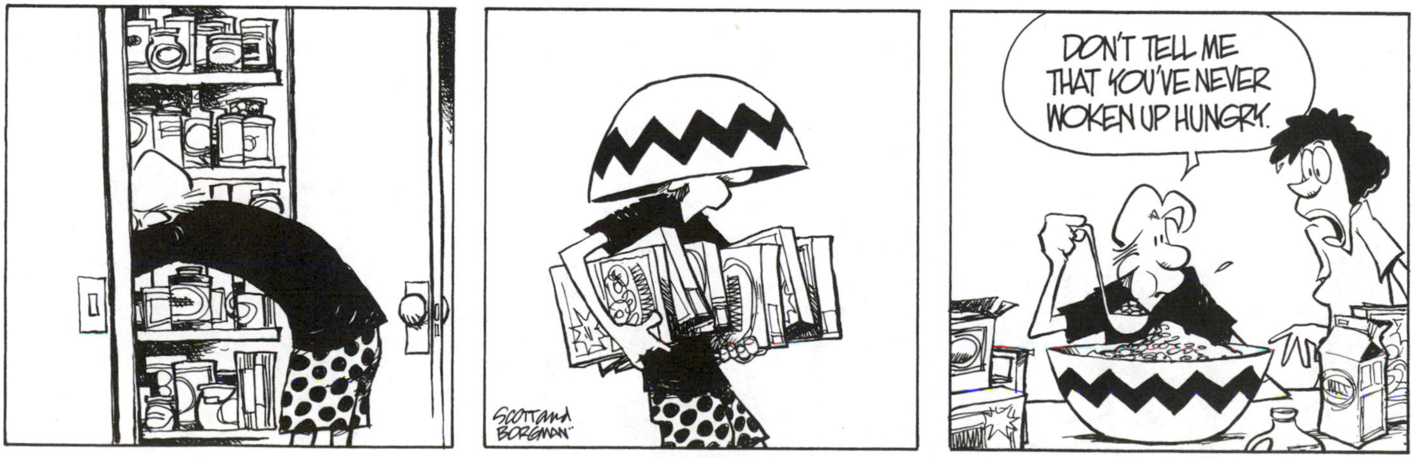
SCOTT and BORGMAN
DON'T TELL ME THAT YOU'VE NEVER WOKEN UP HUNGRY.

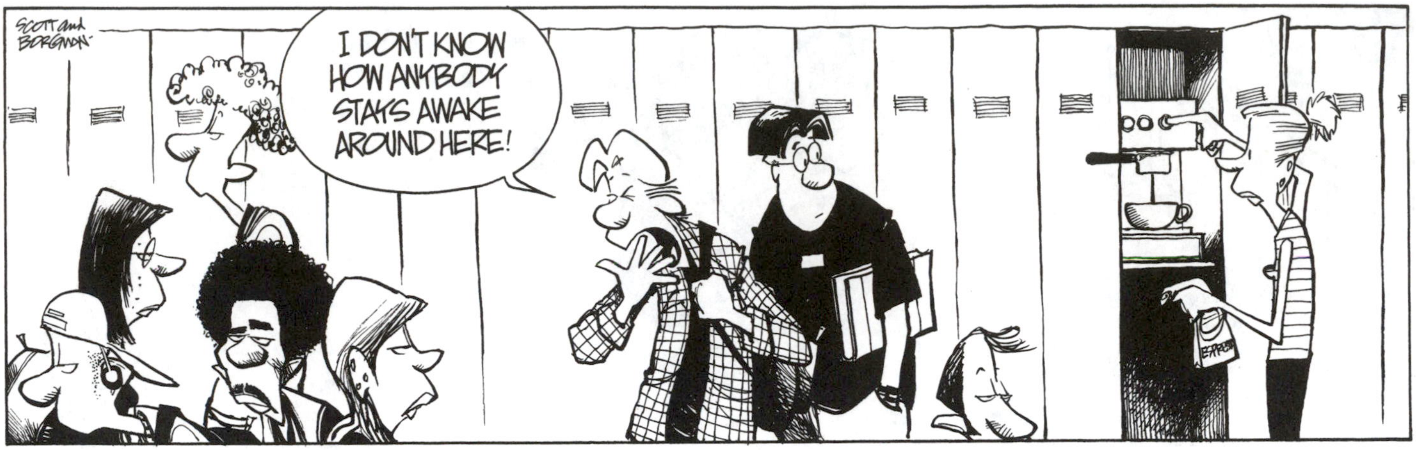
SCOTT and BORGMAN
I DON'T KNOW HOW ANYBODY STAYS AWAKE AROUND HERE!

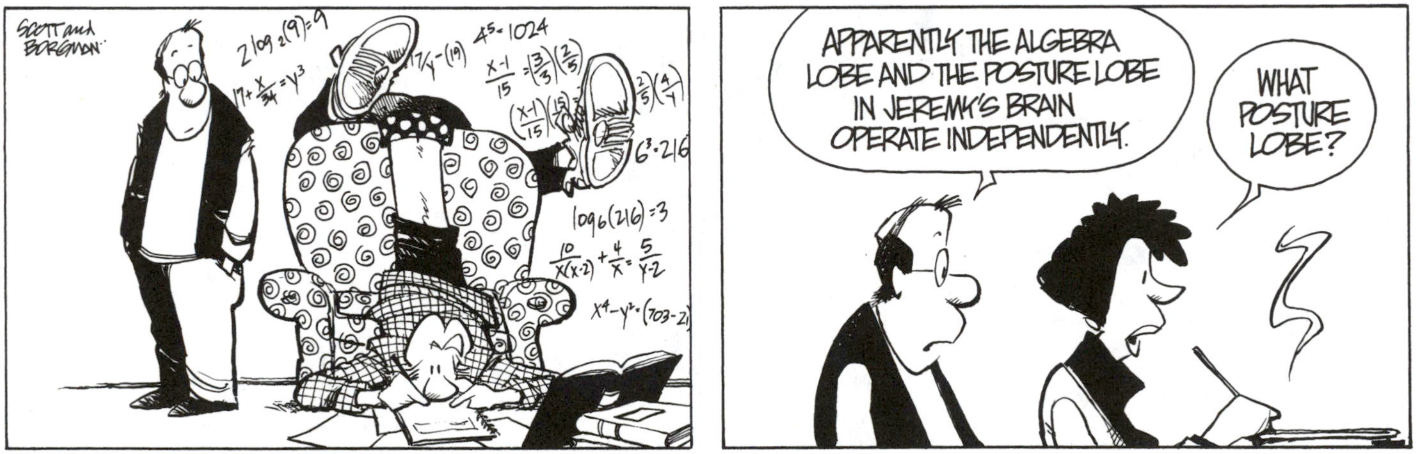
SCOTT and BORGMAN
APPARENTLY THE ALGEBRA LOBE AND THE POSTURE LOBE IN JEREMY'S BRAIN OPERATE INDEPENDENTLY.
WHAT POSTURE LOBE?

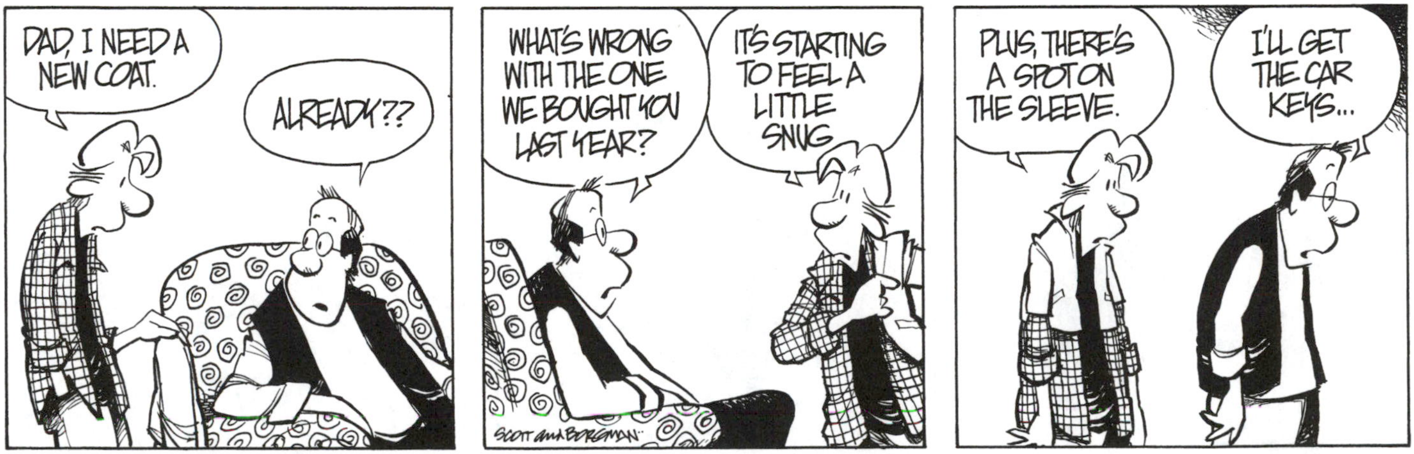
DAD, I NEED A NEW COAT.
ALREADY??
WHAT'S WRONG WITH THE ONE WE BOUGHT YOU LAST YEAR?
IT'S STARTING TO FEEL A LITTLE SNUG
SCOTT and BORGMAN
PLUS, THERE'S A SPOT ON THE SLEEVE.
I'LL GET THE CAR KEYS...

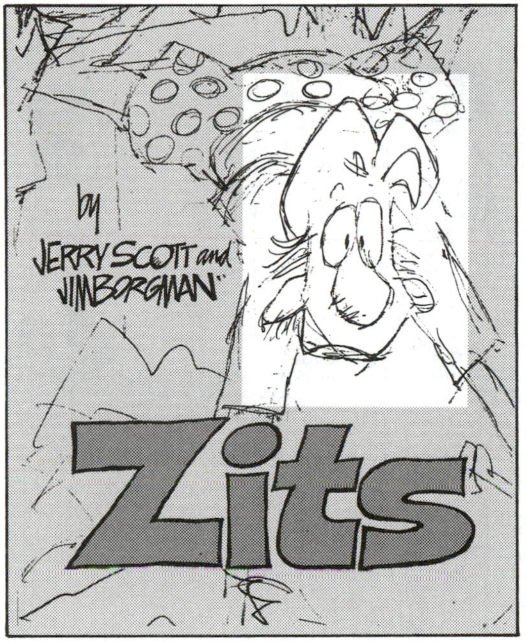
by
JERRY SCOTT and
JIM BORGMAN
Zits

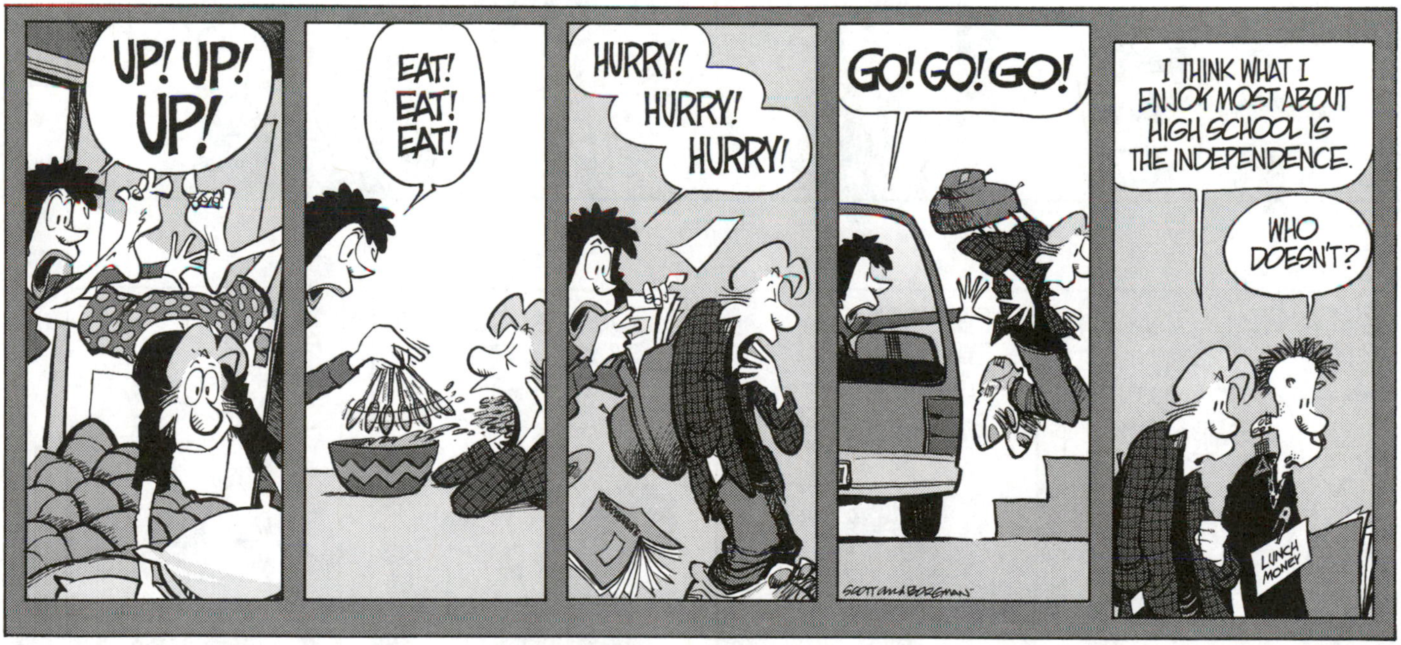
UP! UP! UP!
EAT! EAT! EAT!
HURRY! HURRY! HURRY!
GO! GO! GO!
SCOTT and BORGMAN
I THINK WHAT I ENJOY MOST ABOUT HIGH SCHOOL IS THE INDEPENDENCE.
WHO DOESN'T?
LUNCH MONEY

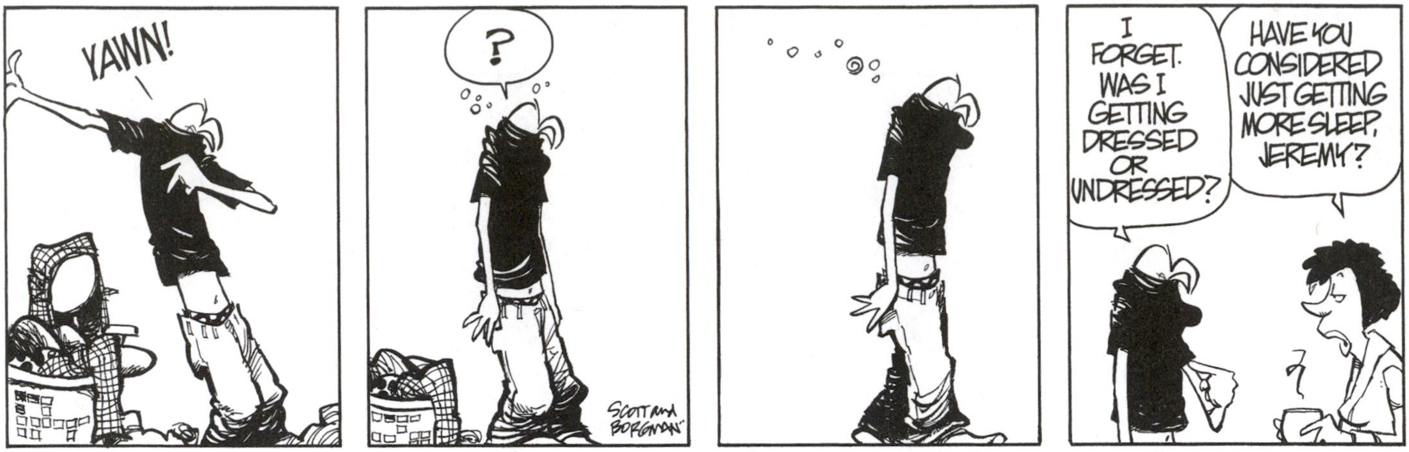
YAWN!
?
I FORGET. WAS I GETTING DRESSED OR UNDRESSED?
HAVE YOU CONSIDERED JUST GETTING MORE SLEEP, JEREMY?

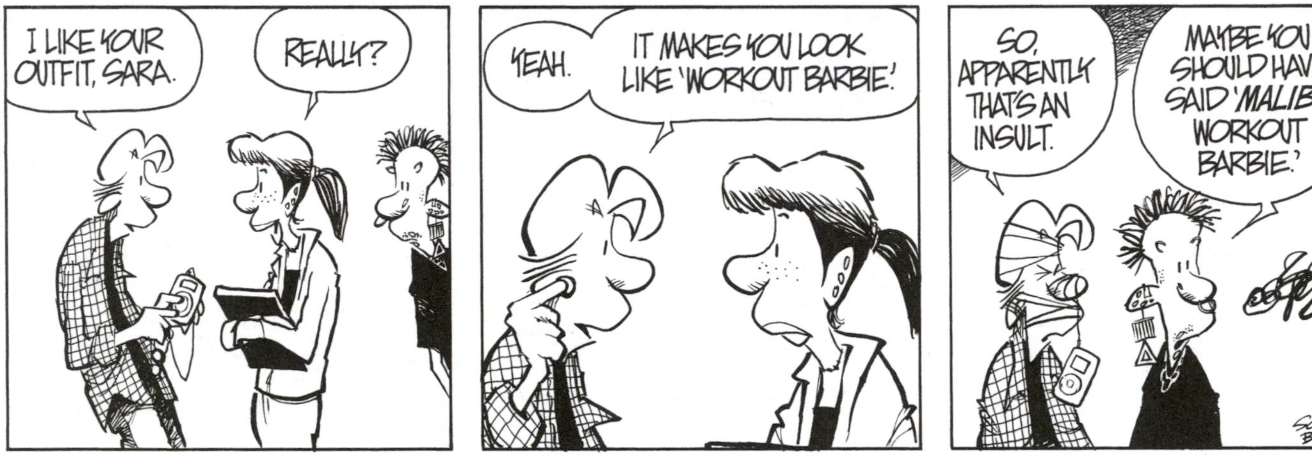
I LIKE YOUR OUTFIT, SARA.
REALLY?
YEAH.
IT MAKES YOU LOOK LIKE 'WORKOUT BARBIE.'
SO, APPARENTLY THAT'S AN INSULT.
MAYBE YOU SHOULD HAVE SAID '*MALIBU* WORKOUT BARBIE.'

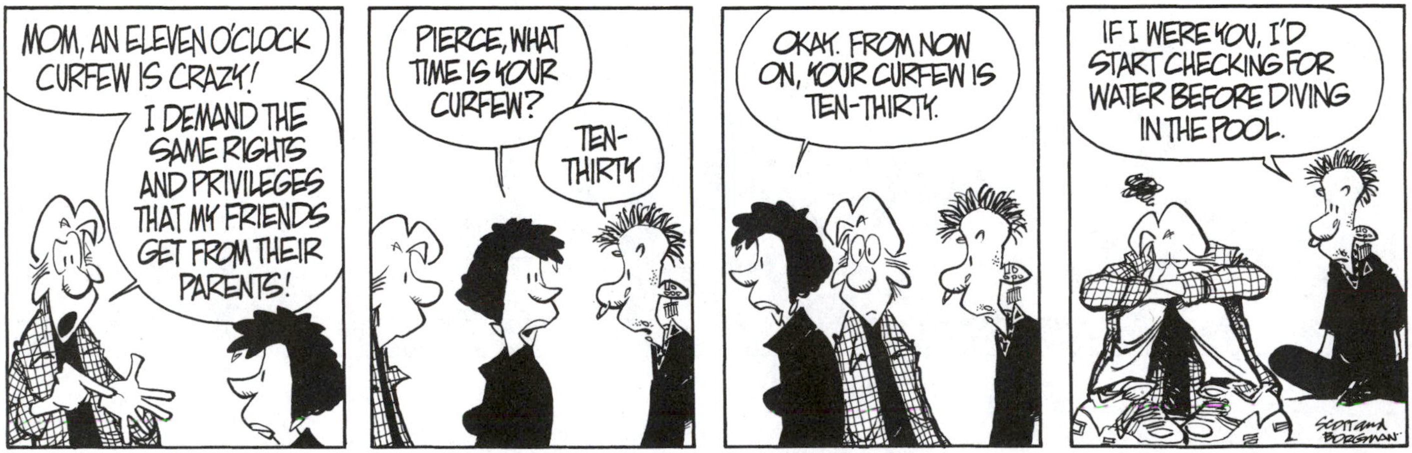
MOM, AN ELEVEN O'CLOCK CURFEW IS CRAZY!
I DEMAND THE SAME RIGHTS AND PRIVILEGES THAT MY FRIENDS GET FROM THEIR PARENTS!
PIERCE, WHAT TIME IS YOUR CURFEW?
TEN-THIRTY
OKAY. FROM NOW ON, YOUR CURFEW IS TEN-THIRTY.
IF I WERE YOU, I'D START CHECKING FOR WATER BEFORE DIVING IN THE POOL.

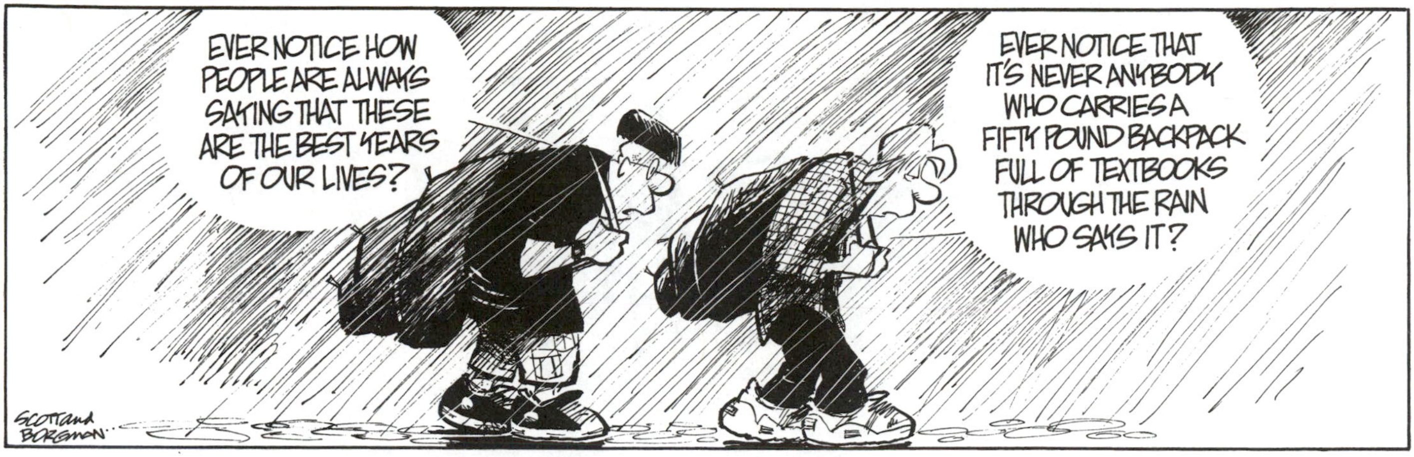
EVER NOTICE HOW PEOPLE ARE ALWAYS SAYING THAT THESE ARE THE BEST YEARS OF OUR LIVES?
EVER NOTICE THAT IT'S NEVER ANYBODY WHO CARRIES A FIFTY POUND BACKPACK FULL OF TEXTBOOKS THROUGH THE RAIN WHO SAYS IT?
SCOTT AND BORGMAN

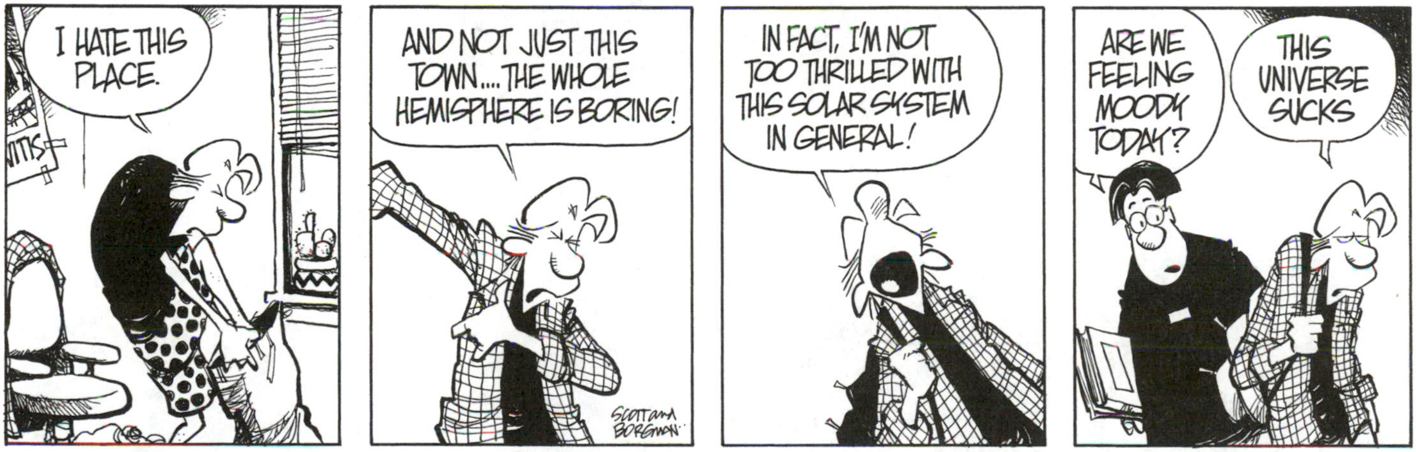
I HATE THIS PLACE.
AND NOT JUST THIS TOWN.... THE WHOLE HEMISPHERE IS BORING!
SCOTT AND BORGMAN
IN FACT, I'M NOT TOO THRILLED WITH THIS SOLAR SYSTEM IN GENERAL!
ARE WE FEELING MOODY TODAY?
THIS UNIVERSE SUCKS

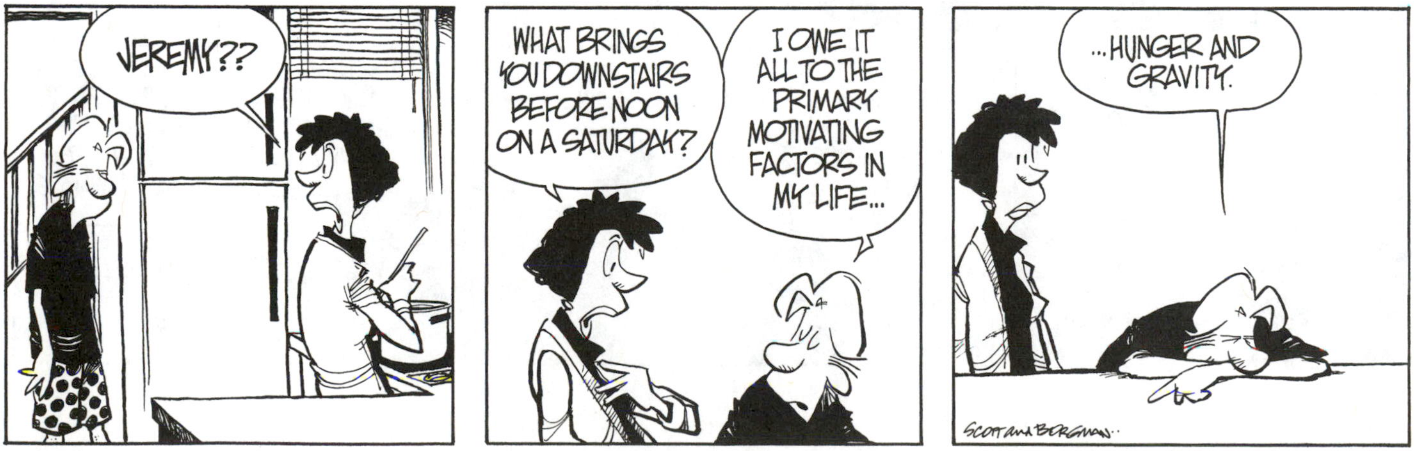
JEREMY??
WHAT BRINGS YOU DOWNSTAIRS BEFORE NOON ON A SATURDAY?
I OWE IT ALL TO THE PRIMARY MOTIVATING FACTORS IN MY LIFE...
...HUNGER AND GRAVITY.
SCOTT AND BORGMAN

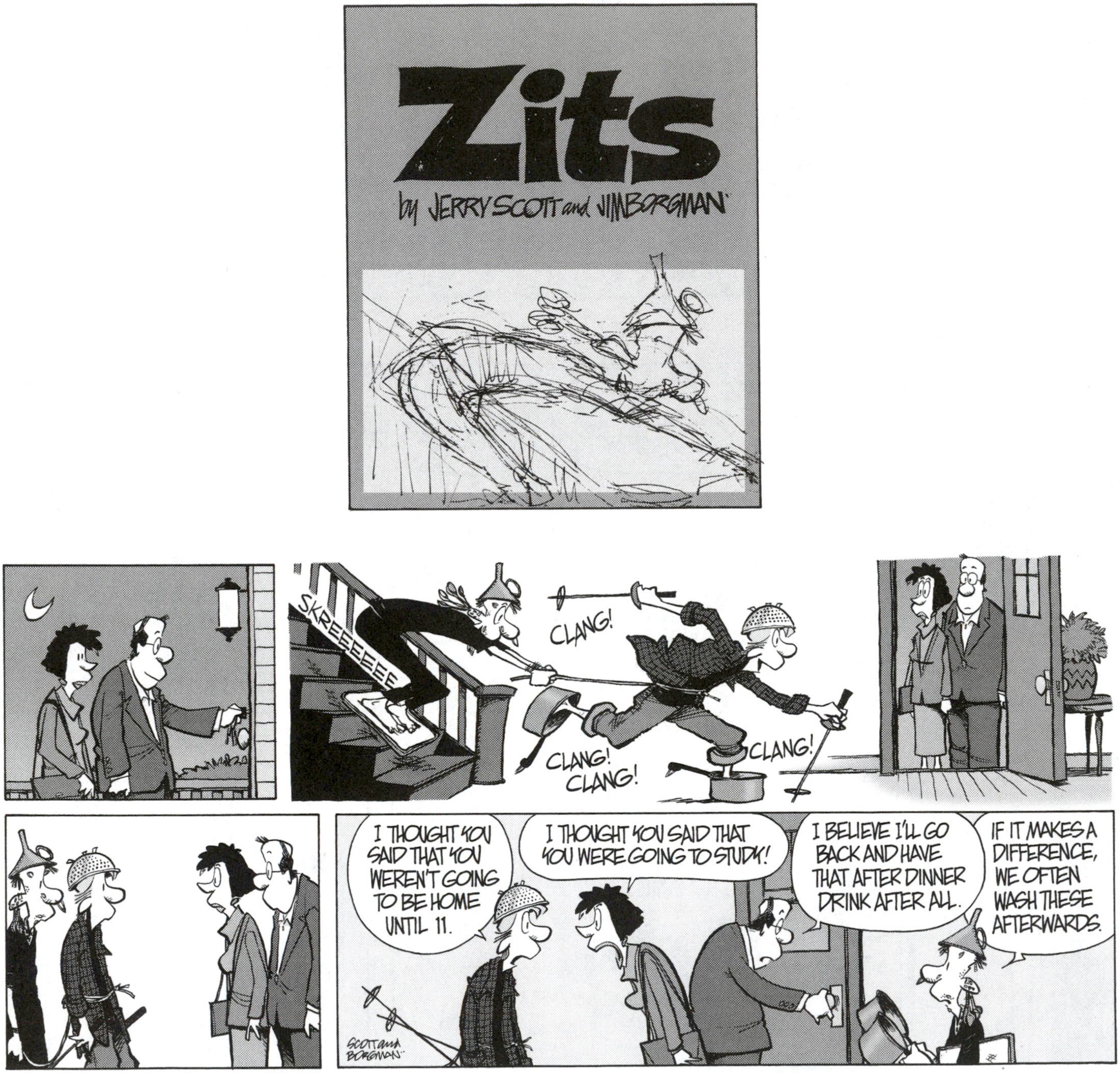
Zits
by JERRY SCOTT and JIM BORGMAN
SKREEEEEEEE
CLANG!
CLANG! CLANG!
CLANG!
I THOUGHT YOU SAID THAT YOU WEREN'T GOING TO BE HOME UNTIL 11.
I THOUGHT YOU SAID THAT YOU WERE GOING TO STUDY!
I BELIEVE I'LL GO BACK AND HAVE THAT AFTER DINNER DRINK AFTER ALL.
IF IT MAKES A DIFFERENCE, WE OFTEN WASH THESE AFTERWARDS.
SCOTT and BORGMAN

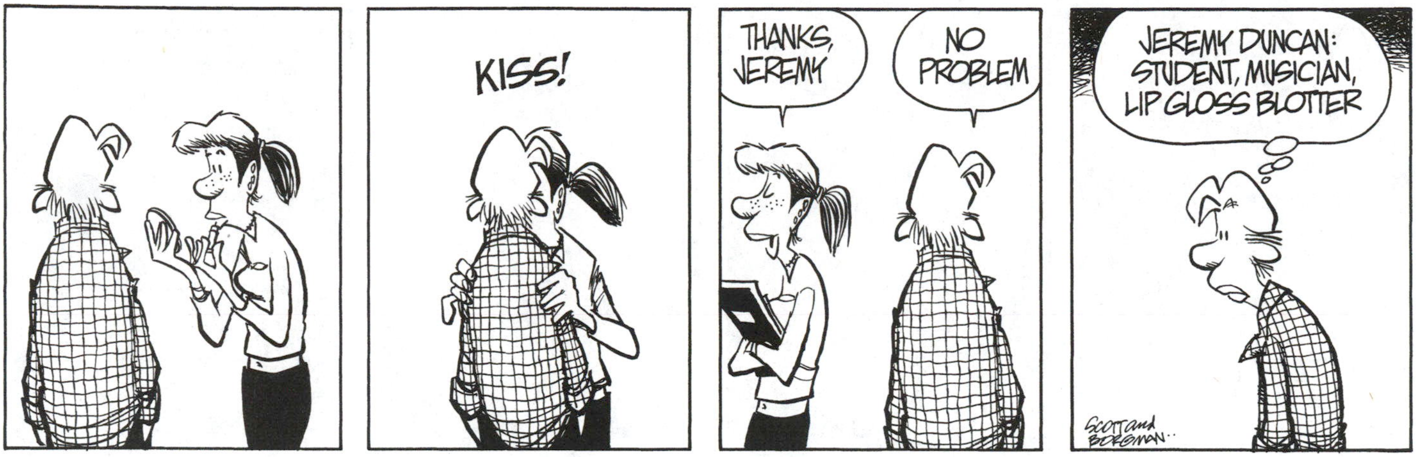
KISS!
THANKS, JEREMY
NO PROBLEM
JEREMY DUNCAN: STUDENT, MUSICIAN, LIP GLOSS BLOTTER

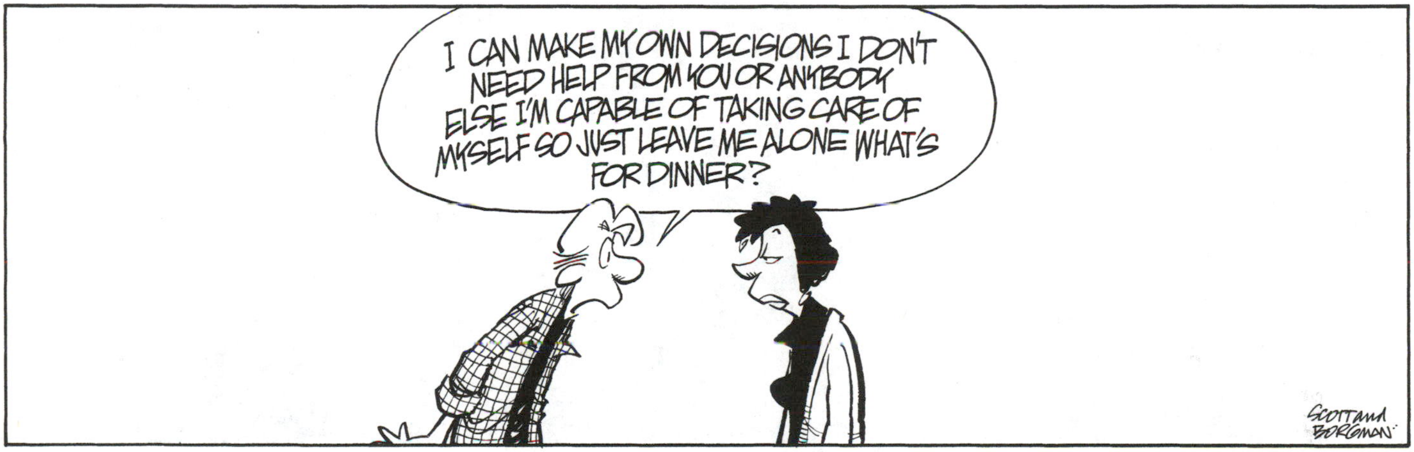
I CAN MAKE MY OWN DECISIONS I DON'T NEED HELP FROM YOU OR ANYBODY ELSE I'M CAPABLE OF TAKING CARE OF MYSELF SO JUST LEAVE ME ALONE WHAT'S FOR DINNER?

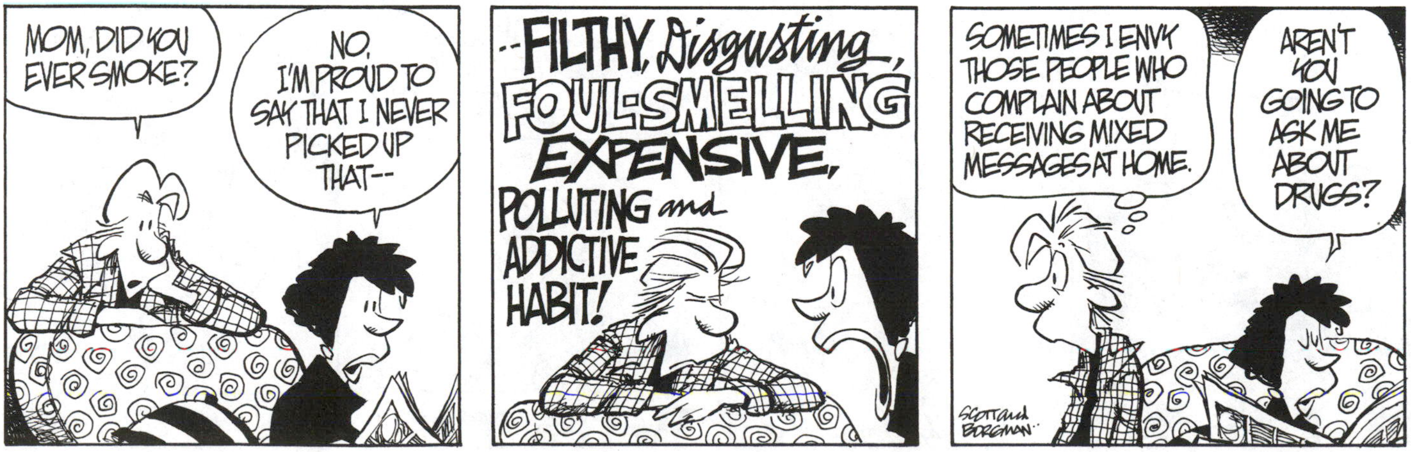
MOM, DID YOU EVER SMOKE?
NO. I'M PROUD TO SAY THAT I NEVER PICKED UP THAT--
--FILTHY, Disgusting, FOUL-SMELLING EXPENSIVE, POLLUTING and ADDICTIVE HABIT!
SOMETIMES I ENVY THOSE PEOPLE WHO COMPLAIN ABOUT RECEIVING MIXED MESSAGES AT HOME.
AREN'T YOU GOING TO ASK ME ABOUT DRUGS?

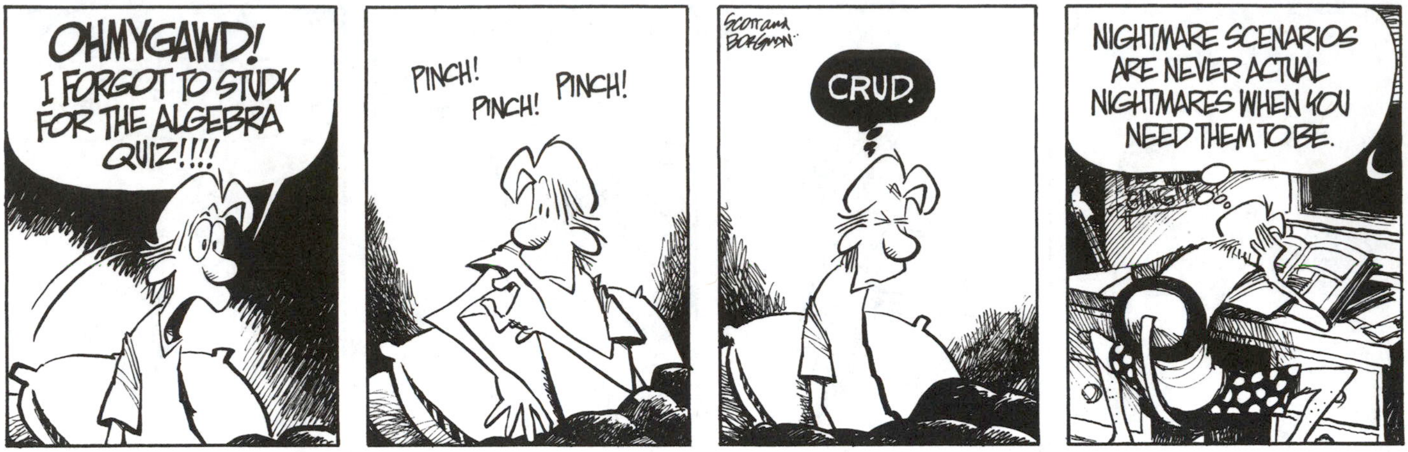
OHMYGAWD! I FORGOT TO STUDY FOR THE ALGEBRA QUIZ!!!!
PINCH!
PINCH!
PINCH!
CRUD.
NIGHTMARE SCENARIOS ARE NEVER ACTUAL NIGHTMARES WHEN YOU NEED THEM TO BE.

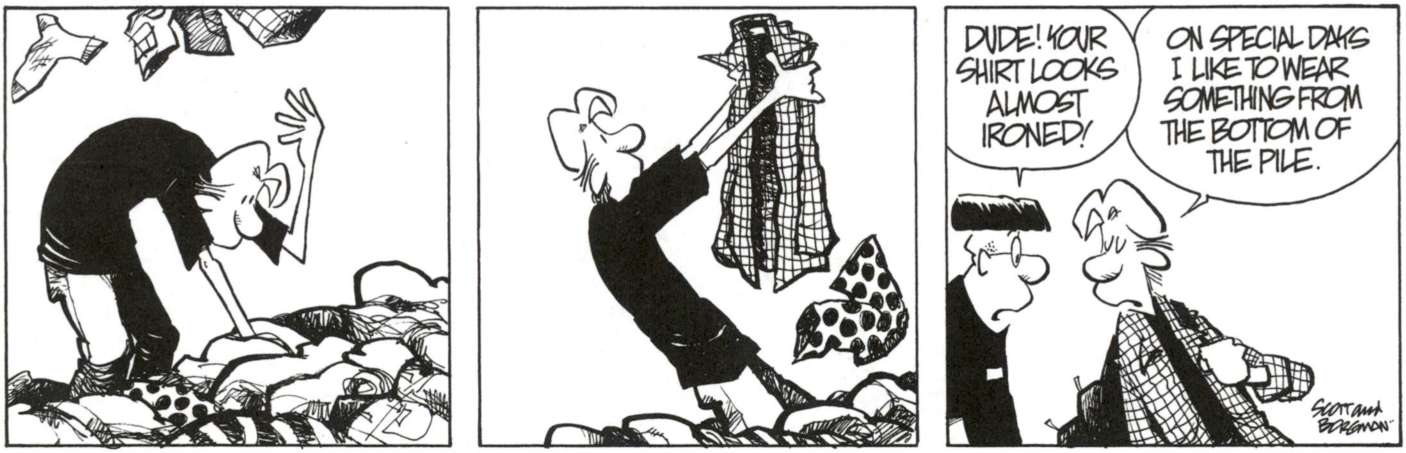
DUDE! YOUR SHIRT LOOKS ALMOST IRONED!
ON SPECIAL DAYS I LIKE TO WEAR SOMETHING FROM THE BOTTOM OF THE PILE.

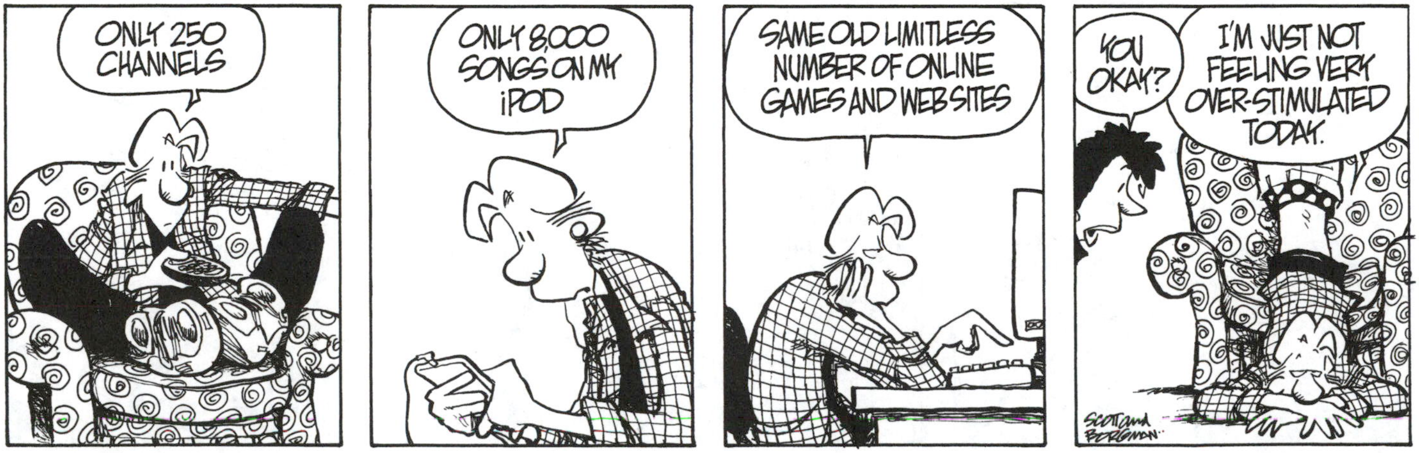
ONLY 250 CHANNELS
ONLY 8,000 SONGS ON MY iPOD
SAME OLD LIMITLESS NUMBER OF ONLINE GAMES AND WEB SITES
YOU OKAY?
I'M JUST NOT FEELING VERY OVER-STIMULATED TODAY.

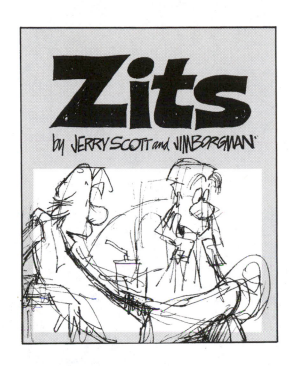

Zits

by JERRY SCOTT and JIM BORGMAN

HI LOW-SELF-ESTEEM GIRL! WANT TO HAVE LUNCH TOGETHER AT SEPARATE TABLES?

THAT WOULD BE LOVELY, NEVER-GOES-TO-HIS-LOCKER-GUY!

I LIKE YOUR MAKEUP, TOO-MUCH-EYESHADOW-GIRL!

THANKS, VOLLEYBALL-IS-MY-LIFE-GIRL!

SCOTT and BORGMAN

PEOPLE DON'T HAVE A NICKNAME FOR ME, DO THEY, GIGGLES-AT-EVERYTHING-GIRL?

NOT THAT I KNOW OF, TOO-MUCH-HAIR-GEL-GUY! (HEE HEE HEE HEE HEE HEE HEE HEE)

THE PEOPLE IN THIS SCHOOL ARE HILARIOUS

YEAH, TALK ABOUT EASY TARGETS!

HOW'S IT GOING, UNFAIRLY-CRITICAL-OF-OTHER-PEOPLE-GUYS?

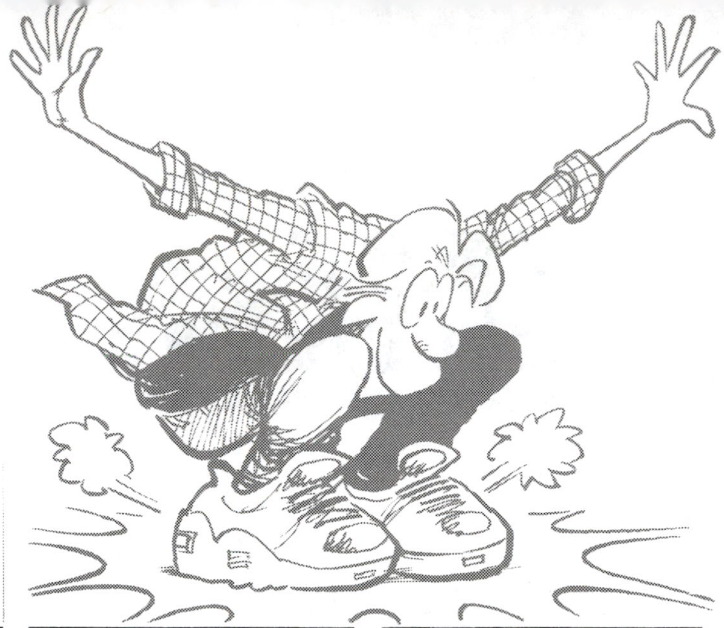

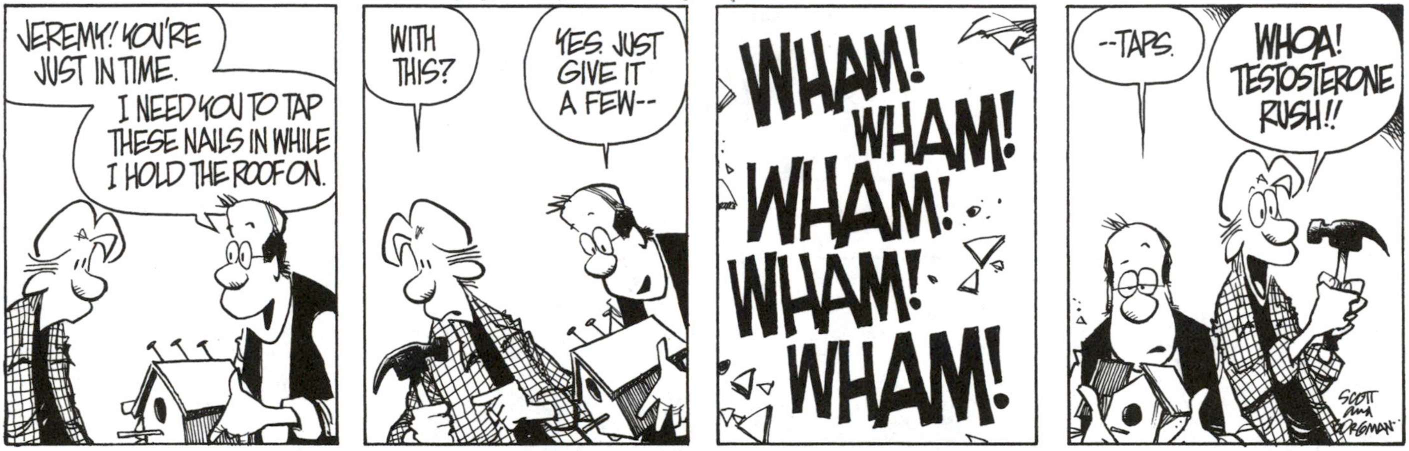
JEREMY! YOU'RE JUST IN TIME.
I NEED YOU TO TAP THESE NAILS IN WHILE I HOLD THE ROOF ON.
WITH THIS?
YES. JUST GIVE IT A FEW--
WHAM! WHAM! WHAM! WHAM! WHAM!
--TAPS.
WHOA! TESTOSTERONE RUSH!!
SCOTT AND BORGMAN

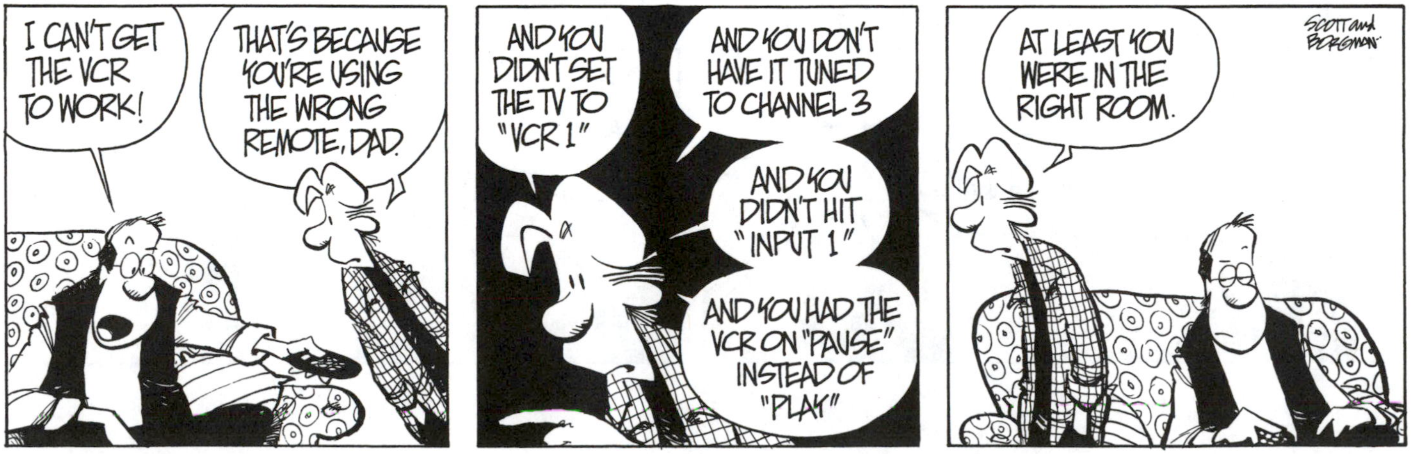
I CAN'T GET THE VCR TO WORK!
THAT'S BECAUSE YOU'RE USING THE WRONG REMOTE, DAD.
AND YOU DIDN'T SET THE TV TO "VCR 1"
AND YOU DON'T HAVE IT TUNED TO CHANNEL 3
AND YOU DIDN'T HIT "INPUT 1"
AND YOU HAD THE VCR ON "PAUSE" INSTEAD OF "PLAY"
AT LEAST YOU WERE IN THE RIGHT ROOM.
SCOTT AND BORGMAN

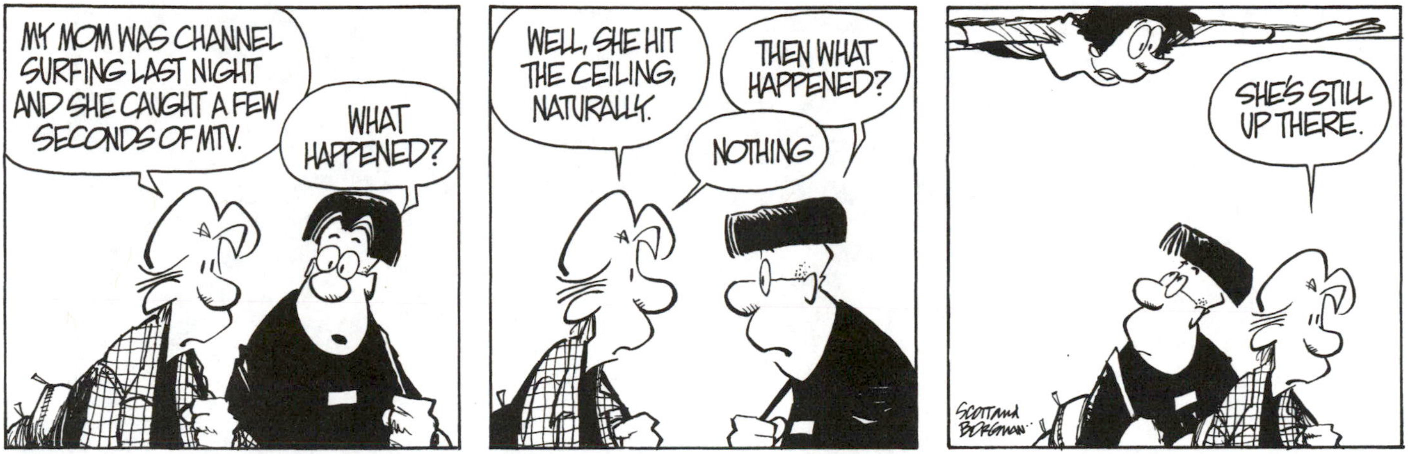
MY MOM WAS CHANNEL SURFING LAST NIGHT AND SHE CAUGHT A FEW SECONDS OF MTV.
WHAT HAPPENED?
WELL, SHE HIT THE CEILING, NATURALLY.
THEN WHAT HAPPENED?
NOTHING
SHE'S STILL UP THERE.

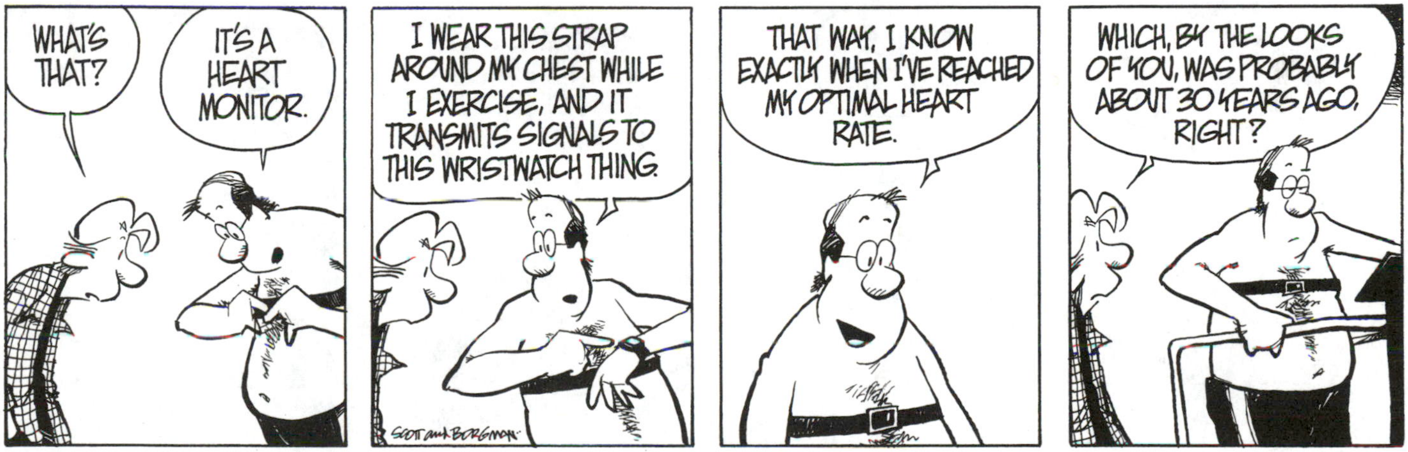
WHAT'S THAT?
IT'S A HEART MONITOR.
I WEAR THIS STRAP AROUND MY CHEST WHILE I EXERCISE, AND IT TRANSMITS SIGNALS TO THIS WRISTWATCH THING.
THAT WAY, I KNOW EXACTLY WHEN I'VE REACHED MY OPTIMAL HEART RATE.
WHICH, BY THE LOOKS OF YOU, WAS PROBABLY ABOUT 30 YEARS AGO, RIGHT?

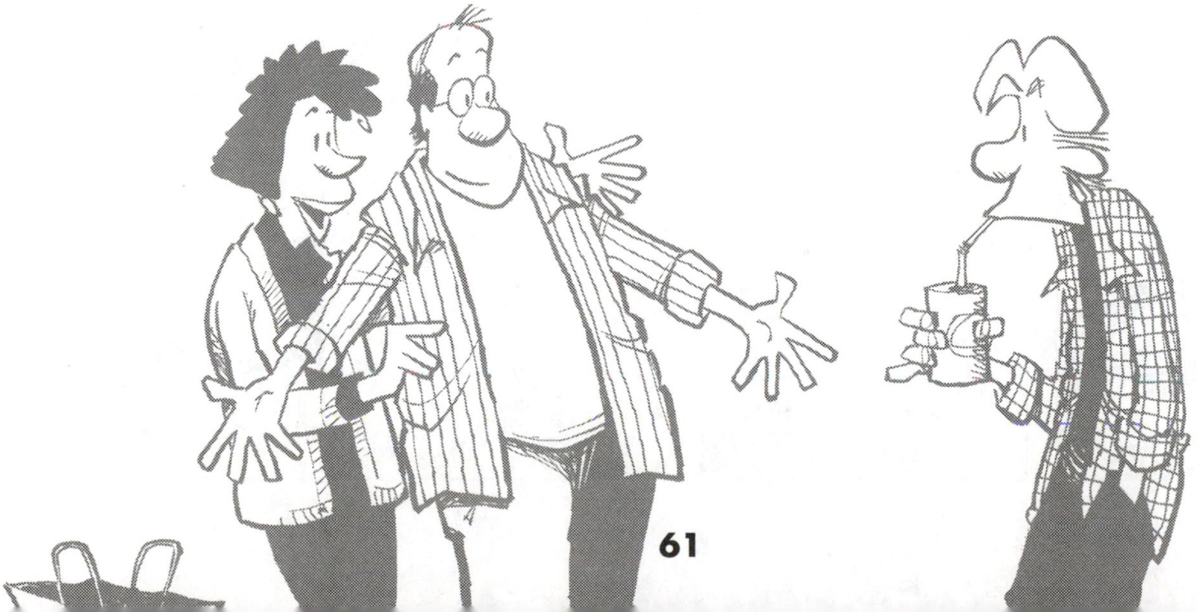

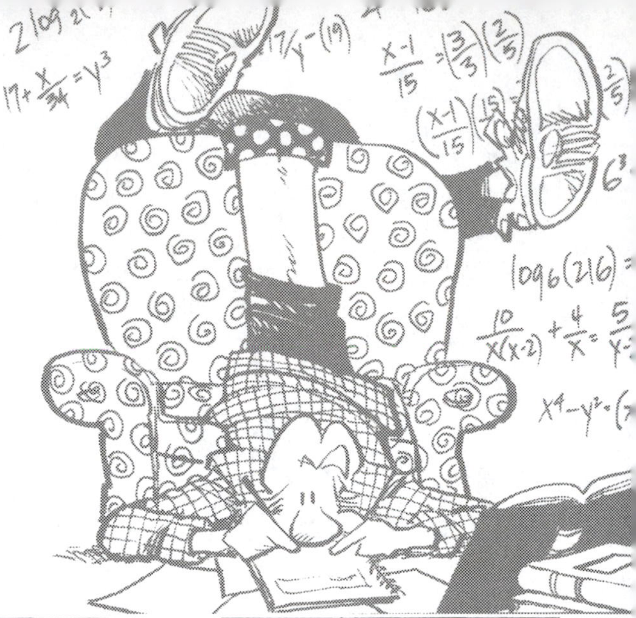

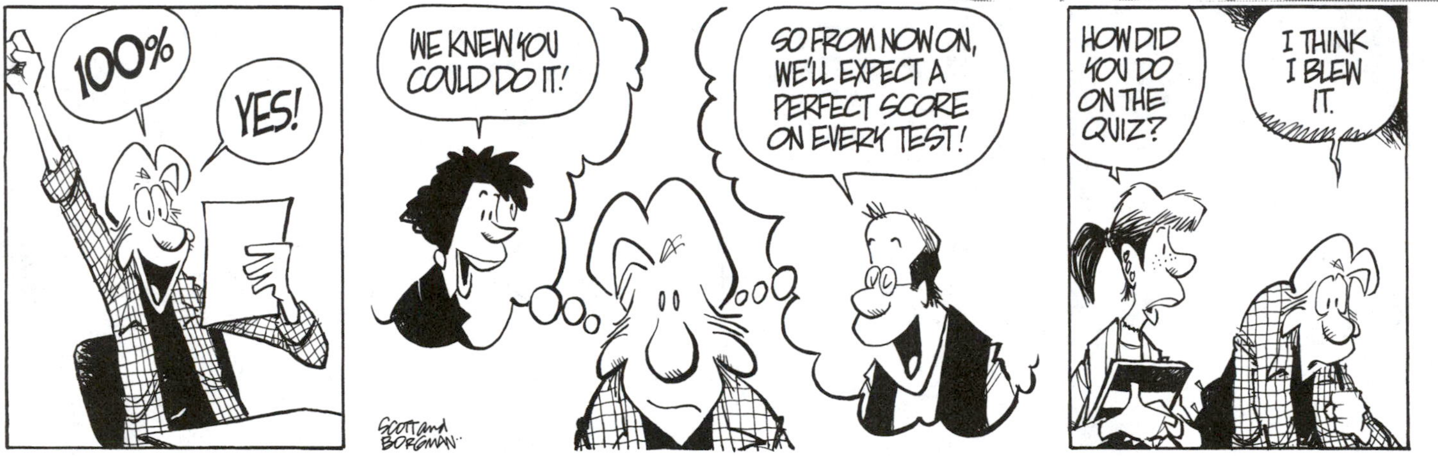
100%
YES!
WE KNEW YOU COULD DO IT!
SO FROM NOW ON, WE'LL EXPECT A PERFECT SCORE ON EVERY TEST!
SCOTT and BORGMAN
HOW DID YOU DO ON THE QUIZ?
I THINK I BLEW IT.

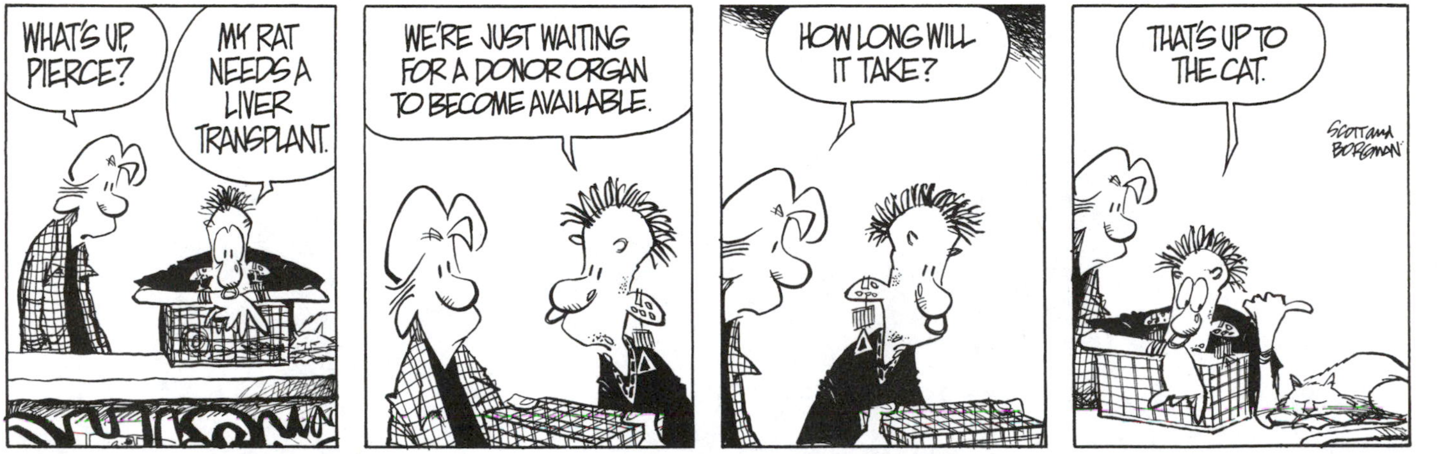
WHAT'S UP, PIERCE?
MY RAT NEEDS A LIVER TRANSPLANT.
WE'RE JUST WAITING FOR A DONOR ORGAN TO BECOME AVAILABLE.
HOW LONG WILL IT TAKE?
THAT'S UP TO THE CAT.
SCOTT and BORGMAN

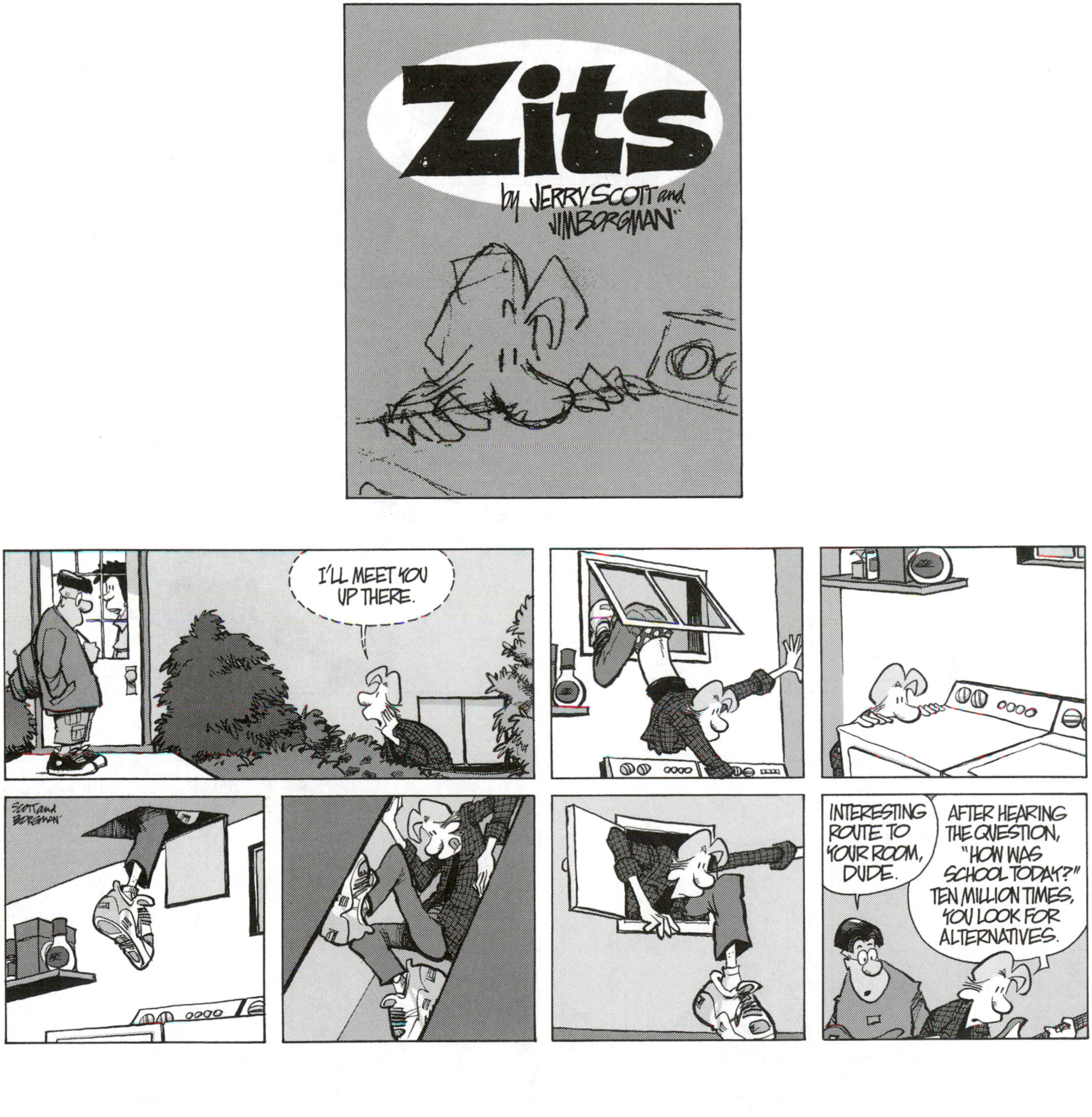
Zits
by JERRY SCOTT and JIM BORGMAN
I'LL MEET YOU UP THERE.
SCOTT and BORGMAN
INTERESTING ROUTE TO YOUR ROOM, DUDE.
AFTER HEARING THE QUESTION, "HOW WAS SCHOOL TODAY?" TEN MILLION TIMES, YOU LOOK FOR ALTERNATIVES.

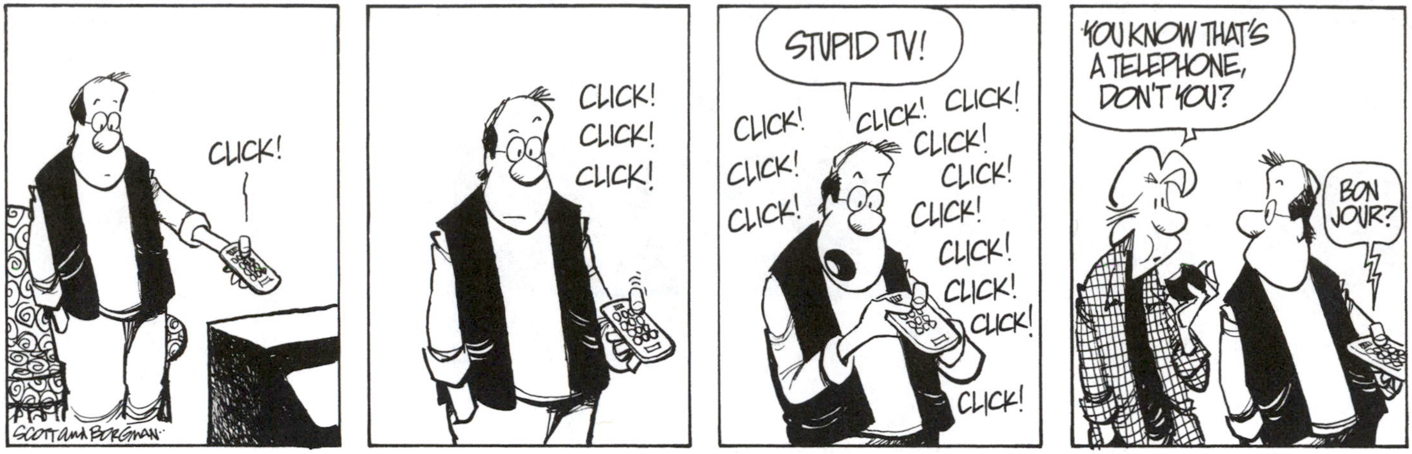
CLICK!
SCOTT and BORGMAN
CLICK! CLICK! CLICK!
STUPID TV!
CLICK! CLICK! CLICK! CLICK! CLICK! CLICK! CLICK! CLICK! CLICK! CLICK! CLICK! CLICK!
YOU KNOW THAT'S A TELEPHONE, DON'T YOU?
BON JOUR?

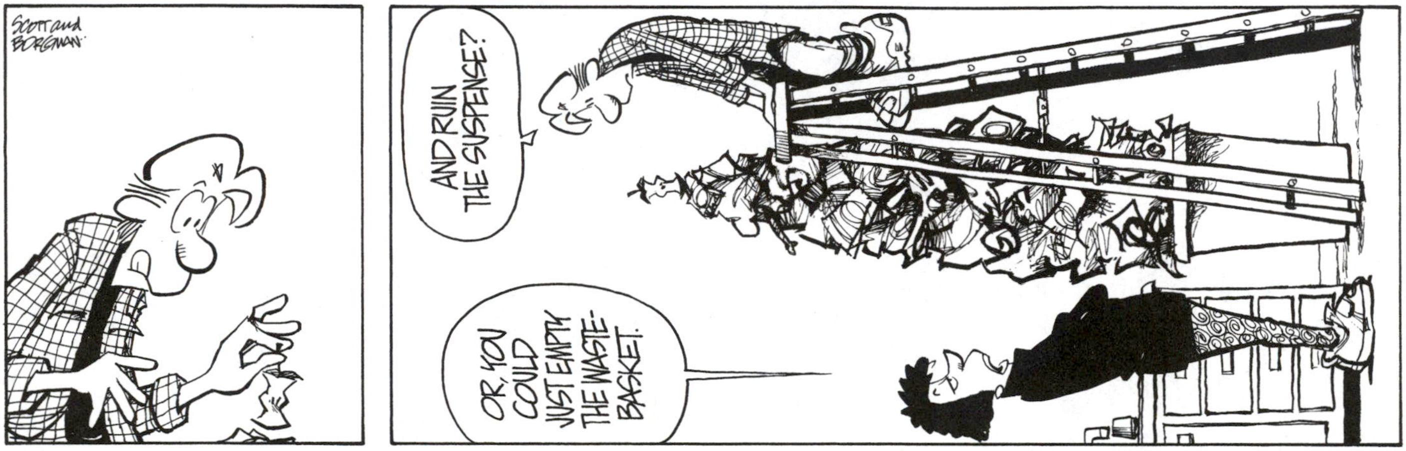
SCOTT and BORGMAN
OR, YOU COULD JUST EMPTY THE WASTE-BASKET.
AND RUIN THE SUSPENSE?

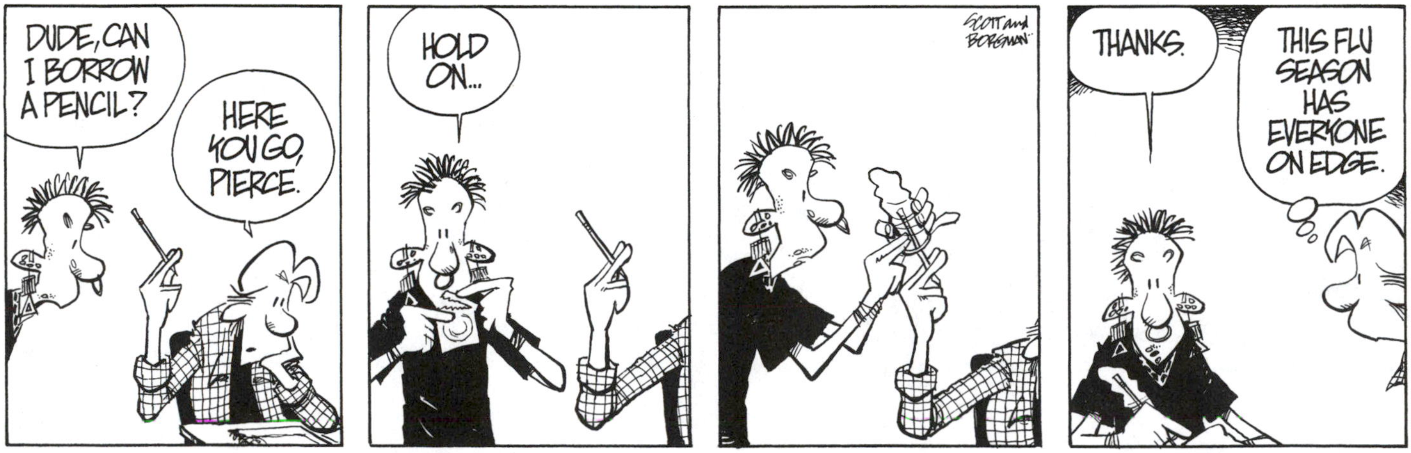
DUDE, CAN I BORROW A PENCIL?
HERE YOU GO, PIERCE.
HOLD ON...
SCOTT and BORGMAN
THANKS.
THIS FLU SEASON HAS EVERYONE ON EDGE.

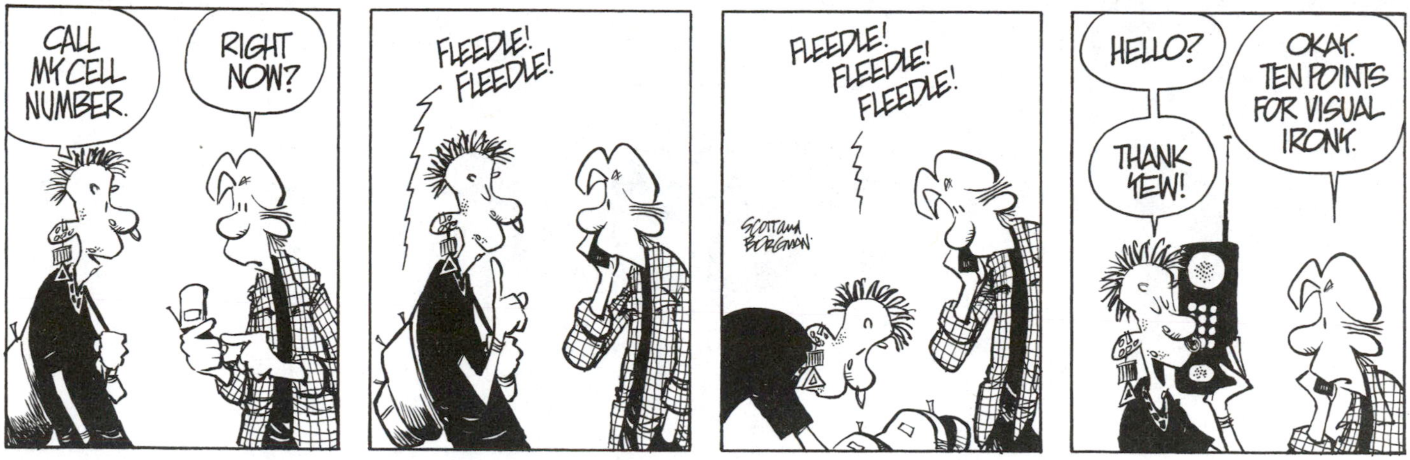
CALL MY CELL NUMBER.
RIGHT NOW?
FLEEDLE! FLEEDLE!
FLEEDLE! FLEEDLE! FLEEDLE!
HELLO?
THANK YEW!
OKAY. TEN POINTS FOR VISUAL IRONY.

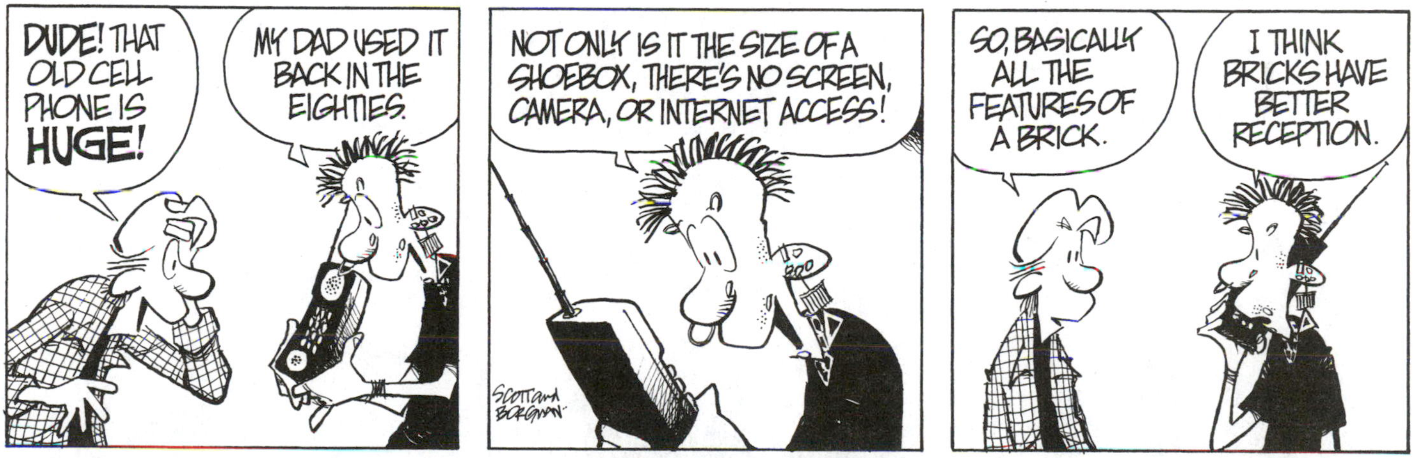
DUDE! THAT OLD CELL PHONE IS HUGE!
MY DAD USED IT BACK IN THE EIGHTIES.
NOT ONLY IS IT THE SIZE OF A SHOEBOX, THERE'S NO SCREEN, CAMERA, OR INTERNET ACCESS!
SO, BASICALLY ALL THE FEATURES OF A BRICK.
I THINK BRICKS HAVE BETTER RECEPTION.

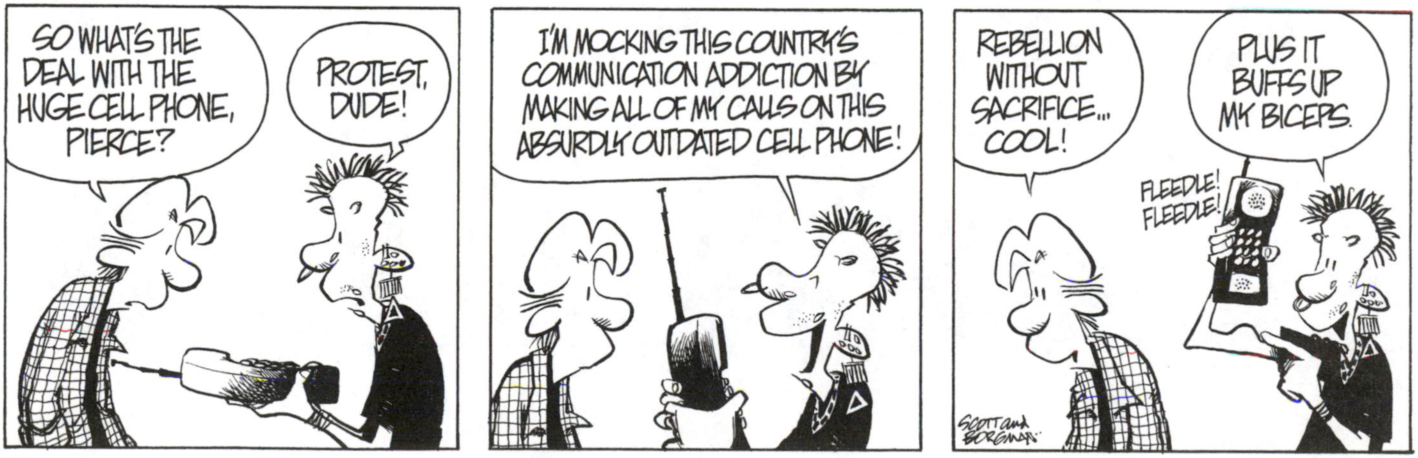
SO WHAT'S THE DEAL WITH THE HUGE CELL PHONE, PIERCE?
PROTEST, DUDE!
I'M MOCKING THIS COUNTRY'S COMMUNICATION ADDICTION BY MAKING ALL OF MY CALLS ON THIS ABSURDLY OUTDATED CELL PHONE!
REBELLION WITHOUT SACRIFICE... COOL!
FLEEDLE! FLEEDLE!
PLUS IT BUFFS UP MY BICEPS.

Zits
by JERRY SCOTT and JIM BORGMAN

YOUR MOTHER SAYS SHE'S TIRED OF ALL THE HOUNDING SHE'S DOING ABOUT YOUR CHORES.
SHE'S TIRED??
SCOTT and BORGMAN

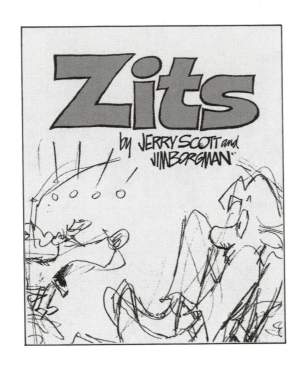

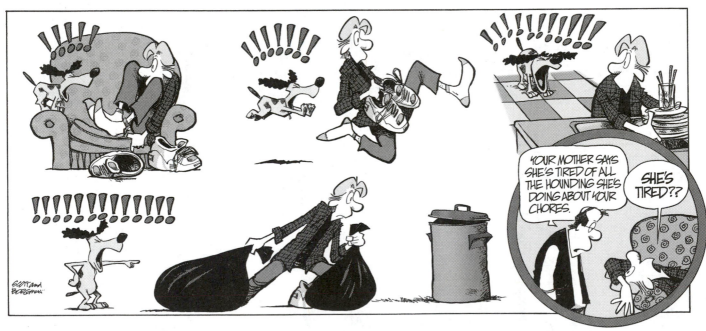

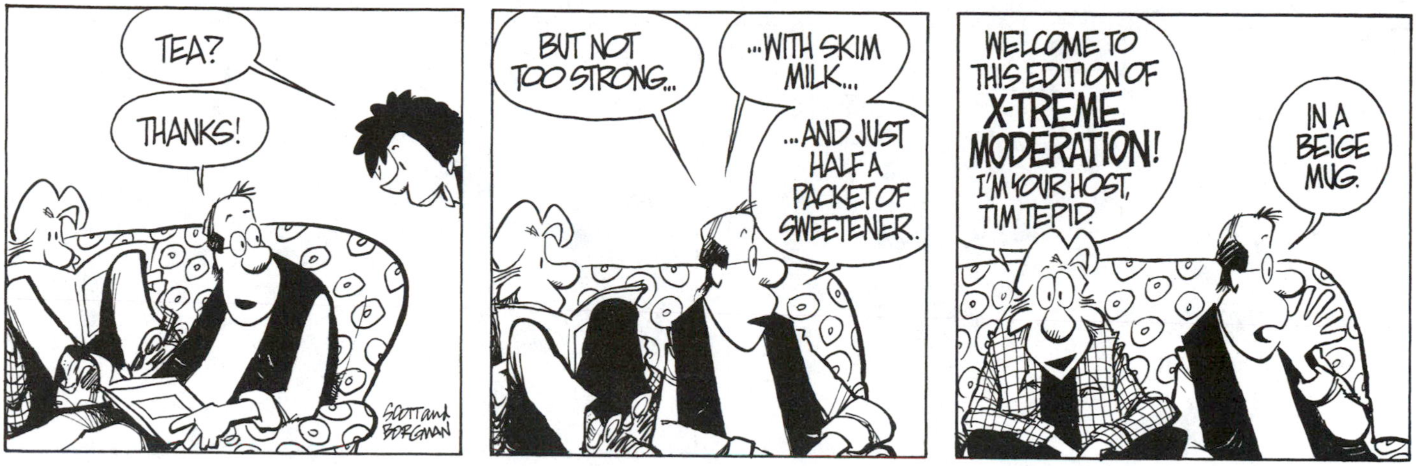
TEA?
THANKS!
SCOTT and BORGMAN
BUT NOT TOO STRONG...
...WITH SKIM MILK...
...AND JUST HALF A PACKET OF SWEETENER.
WELCOME TO THIS EDITION OF X-TREME MODERATION! I'M YOUR HOST, TIM TEPID.
IN A BEIGE MUG.

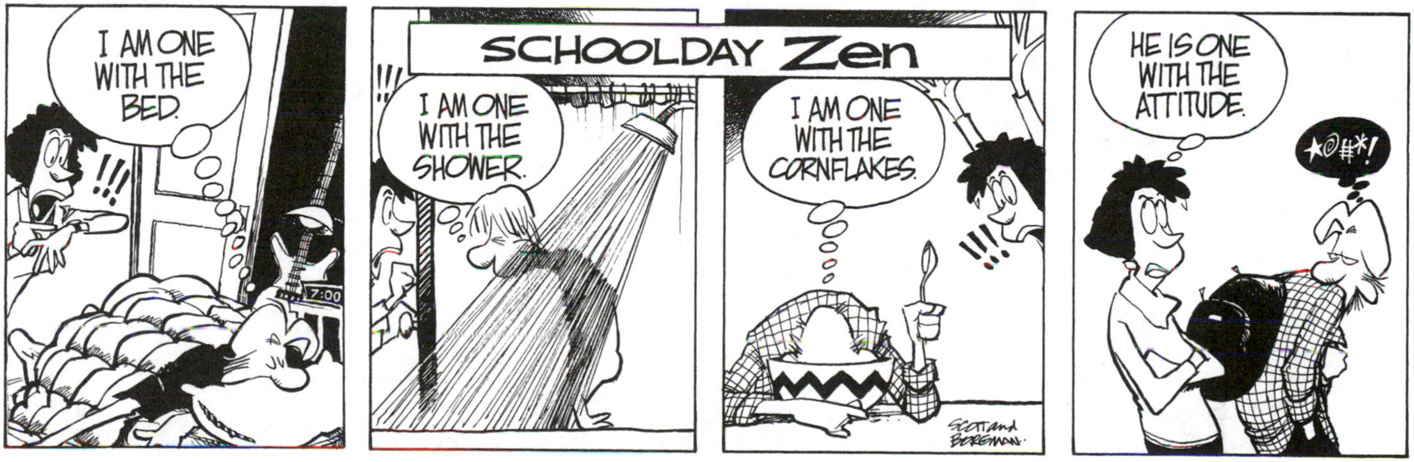
SCHOOLDAY Zen
I AM ONE WITH THE BED.
!!!
7:00
!!!
I AM ONE WITH THE SHOWER.
I AM ONE WITH THE CORNFLAKES.
!!!
SCOTT and BORGMAN
HE IS ONE WITH THE ATTITUDE.
★@#*!

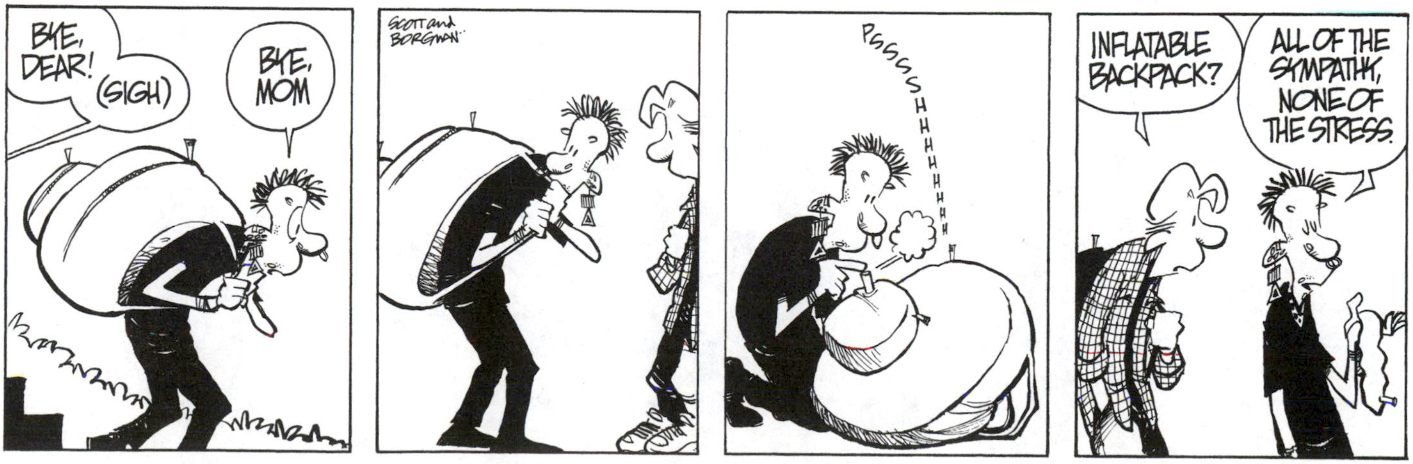
BYE, DEAR!
(SIGH)
BYE, MOM
SCOTT and BORGMAN
PSSSSHHHHHHHH
INFLATABLE BACKPACK?
ALL OF THE SYMPATHY, NONE OF THE STRESS.

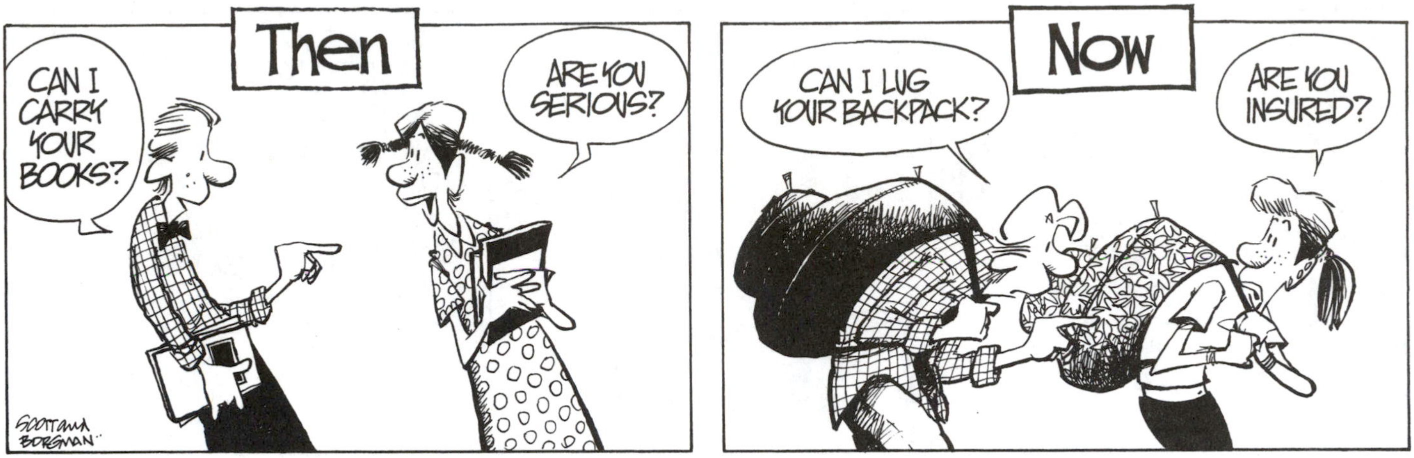
Then
CAN I CARRY YOUR BOOKS?
ARE YOU SERIOUS?
SCOTT and BORGMAN
Now
CAN I LUG YOUR BACKPACK?
ARE YOU INSURED?

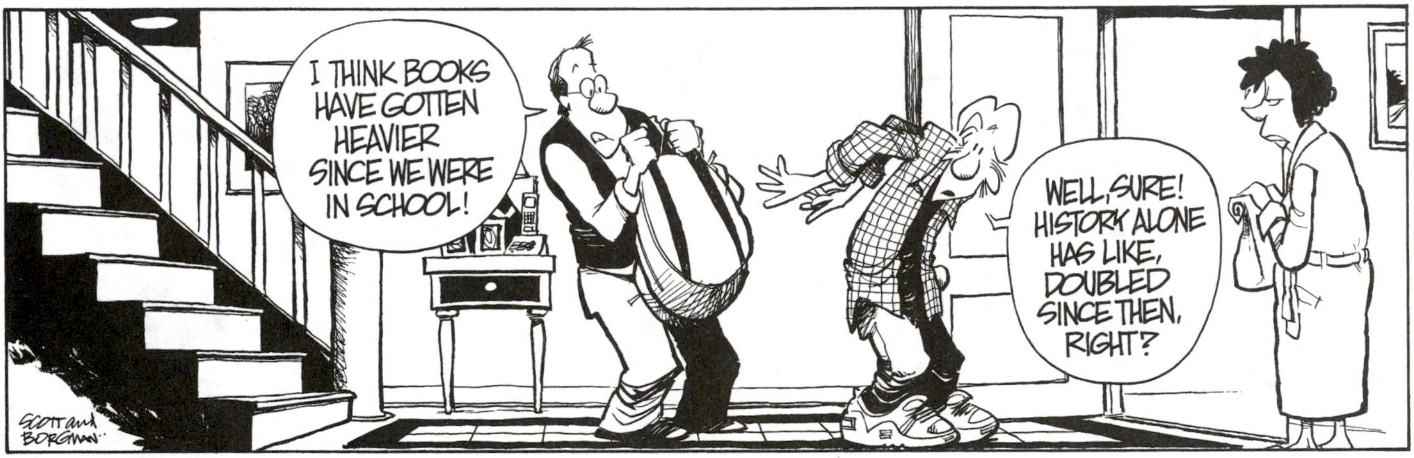
I THINK BOOKS HAVE GOTTEN HEAVIER SINCE WE WERE IN SCHOOL!
WELL, SURE! HISTORY ALONE HAS LIKE, DOUBLED SINCE THEN, RIGHT?
SCOTT and BORGMAN

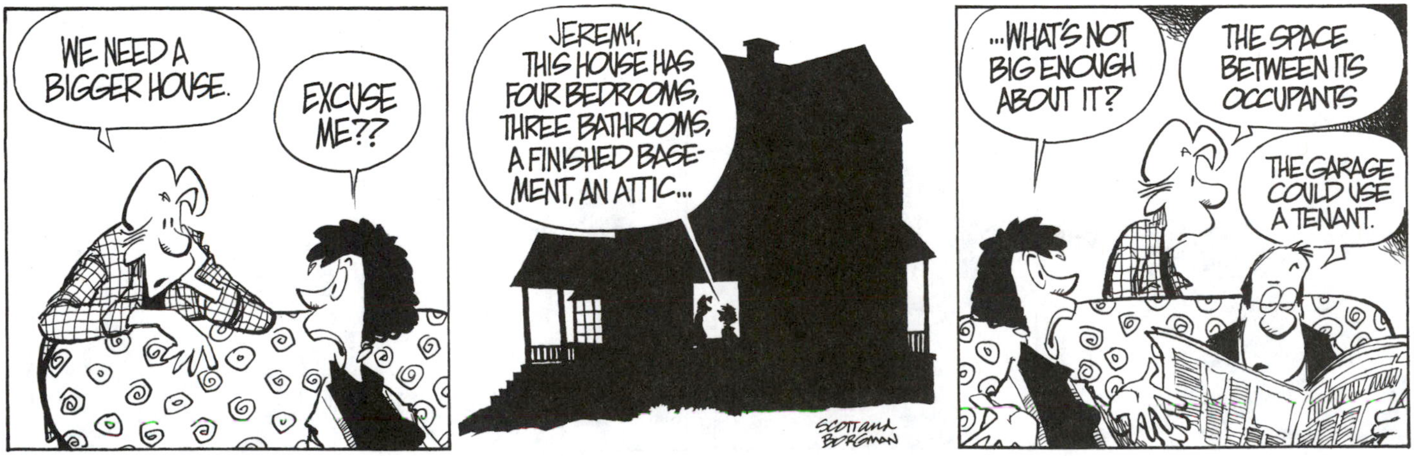
WE NEED A BIGGER HOUSE.
EXCUSE ME??
JEREMY, THIS HOUSE HAS FOUR BEDROOMS, THREE BATHROOMS, A FINISHED BASEMENT, AN ATTIC...
SCOTT and BORGMAN
...WHAT'S NOT BIG ENOUGH ABOUT IT?
THE SPACE BETWEEN ITS OCCUPANTS
THE GARAGE COULD USE A TENANT.

Zits
by JERRY SCOTT and JIM BORGMAN

JEREMY! IT'S FREEZING OUT THERE! WHERE IS YOUR COAT?
NOBODY WEARS COATS ANYMORE, MOM.
WELL, YOU'RE GOING TO WEAR YOURS!
SIGH!
SCOTT and BORGMAN
NOW PUT IT ON.
ON YOUR BODY.
WITH YOUR ARMS IN THE SLEEVES.
WHY MUST YOU MAKE MY LIFE SO DIFFICULT?

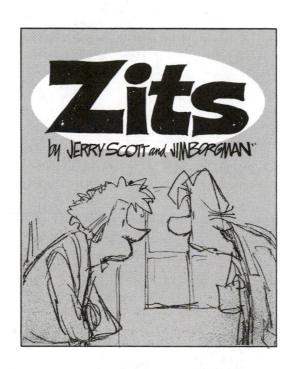

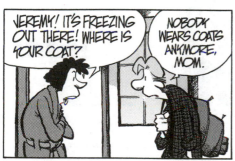

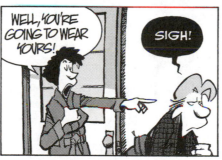

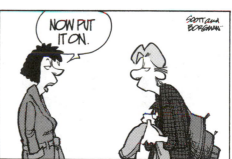

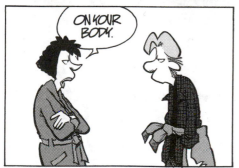

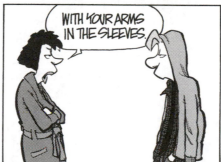

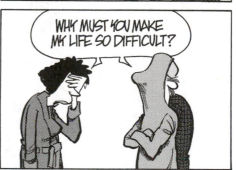

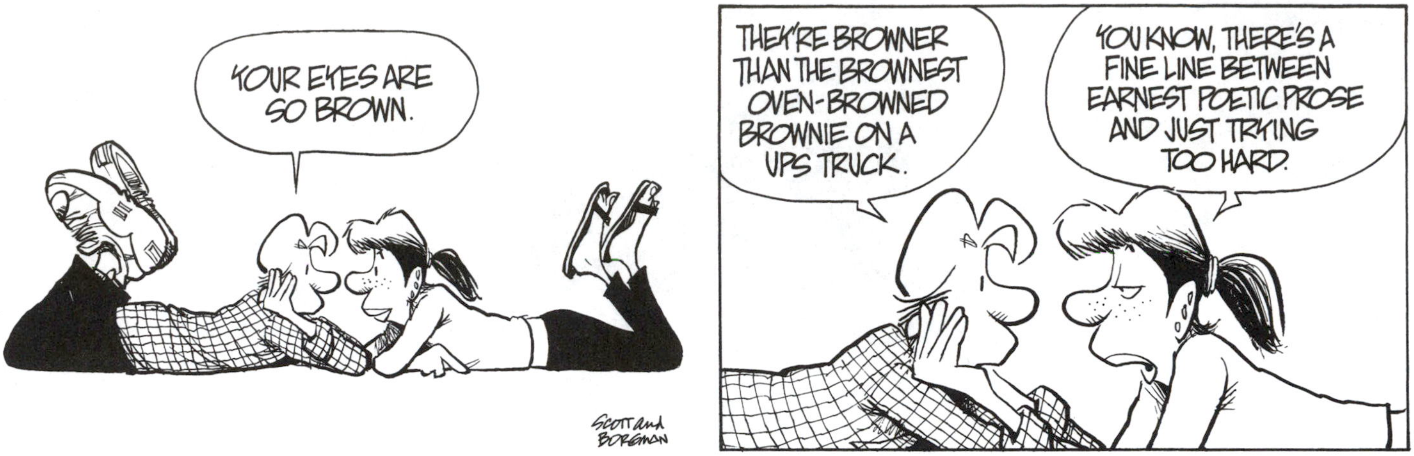
YOUR EYES ARE SO BROWN.
THEY'RE BROWNER THAN THE BROWNEST OVEN-BROWNED BROWNIE ON A UPS TRUCK.
YOU KNOW, THERE'S A FINE LINE BETWEEN EARNEST POETIC PROSE AND JUST TRYING TOO HARD.
SCOTT AND BORGMAN

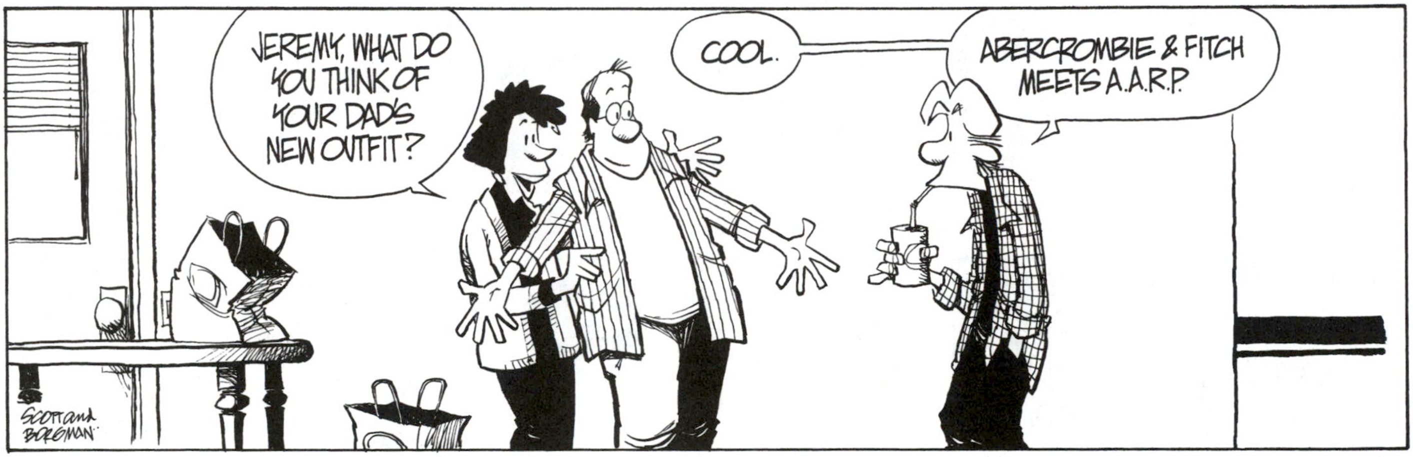
JEREMY, WHAT DO YOU THINK OF YOUR DAD'S NEW OUTFIT?
ABERCROMBIE & FITCH MEETS A.A.R.P.
COOL.
SCOTT AND BORGMAN

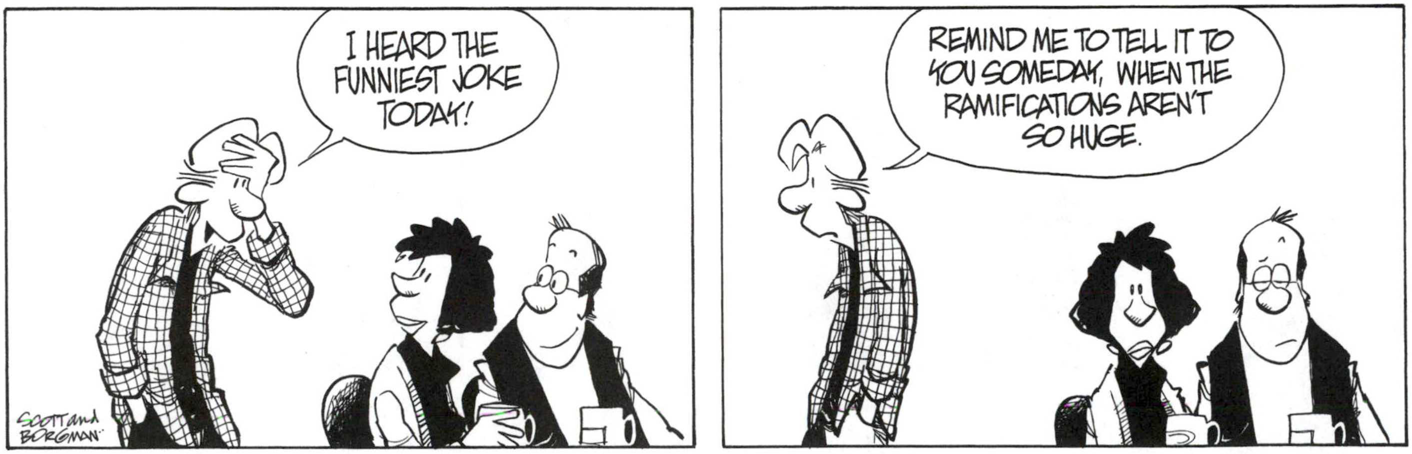
I HEARD THE FUNNIEST JOKE TODAY!
REMIND ME TO TELL IT TO YOU SOMEDAY, WHEN THE RAMIFICATIONS AREN'T SO HUGE.
SCOTT AND BORGMAN

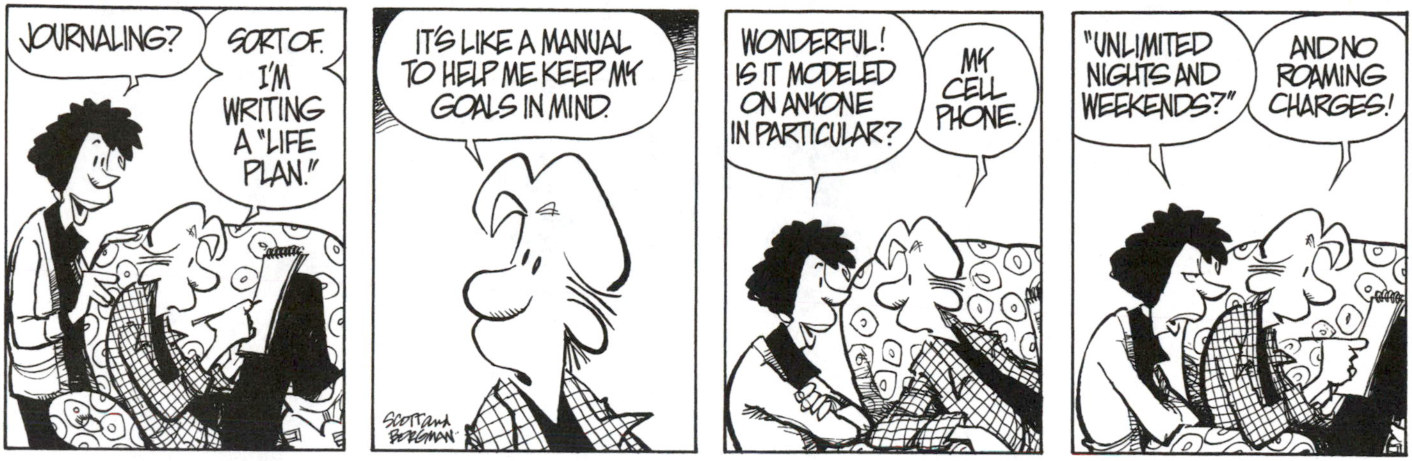
JOURNALING?
SORT OF. I'M WRITING A "LIFE PLAN."
IT'S LIKE A MANUAL TO HELP ME KEEP MY GOALS IN MIND.
WONDERFUL! IS IT MODELED ON ANYONE IN PARTICULAR?
MY CELL PHONE.
"UNLIMITED NIGHTS AND WEEKENDS?"
AND NO ROAMING CHARGES!

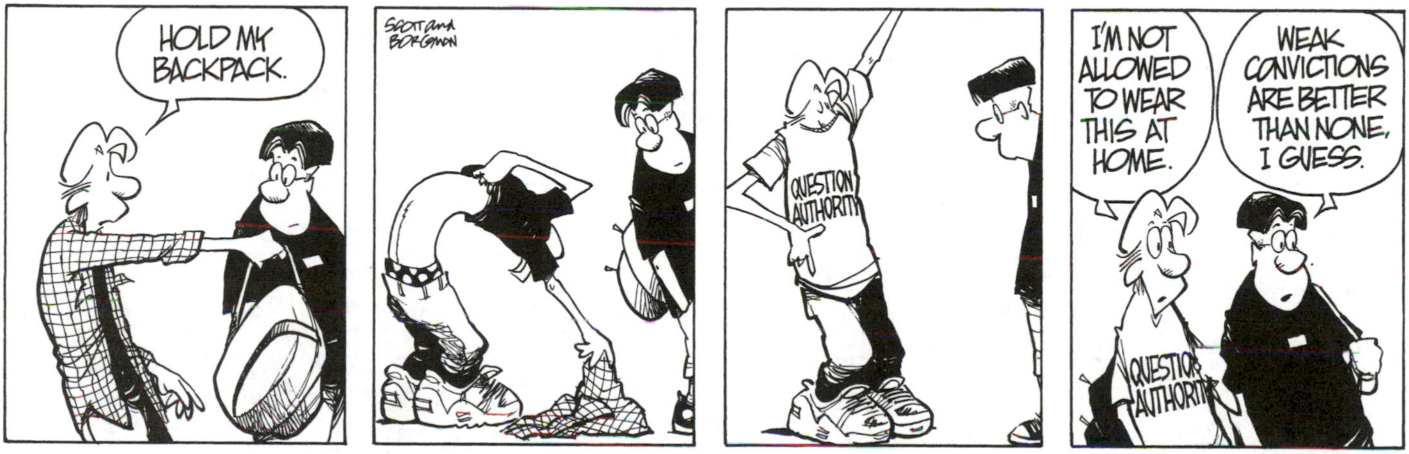
HOLD MY BACKPACK.
QUESTION AUTHORITY
I'M NOT ALLOWED TO WEAR THIS AT HOME.
WEAK CONVICTIONS ARE BETTER THAN NONE, I GUESS.

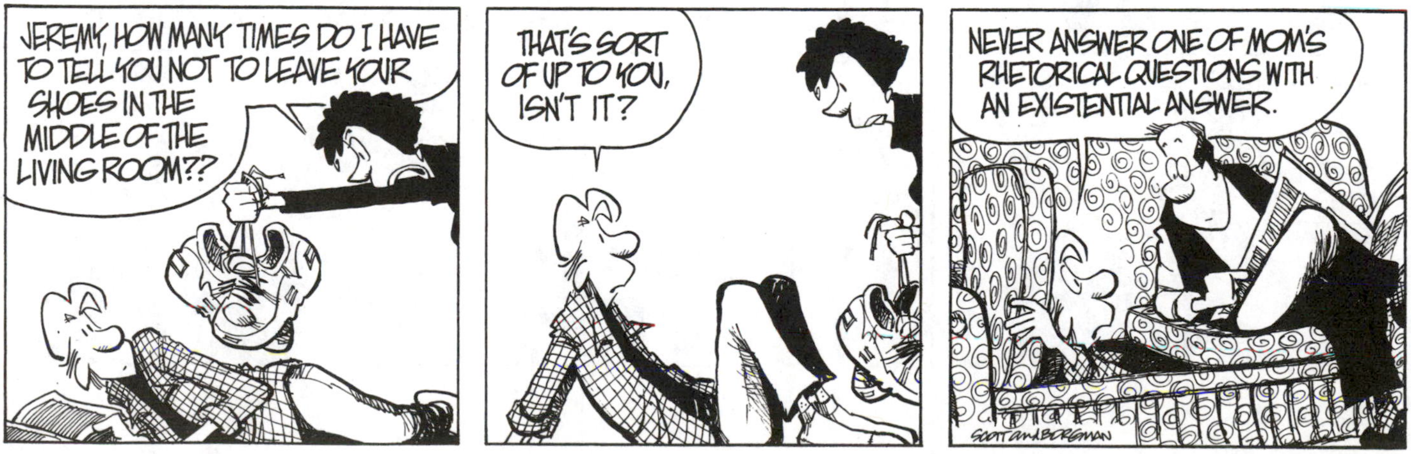
JEREMY, HOW MANY TIMES DO I HAVE TO TELL YOU NOT TO LEAVE YOUR SHOES IN THE MIDDLE OF THE LIVING ROOM??
THAT'S SORT OF UP TO YOU, ISN'T IT?
NEVER ANSWER ONE OF MOM'S RHETORICAL QUESTIONS WITH AN EXISTENTIAL ANSWER.

Zits

by JERRY SCOTT and JIM BORGMAN

WOW... SO YOU AND SARA HAD A FIGHT, HUH?

JUST NOW. HOW DID YOU--?

OOH. YOU SHOULDN'T HAVE CALLED HER "IRRATIONAL," JEREMY.

I DIDN'T CALL HER IRRATIONAL!

ACCORDING TO THE TRANSCRIPT YOU DID... AND YOU DO LOOK PRETTY MAD IN THE PICTURES.

OKAY, BUT SHE-- WHAT PICTURES??

HOWEVER, THE GOOD NEWS IS THAT POPULAR OPINION SEEMS TO INDICATE THAT YOU TWO SHOULD STAY TOGETHER.

CONGRATULATIONS!

HOLD ON... MORE POLL RESULTS ARE COMING IN FROM NEW ZEALAND......

SCROLL SCROLL SCROLL

SOMETIMES I REALLY HATE THE INTERNET.

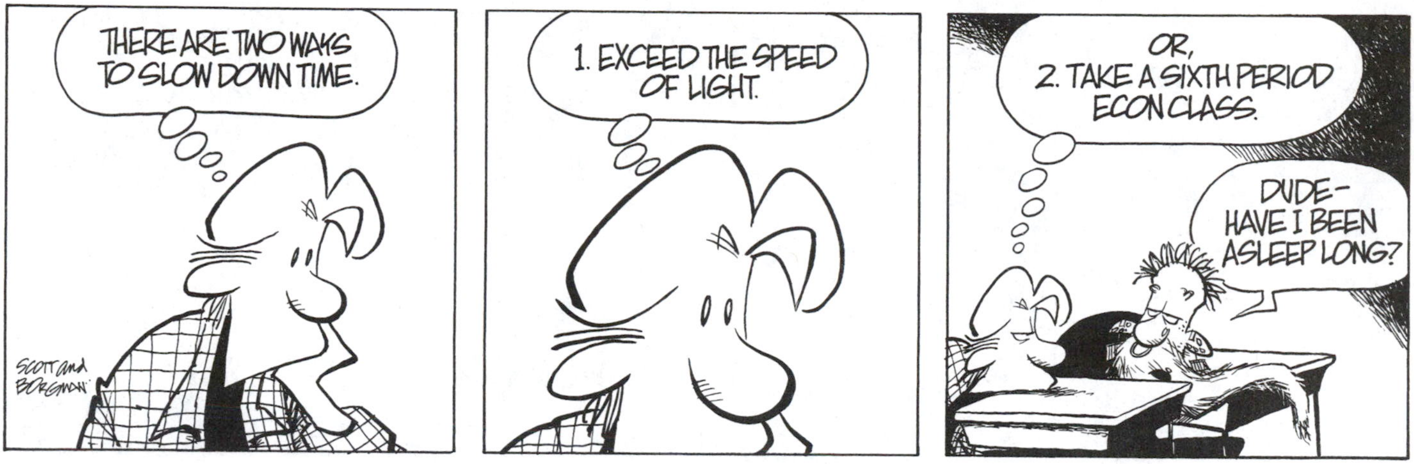
THERE ARE TWO WAYS TO SLOW DOWN TIME.
SCOTT and BORGMAN
1. EXCEED THE SPEED OF LIGHT.
OR, 2. TAKE A SIXTH PERIOD ECON CLASS.
DUDE- HAVE I BEEN ASLEEP LONG?

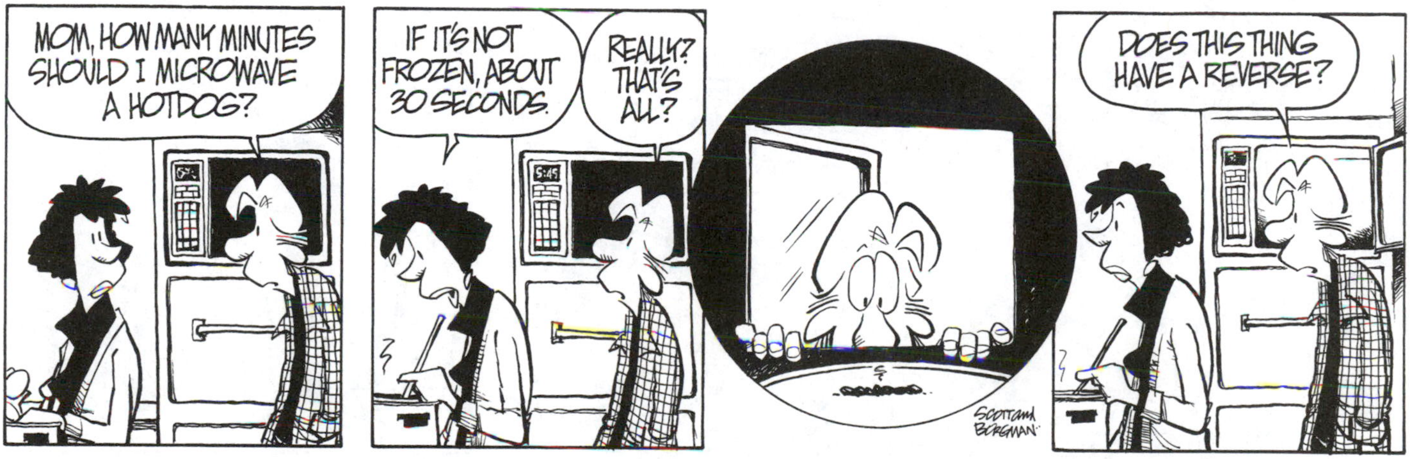
MOM, HOW MANY MINUTES SHOULD I MICROWAVE A HOTDOG?
IF IT'S NOT FROZEN, ABOUT 30 SECONDS.
REALLY? THAT'S ALL?
SCOTT and BORGMAN
DOES THIS THING HAVE A REVERSE?

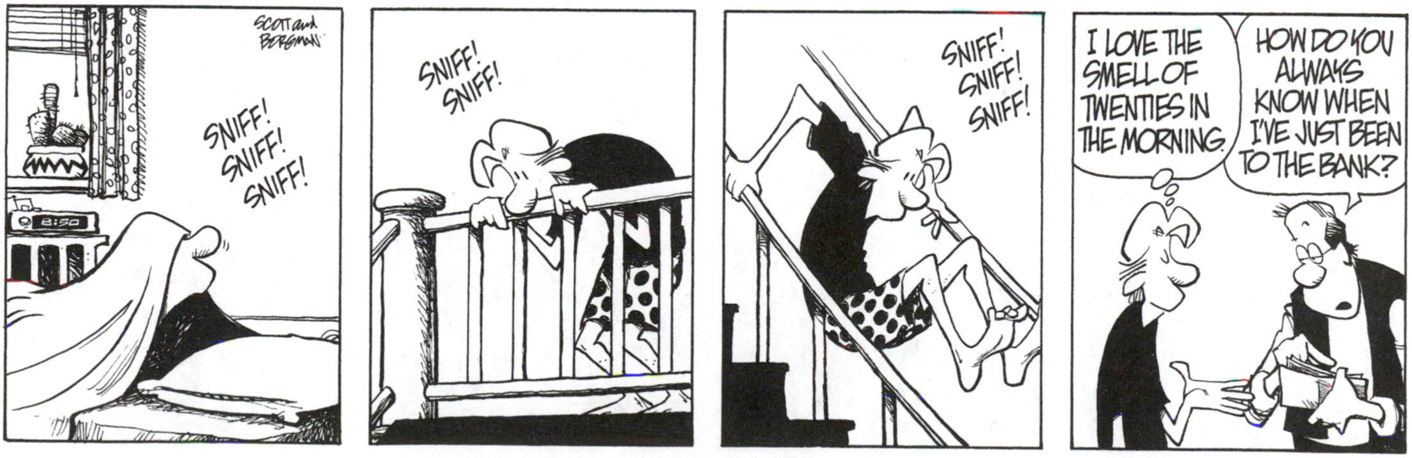
SCOTT and BORGMAN
SNIFF! SNIFF! SNIFF!
SNIFF! SNIFF!
SNIFF! SNIFF! SNIFF!
I LOVE THE SMELL OF TWENTIES IN THE MORNING.
HOW DO YOU ALWAYS KNOW WHEN I'VE JUST BEEN TO THE BANK?

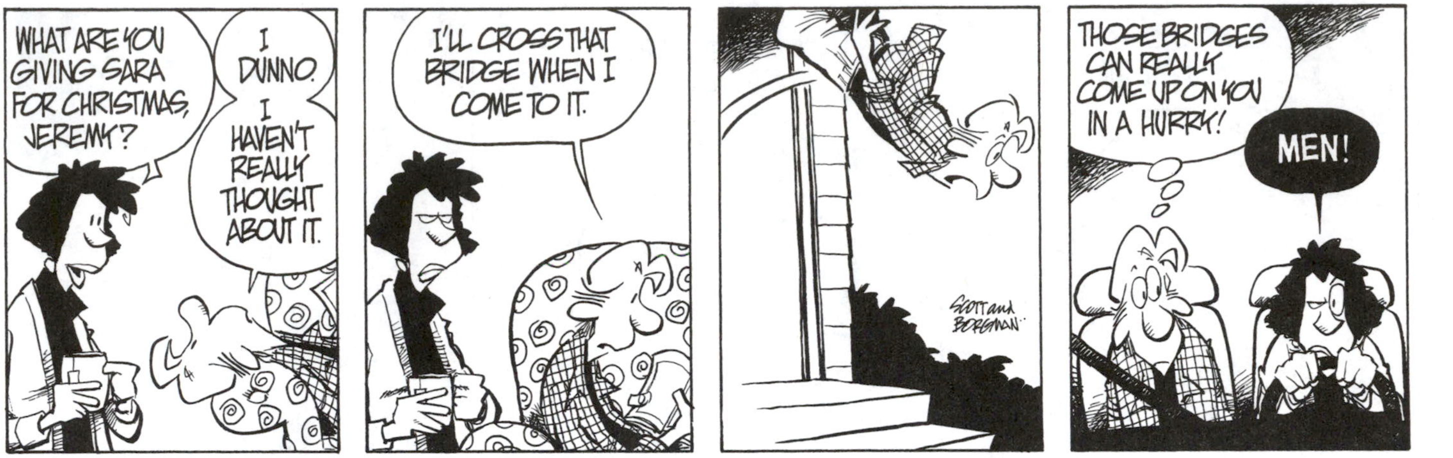
WHAT ARE YOU GIVING SARA FOR CHRISTMAS, JEREMY?
I DUNNO. I HAVEN'T REALLY THOUGHT ABOUT IT.
I'LL CROSS THAT BRIDGE WHEN I COME TO IT.
SCOTT and BORGMAN
THOSE BRIDGES CAN REALLY COME UP ON YOU IN A HURRY!
MEN!

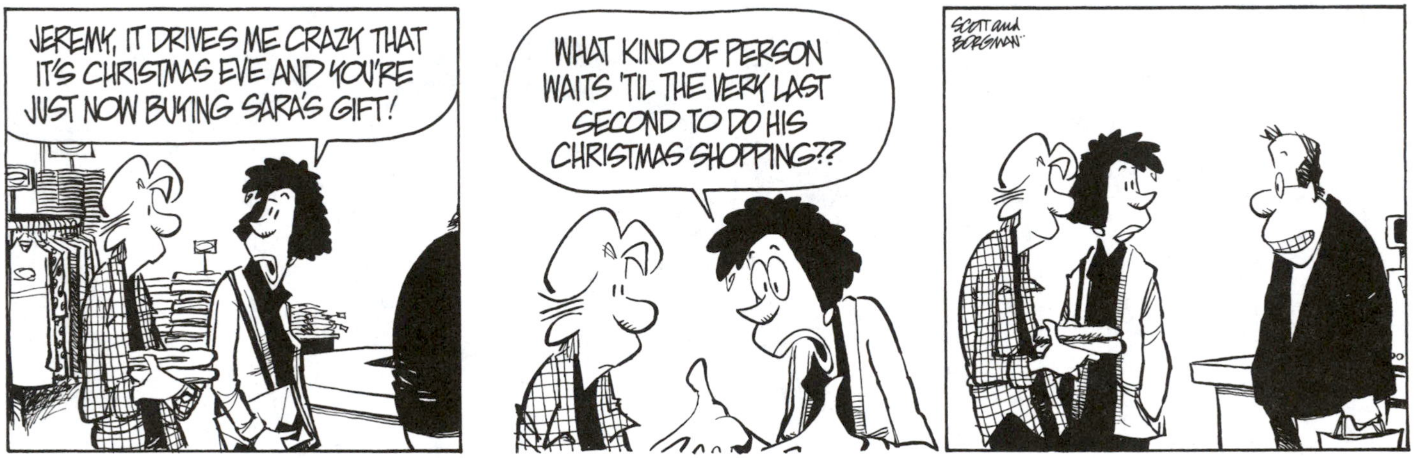
JEREMY, IT DRIVES ME CRAZY THAT IT'S CHRISTMAS EVE AND YOU'RE JUST NOW BUYING SARA'S GIFT!
WHAT KIND OF PERSON WAITS 'TIL THE VERY LAST SECOND TO DO HIS CHRISTMAS SHOPPING??
SCOTT and BORGMAN

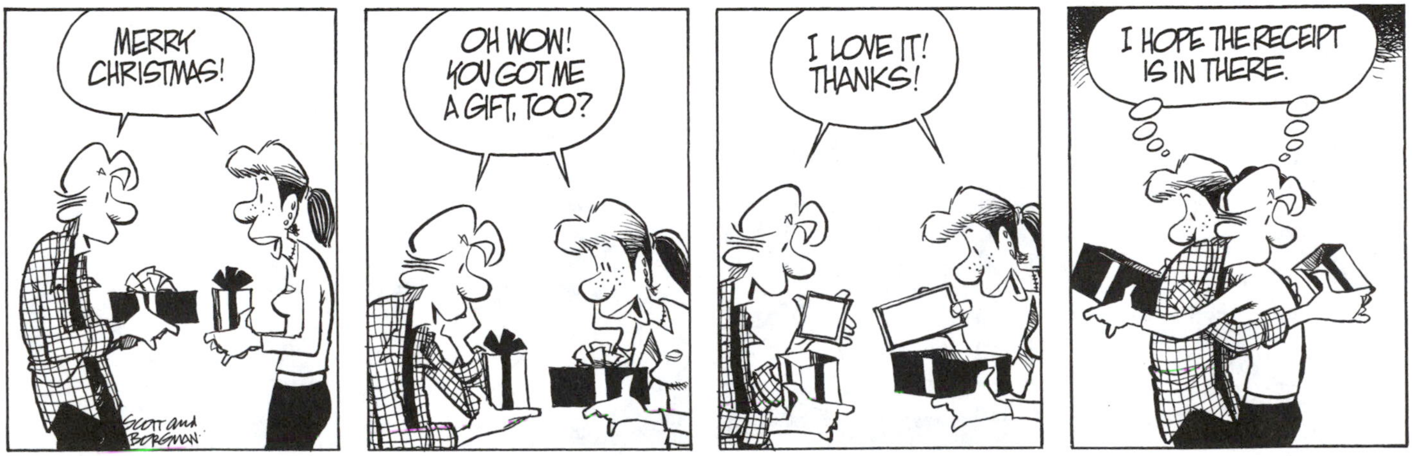
MERRY CHRISTMAS!
SCOTT and BORGMAN
OH WOW! YOU GOT ME A GIFT, TOO?
I LOVE IT! THANKS!
I HOPE THE RECEIPT IS IN THERE.

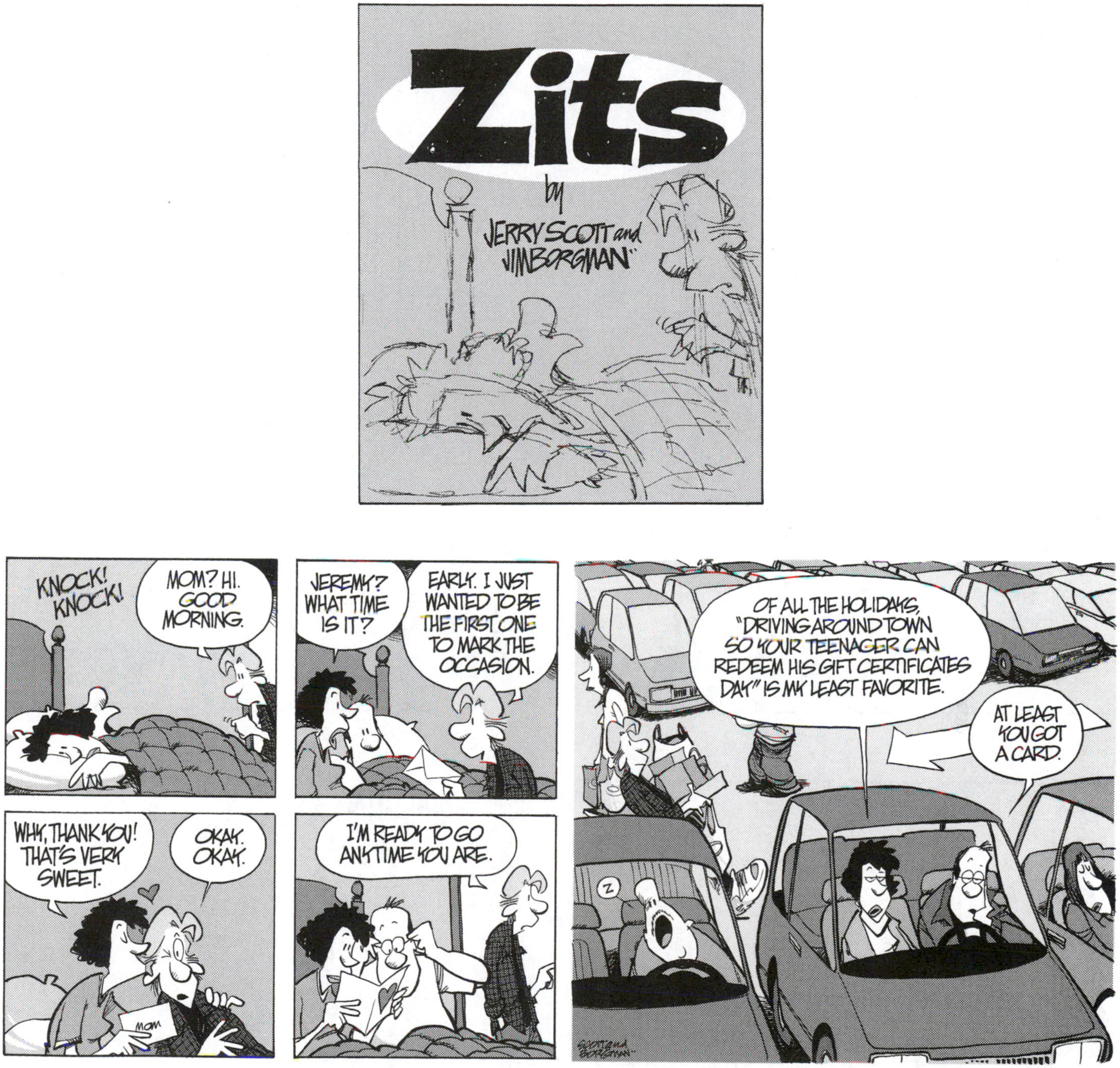
Zits
by
JERRY SCOTT and
JIM BORGMAN
KNOCK! KNOCK!
MOM? HI. GOOD MORNING.
JEREMY? WHAT TIME IS IT?
EARLY. I JUST WANTED TO BE THE FIRST ONE TO MARK THE OCCASION.
WHY, THANK YOU! THAT'S VERY SWEET.
OKAY. OKAY.
MOM
I'M READY TO GO ANYTIME YOU ARE.
OF ALL THE HOLIDAYS, "DRIVING AROUND TOWN SO YOUR TEENAGER CAN REDEEM HIS GIFT CERTIFICATES DAY" IS MY LEAST FAVORITE.
AT LEAST YOU GOT A CARD.
Z

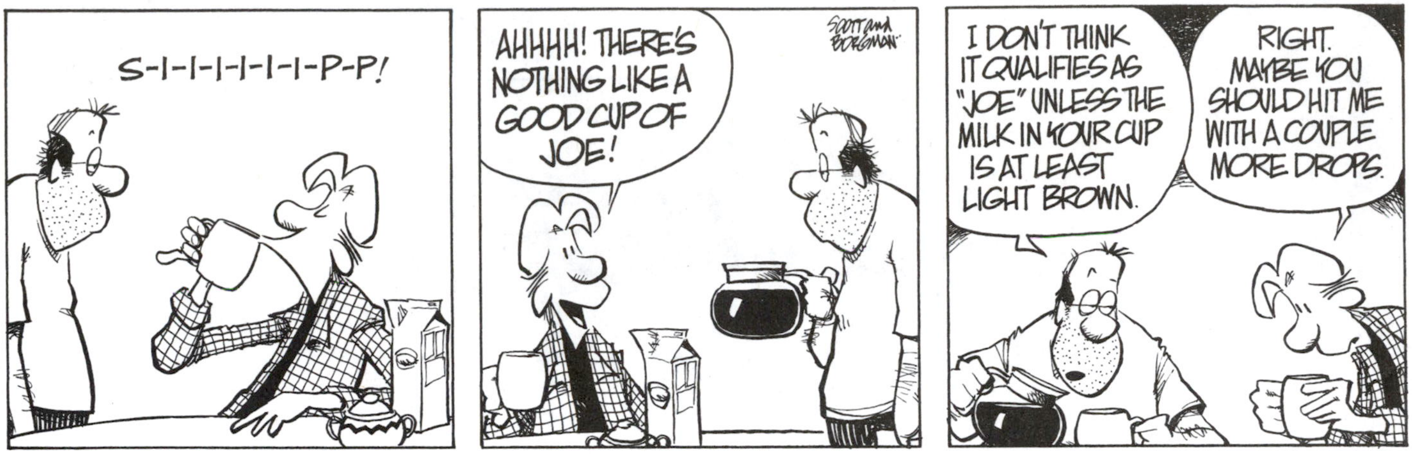
S-I-I-I-I-I-I-P-P!
AHHHH! THERE'S NOTHING LIKE A GOOD CUP OF JOE!
I DON'T THINK IT QUALIFIES AS "JOE" UNLESS THE MILK IN YOUR CUP IS AT LEAST LIGHT BROWN.
RIGHT. MAYBE YOU SHOULD HIT ME WITH A COUPLE MORE DROPS.

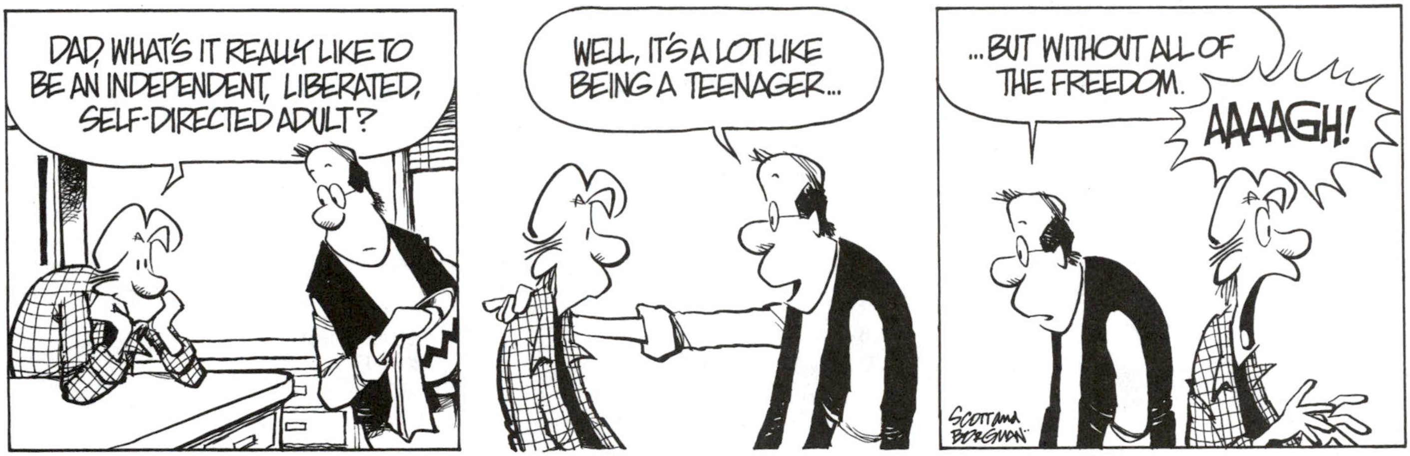
DAD, WHAT'S IT REALLY LIKE TO BE AN INDEPENDENT, LIBERATED, SELF-DIRECTED ADULT?
WELL, IT'S A LOT LIKE BEING A TEENAGER...
...BUT WITHOUT ALL OF THE FREEDOM.
AAAAGH!

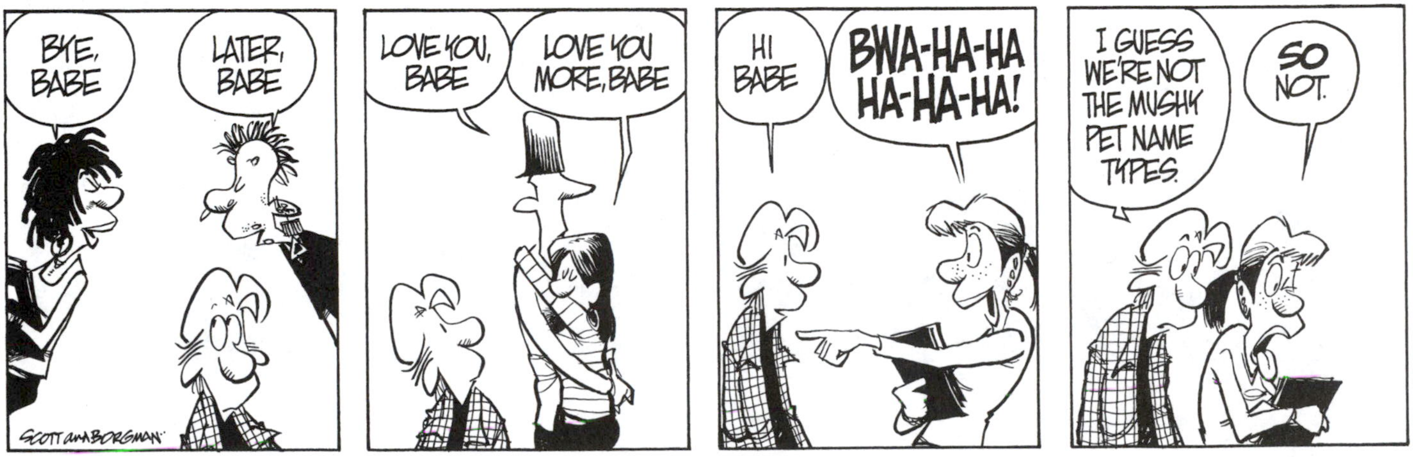
BYE, BABE
LATER, BABE
LOVE YOU, BABE
LOVE YOU MORE, BABE
HI BABE
BWA-HA-HA HA-HA-HA!
I GUESS WE'RE NOT THE MUSHY PET NAME TYPES.
SO NOT.

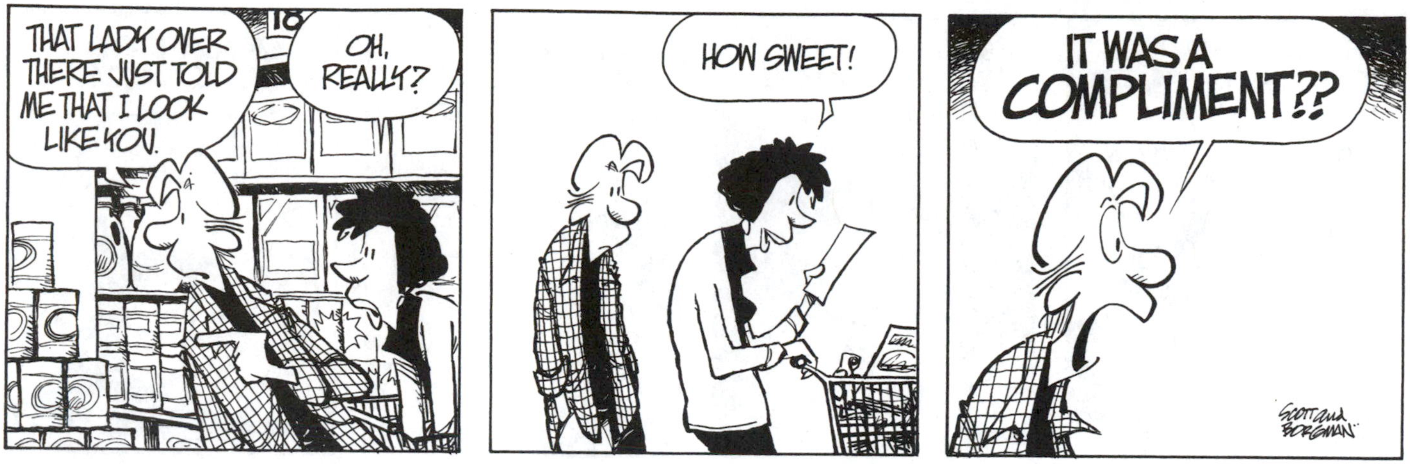
THAT LADY OVER THERE JUST TOLD ME THAT I LOOK LIKE YOU.
OH, REALLY?
HOW SWEET!
IT WAS A COMPLIMENT??
SCOTT and BORGMAN

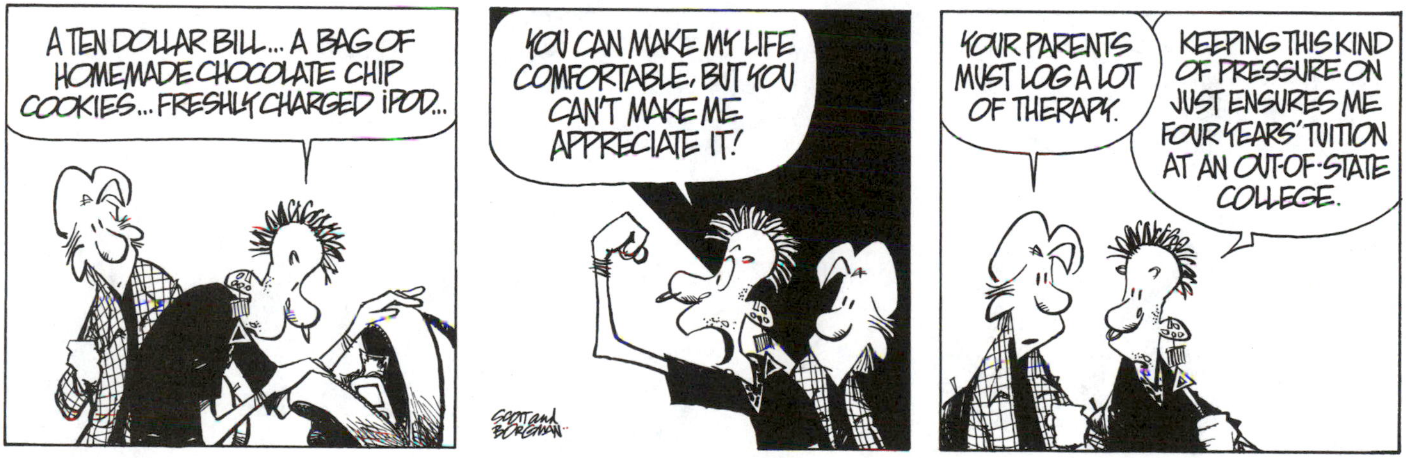
A TEN DOLLAR BILL... A BAG OF HOMEMADE CHOCOLATE CHIP COOKIES... FRESHLY CHARGED iPOD...
YOU CAN MAKE MY LIFE COMFORTABLE, BUT YOU CAN'T MAKE ME APPRECIATE IT!
SCOTT and BORGMAN
YOUR PARENTS MUST LOG A LOT OF THERAPY.
KEEPING THIS KIND OF PRESSURE ON JUST ENSURES ME FOUR YEARS' TUITION AT AN OUT-OF-STATE COLLEGE.

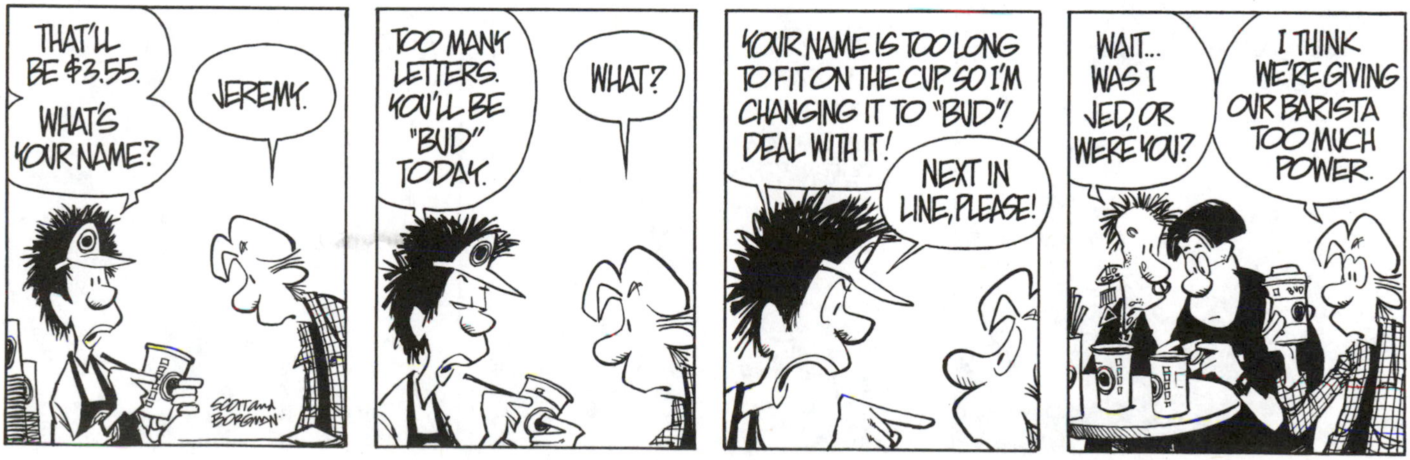
THAT'LL BE $3.55.
WHAT'S YOUR NAME?
JEREMY.
SCOTT and BORGMAN
TOO MANY LETTERS. YOU'LL BE "BUD" TODAY.
WHAT?
YOUR NAME IS TOO LONG TO FIT ON THE CUP, SO I'M CHANGING IT TO "BUD"! DEAL WITH IT!
NEXT IN LINE, PLEASE!
WAIT... WAS I JED, OR WERE YOU?
I THINK WE'RE GIVING OUR BARISTA TOO MUCH POWER.

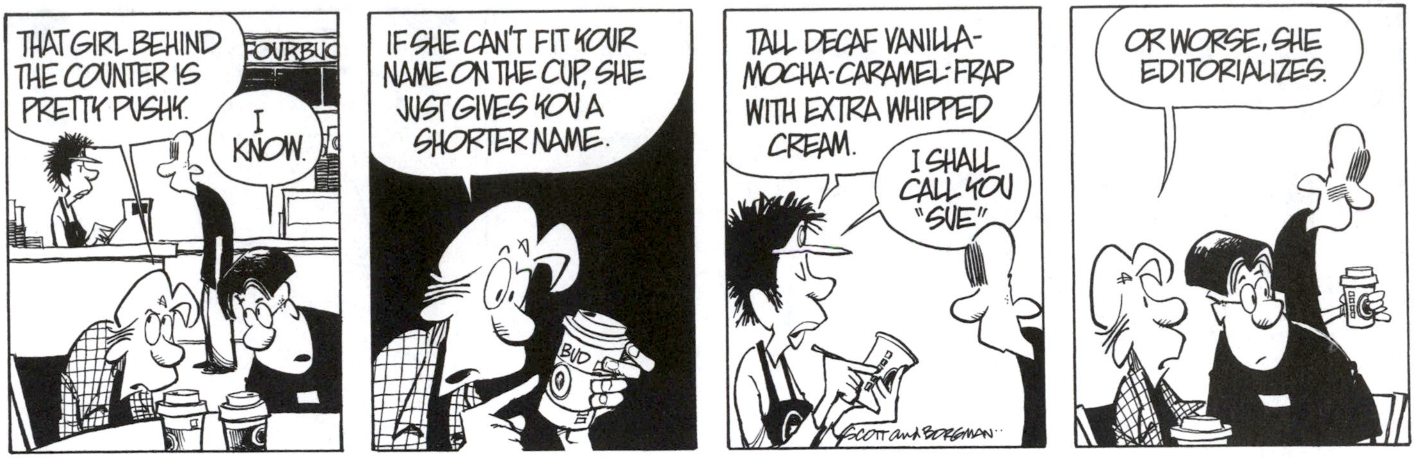
THAT GIRL BEHIND THE COUNTER IS PRETTY PUSHY.
FOURBUC
I KNOW.
IF SHE CAN'T FIT YOUR NAME ON THE CUP, SHE JUST GIVES YOU A SHORTER NAME.
BUD
TALL DECAF VANILLA-MOCHA-CARAMEL-FRAP WITH EXTRA WHIPPED CREAM.
I SHALL CALL YOU "SUE"
SCOTT and BORGMAN
OR WORSE, SHE EDITORIALIZES.

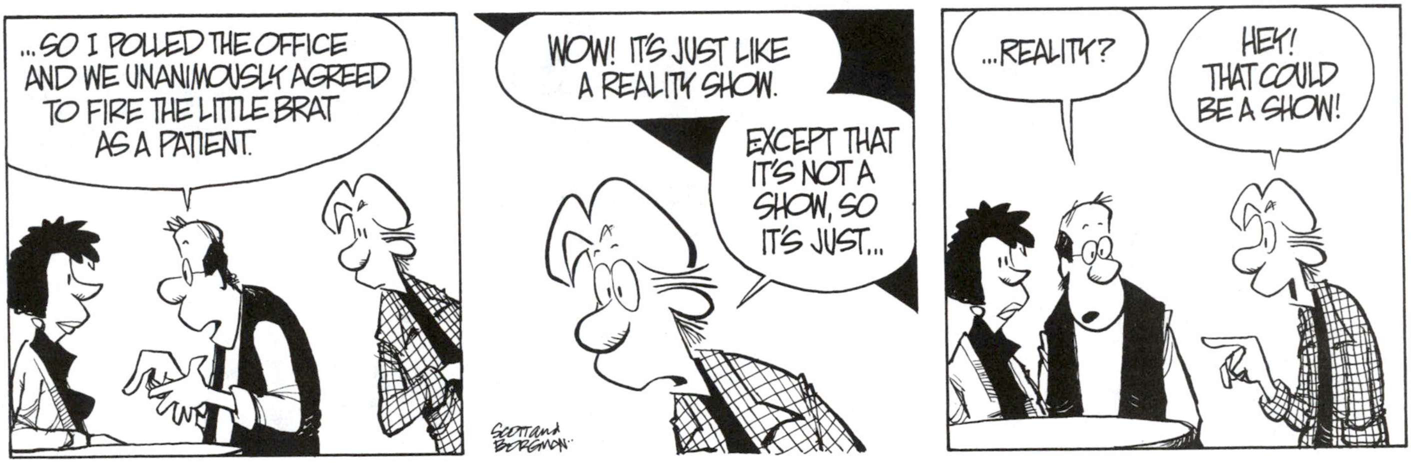
...SO I POLLED THE OFFICE AND WE UNANIMOUSLY AGREED TO FIRE THE LITTLE BRAT AS A PATIENT.
SCOTT and BORGMAN
WOW! IT'S JUST LIKE A REALITY SHOW.
EXCEPT THAT IT'S NOT A SHOW, SO IT'S JUST...
...REALITY?
HEY! THAT COULD BE A SHOW!

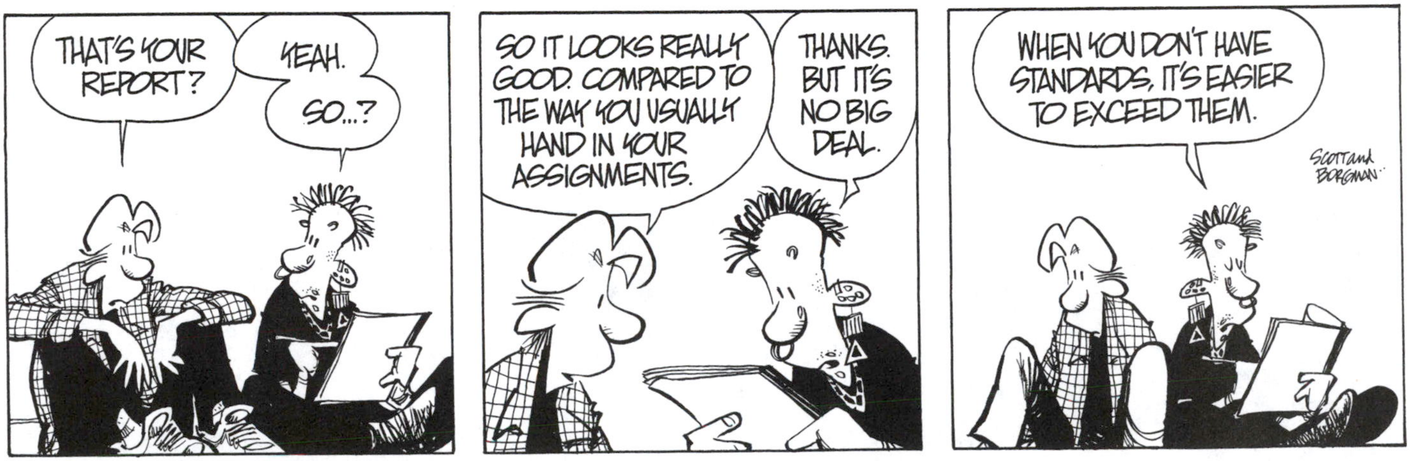
THAT'S YOUR REPORT?
YEAH.
SO...?
SO IT LOOKS REALLY GOOD, COMPARED TO THE WAY YOU USUALLY HAND IN YOUR ASSIGNMENTS.
THANKS. BUT IT'S NO BIG DEAL.
WHEN YOU DON'T HAVE STANDARDS, IT'S EASIER TO EXCEED THEM.
SCOTT and BORGMAN

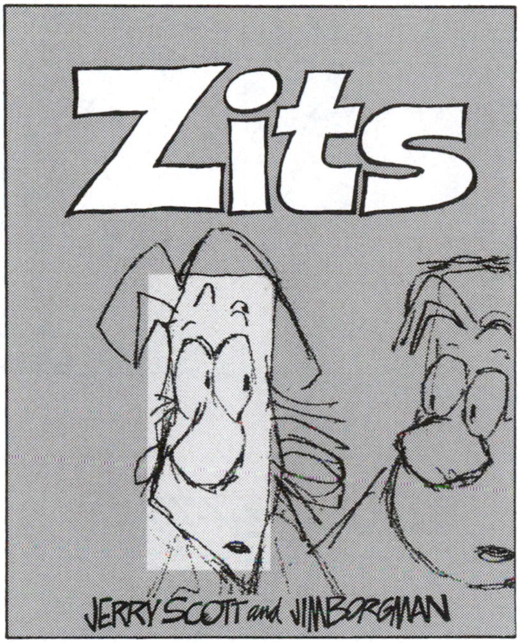
Zits
JERRY SCOTT and JIM BORGMAN

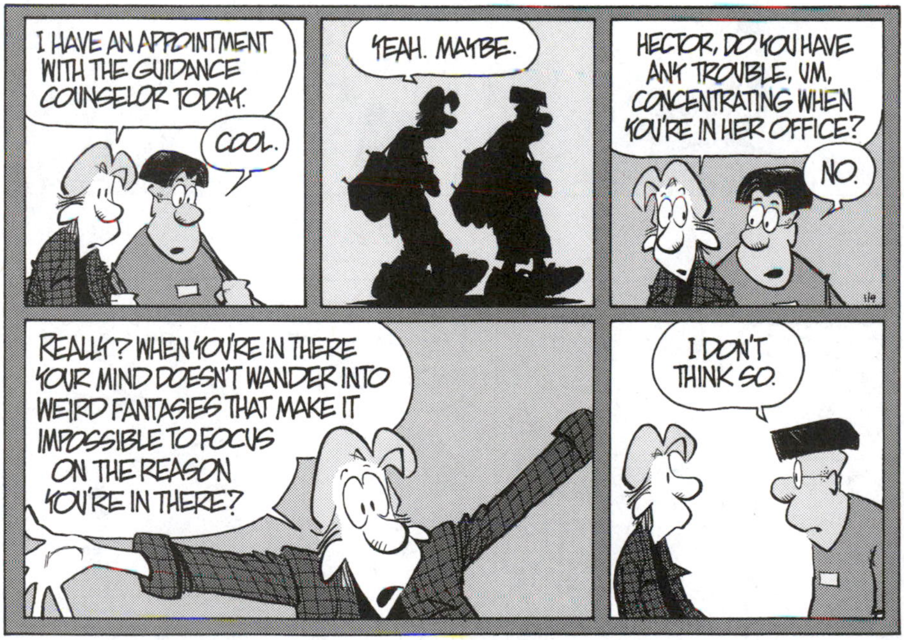
I HAVE AN APPOINTMENT WITH THE GUIDANCE COUNSELOR TODAY.
COOL.
YEAH. MAYBE.
HECTOR, DO YOU HAVE ANY TROUBLE, UM, CONCENTRATING WHEN YOU'RE IN HER OFFICE?
NO.
REALLY? WHEN YOU'RE IN THERE YOUR MIND DOESN'T WANDER INTO WEIRD FANTASIES THAT MAKE IT IMPOSSIBLE TO FOCUS ON THE REASON YOU'RE IN THERE?
I DON'T THINK SO.

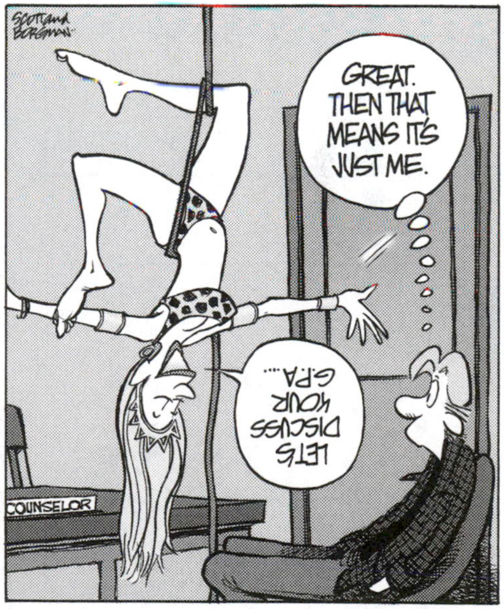
SCOTT and BORGMAN
GREAT. THEN THAT MEANS IT'S JUST ME.
LET'S DISCUSS YOUR G.P.A....
COUNSELOR

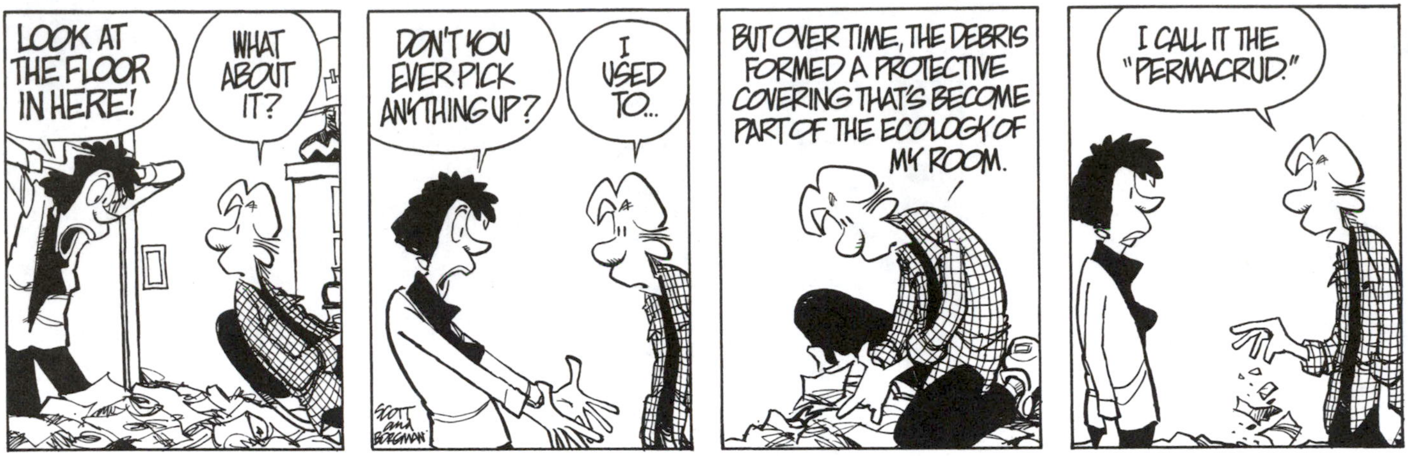
LOOK AT THE FLOOR IN HERE!
WHAT ABOUT IT?
DON'T YOU EVER PICK ANYTHING UP?
I USED TO...
BUT OVER TIME, THE DEBRIS FORMED A PROTECTIVE COVERING THAT'S BECOME PART OF THE ECOLOGY OF MY ROOM.
I CALL IT THE "PERMACRUD."

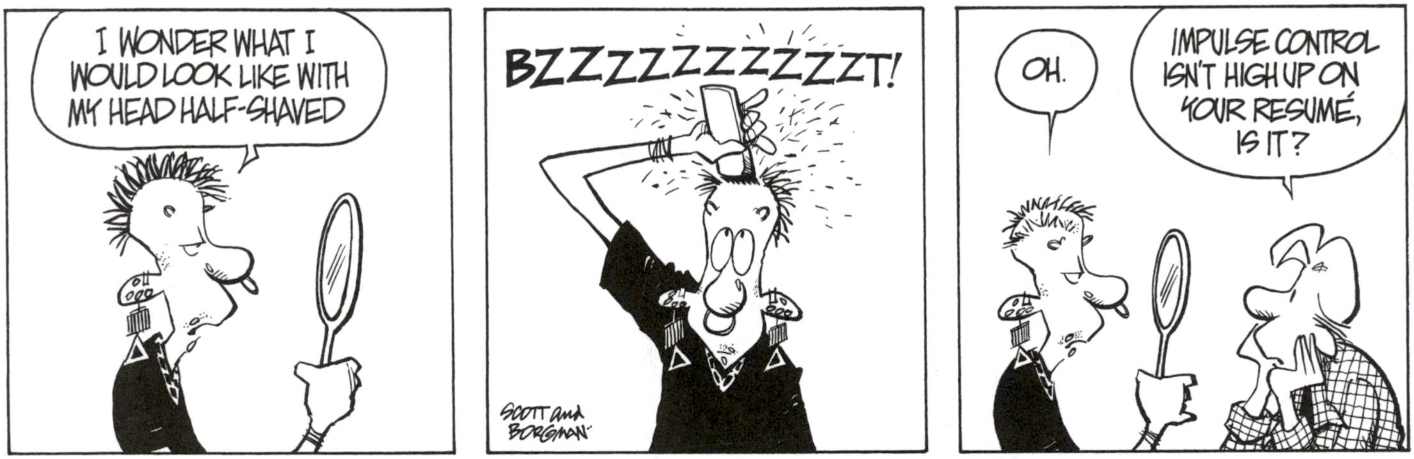
I WONDER WHAT I WOULD LOOK LIKE WITH MY HEAD HALF-SHAVED
BZZZZZZZZZZZT!
OH.
IMPULSE CONTROL ISN'T HIGH UP ON YOUR RESUMÉ, IS IT?

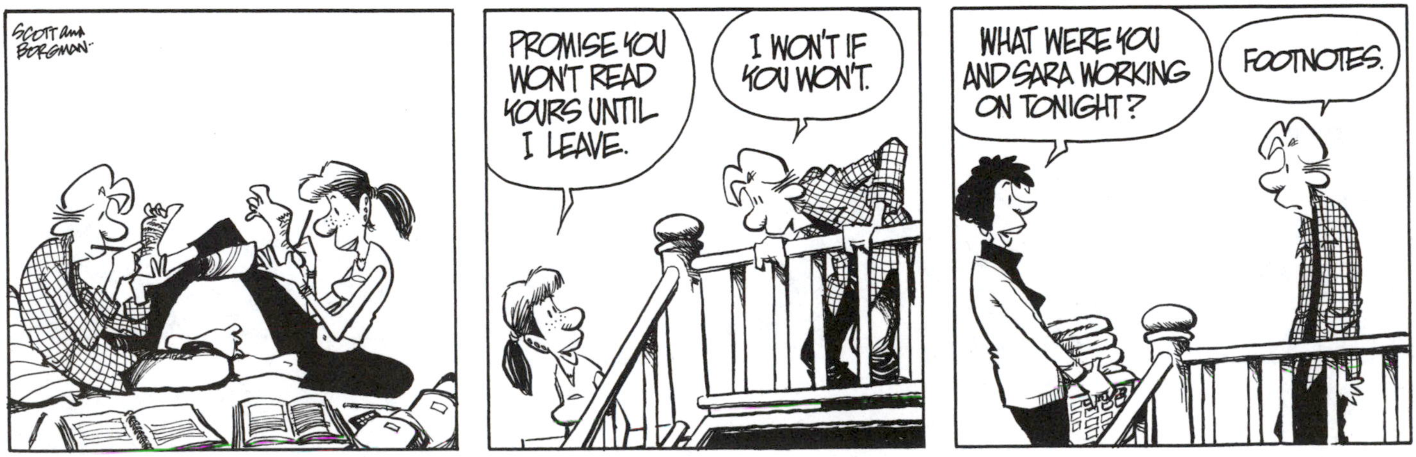
PROMISE YOU WON'T READ YOURS UNTIL I LEAVE.
I WON'T IF YOU WON'T.
WHAT WERE YOU AND SARA WORKING ON TONIGHT?
FOOTNOTES.

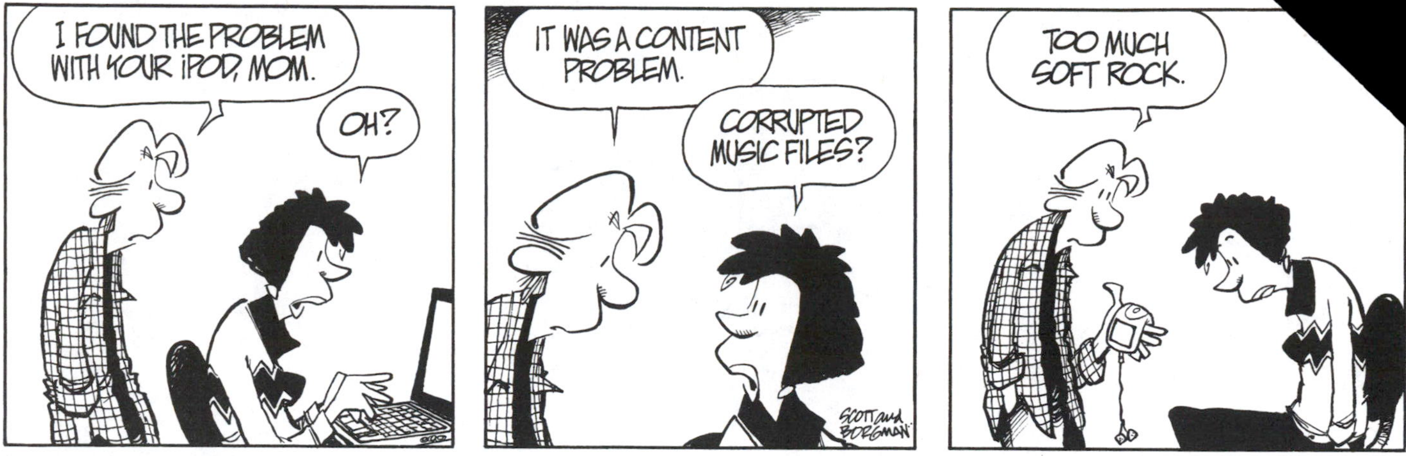
I FOUND THE PROBLEM WITH YOUR iPOD, MOM.
OH?
IT WAS A CONTENT PROBLEM.
CORRUPTED MUSIC FILES?
SCOTT and BORGMAN
TOO MUCH SOFT ROCK.

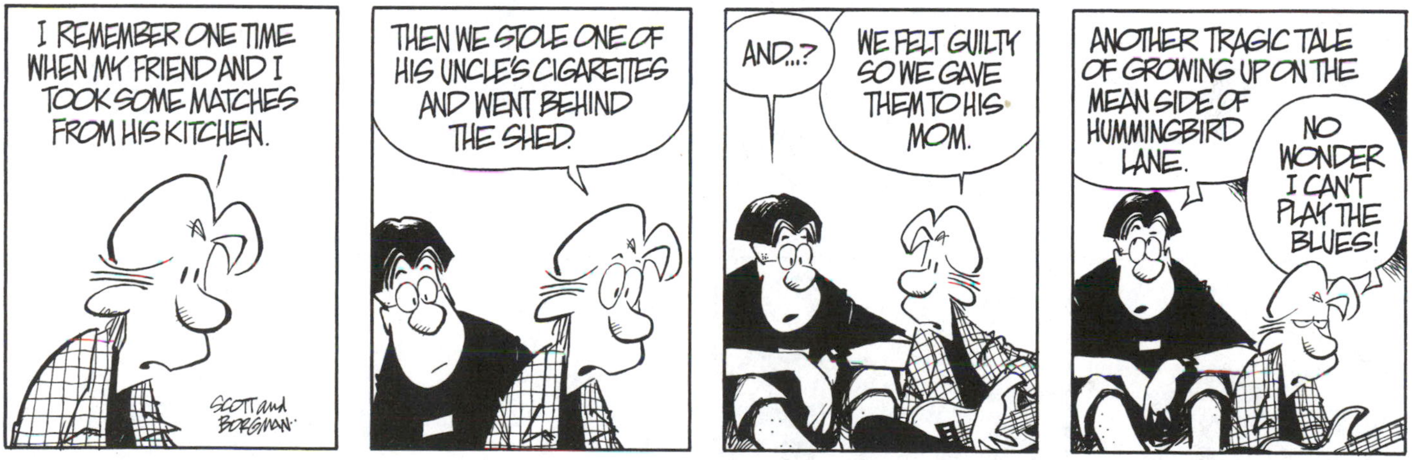
I REMEMBER ONE TIME WHEN MY FRIEND AND I TOOK SOME MATCHES FROM HIS KITCHEN.
SCOTT and BORGMAN
THEN WE STOLE ONE OF HIS UNCLE'S CIGARETTES AND WENT BEHIND THE SHED.
AND...?
WE FELT GUILTY SO WE GAVE THEM TO HIS MOM.
ANOTHER TRAGIC TALE OF GROWING UP ON THE MEAN SIDE OF HUMMINGBIRD LANE.
NO WONDER I CAN'T PLAY THE BLUES!

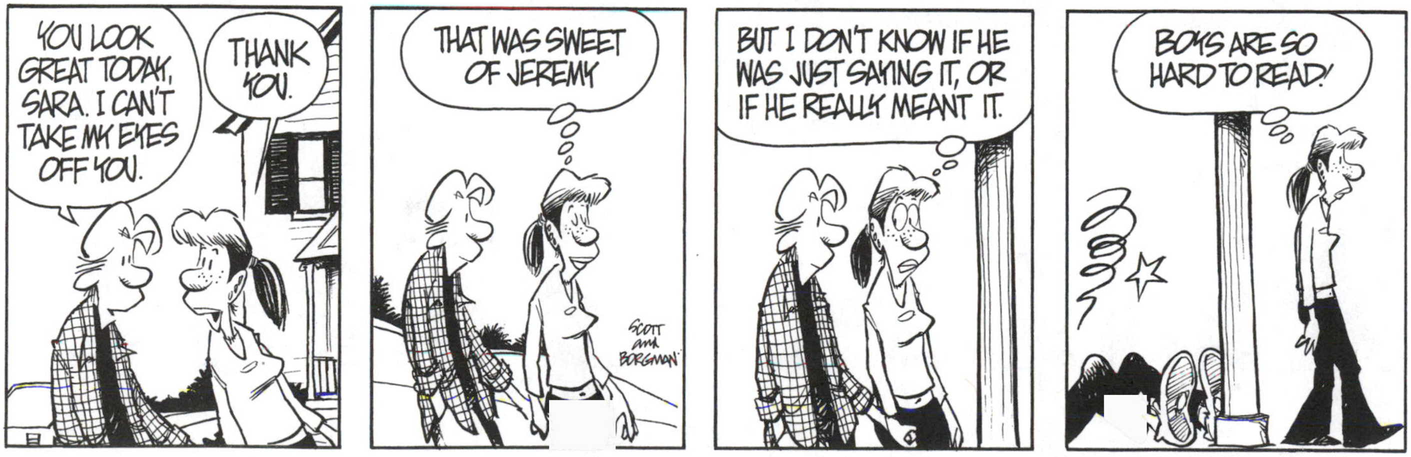
YOU LOOK GREAT TODAY, SARA. I CAN'T TAKE MY EYES OFF YOU.
THANK YOU.
THAT WAS SWEET OF JEREMY.
SCOTT and BORGMAN
BUT I DON'T KNOW IF HE WAS JUST SAYING IT, OR IF HE REALLY MEANT IT.
BOYS ARE SO HARD TO READ!

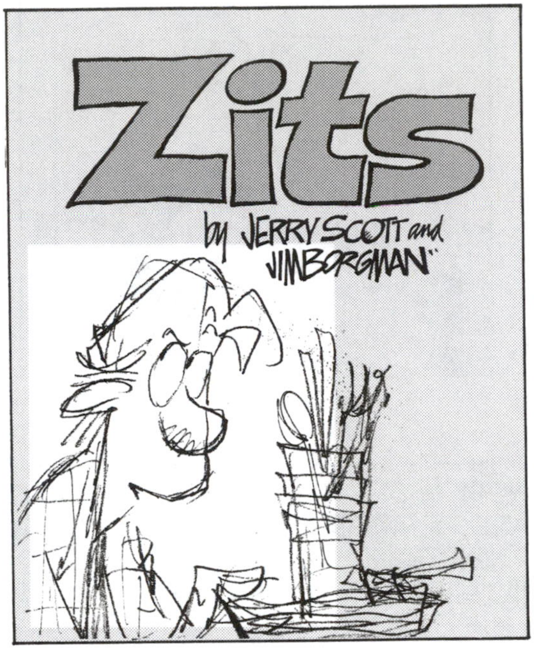
Zits
by JERRY SCOTT and
JIM BORGMAN

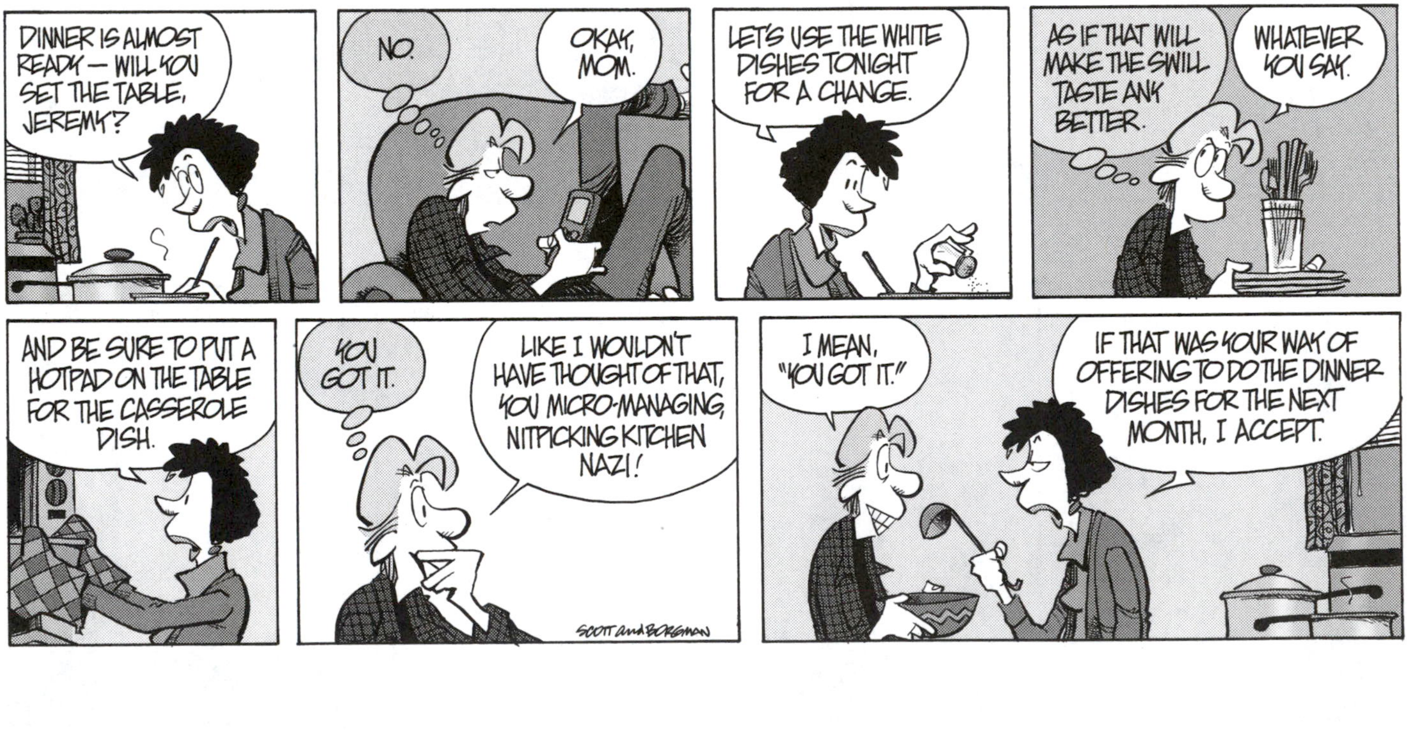
DINNER IS ALMOST READY — WILL YOU SET THE TABLE, JEREMY?
NO.
OKAY, MOM.
LET'S USE THE WHITE DISHES TONIGHT FOR A CHANGE.
AS IF THAT WILL MAKE THE SWILL TASTE ANY BETTER.
WHATEVER YOU SAY.
AND BE SURE TO PUT A HOTPAD ON THE TABLE FOR THE CASSEROLE DISH.
YOU GOT IT.
LIKE I WOULDN'T HAVE THOUGHT OF THAT, YOU MICRO-MANAGING, NITPICKING KITCHEN NAZI!
SCOTT AND BORGMAN
I MEAN, "YOU GOT IT."
IF THAT WAS YOUR WAY OF OFFERING TO DO THE DINNER DISHES FOR THE NEXT MONTH, I ACCEPT.

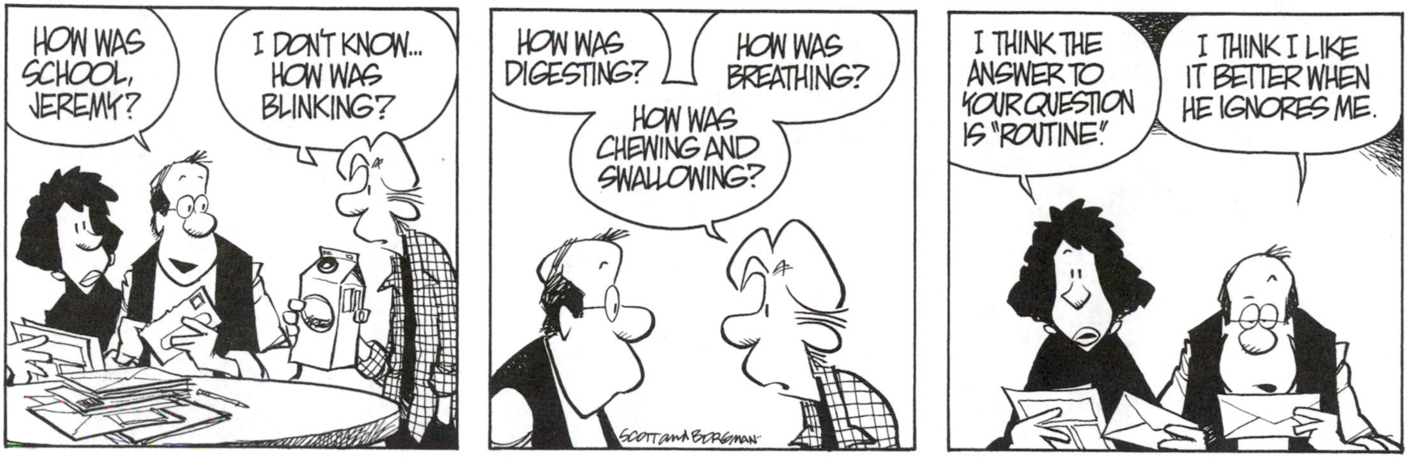
HOW WAS SCHOOL, JEREMY?
I DON'T KNOW... HOW WAS BLINKING?
HOW WAS DIGESTING?
HOW WAS BREATHING?
HOW WAS CHEWING AND SWALLOWING?
SCOTT and BORGMAN
I THINK THE ANSWER TO YOUR QUESTION IS "ROUTINE."
I THINK I LIKE IT BETTER WHEN HE IGNORES ME.

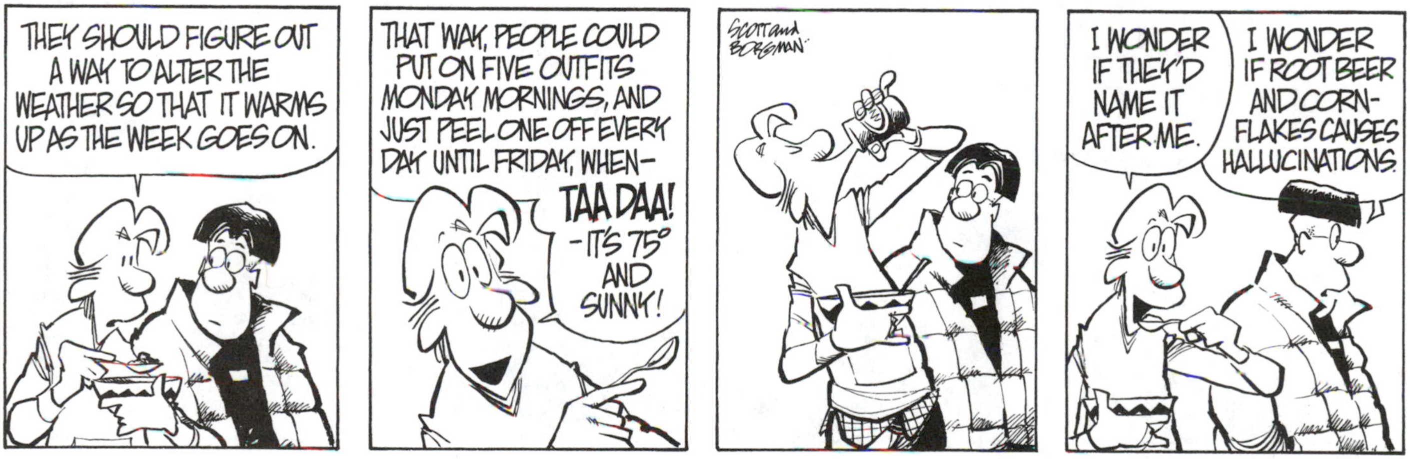
THEY SHOULD FIGURE OUT A WAY TO ALTER THE WEATHER SO THAT IT WARMS UP AS THE WEEK GOES ON.
THAT WAY, PEOPLE COULD PUT ON FIVE OUTFITS MONDAY MORNINGS, AND JUST PEEL ONE OFF EVERY DAY UNTIL FRIDAY, WHEN–
TAA DAA! –IT'S 75° AND SUNNY!
SCOTT and BORGMAN
I WONDER IF THEY'D NAME IT AFTER ME.
I WONDER IF ROOT BEER AND CORN-FLAKES CAUSES HALLUCINATIONS.

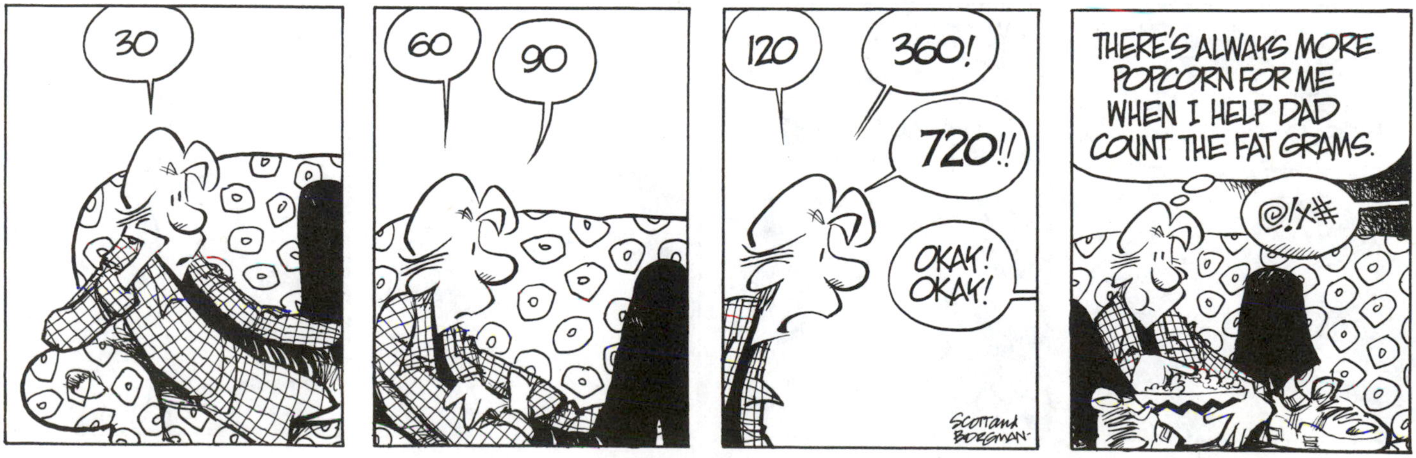
30
60
90
120
360!
720!!
OKAY! OKAY!
SCOTT and BORGMAN
THERE'S ALWAYS MORE POPCORN FOR ME WHEN I HELP DAD COUNT THE FAT GRAMS.
@!x#

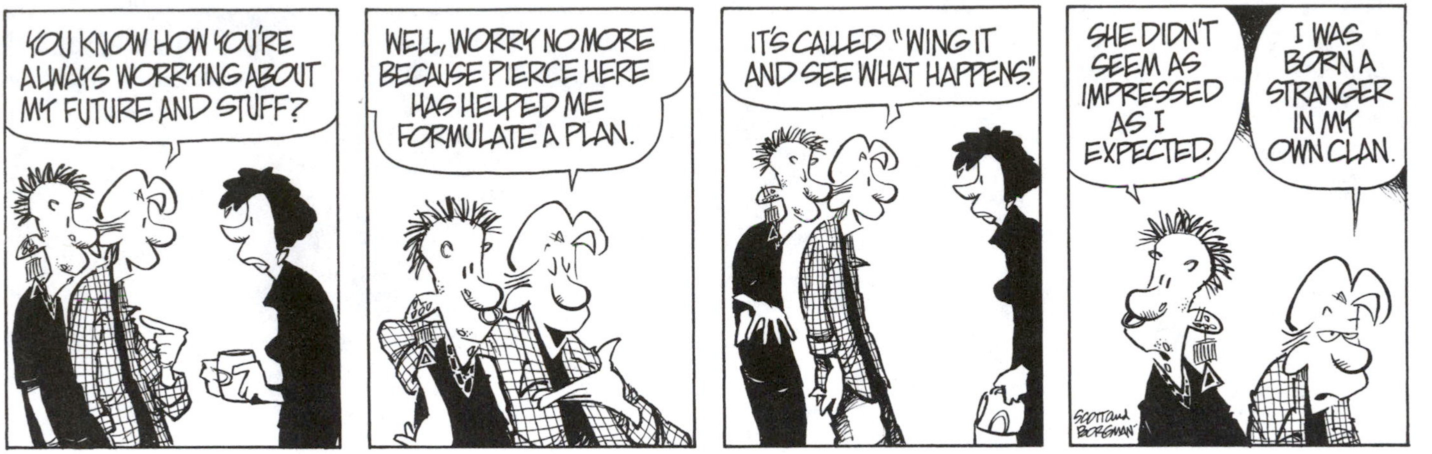
YOU KNOW HOW YOU'RE ALWAYS WORRYING ABOUT MY FUTURE AND STUFF?
WELL, WORRY NO MORE BECAUSE PIERCE HERE HAS HELPED ME FORMULATE A PLAN.
IT'S CALLED "WING IT AND SEE WHAT HAPPENS."
SHE DIDN'T SEEM AS IMPRESSED AS I EXPECTED.
I WAS BORN A STRANGER IN MY OWN CLAN.

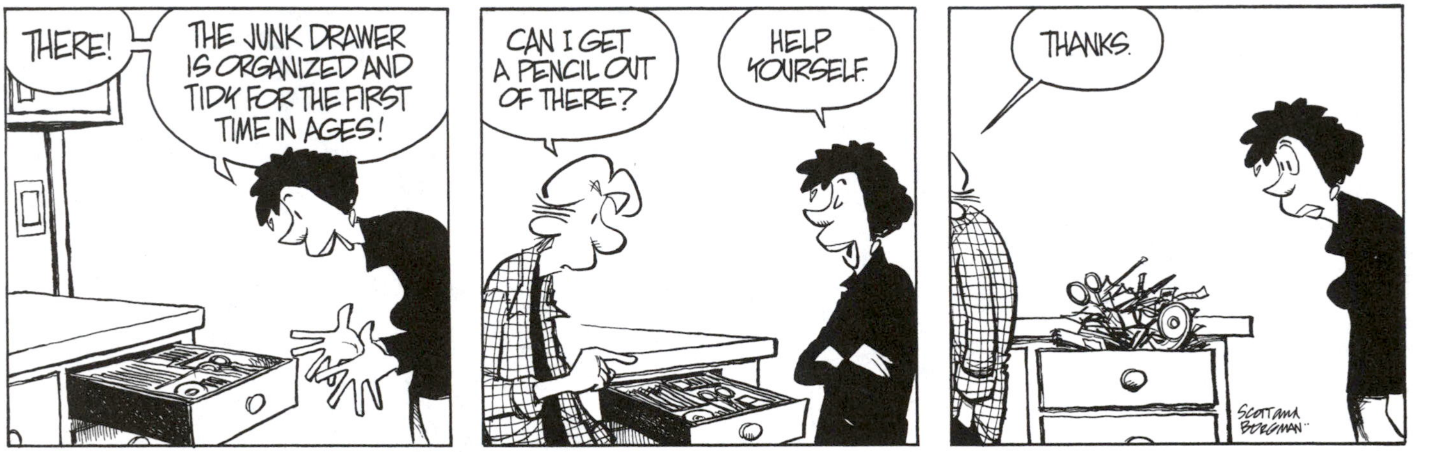
THERE!
THE JUNK DRAWER IS ORGANIZED AND TIDY FOR THE FIRST TIME IN AGES!
CAN I GET A PENCIL OUT OF THERE?
HELP YOURSELF.
THANKS.

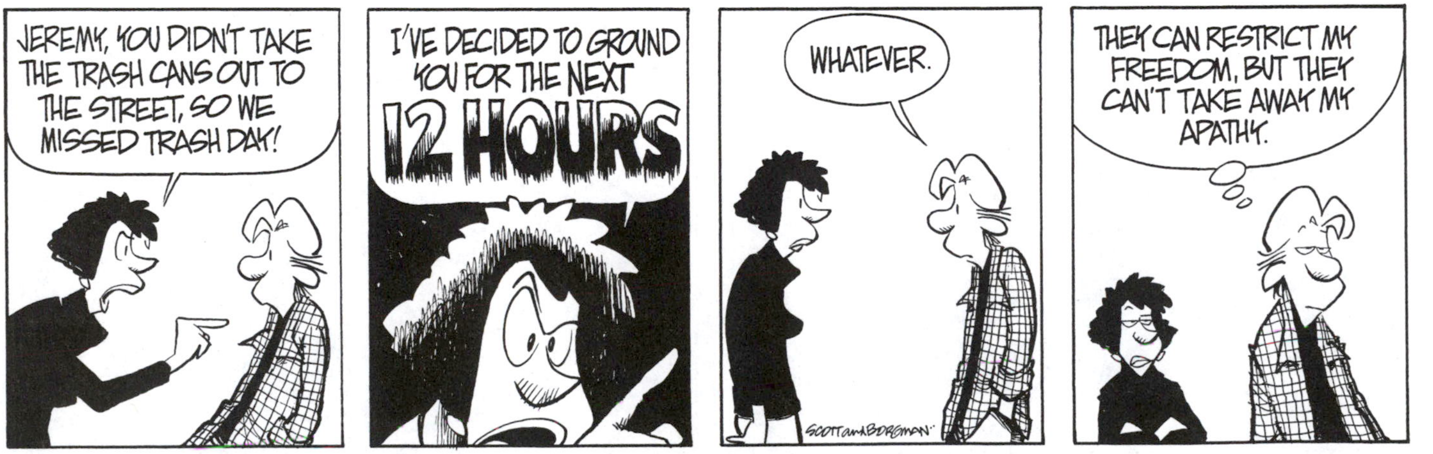
JEREMY, YOU DIDN'T TAKE THE TRASH CANS OUT TO THE STREET, SO WE MISSED TRASH DAY!
I'VE DECIDED TO GROUND YOU FOR THE NEXT
12 HOURS
WHATEVER.
THEY CAN RESTRICT MY FREEDOM, BUT THEY CAN'T TAKE AWAY MY APATHY.

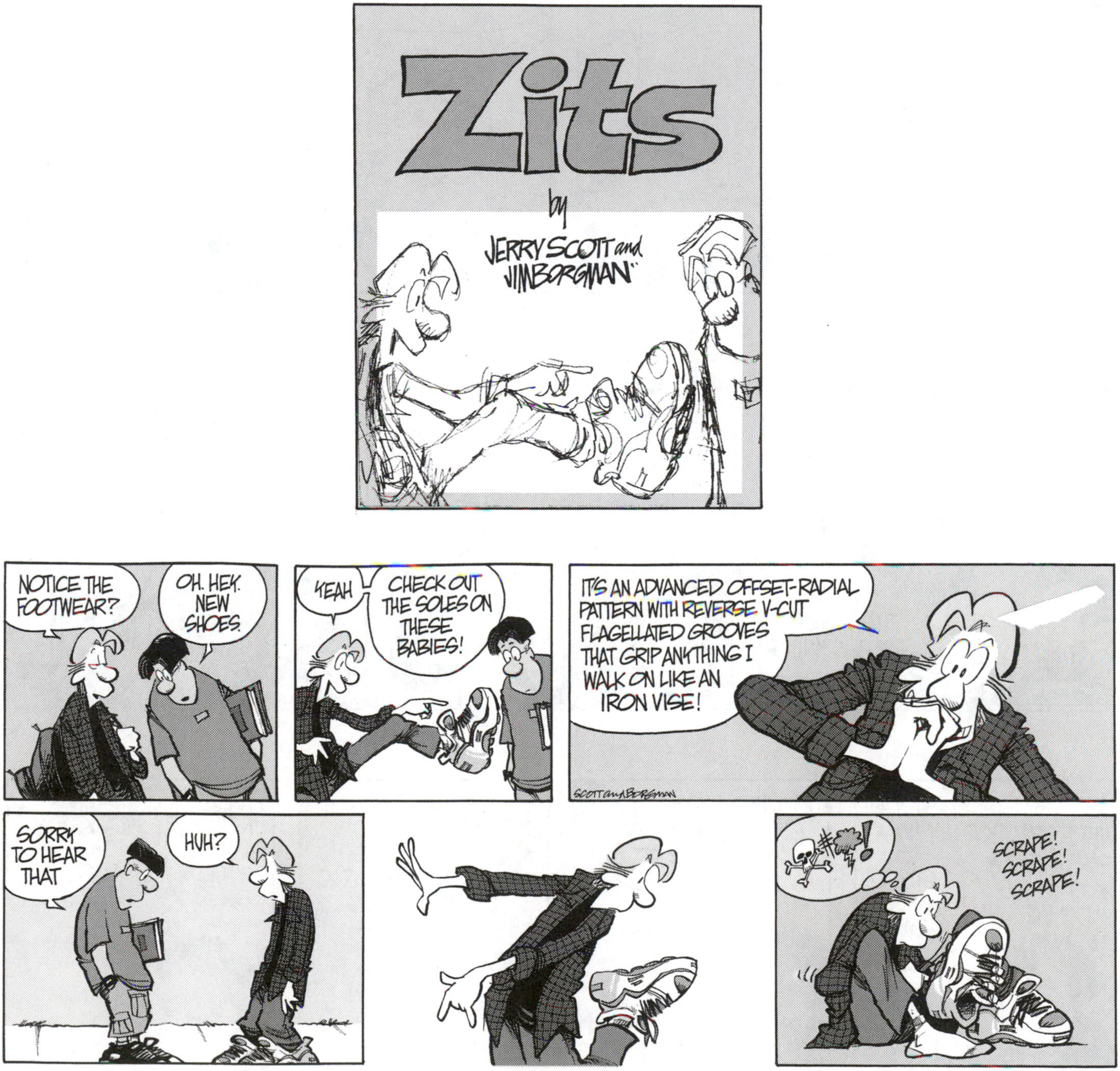
Zits
by
JERRY SCOTT and
JIM BORGMAN
NOTICE THE FOOTWEAR?
OH. HEY. NEW SHOES.
YEAH
CHECK OUT THE SOLES ON THESE BABIES!
IT'S AN ADVANCED OFFSET-RADIAL PATTERN WITH REVERSE V-CUT FLAGELLATED GROOVES THAT GRIP ANYTHING I WALK ON LIKE AN IRON VISE!
SCOTT and BORGMAN
SORRY TO HEAR THAT
HUH?
SCRAPE! SCRAPE! SCRAPE!

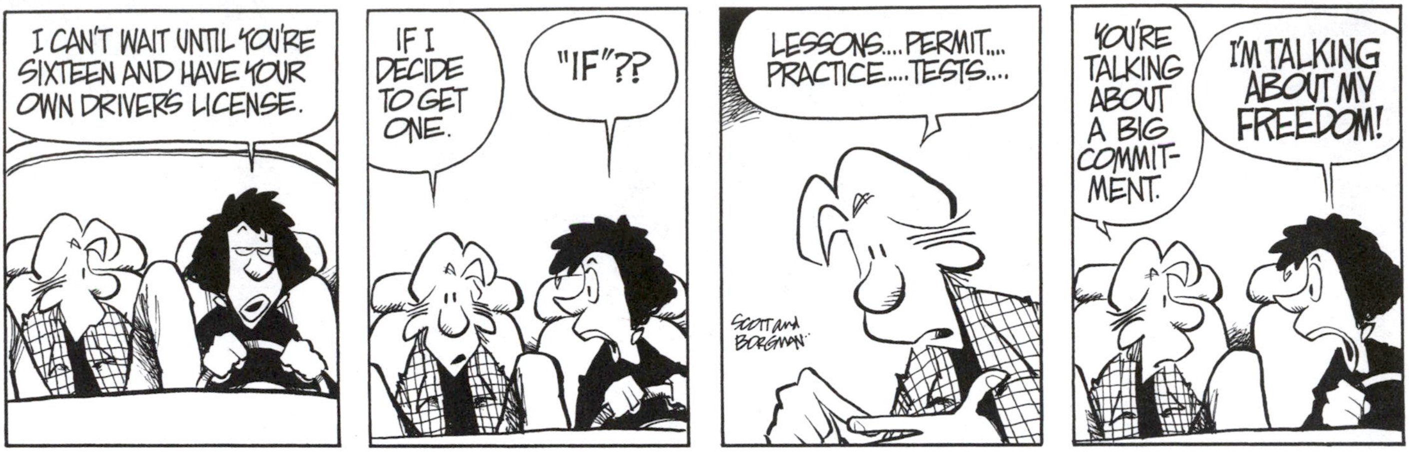
I CAN'T WAIT UNTIL YOU'RE SIXTEEN AND HAVE YOUR OWN DRIVER'S LICENSE.
IF I DECIDE TO GET ONE.
"IF"??
LESSONS.... PERMIT.... PRACTICE.... TESTS....
YOU'RE TALKING ABOUT A BIG COMMIT-MENT.
I'M TALKING ABOUT MY FREEDOM!

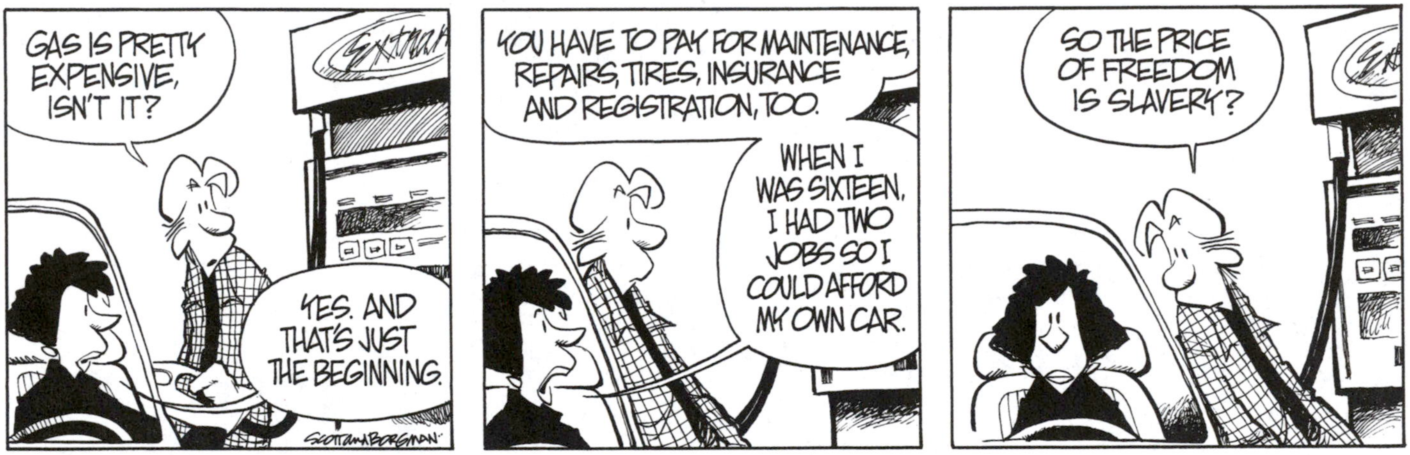
GAS IS PRETTY EXPENSIVE, ISN'T IT?
YES. AND THAT'S JUST THE BEGINNING.
YOU HAVE TO PAY FOR MAINTENANCE, REPAIRS, TIRES, INSURANCE AND REGISTRATION, TOO.
WHEN I WAS SIXTEEN, I HAD TWO JOBS SO I COULD AFFORD MY OWN CAR.
SO THE PRICE OF FREEDOM IS SLAVERY?

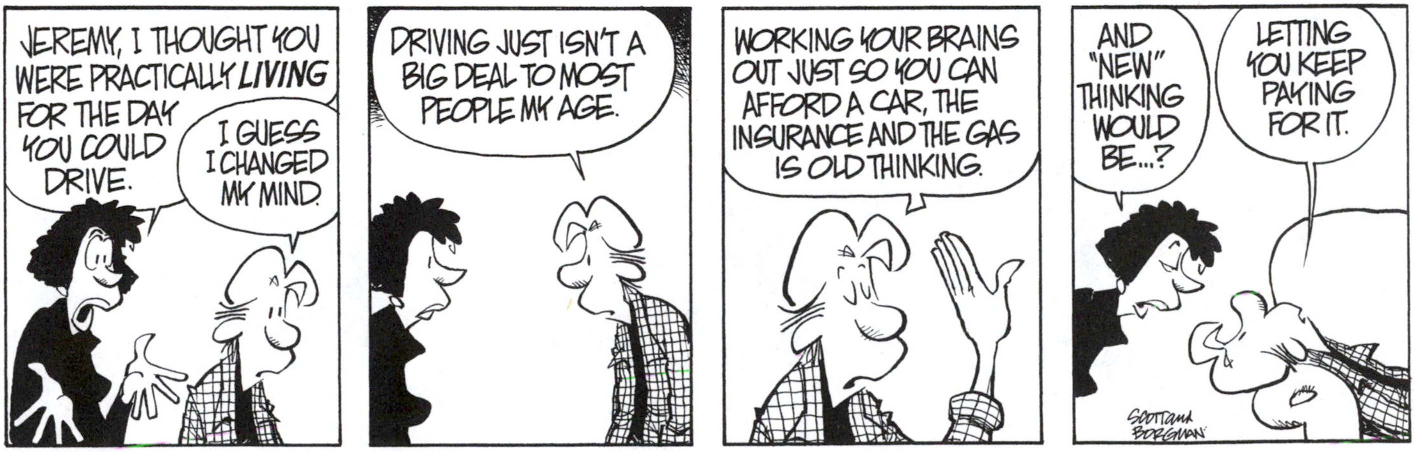
JEREMY, I THOUGHT YOU WERE PRACTICALLY *LIVING* FOR THE DAY YOU COULD DRIVE.
I GUESS I CHANGED MY MIND.
DRIVING JUST ISN'T A BIG DEAL TO MOST PEOPLE MY AGE.
WORKING YOUR BRAINS OUT JUST SO YOU CAN AFFORD A CAR, THE INSURANCE AND THE GAS IS OLD THINKING.
AND "NEW" THINKING WOULD BE...?
LETTING YOU KEEP PAYING FOR IT.

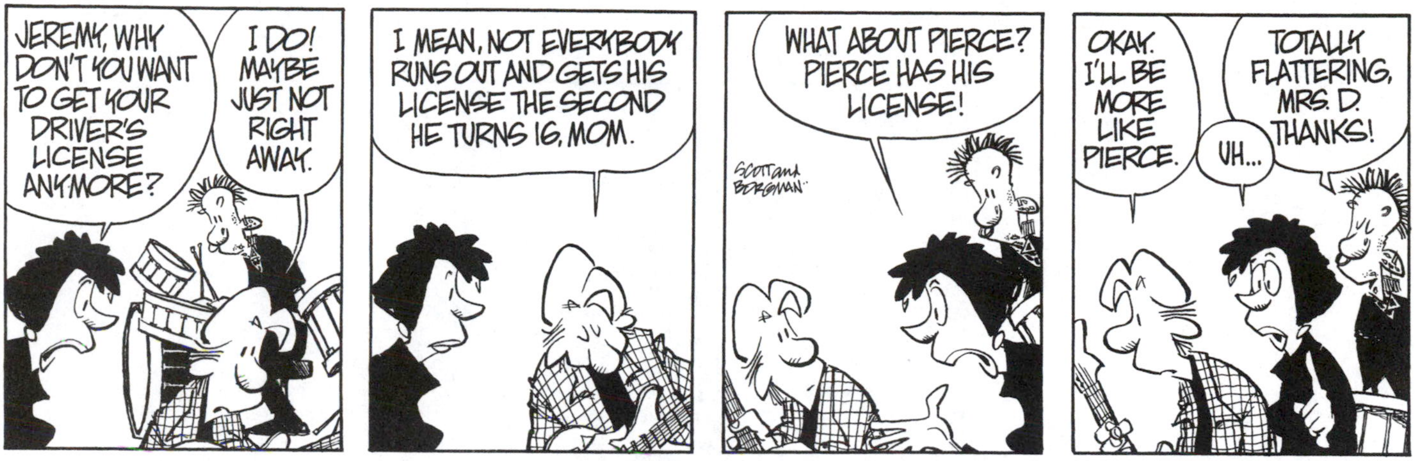
JEREMY, WHY DON'T YOU WANT TO GET YOUR DRIVER'S LICENSE ANYMORE?
I DO! MAYBE JUST NOT RIGHT AWAY.
I MEAN, NOT EVERYBODY RUNS OUT AND GETS HIS LICENSE THE SECOND HE TURNS 16, MOM.
WHAT ABOUT PIERCE? PIERCE HAS HIS LICENSE!
SCOTT and BORGMAN
OKAY. I'LL BE MORE LIKE PIERCE.
UH...
TOTALLY FLATTERING, MRS. D. THANKS!

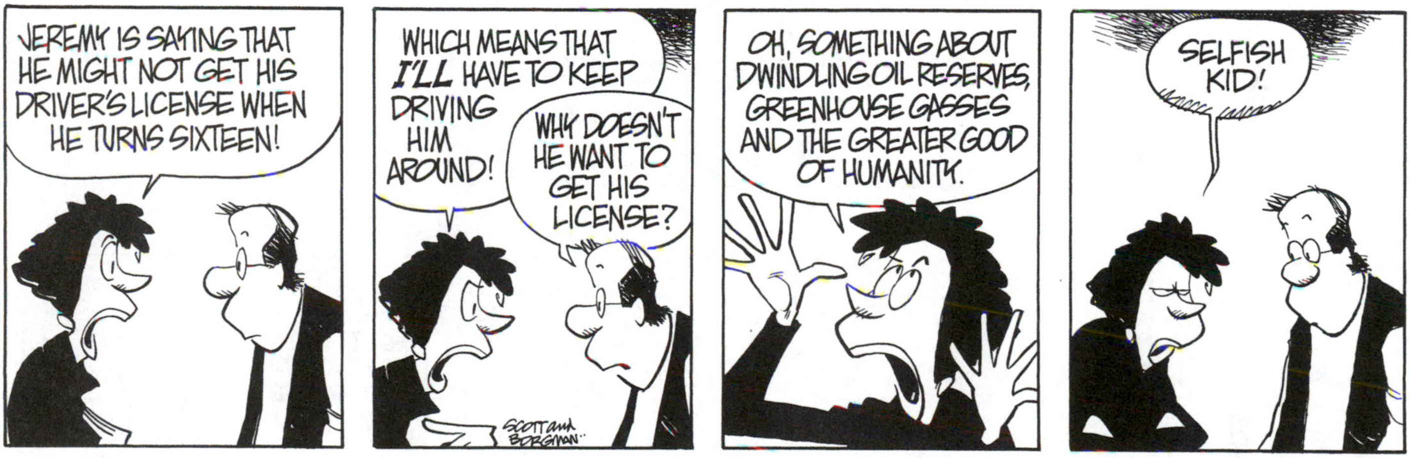
JEREMY IS SAYING THAT HE MIGHT NOT GET HIS DRIVER'S LICENSE WHEN HE TURNS SIXTEEN!
WHICH MEANS THAT I'LL HAVE TO KEEP DRIVING HIM AROUND!
WHY DOESN'T HE WANT TO GET HIS LICENSE?
SCOTT and BORGMAN
OH, SOMETHING ABOUT DWINDLING OIL RESERVES, GREENHOUSE GASSES AND THE GREATER GOOD OF HUMANITY.
SELFISH KID!

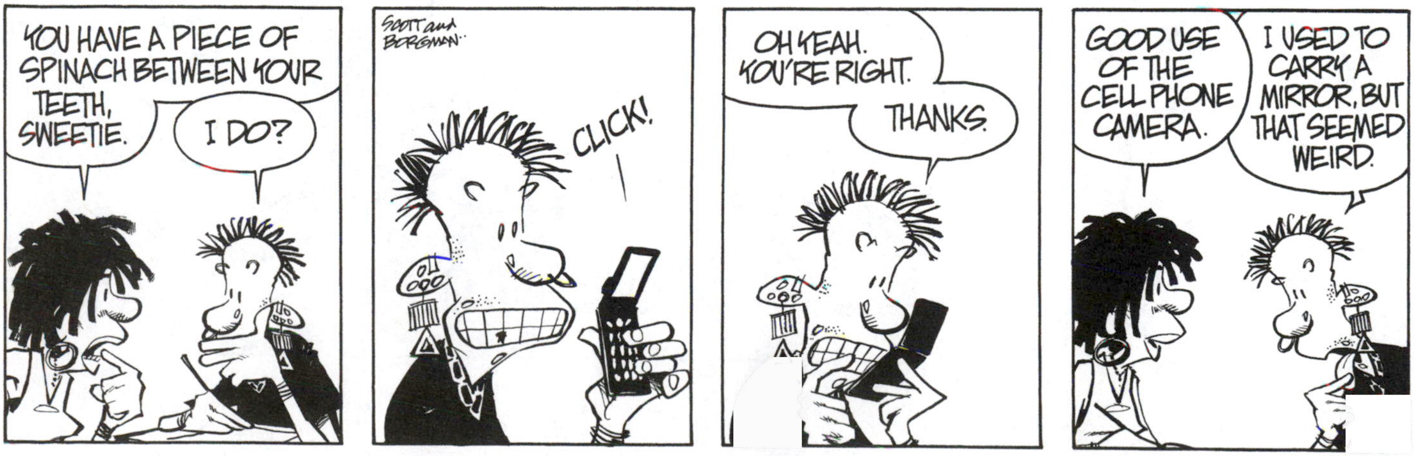
YOU HAVE A PIECE OF SPINACH BETWEEN YOUR TEETH, SWEETIE.
I DO?
SCOTT and BORGMAN
CLICK!
OH YEAH. YOU'RE RIGHT.
THANKS.
GOOD USE OF THE CELL PHONE CAMERA.
I USED TO CARRY A MIRROR, BUT THAT SEEMED WEIRD.

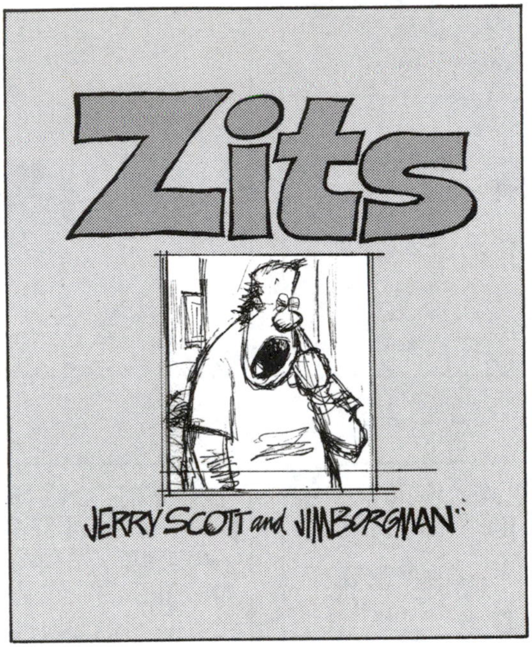
Zits
JERRY SCOTT and JIM BORGMAN

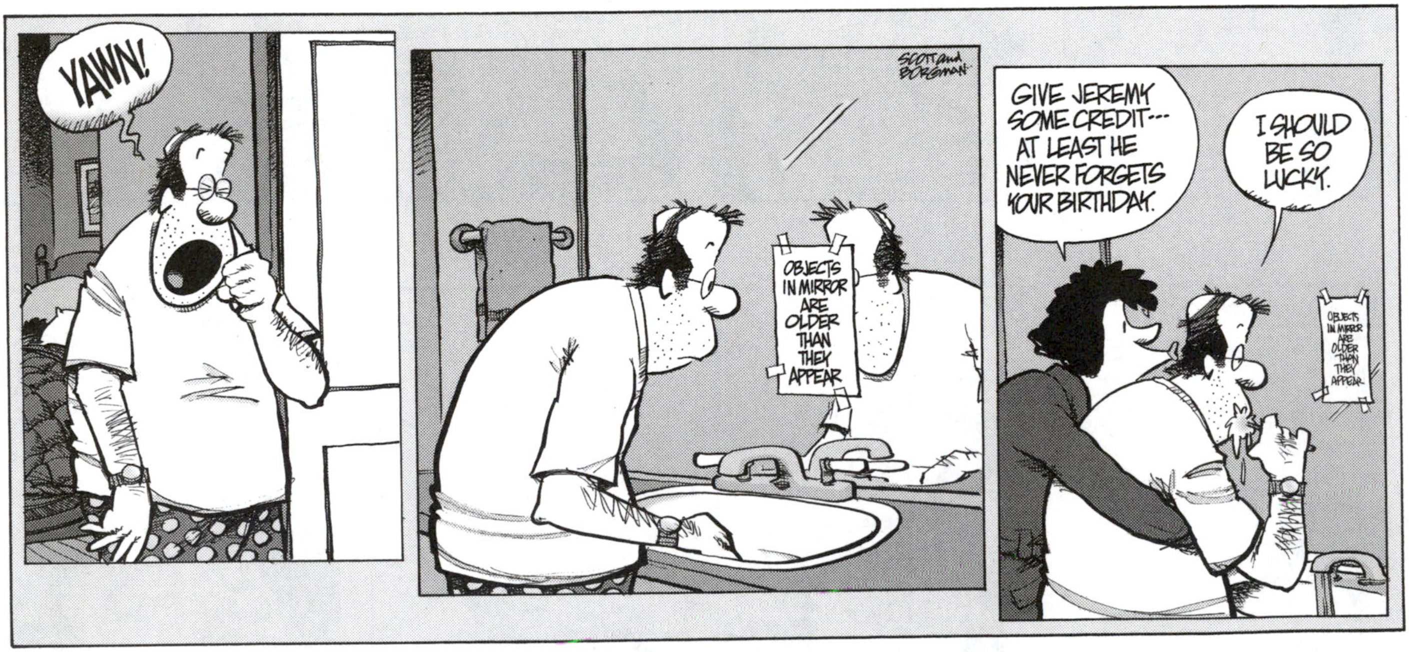
YAWN!
SCOTT and BORGMAN
OBJECTS IN MIRROR ARE OLDER THAN THEY APPEAR
GIVE JEREMY SOME CREDIT--- AT LEAST HE NEVER FORGETS YOUR BIRTHDAY.
I SHOULD BE SO LUCKY.

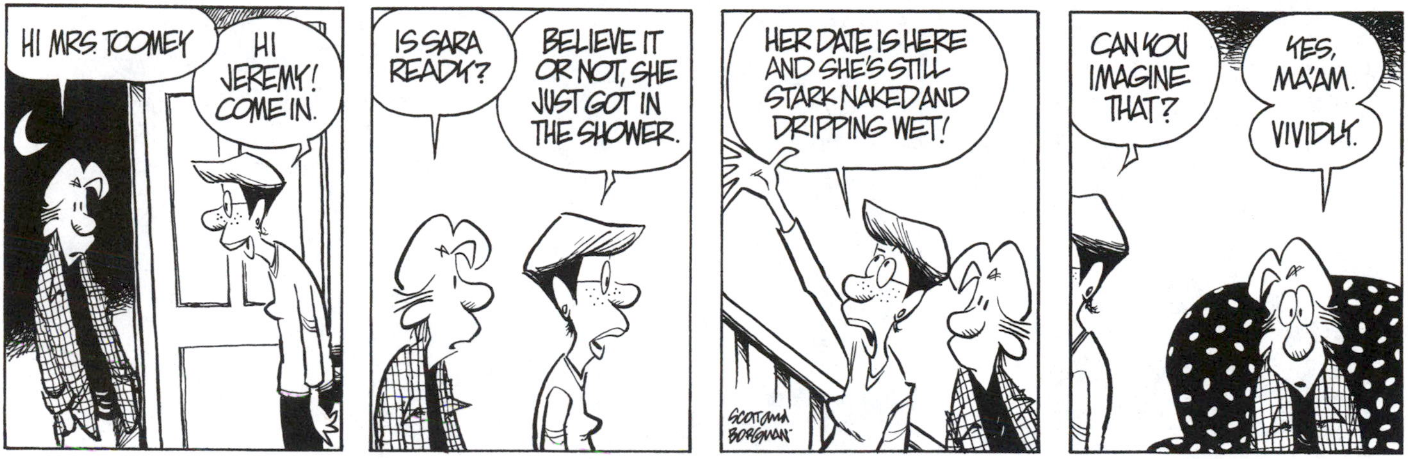
HI MRS. TOOMEY
HI JEREMY! COME IN.
IS SARA READY?
BELIEVE IT OR NOT, SHE JUST GOT IN THE SHOWER.
HER DATE IS HERE AND SHE'S STILL STARK NAKED AND DRIPPING WET!
CAN YOU IMAGINE THAT?
YES, MA'AM.
VIVIDLY.

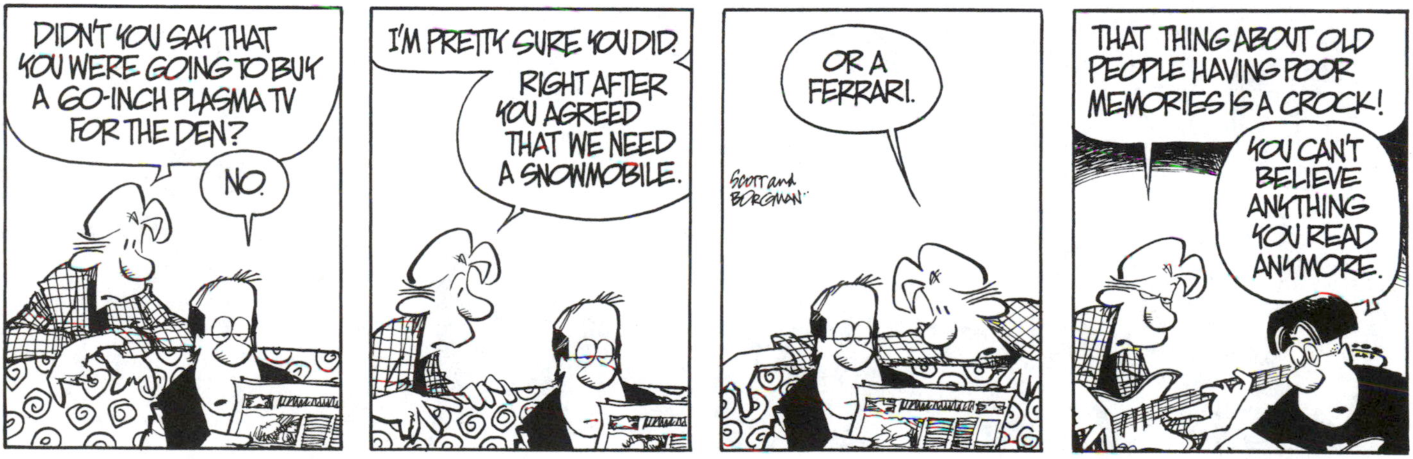
DIDN'T YOU SAY THAT YOU WERE GOING TO BUY A 60-INCH PLASMA TV FOR THE DEN?
NO.
I'M PRETTY SURE YOU DID.
RIGHT AFTER YOU AGREED THAT WE NEED A SNOWMOBILE.
OR A FERRARI.
THAT THING ABOUT OLD PEOPLE HAVING POOR MEMORIES IS A CROCK!
YOU CAN'T BELIEVE ANYTHING YOU READ ANYMORE.

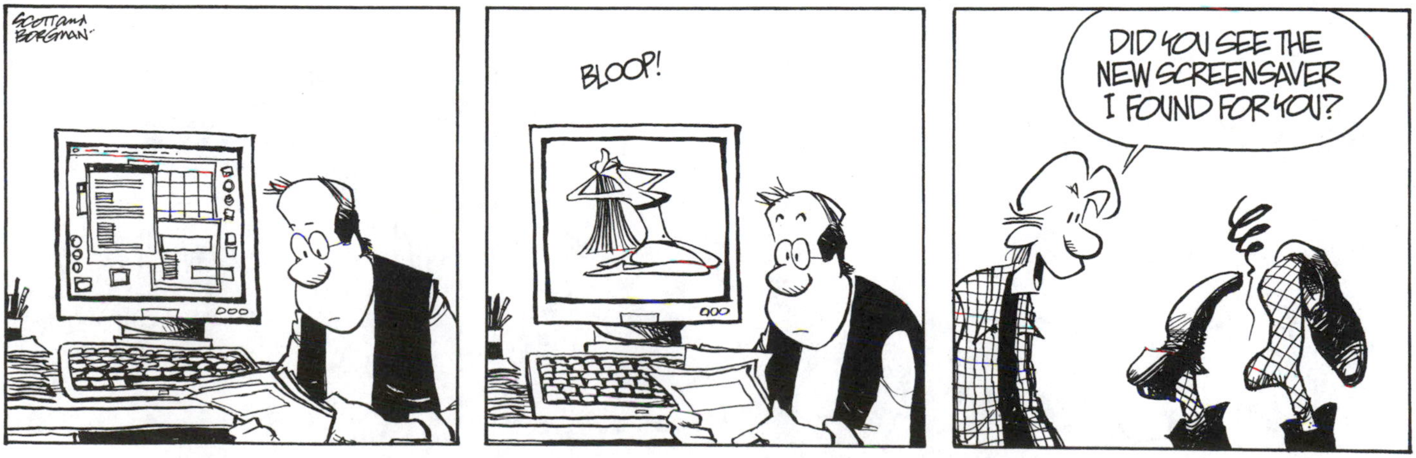
BLOOP!
DID YOU SEE THE NEW SCREENSAVER I FOUND FOR YOU?

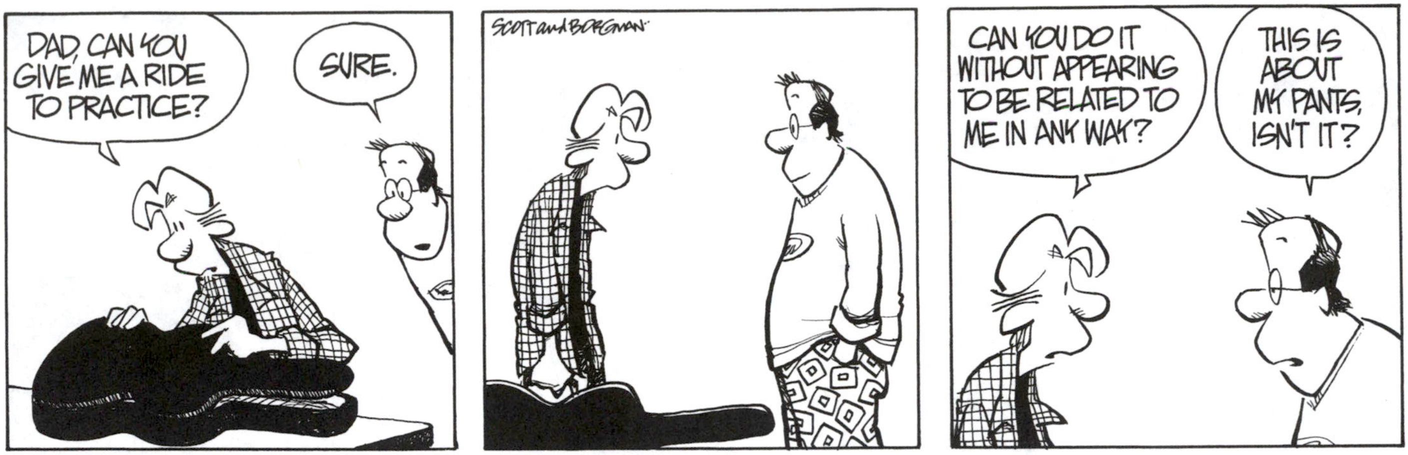
DAD, CAN YOU GIVE ME A RIDE TO PRACTICE?
SURE.
SCOTT and BORGMAN
CAN YOU DO IT WITHOUT APPEARING TO BE RELATED TO ME IN ANY WAY?
THIS IS ABOUT MY PANTS, ISN'T IT?

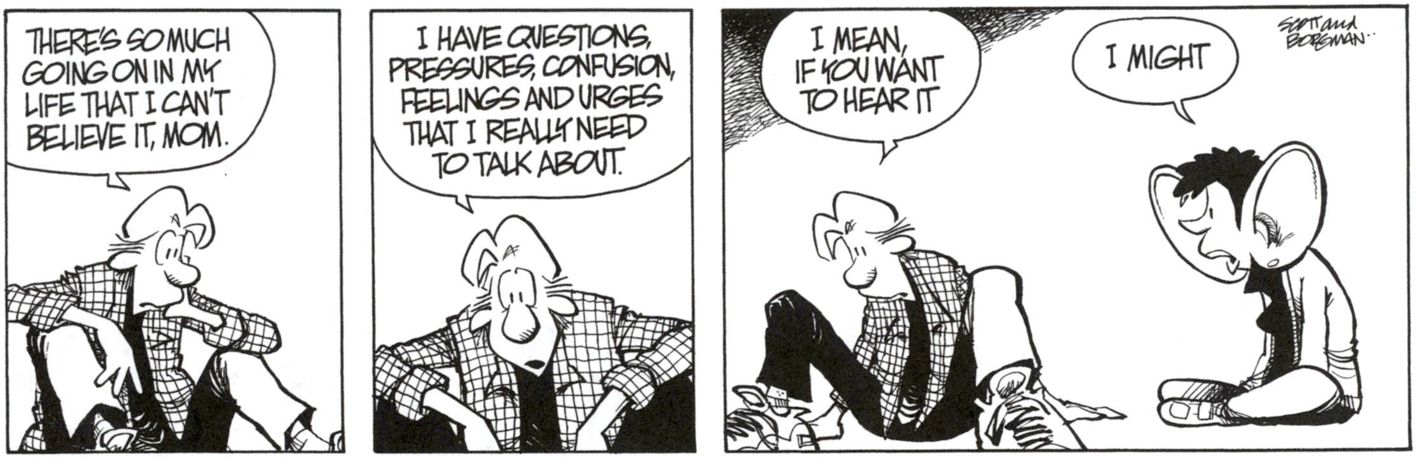
THERE'S SO MUCH GOING ON IN MY LIFE THAT I CAN'T BELIEVE IT, MOM.
I HAVE QUESTIONS, PRESSURES, CONFUSION, FEELINGS AND URGES THAT I REALLY NEED TO TALK ABOUT.
I MEAN, IF YOU WANT TO HEAR IT
I MIGHT
SCOTT and BORGMAN

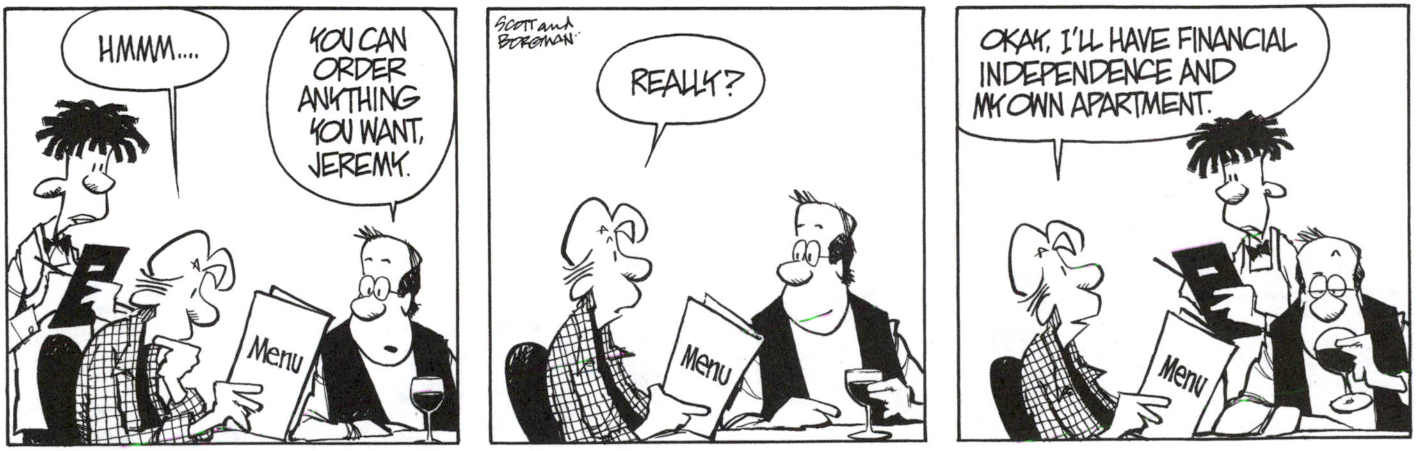
HMMM....
YOU CAN ORDER ANYTHING YOU WANT, JEREMY.
Menu
SCOTT and BORGMAN
REALLY?
Menu
OKAY, I'LL HAVE FINANCIAL INDEPENDENCE AND MY OWN APARTMENT.
Menu

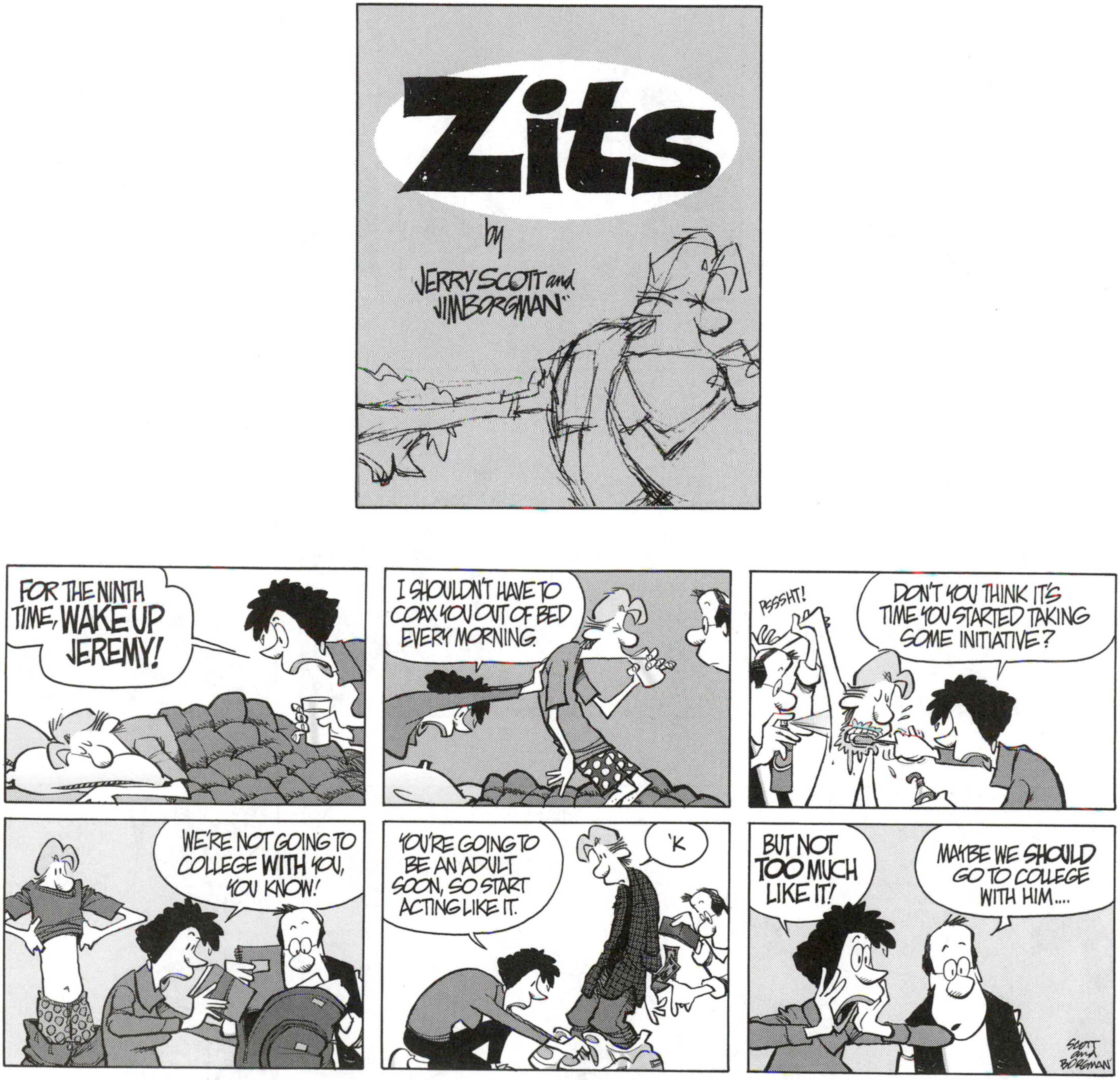
Zits
by
JERRY SCOTT and JIM BORGMAN
FOR THE NINTH TIME, WAKE UP JEREMY!
I SHOULDN'T HAVE TO COAX YOU OUT OF BED EVERY MORNING.
PSSSHT!
DON'T YOU THINK IT'S TIME YOU STARTED TAKING SOME INITIATIVE?
WE'RE NOT GOING TO COLLEGE WITH YOU, YOU KNOW!
YOU'RE GOING TO BE AN ADULT SOON, SO START ACTING LIKE IT.
'K
BUT NOT TOO MUCH LIKE IT!
MAYBE WE SHOULD GO TO COLLEGE WITH HIM....
SCOTT and BORGMAN

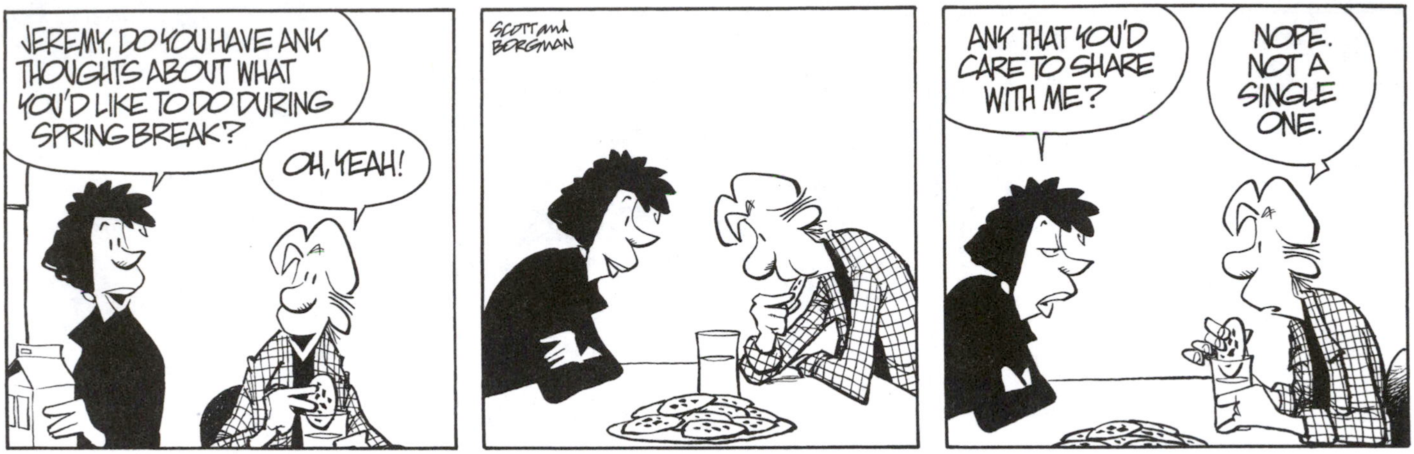
JEREMY, DO YOU HAVE ANY THOUGHTS ABOUT WHAT YOU'D LIKE TO DO DURING SPRING BREAK?
OH, YEAH!
SCOTT and BORGMAN
ANY THAT YOU'D CARE TO SHARE WITH ME?
NOPE. NOT A SINGLE ONE.

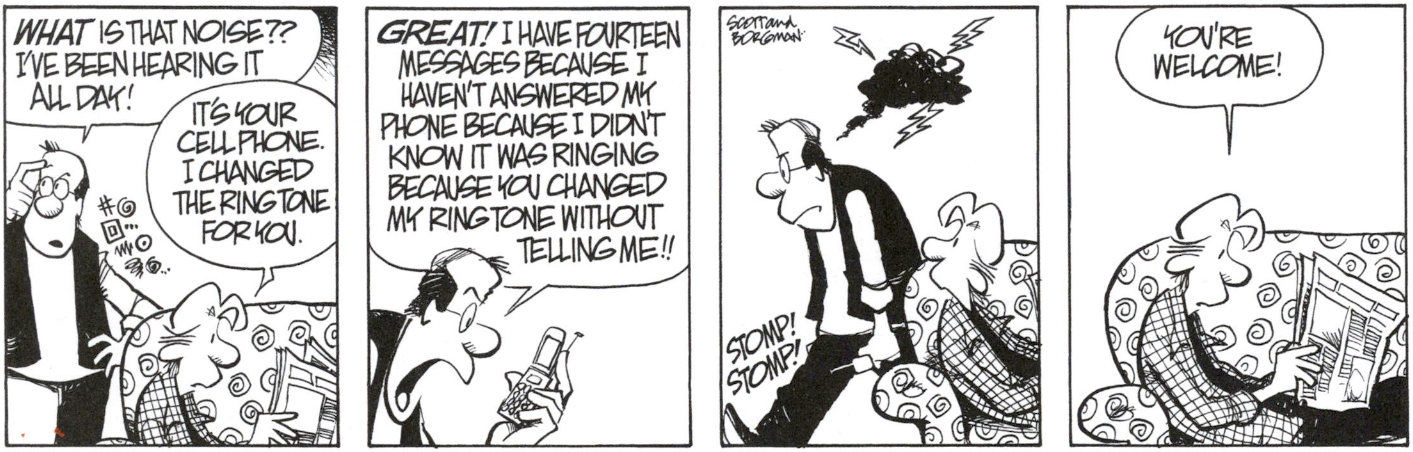
WHAT IS THAT NOISE?? I'VE BEEN HEARING IT ALL DAY!
IT'S YOUR CELL PHONE. I CHANGED THE RINGTONE FOR YOU.
GREAT! I HAVE FOURTEEN MESSAGES BECAUSE I HAVEN'T ANSWERED MY PHONE BECAUSE I DIDN'T KNOW IT WAS RINGING BECAUSE YOU CHANGED MY RINGTONE WITHOUT TELLING ME!!
SCOTT and BORGMAN
STOMP! STOMP!
YOU'RE WELCOME!

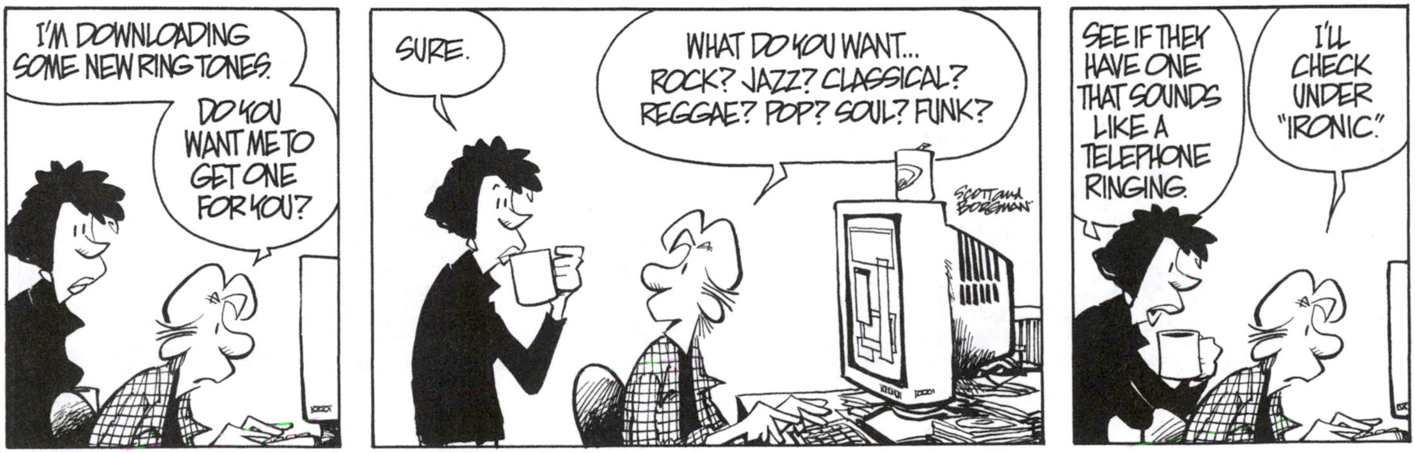
I'M DOWNLOADING SOME NEW RINGTONES.
DO YOU WANT ME TO GET ONE FOR YOU?
SURE.
WHAT DO YOU WANT... ROCK? JAZZ? CLASSICAL? REGGAE? POP? SOUL? FUNK?
SCOTT and BORGMAN
SEE IF THEY HAVE ONE THAT SOUNDS LIKE A TELEPHONE RINGING.
I'LL CHECK UNDER "IRONIC."

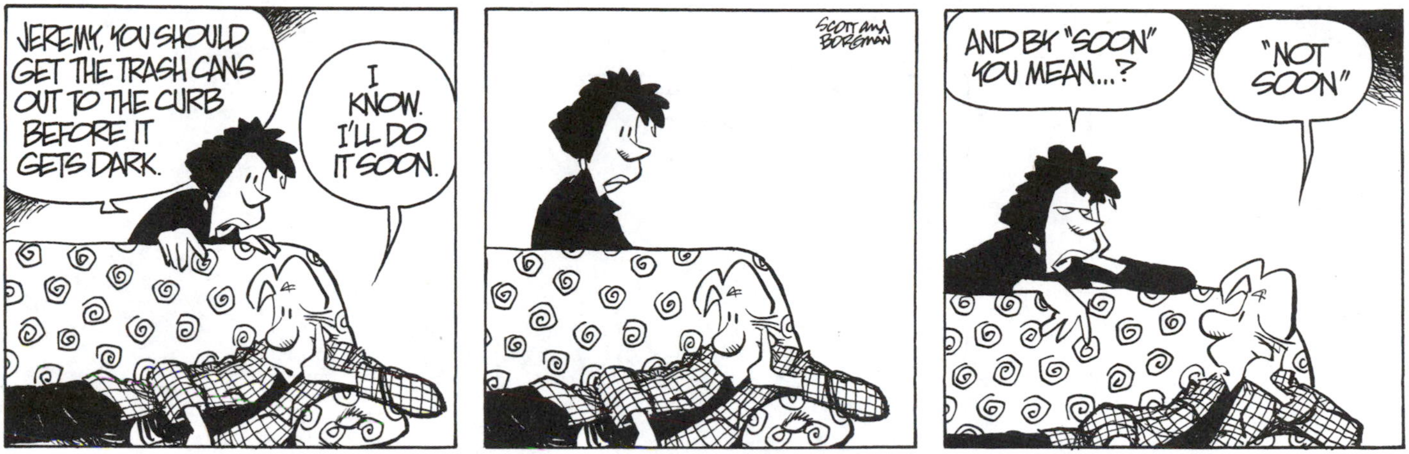
JEREMY, YOU SHOULD GET THE TRASH CANS OUT TO THE CURB BEFORE IT GETS DARK.
I KNOW. I'LL DO IT SOON.
SCOTT AND BORGMAN
AND BY "SOON" YOU MEAN...?
"NOT SOON"

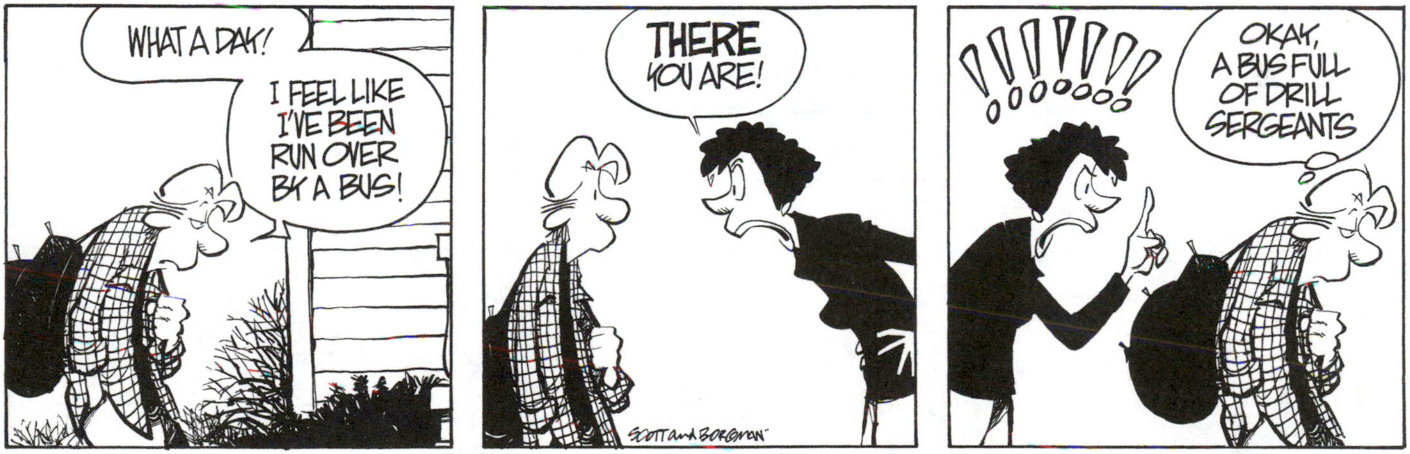
WHAT A DAY!
I FEEL LIKE I'VE BEEN RUN OVER BY A BUS!
THERE YOU ARE!
SCOTT AND BORGMAN
!!!!!!!
OKAY, A BUS FULL OF DRILL SERGEANTS

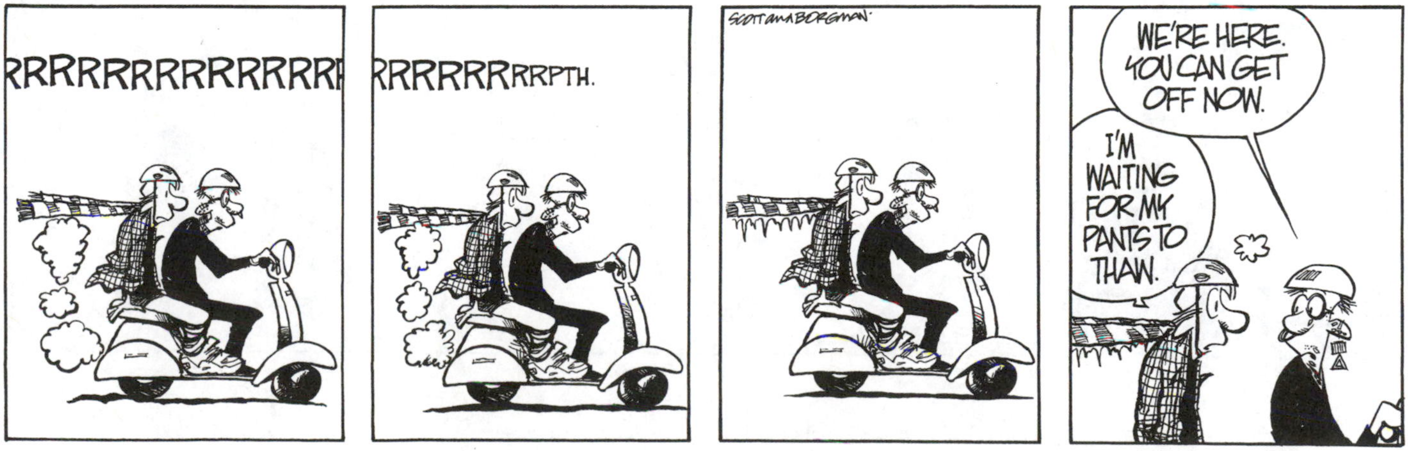
RRRRRRRRRRRRRR
RRRRRRRRPTH.
SCOTT AND BORGMAN
WE'RE HERE. YOU CAN GET OFF NOW.
I'M WAITING FOR MY PANTS TO THAW.

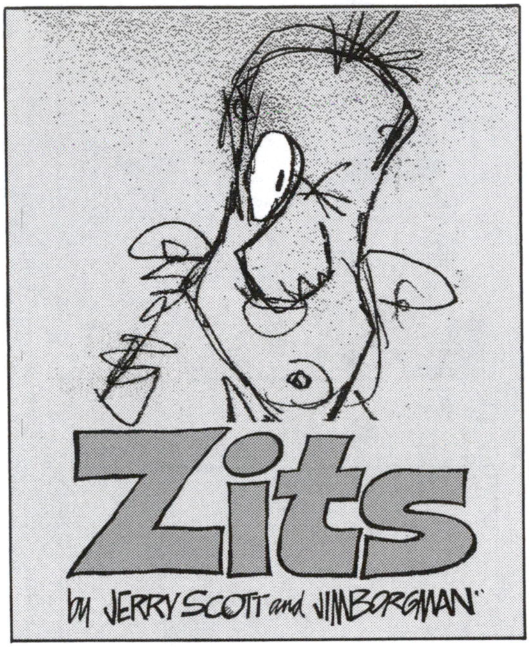
Zits
by JERRY SCOTT and JIM BORGMAN

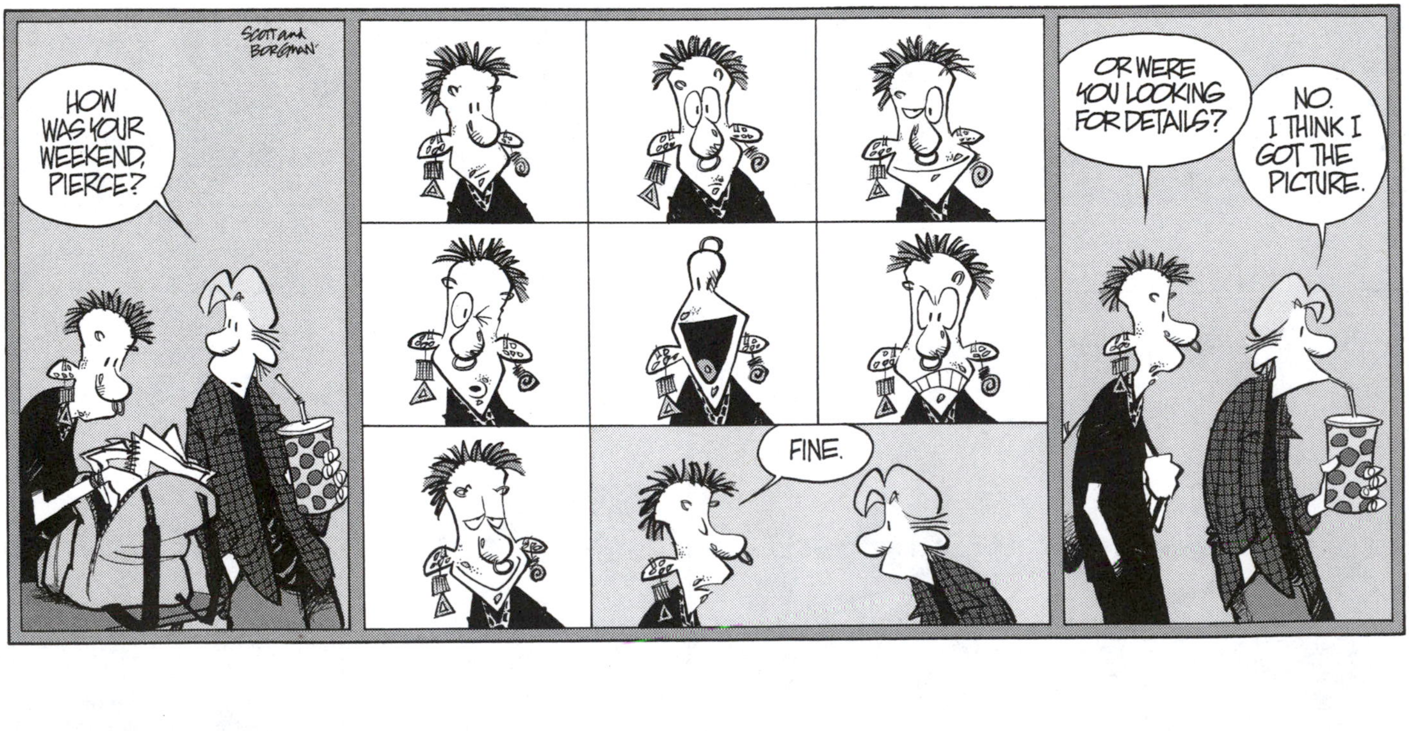
SCOTT and BORGMAN
HOW WAS YOUR WEEKEND, PIERCE?
FINE.
OR WERE YOU LOOKING FOR DETAILS?
NO. I THINK I GOT THE PICTURE.

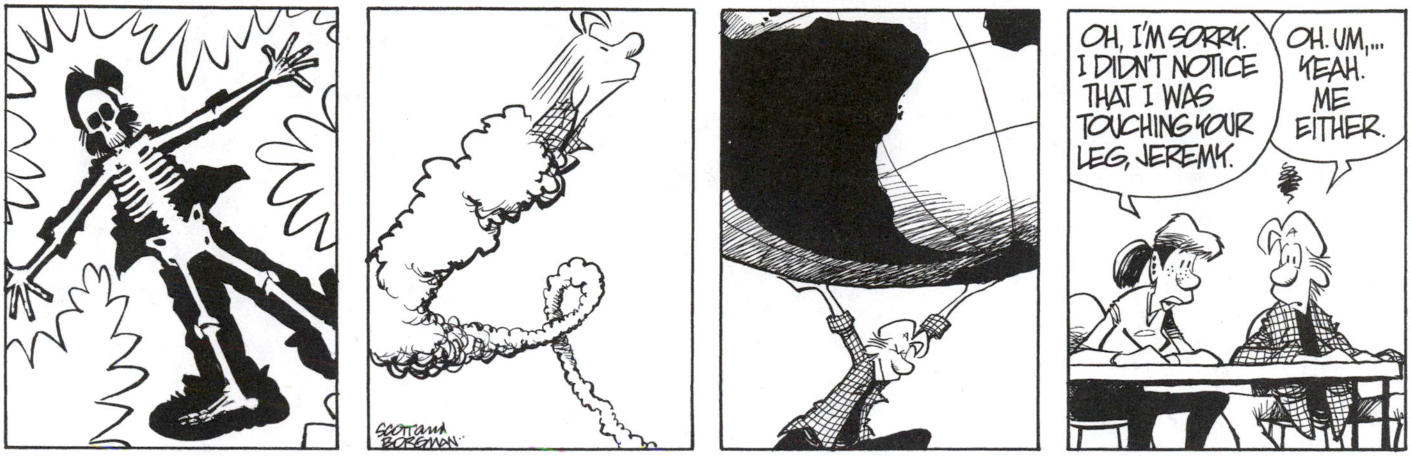
OH, I'M SORRY. I DIDN'T NOTICE THAT I WAS TOUCHING YOUR LEG, JEREMY.
OH. UM,... YEAH. ME EITHER.

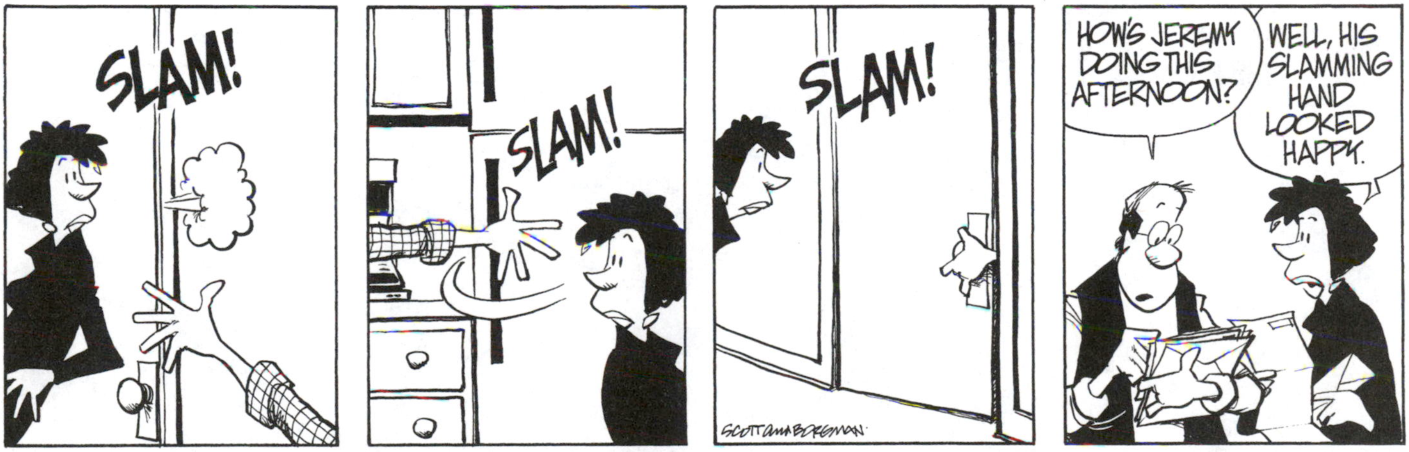
SLAM!
SLAM!
SLAM!
HOW'S JEREMY DOING THIS AFTERNOON?
WELL, HIS SLAMMING HAND LOOKED HAPPY.

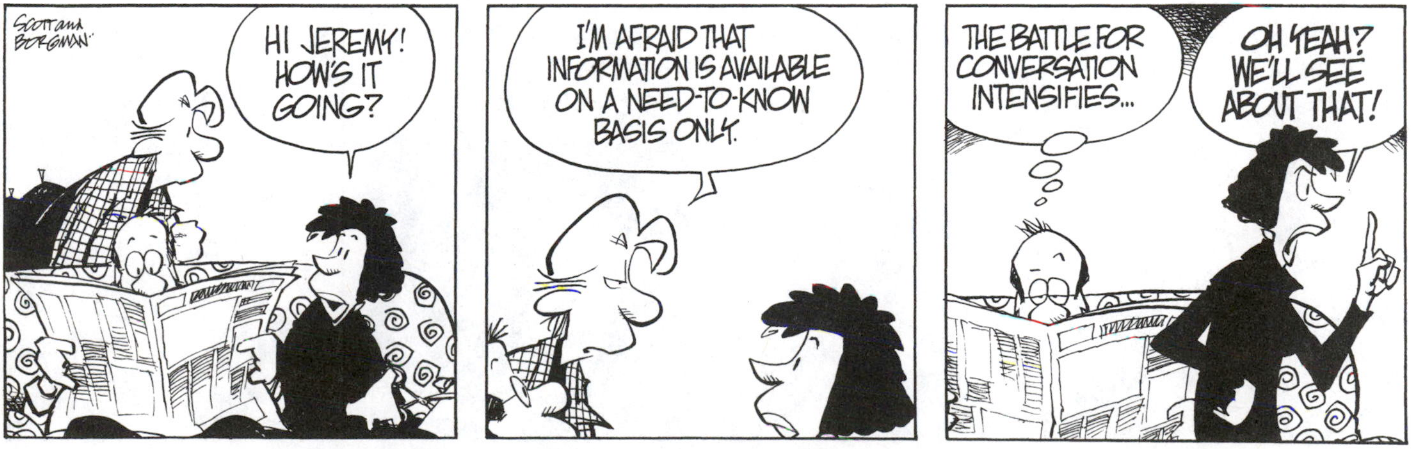
HI JEREMY! HOW'S IT GOING?
I'M AFRAID THAT INFORMATION IS AVAILABLE ON A NEED-TO-KNOW BASIS ONLY.
THE BATTLE FOR CONVERSATION INTENSIFIES...
OH YEAH? WE'LL SEE ABOUT THAT!

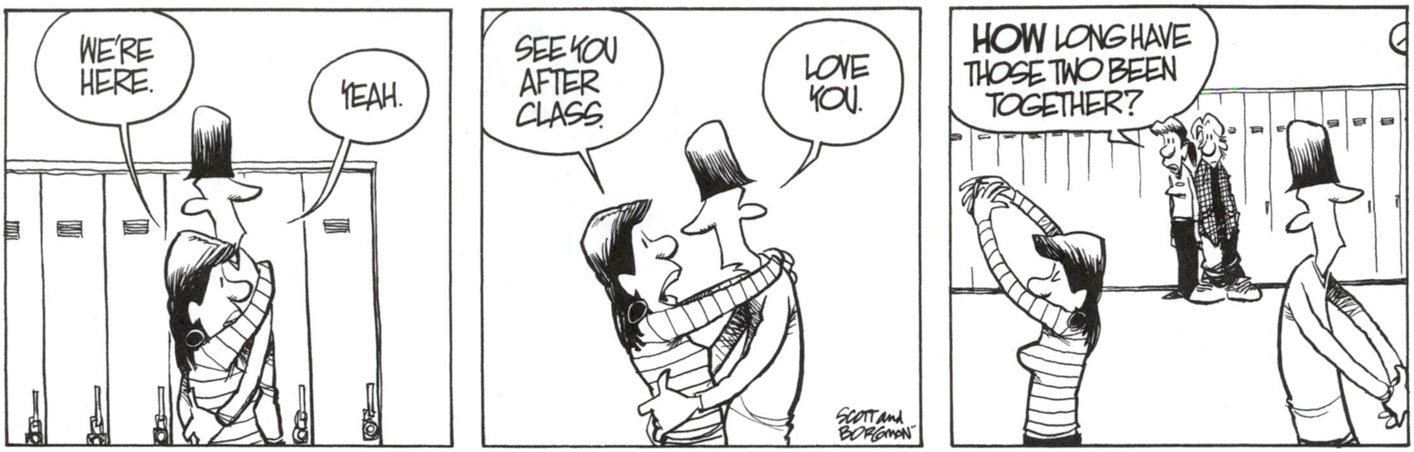
WE'RE HERE.
YEAH.
SEE YOU AFTER CLASS.
LOVE YOU.
HOW LONG HAVE THOSE TWO BEEN TOGETHER?

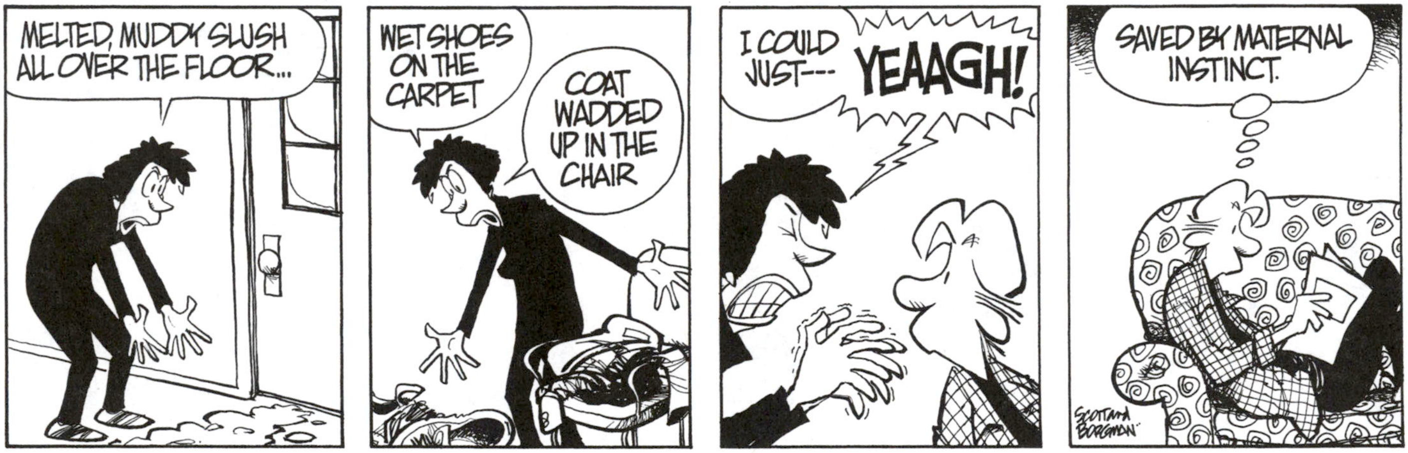
MELTED, MUDDY SLUSH ALL OVER THE FLOOR...
WET SHOES ON THE CARPET
COAT WADDED UP IN THE CHAIR
I COULD JUST---
YEAAGH!
SAVED BY MATERNAL INSTINCT.

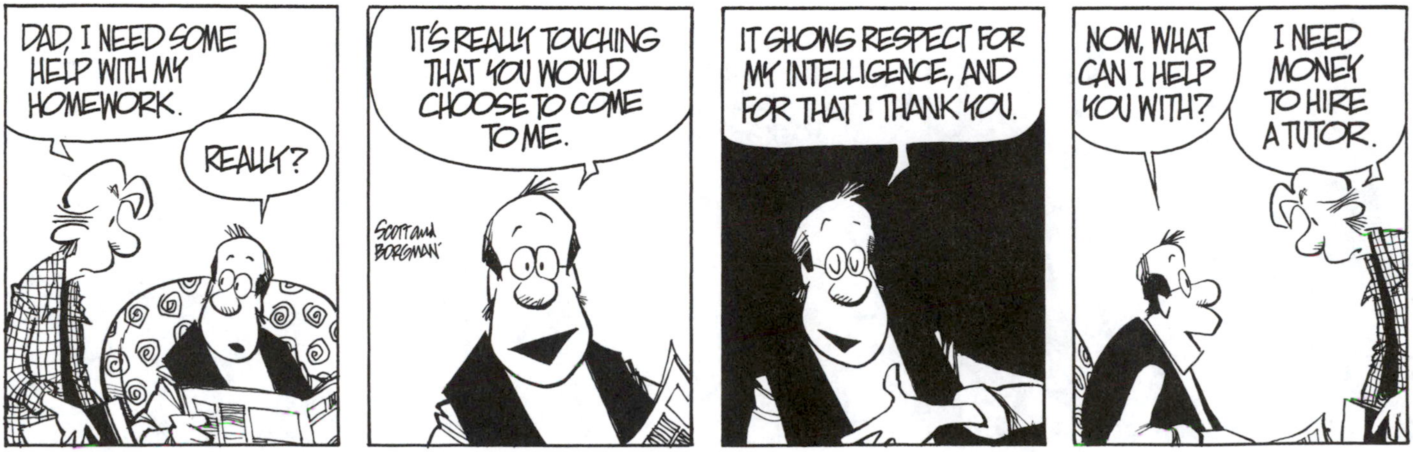
DAD, I NEED SOME HELP WITH MY HOMEWORK.
REALLY?
IT'S REALLY TOUCHING THAT YOU WOULD CHOOSE TO COME TO ME.
IT SHOWS RESPECT FOR MY INTELLIGENCE, AND FOR THAT I THANK YOU.
NOW, WHAT CAN I HELP YOU WITH?
I NEED MONEY TO HIRE A TUTOR.

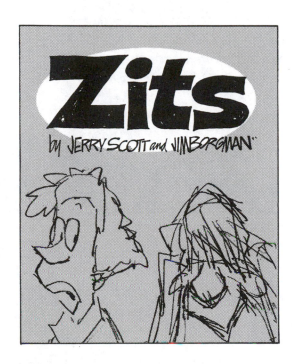

Zits
by JERRY SCOTT and JIM BORGMAN™

YAWN!

GOOD MORNING, JEREMY!

Hi

BIG DAY AT SCHOOL TODAY?

Not really

I have an Algebra Quiz.

But other than that, it looks pretty routine.

YOU'RE WELCOME.

Thanks for

I THINK HE MUMBLES LIKE THAT JUST TO BUG ME.

EVERY TEENAGER SHOULD COME WITH SUBTITLES.

asking.

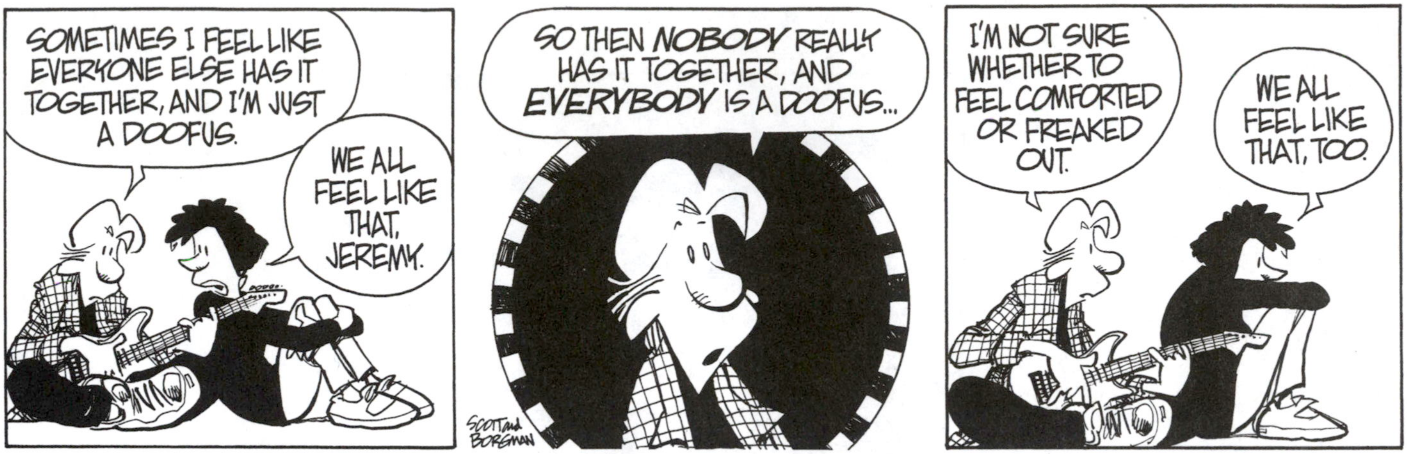
SOMETIMES I FEEL LIKE EVERYONE ELSE HAS IT TOGETHER, AND I'M JUST A DOOFUS.
WE ALL FEEL LIKE THAT, JEREMY.
SO THEN NOBODY REALLY HAS IT TOGETHER, AND EVERYBODY IS A DOOFUS...
I'M NOT SURE WHETHER TO FEEL COMFORTED OR FREAKED OUT.
WE ALL FEEL LIKE THAT, TOO.

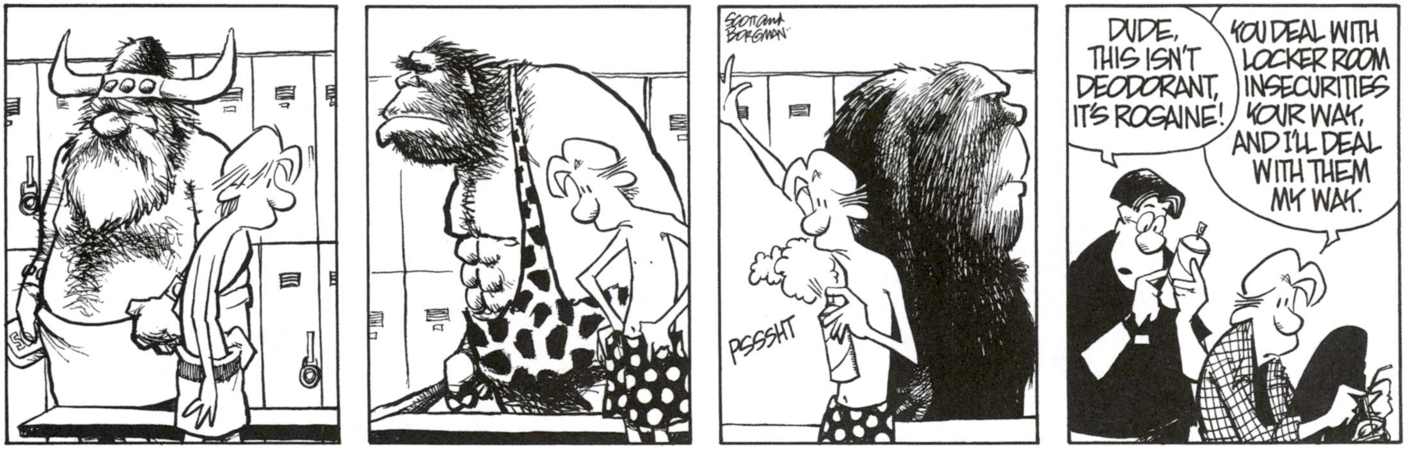
PSSSHT
DUDE, THIS ISN'T DEODORANT, IT'S ROGAINE!
YOU DEAL WITH LOCKER ROOM INSECURITIES YOUR WAY, AND I'LL DEAL WITH THEM MY WAY.

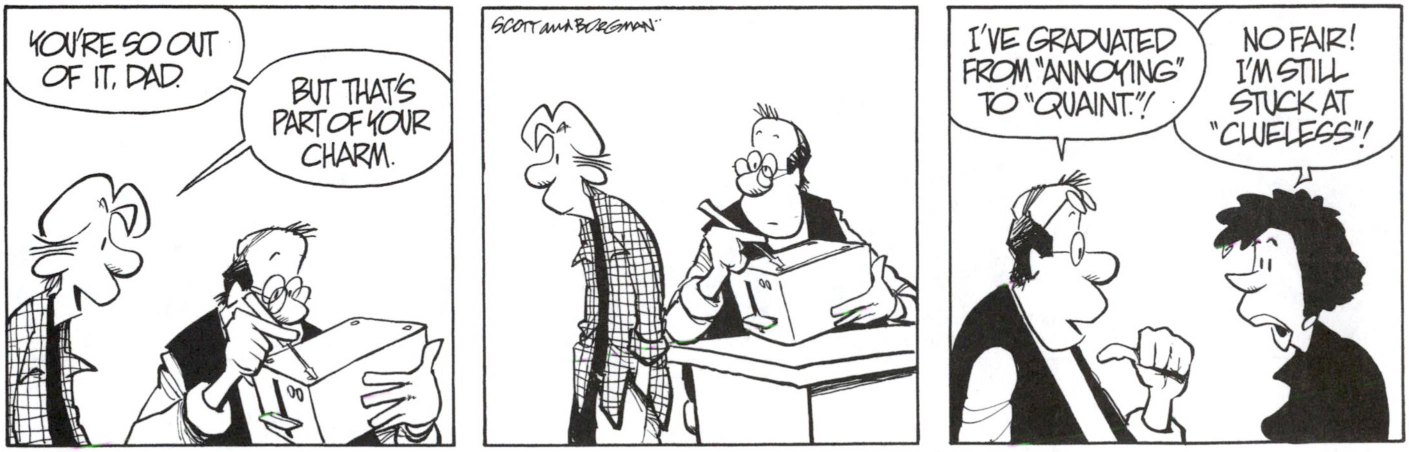
YOU'RE SO OUT OF IT, DAD.
BUT THAT'S PART OF YOUR CHARM.
I'VE GRADUATED FROM "ANNOYING" TO "QUAINT."!
NO FAIR! I'M STILL STUCK AT "CLUELESS"!

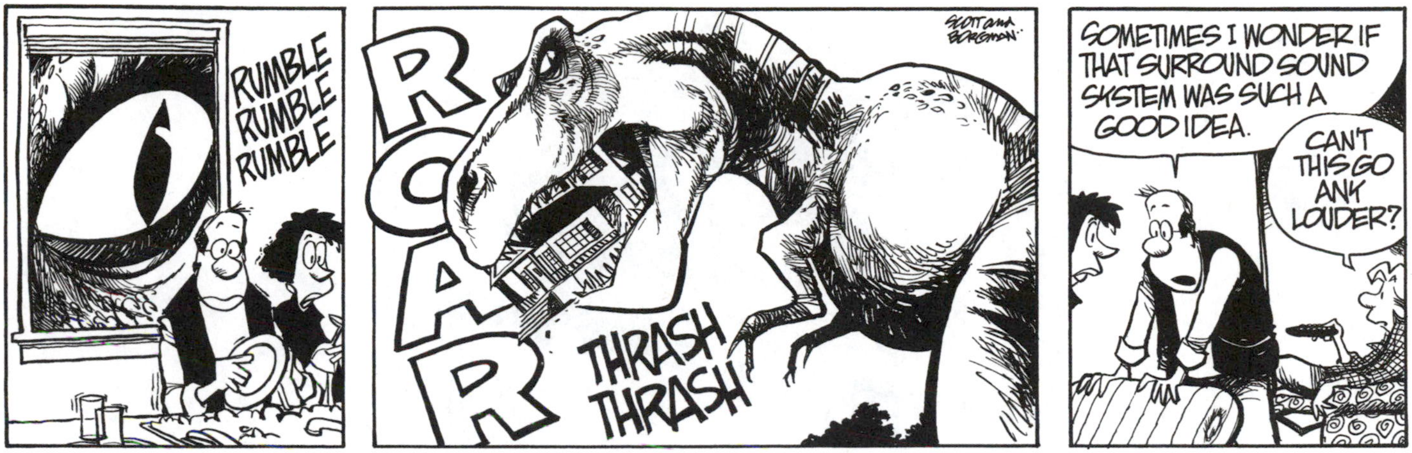
RUMBLE RUMBLE RUMBLE
ROAR
THRASH THRASH
SOMETIMES I WONDER IF THAT SURROUND SOUND SYSTEM WAS SUCH A GOOD IDEA.
CAN'T THIS GO ANY LOUDER?

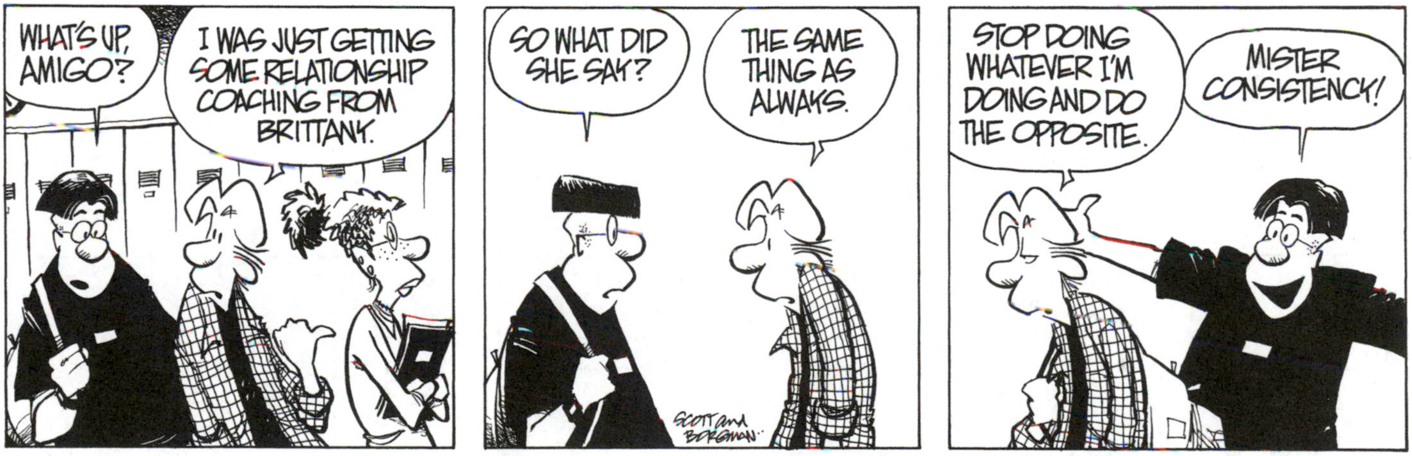
WHAT'S UP, AMIGO?
I WAS JUST GETTING SOME RELATIONSHIP COACHING FROM BRITTANY.
SO WHAT DID SHE SAY?
THE SAME THING AS ALWAYS.
STOP DOING WHATEVER I'M DOING AND DO THE OPPOSITE.
MISTER CONSISTENCY!

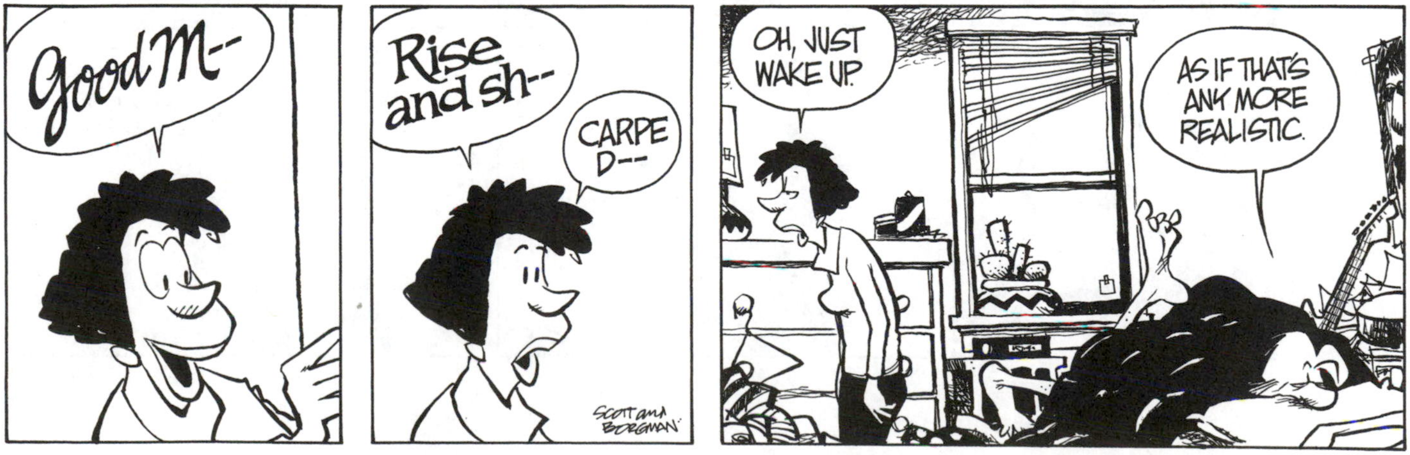
Good M--
Rise and sh--
CARPE D--
OH, JUST WAKE UP.
AS IF THAT'S ANY MORE REALISTIC.

Zits
by Jerry Scott and Jim Borgman

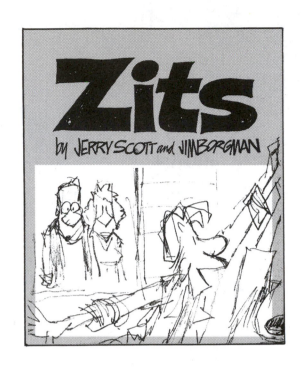

JEREMY KNOWS SO MUCH ABOUT TECHNOLOGY THAT IT'S ALMOST SCARY!

YUP.

AND HIS GRADES ARE AMAZING, TOO.

HE'S HOLDING A 4.0 GPA WITH THREE A.P. CLASSES.

I'VE NOTICED THAT HE'S GETTING PRETTY TALL, TOO.

PLUS, HE HAS GREAT HAIR, A HANDSOME FACE, AND MUSICAL TALENT COMING OUT OF HIS EARS!

SCOTT AND BORGMAN

MAKES YOU PROUD, DOESN'T HE?

YOU BET.

AND IF HE WASN'T MY SON, I'D HATE HIS GUTS.

NOW, NOW... THAT'S JUST THE CHOLESTEROL TALKING.

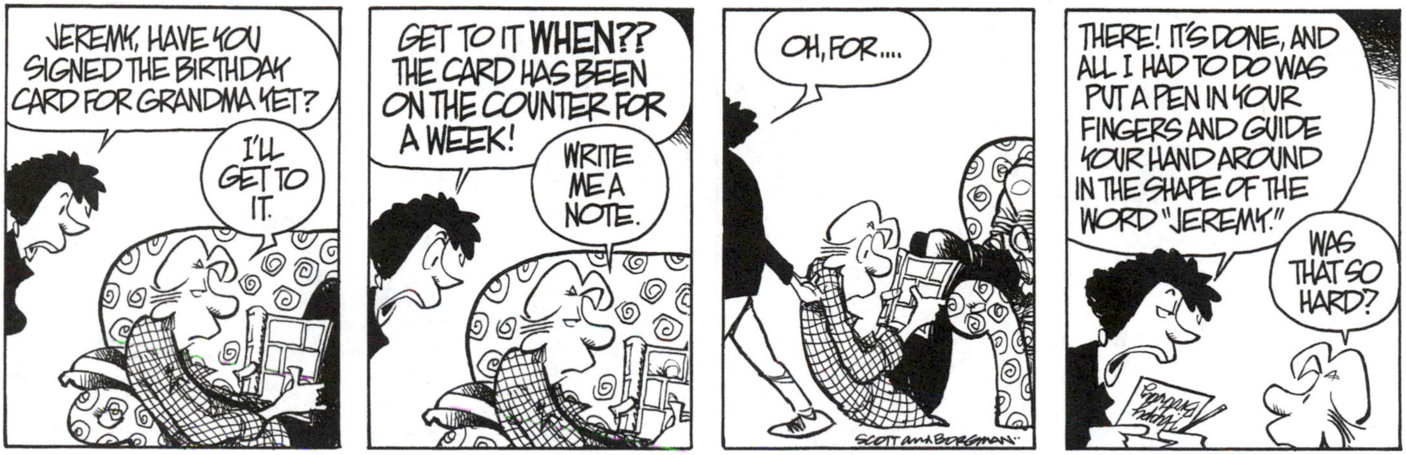
JEREMY, HAVE YOU SIGNED THE BIRTHDAY CARD FOR GRANDMA YET?
I'LL GET TO IT.
GET TO IT **WHEN??** THE CARD HAS BEEN ON THE COUNTER FOR A WEEK!
WRITE ME A NOTE.
OH, FOR....
THERE! IT'S DONE, AND ALL I HAD TO DO WAS PUT A PEN IN YOUR FINGERS AND GUIDE YOUR HAND AROUND IN THE SHAPE OF THE WORD "JEREMY."
WAS THAT SO HARD?

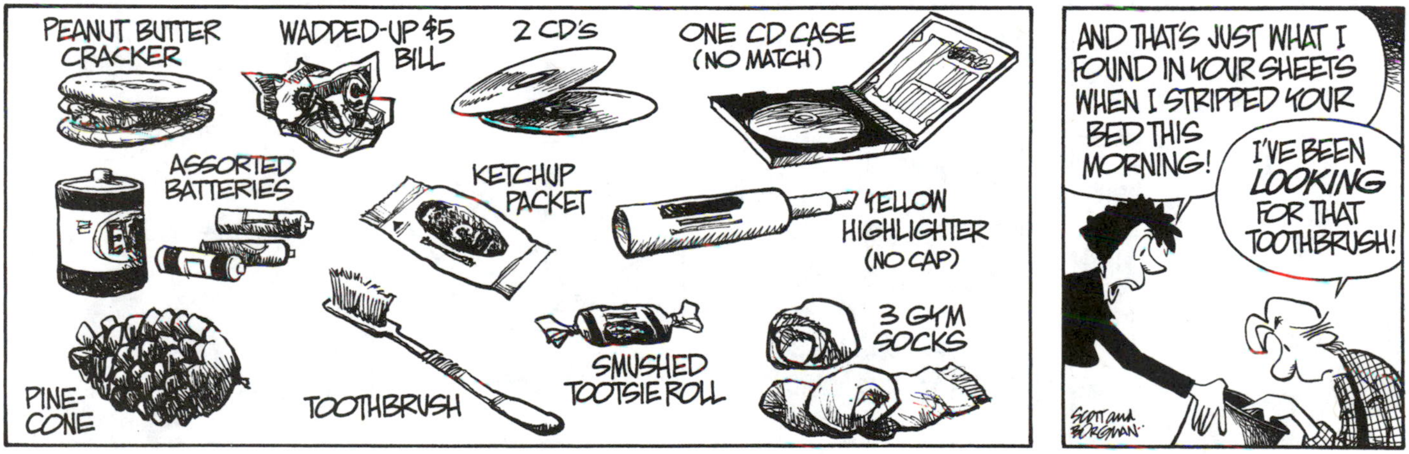
PEANUT BUTTER CRACKER
WADDED-UP $5 BILL
2 CD'S
ONE CD CASE (NO MATCH)
ASSORTED BATTERIES
KETCHUP PACKET
YELLOW HIGHLIGHTER (NO CAP)
PINE-CONE
TOOTHBRUSH
SMUSHED TOOTSIE ROLL
3 GYM SOCKS
AND THAT'S JUST WHAT I FOUND IN YOUR SHEETS WHEN I STRIPPED YOUR BED THIS MORNING!
I'VE BEEN *LOOKING* FOR THAT TOOTHBRUSH!

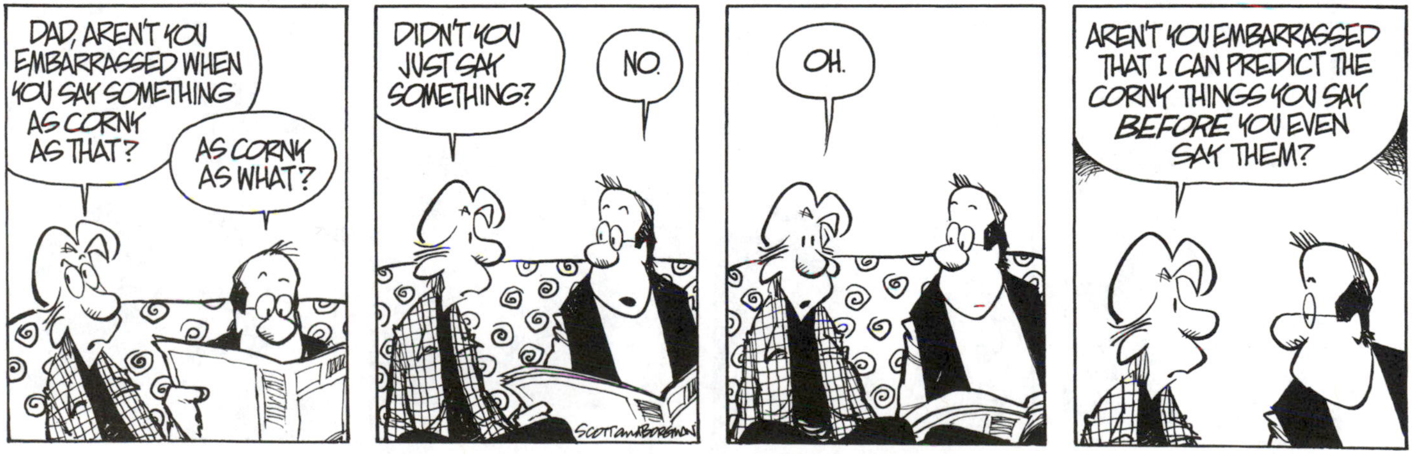
DAD, AREN'T YOU EMBARRASSED WHEN YOU SAY SOMETHING AS CORNY AS THAT?
AS CORNY AS WHAT?
DIDN'T YOU JUST SAY SOMETHING?
NO.
OH.
AREN'T YOU EMBARRASSED THAT I CAN PREDICT THE CORNY THINGS YOU SAY *BEFORE* YOU EVEN SAY THEM?

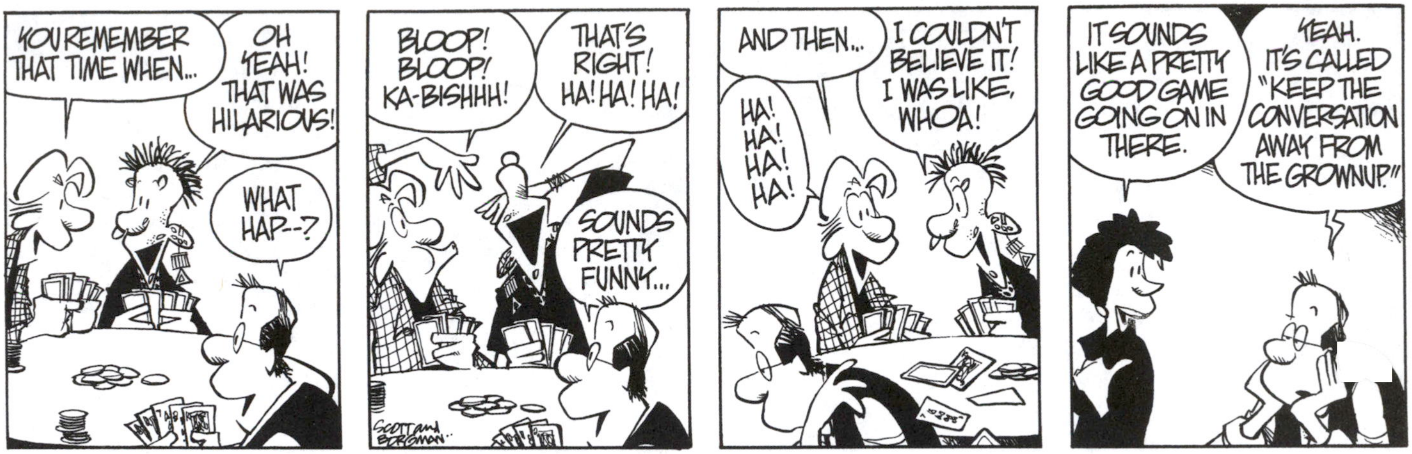
YOU REMEMBER THAT TIME WHEN...
OH YEAH! THAT WAS HILARIOUS!
WHAT HAP--?
BLOOP! BLOOP! KA-BISHHH!
THAT'S RIGHT! HA! HA! HA!
SOUNDS PRETTY FUNNY...
SCOTT and BORGMAN
AND THEN...
HA! HA! HA! HA!
I COULDN'T BELIEVE IT! I WAS LIKE, WHOA!
IT SOUNDS LIKE A PRETTY GOOD GAME GOING ON IN THERE.
YEAH. IT'S CALLED "KEEP THE CONVERSATION AWAY FROM THE GROWNUP."

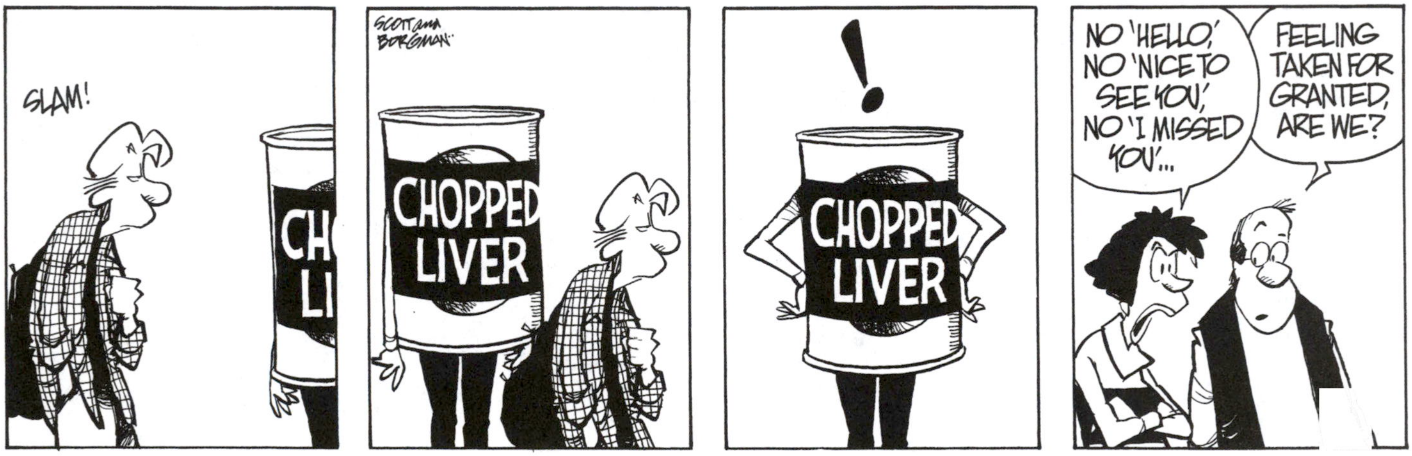
SLAM!
SCOTT and BORGMAN
CHOPPED LIVER
!
CHOPPED LIVER
NO 'HELLO,' NO 'NICE TO SEE YOU,' NO 'I MISSED YOU'...
FEELING TAKEN FOR GRANTED, ARE WE?

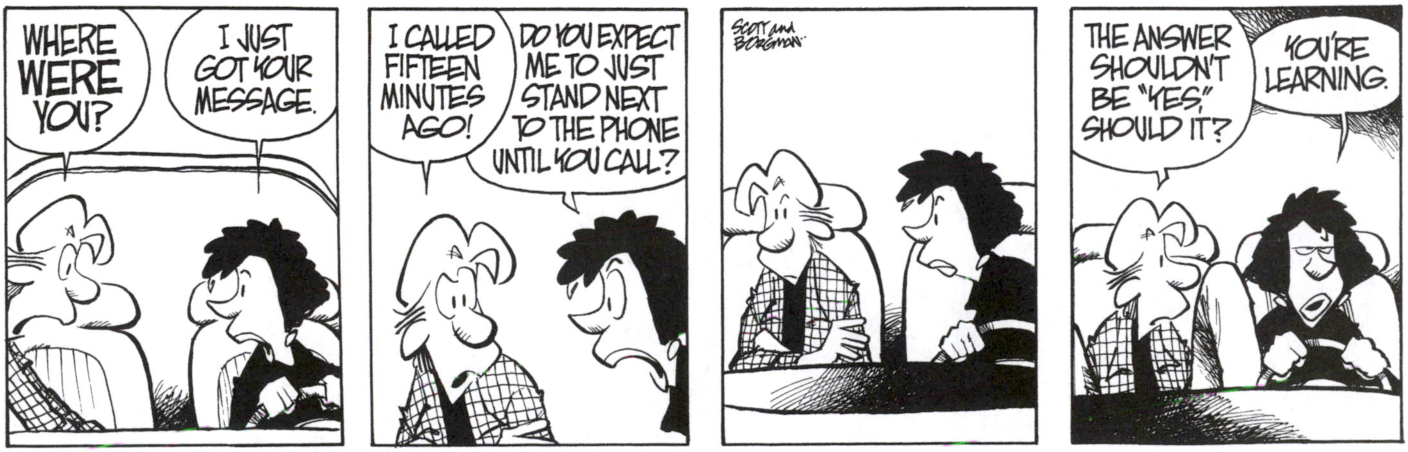
WHERE WERE YOU?
I JUST GOT YOUR MESSAGE.
I CALLED FIFTEEN MINUTES AGO!
DO YOU EXPECT ME TO JUST STAND NEXT TO THE PHONE UNTIL YOU CALL?
SCOTT and BORGMAN
THE ANSWER SHOULDN'T BE "YES," SHOULD IT?
YOU'RE LEARNING.

Zits
by
JERRY SCOTT and
JIM BORGMAN

THERE'S THAT ANNOYING NOISE AGAIN!
I THINK IT'S COMING FROM UPSTAIRS
THUNK!
THUNK!
THUNK!
OH, HI
I GOT REALLY COMFORTABLE AND DIDN'T WANT TO GET UP TO TURN OUT THE LIGHT, SO I'VE BEEN TRYING TO HIT THE LIGHT SWITCH WITH MY SHOE.
BUT NOW THAT YOU'RE HERE, COULD YOU TURN IT OFF FOR ME?
THANKS.
THUNK!
THUNK!
SCOTT and BORGMAN
DO YOU HAVE ANY IDEA HOW ANNOYING THAT IS?
THUNK!
THUNK!

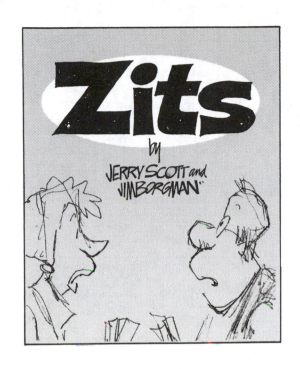

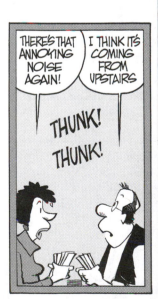

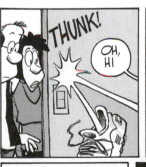

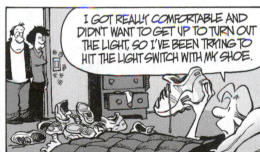

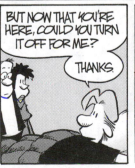

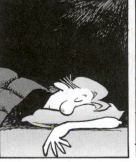

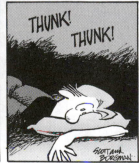

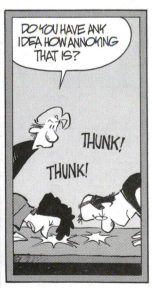

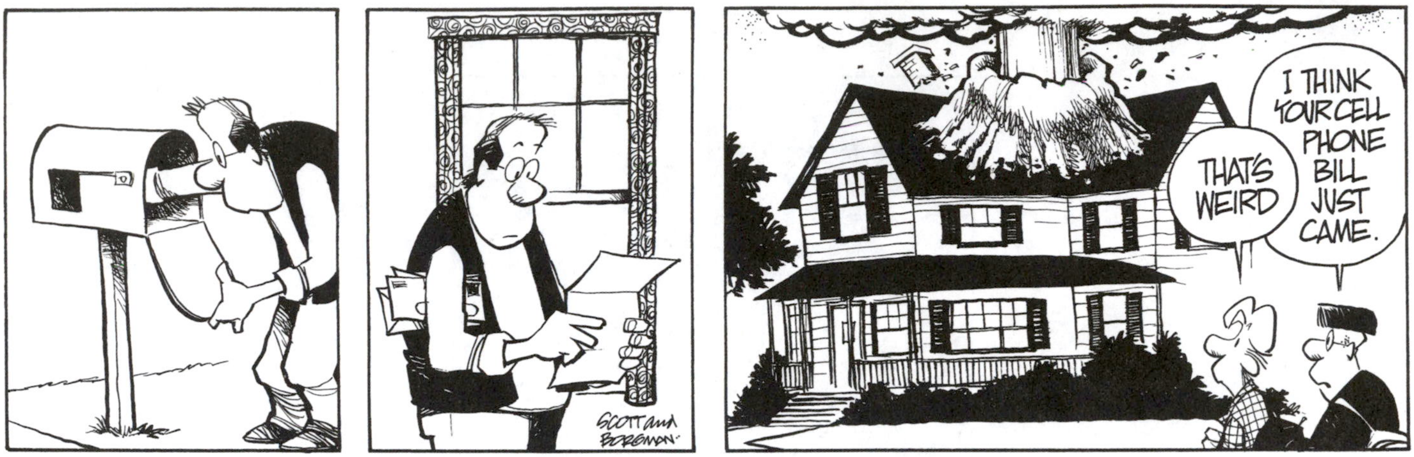
THAT'S WEIRD
I THINK YOUR CELL PHONE BILL JUST CAME.

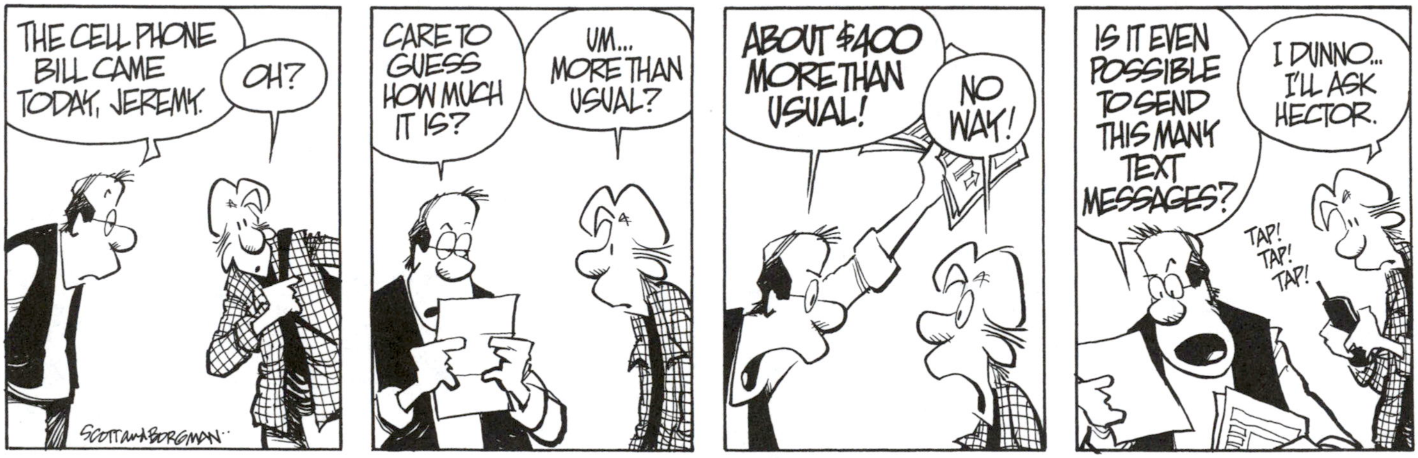
THE CELL PHONE BILL CAME TODAY, JEREMY.
OH?
CARE TO GUESS HOW MUCH IT IS?
UM... MORE THAN USUAL?
ABOUT $400 MORE THAN USUAL!
NO WAY!
IS IT EVEN POSSIBLE TO SEND THIS MANY TEXT MESSAGES?
I DUNNO... I'LL ASK HECTOR.
TAP! TAP! TAP!

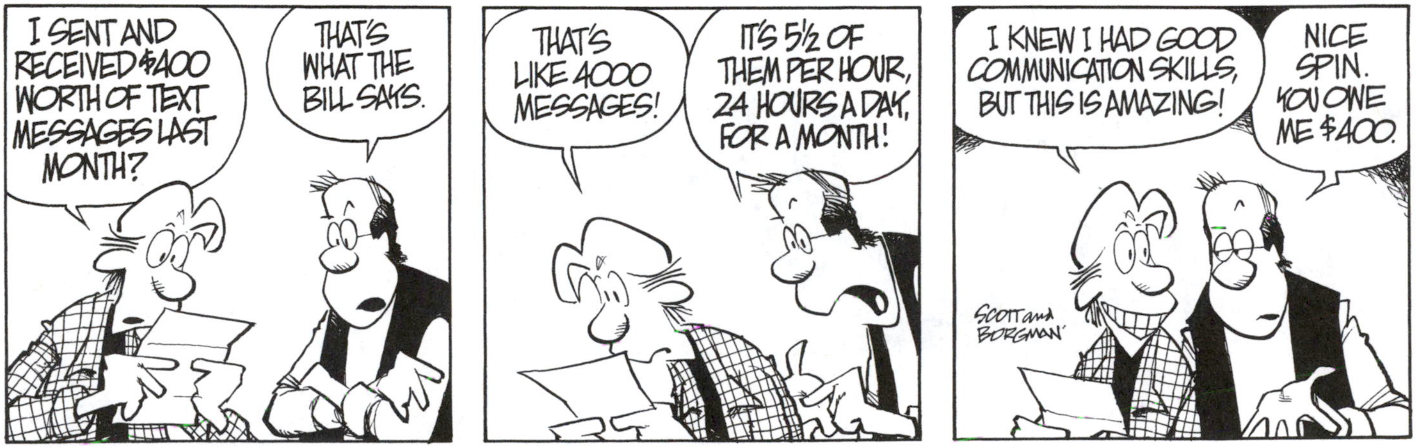
I SENT AND RECEIVED $400 WORTH OF TEXT MESSAGES LAST MONTH?
THAT'S WHAT THE BILL SAYS.
THAT'S LIKE 4000 MESSAGES!
IT'S 5½ OF THEM PER HOUR, 24 HOURS A DAY, FOR A MONTH!
I KNEW I HAD GOOD COMMUNICATION SKILLS, BUT THIS IS AMAZING!
NICE SPIN. YOU OWE ME $400.

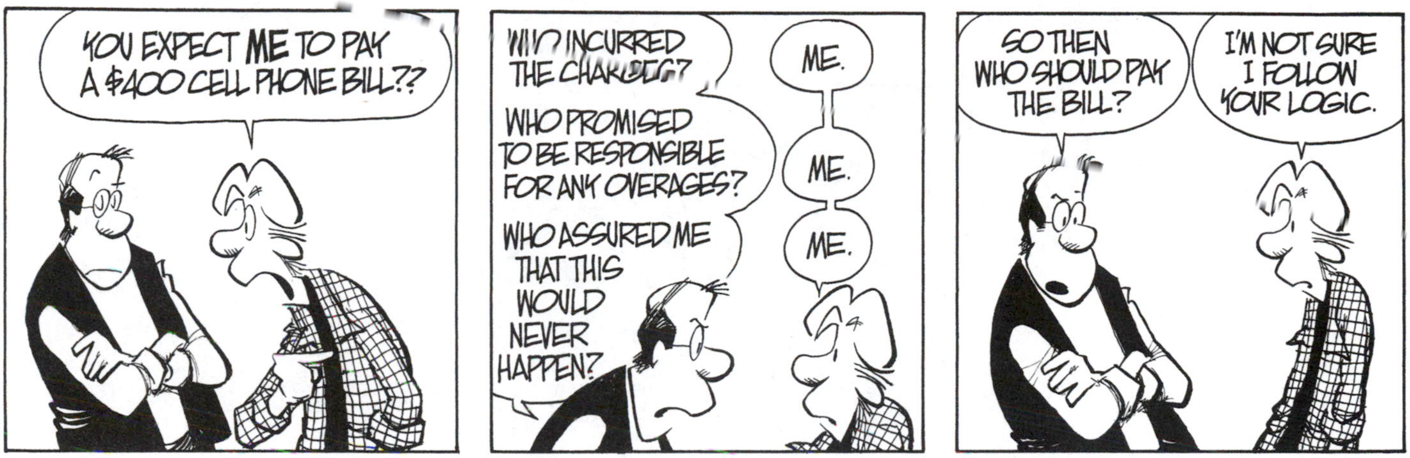
YOU EXPECT ME TO PAY A $400 CELL PHONE BILL??
WHO INCURRED THE CHARGES?
ME.
WHO PROMISED TO BE RESPONSIBLE FOR ANY OVERAGES?
ME.
WHO ASSURED ME THAT THIS WOULD NEVER HAPPEN?
ME.
SO THEN WHO SHOULD PAY THE BILL?
I'M NOT SURE I FOLLOW YOUR LOGIC.

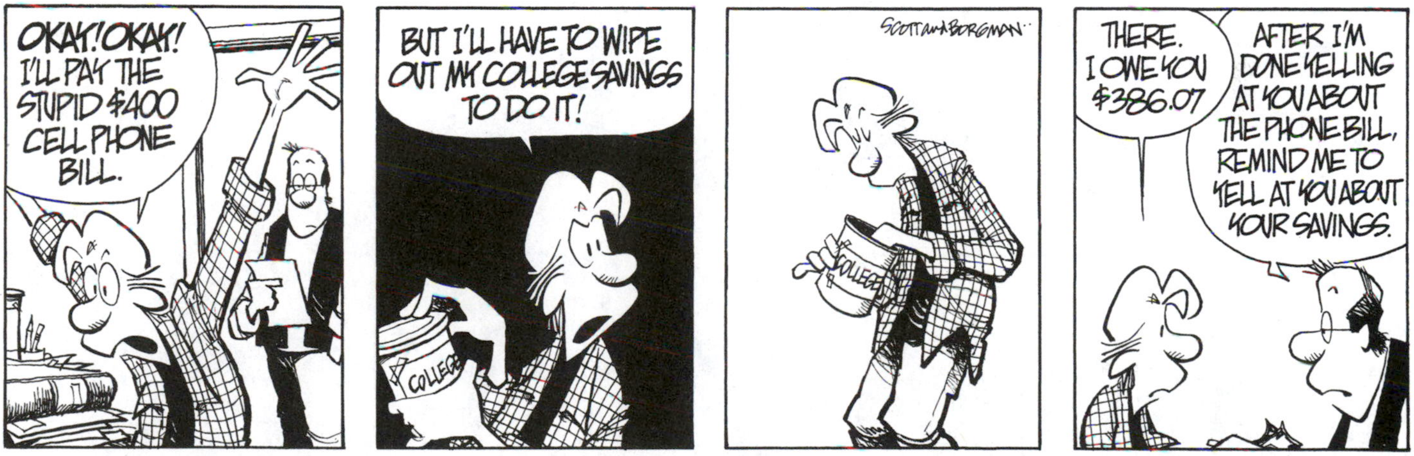
OKAY! OKAY! I'LL PAY THE STUPID $400 CELL PHONE BILL.
BUT I'LL HAVE TO WIPE OUT MY COLLEGE SAVINGS TO DO IT!
COLLEGE
THERE. I OWE YOU $386.07
AFTER I'M DONE YELLING AT YOU ABOUT THE PHONE BILL, REMIND ME TO YELL AT YOU ABOUT YOUR SAVINGS.

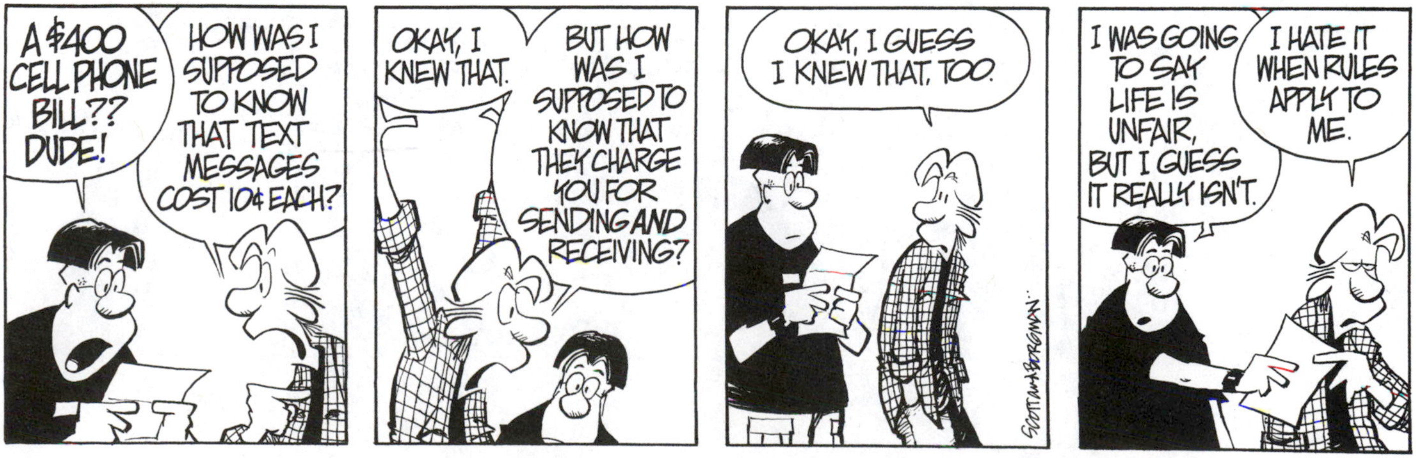
A $400 CELL PHONE BILL?? DUDE!
HOW WAS I SUPPOSED TO KNOW THAT TEXT MESSAGES COST 10¢ EACH?
OKAY, I KNEW THAT.
BUT HOW WAS I SUPPOSED TO KNOW THAT THEY CHARGE YOU FOR SENDING AND RECEIVING?
OKAY, I GUESS I KNEW THAT, TOO.
I WAS GOING TO SAY LIFE IS UNFAIR, BUT I GUESS IT REALLY ISN'T.
I HATE IT WHEN RULES APPLY TO ME.

Zits
by
JERRY SCOTT and
JIM BORGMAN

DEEDLE! DEEDLE! DEEDLE!
DEEDLE! DEEDLE! DEEDLE!
OW!
DEEDLE! DEEDLE! DEEDLE!
BAM!
DEEDLE! DEEDLE! DEEDLE!
WHUMP!
DEEDLE! DEEDLE! DEEDLE!
HELLO?
HELLO?
JEREMY, DID YOU CALL YOUR FATHER FOR DINNER LIKE I ASKED YOU TO?
YEAH. BUT FOR SOME REASON HE HUNG UP ON ME.
SCOTT and BORGMAN

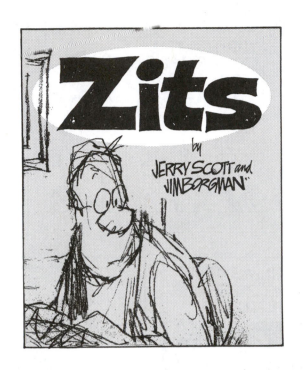

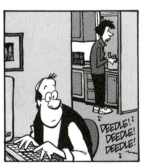

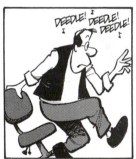

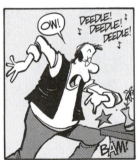

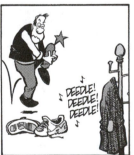

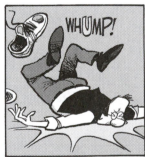

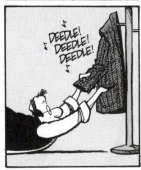

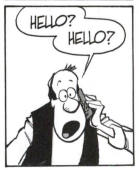

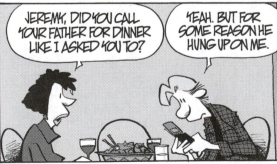

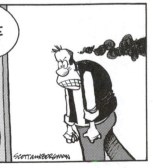

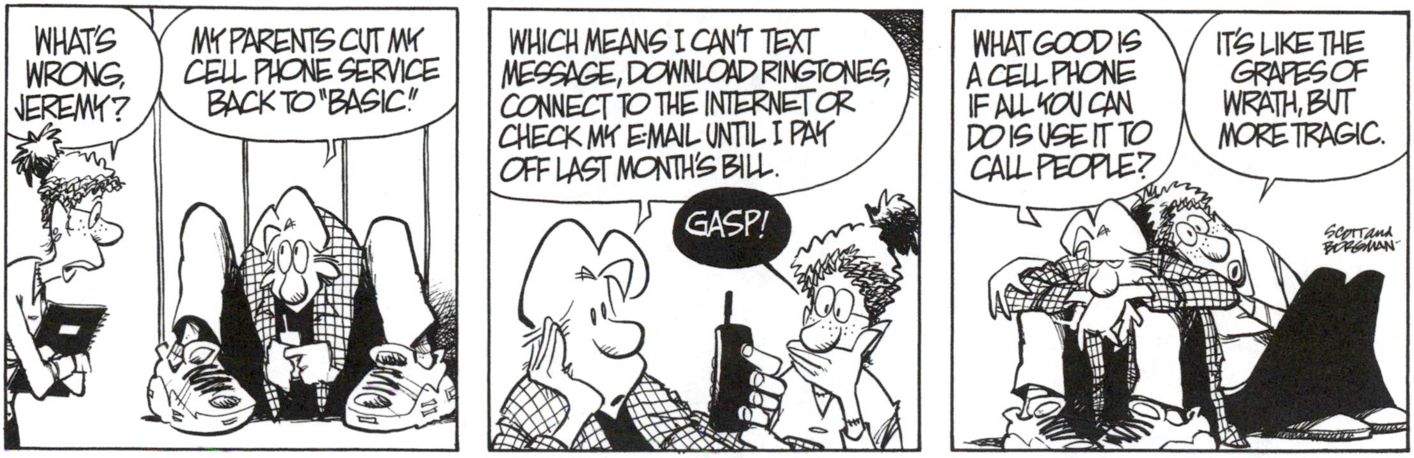
WHAT'S WRONG, JEREMY?
MY PARENTS CUT MY CELL PHONE SERVICE BACK TO "BASIC."
WHICH MEANS I CAN'T TEXT MESSAGE, DOWNLOAD RINGTONES, CONNECT TO THE INTERNET OR CHECK MY E-MAIL UNTIL I PAY OFF LAST MONTH'S BILL.
GASP!
WHAT GOOD IS A CELL PHONE IF ALL YOU CAN DO IS USE IT TO CALL PEOPLE?
IT'S LIKE THE GRAPES OF WRATH, BUT MORE TRAGIC.
SCOTT AND BORGMAN

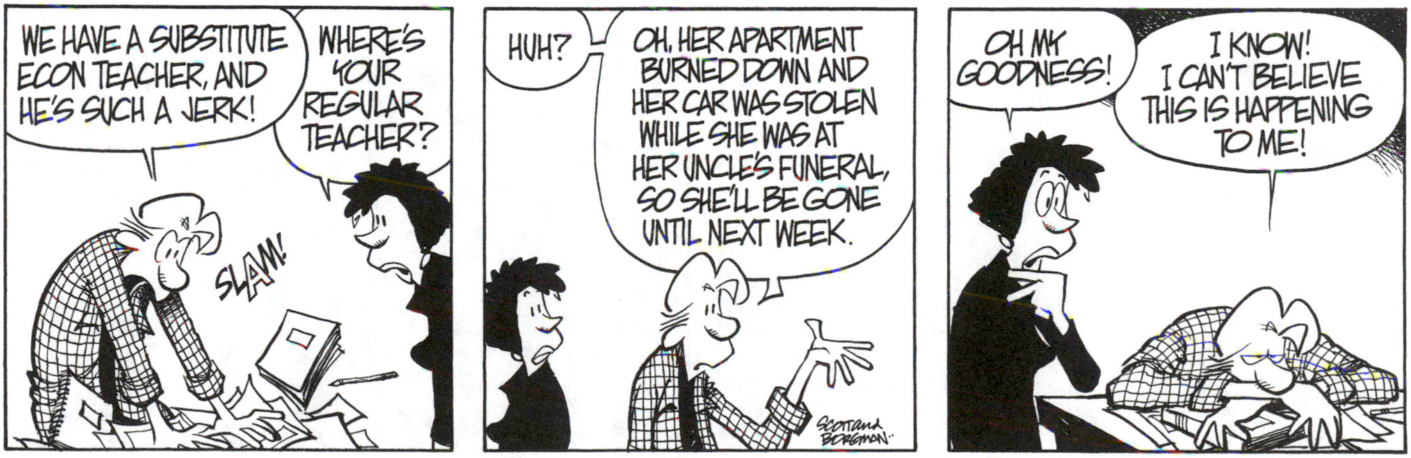
WE HAVE A SUBSTITUTE ECON TEACHER, AND HE'S SUCH A JERK!
WHERE'S YOUR REGULAR TEACHER?
SLAM!
HUH?
OH, HER APARTMENT BURNED DOWN AND HER CAR WAS STOLEN WHILE SHE WAS AT HER UNCLE'S FUNERAL, SO SHE'LL BE GONE UNTIL NEXT WEEK.
SCOTT AND BORGMAN
OH MY GOODNESS!
I KNOW! I CAN'T BELIEVE THIS IS HAPPENING TO ME!

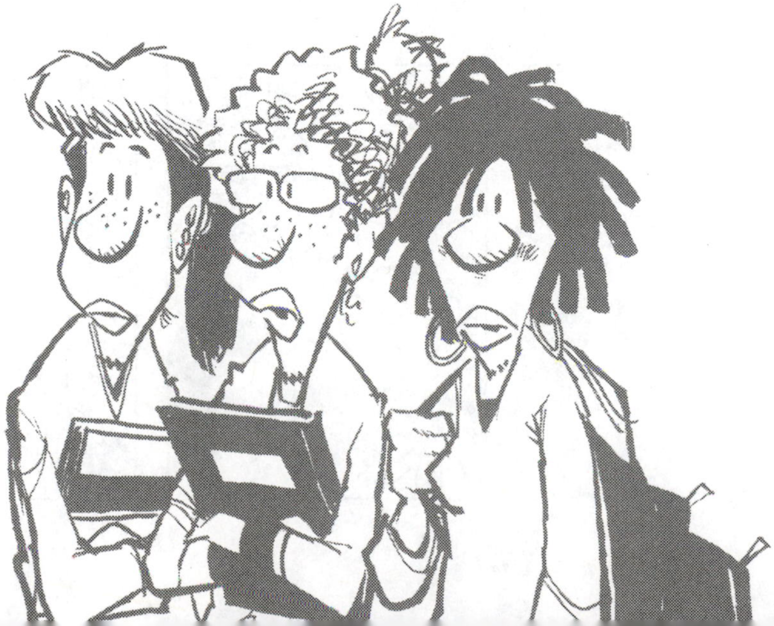

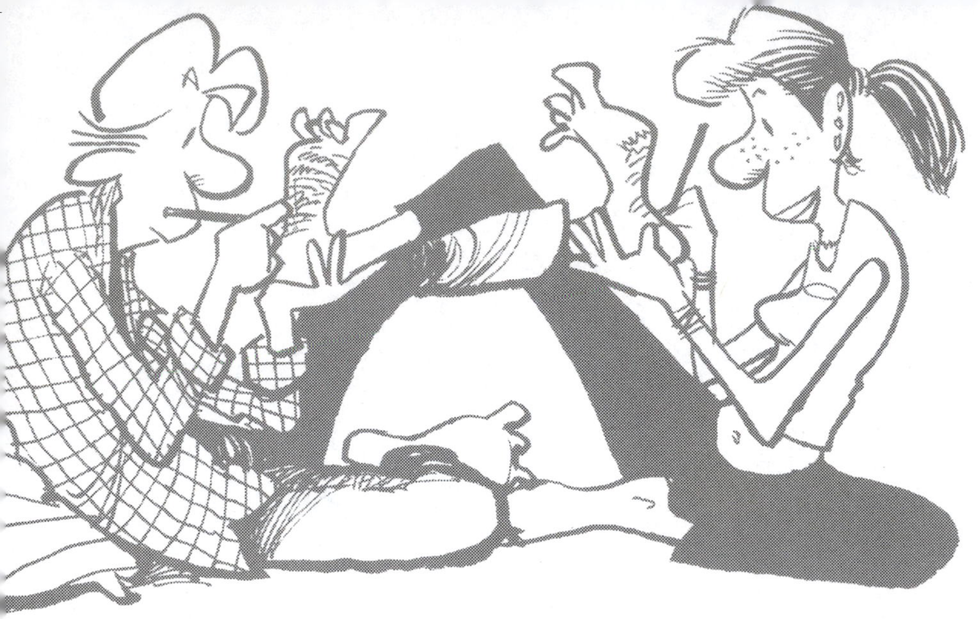

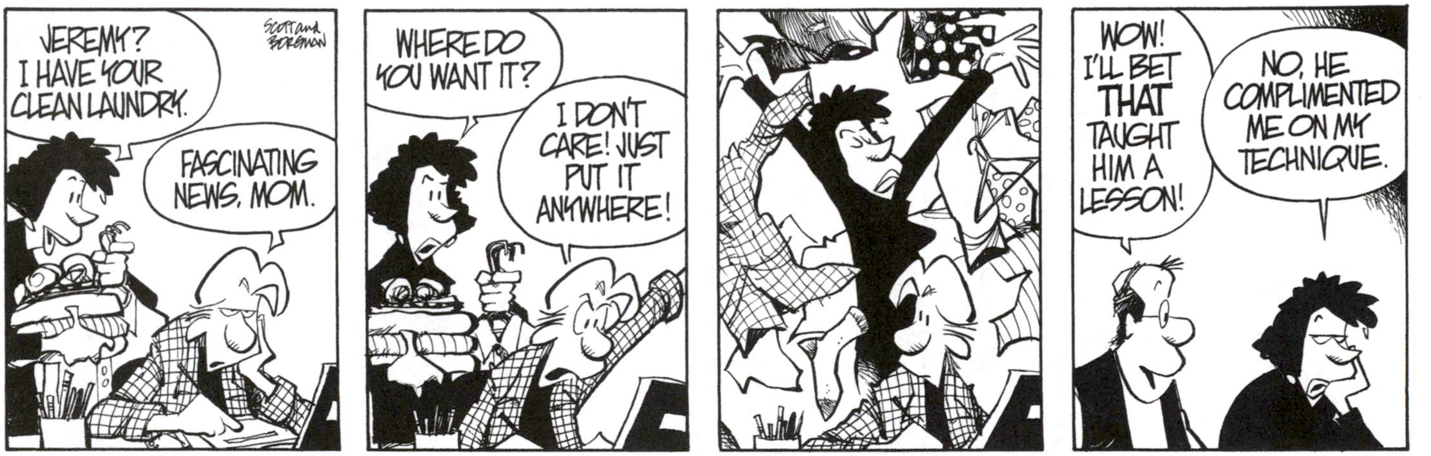
JEREMY? I HAVE YOUR CLEAN LAUNDRY.
FASCINATING NEWS, MOM.
WHERE DO YOU WANT IT?
I DON'T CARE! JUST PUT IT ANYWHERE!
WOW! I'LL BET THAT TAUGHT HIM A LESSON!
NO, HE COMPLIMENTED ME ON MY TECHNIQUE.

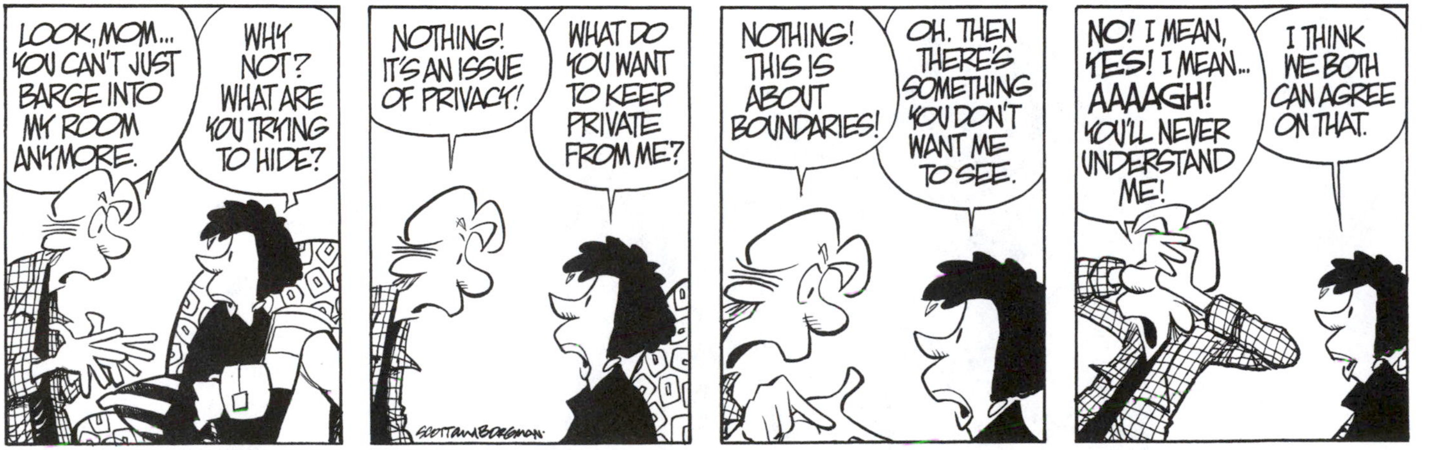
LOOK, MOM... YOU CAN'T JUST BARGE INTO MY ROOM ANYMORE.
WHY NOT? WHAT ARE YOU TRYING TO HIDE?
NOTHING! IT'S AN ISSUE OF PRIVACY!
WHAT DO YOU WANT TO KEEP PRIVATE FROM ME?
NOTHING! THIS IS ABOUT BOUNDARIES!
OH. THEN THERE'S SOMETHING YOU DON'T WANT ME TO SEE.
NO! I MEAN, YES! I MEAN... AAAAGH! YOU'LL NEVER UNDERSTAND ME!
I THINK WE BOTH CAN AGREE ON THAT.

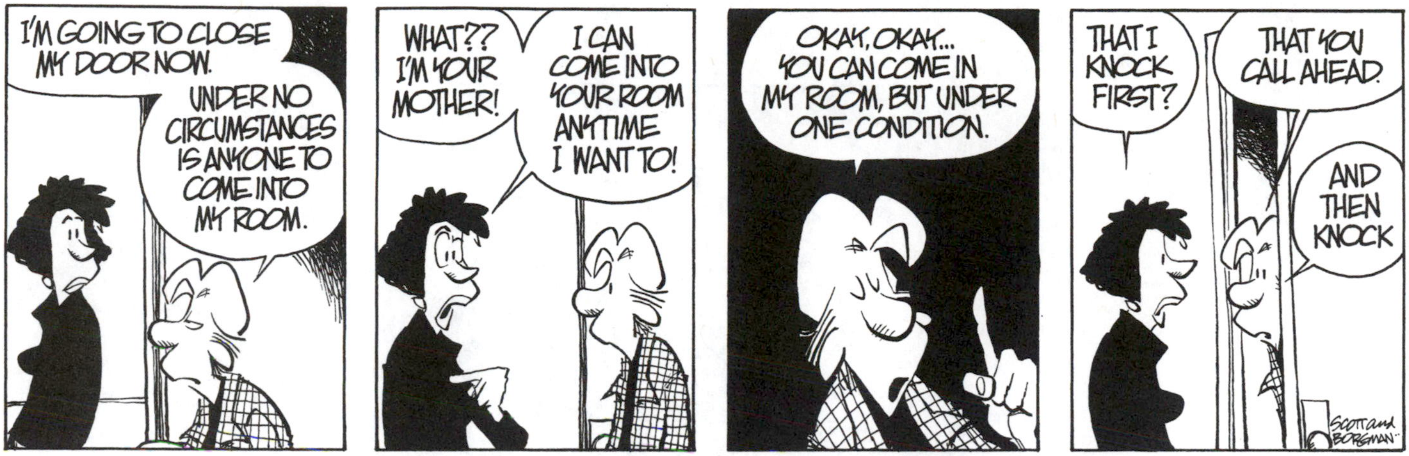
I'M GOING TO CLOSE MY DOOR NOW.
UNDER NO CIRCUMSTANCES IS ANYONE TO COME INTO MY ROOM.
WHAT?? I'M YOUR MOTHER!
I CAN COME INTO YOUR ROOM ANYTIME I WANT TO!
OKAY, OKAY... YOU CAN COME IN MY ROOM, BUT UNDER ONE CONDITION.
THAT I KNOCK FIRST?
THAT YOU CALL AHEAD.
AND THEN KNOCK
SCOTT and BORGMAN

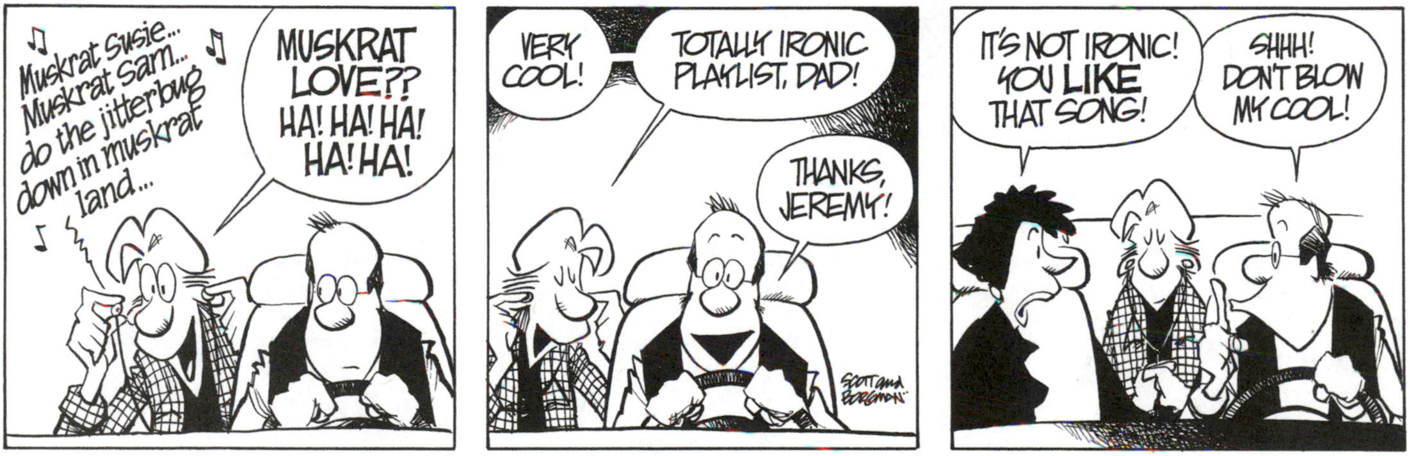
Muskrat Susie... Muskrat Sam... do the jitterbug down in muskrat land...
MUSKRAT LOVE?? HA! HA! HA! HA! HA!
VERY COOL!
TOTALLY IRONIC PLAYLIST, DAD!
THANKS, JEREMY!
SCOTT and BORGMAN
IT'S NOT IRONIC! YOU LIKE THAT SONG!
SHHH! DON'T BLOW MY COOL!

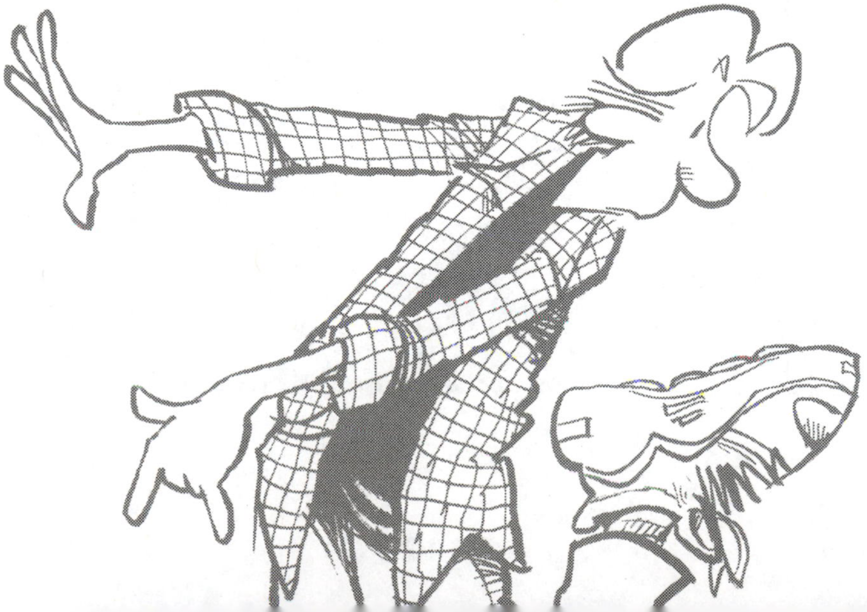

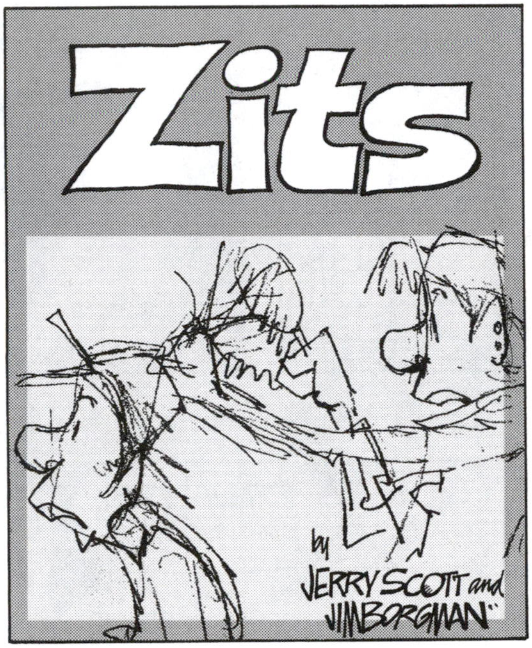
Zits
by JERRY SCOTT and JIM BORGMAN

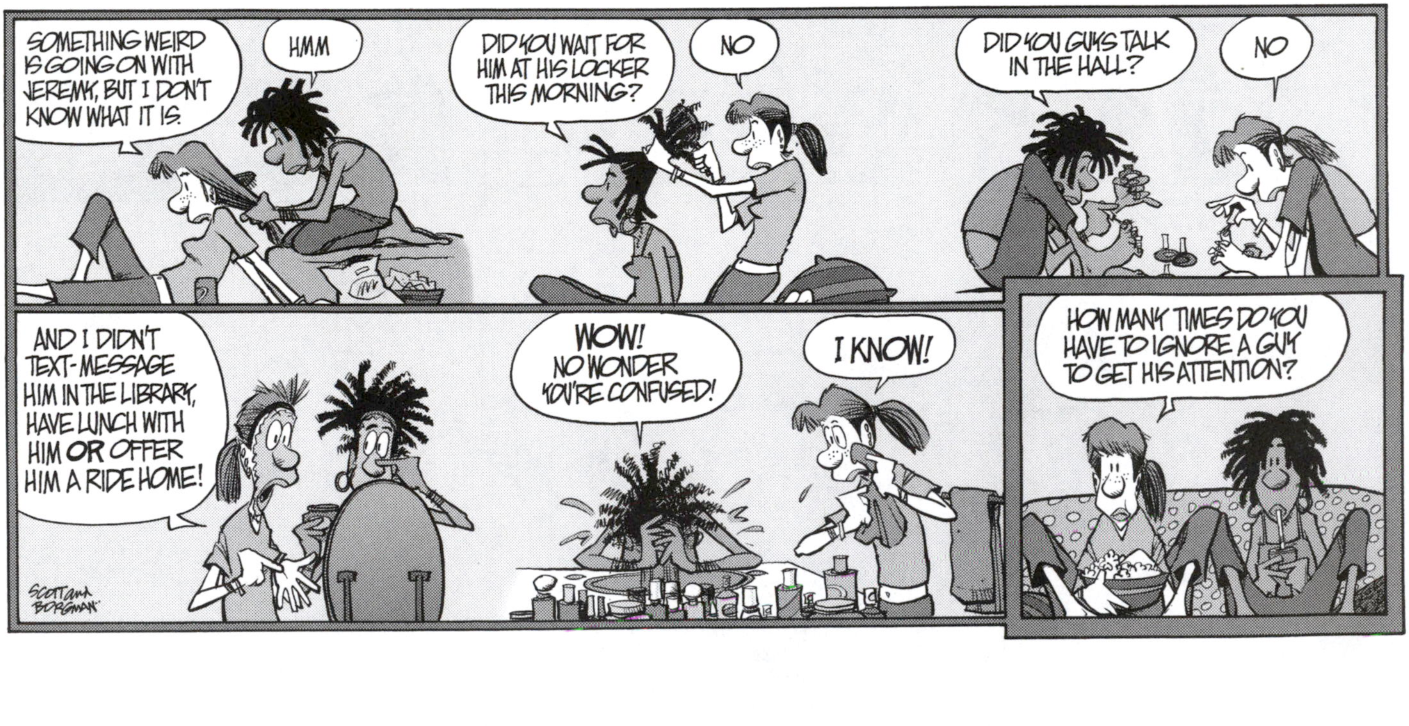
SOMETHING WEIRD IS GOING ON WITH JEREMY, BUT I DON'T KNOW WHAT IT IS.
HMM
DID YOU WAIT FOR HIM AT HIS LOCKER THIS MORNING?
NO
DID YOU GUYS TALK IN THE HALL?
NO
AND I DIDN'T TEXT-MESSAGE HIM IN THE LIBRARY, HAVE LUNCH WITH HIM OR OFFER HIM A RIDE HOME!
WOW! NO WONDER YOU'RE CONFUSED!
I KNOW!
HOW MANY TIMES DO YOU HAVE TO IGNORE A GUY TO GET HIS ATTENTION?

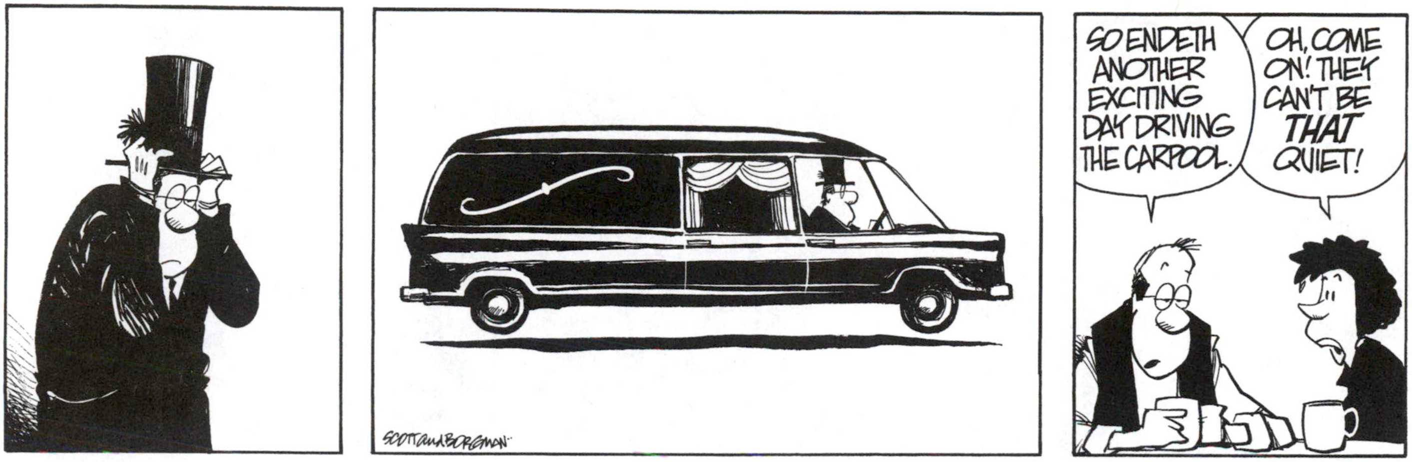
SO ENDETH ANOTHER EXCITING DAY DRIVING THE CARPOOL.
OH, COME ON! THEY CAN'T BE *THAT* QUIET!

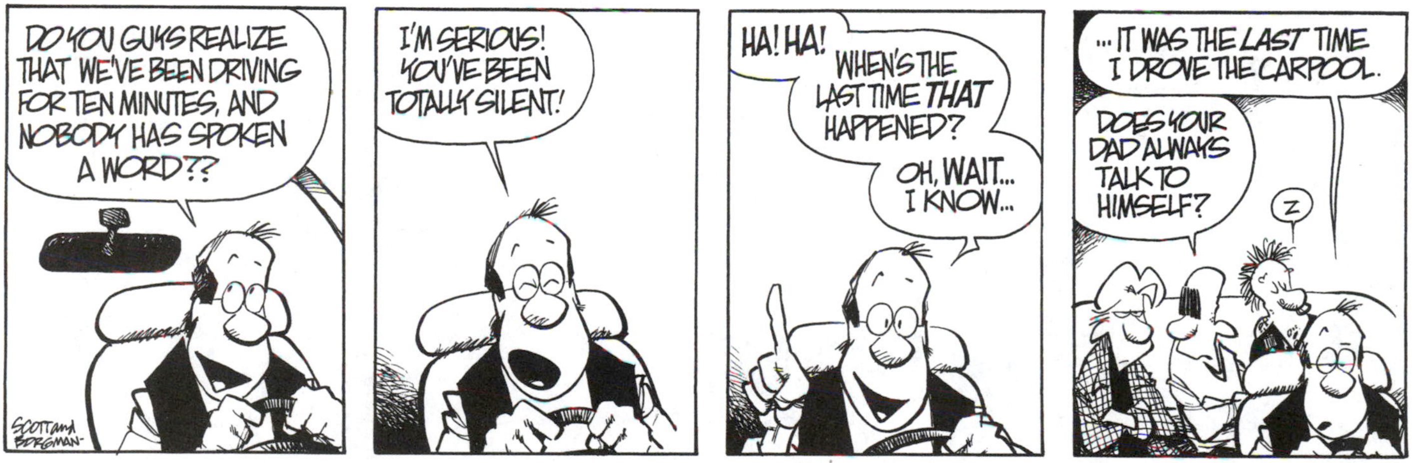
DO YOU GUYS REALIZE THAT WE'VE BEEN DRIVING FOR TEN MINUTES, AND NOBODY HAS SPOKEN A WORD??
I'M SERIOUS! YOU'VE BEEN TOTALLY SILENT!
HA! HA!
WHEN'S THE LAST TIME *THAT* HAPPENED?
OH, WAIT... I KNOW...
...IT WAS THE *LAST* TIME I DROVE THE CARPOOL.
DOES YOUR DAD ALWAYS TALK TO HIMSELF?
Z

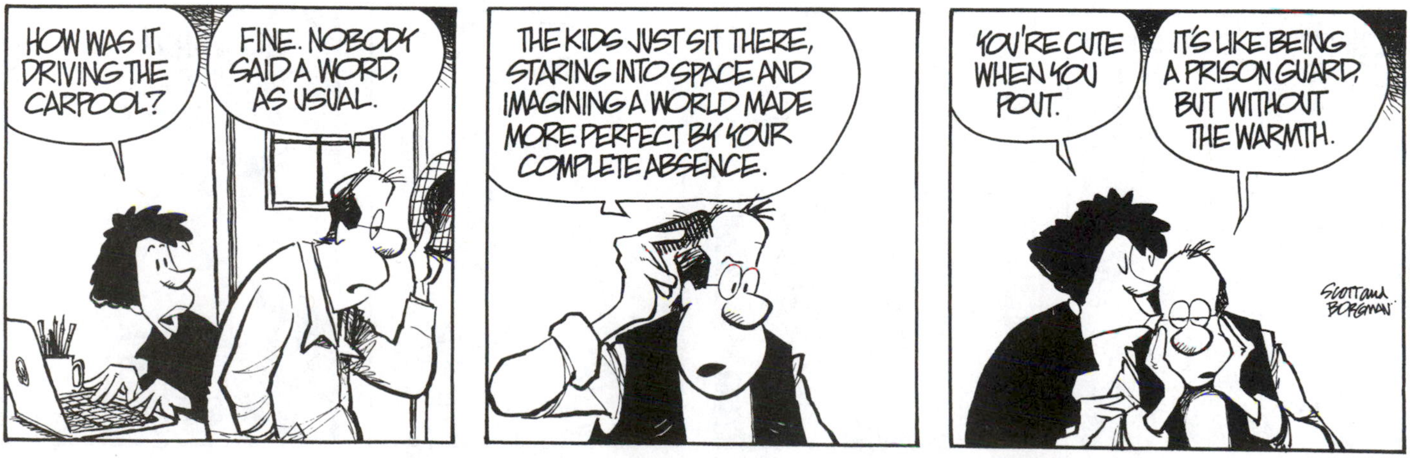
HOW WAS IT DRIVING THE CARPOOL?
FINE. NOBODY SAID A WORD, AS USUAL.
THE KIDS JUST SIT THERE, STARING INTO SPACE AND IMAGINING A WORLD MADE MORE PERFECT BY YOUR COMPLETE ABSENCE.
YOU'RE CUTE WHEN YOU POUT.
IT'S LIKE BEING A PRISON GUARD, BUT WITHOUT THE WARMTH.

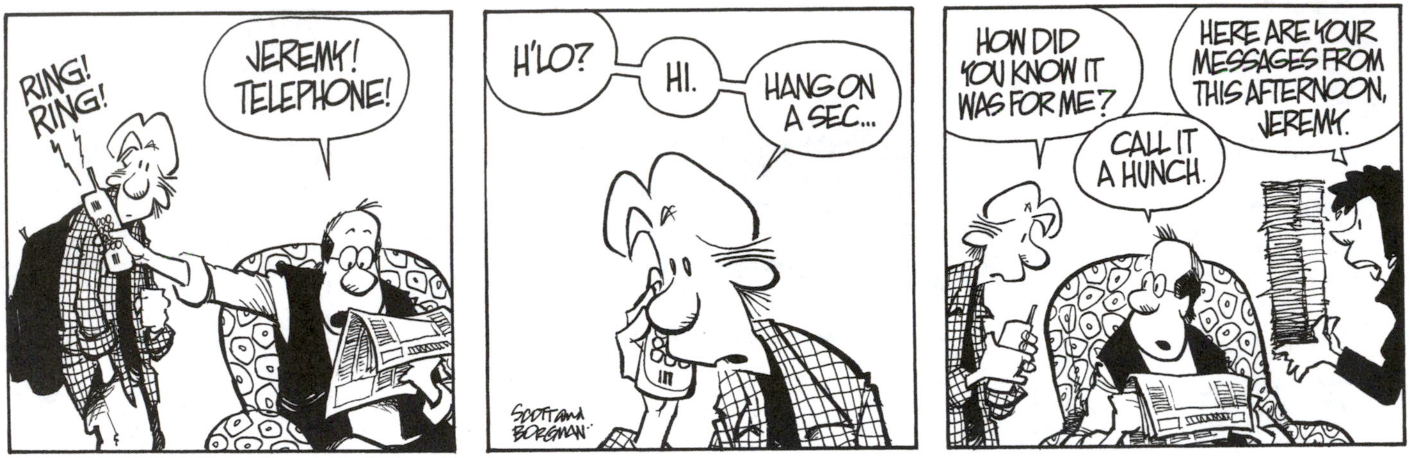
RING! RING!
JEREMY! TELEPHONE!
H'LO?
HI.
HANG ON A SEC...
HOW DID YOU KNOW IT WAS FOR ME?
CALL IT A HUNCH.
HERE ARE YOUR MESSAGES FROM THIS AFTERNOON, JEREMY.

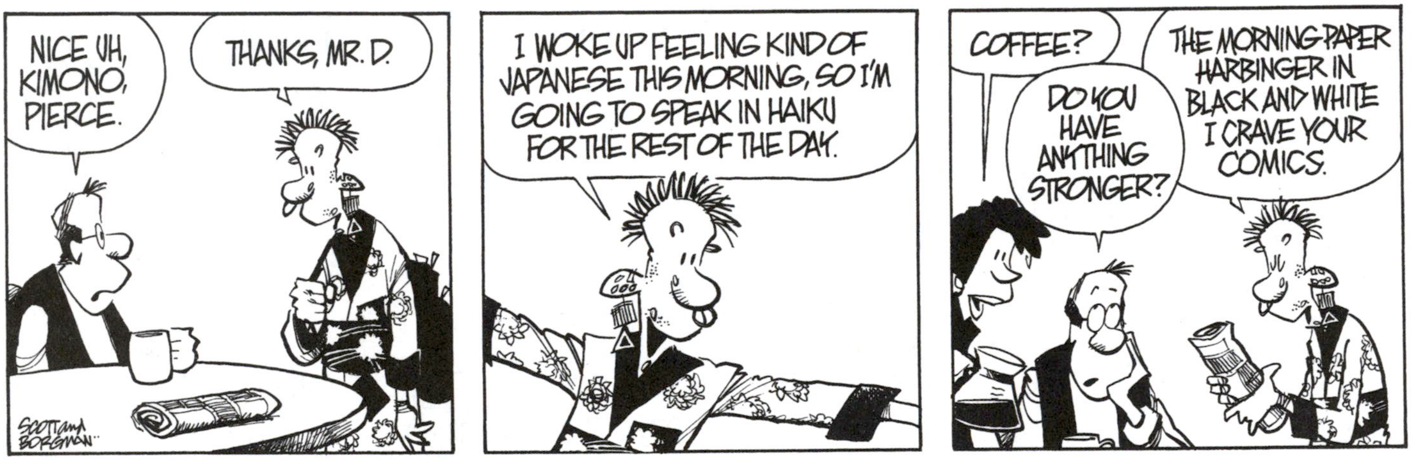
NICE UH, KIMONO, PIERCE.
THANKS, MR. D.
I WOKE UP FEELING KIND OF JAPANESE THIS MORNING, SO I'M GOING TO SPEAK IN HAIKU FOR THE REST OF THE DAY.
COFFEE?
DO YOU HAVE ANYTHING STRONGER?
THE MORNING PAPER HARBINGER IN BLACK AND WHITE I CRAVE YOUR COMICS.

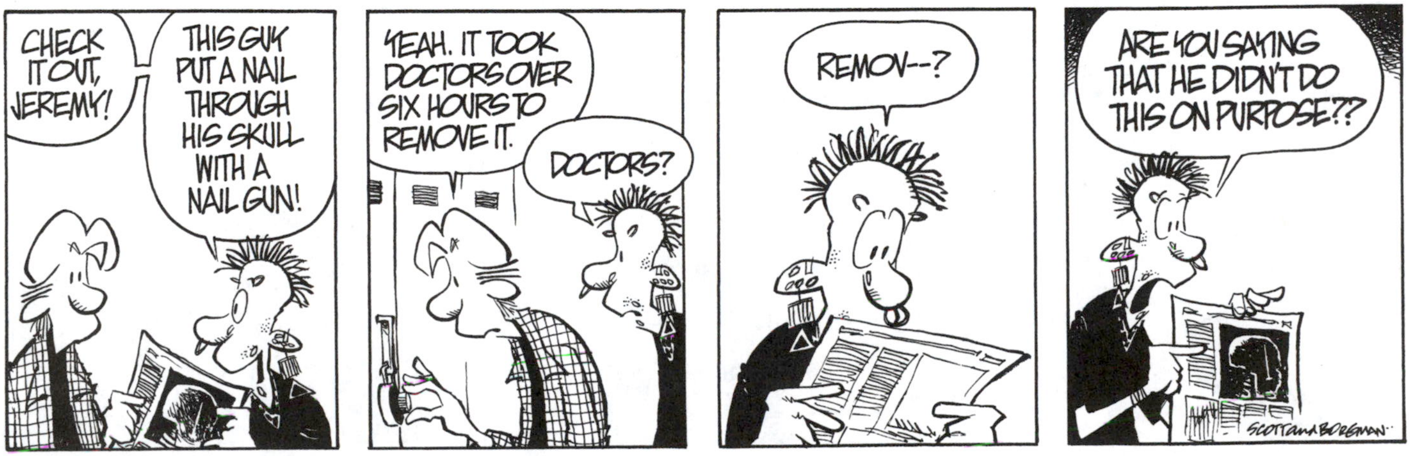
CHECK IT OUT, JEREMY!
THIS GUY PUT A NAIL THROUGH HIS SKULL WITH A NAIL GUN!
YEAH. IT TOOK DOCTORS OVER SIX HOURS TO REMOVE IT.
DOCTORS?
REMOV--?
ARE YOU SAYING THAT HE DIDN'T DO THIS ON PURPOSE??

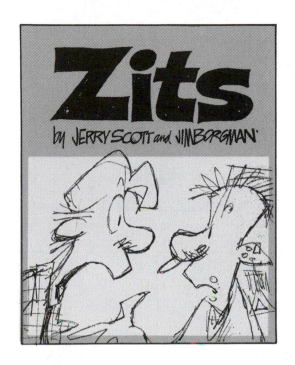

(YAWN!) I DON'T KNOW WHY I'M ALWAYS SO TIRED.

DUH. YOU PROBABLY NEED TO GET MORE REST, LIKE ME.

HOW MUCH SLEEP DO YOU GET, PIERCE?

OH, I AVERAGE ABOUT SIXTEEN HOURS.

A DAY??

YEAH. NINE AT NIGHT, AND AROUND SEVEN AT SCHOOL.

Scott and Borgman

HOW CAN YOU SLEEP SEVEN HOURS AT SCHOOL WITHOUT GETTING CAUGHT?

SIMPLE....

IF YOU LOOK CLOSELY, YOU'LL SEE THAT I'VE HAD EXACT DUPLICATES OF MY IRISES TATTOOED ON MY EYELIDS WHICH MAKE ME APPEAR TO BE AWAKE WHILE MY EYES ARE ACTUALLY SHUT.

AND THAT WORKS??

WELL, I WON'T SAY MY DRIVER'S ED GRADES HAVEN'T SUFFERED....

STUDENT DRIVER

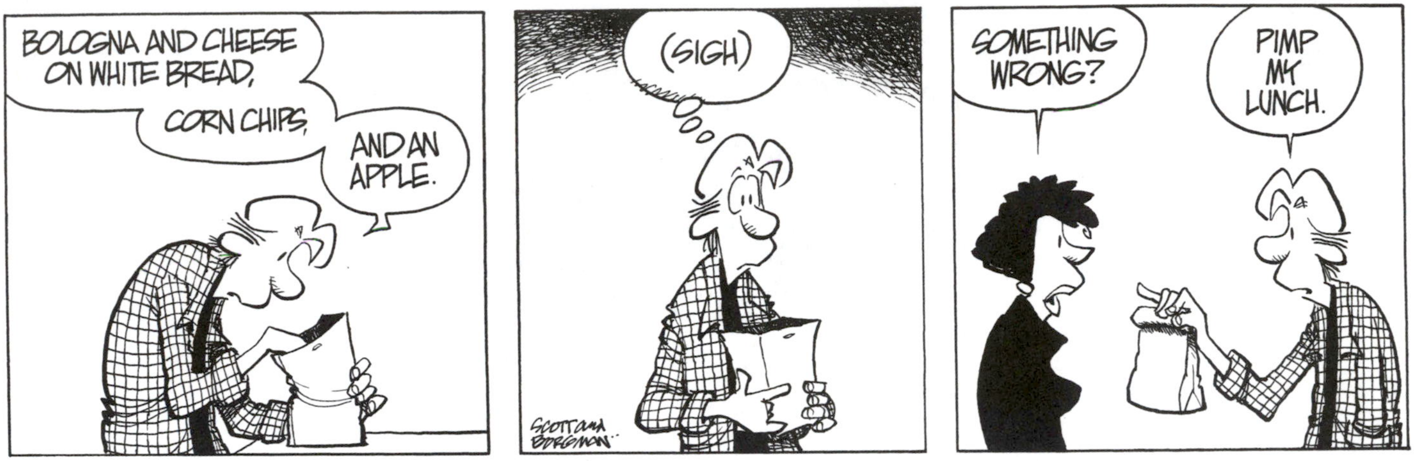
BOLOGNA AND CHEESE ON WHITE BREAD,
CORN CHIPS,
AND AN APPLE.
(SIGH)
SOMETHING WRONG?
PIMP MY LUNCH.

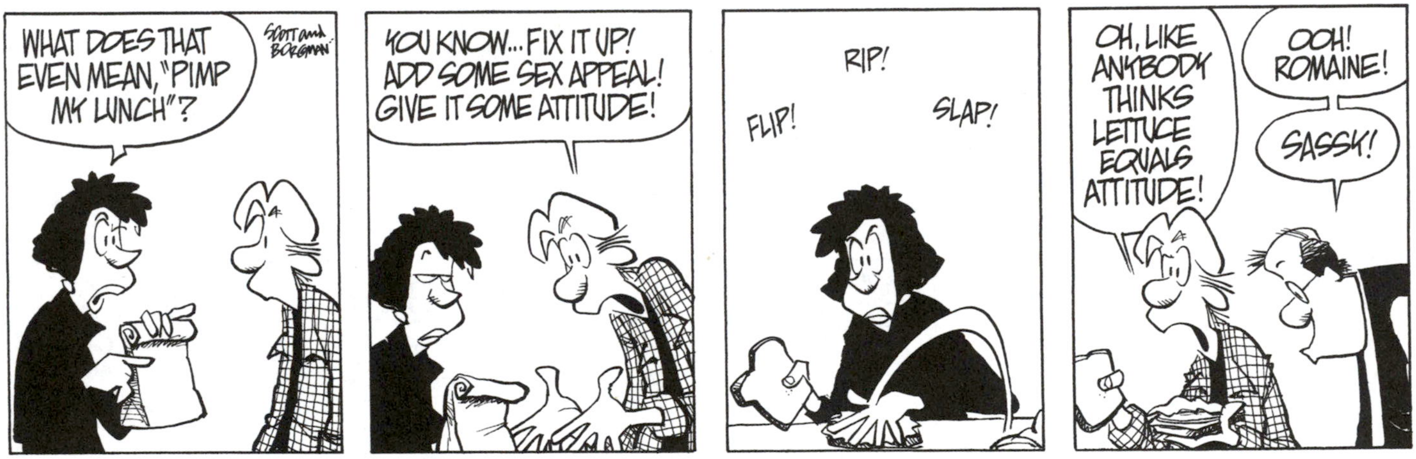
WHAT DOES THAT EVEN MEAN, "PIMP MY LUNCH"?
YOU KNOW... FIX IT UP! ADD SOME SEX APPEAL! GIVE IT SOME ATTITUDE!
FLIP!
RIP!
SLAP!
OH, LIKE ANYBODY THINKS LETTUCE EQUALS ATTITUDE!
OOH! ROMAINE!
SASSY!

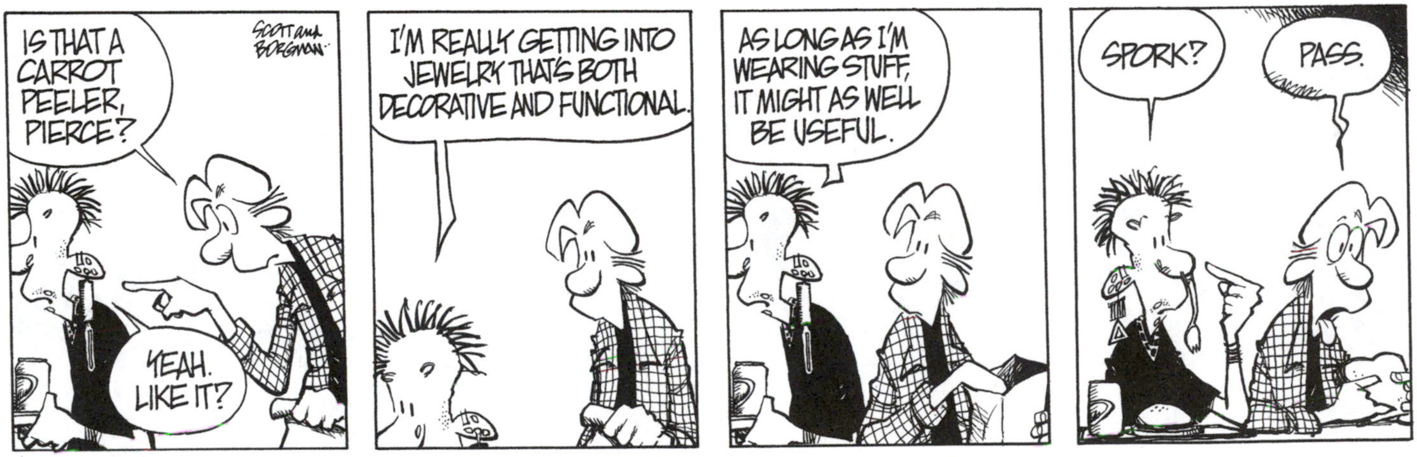
IS THAT A CARROT PEELER, PIERCE?
YEAH. LIKE IT?
I'M REALLY GETTING INTO JEWELRY THAT'S BOTH DECORATIVE AND FUNCTIONAL.
AS LONG AS I'M WEARING STUFF, IT MIGHT AS WELL BE USEFUL.
SPORK?
PASS.

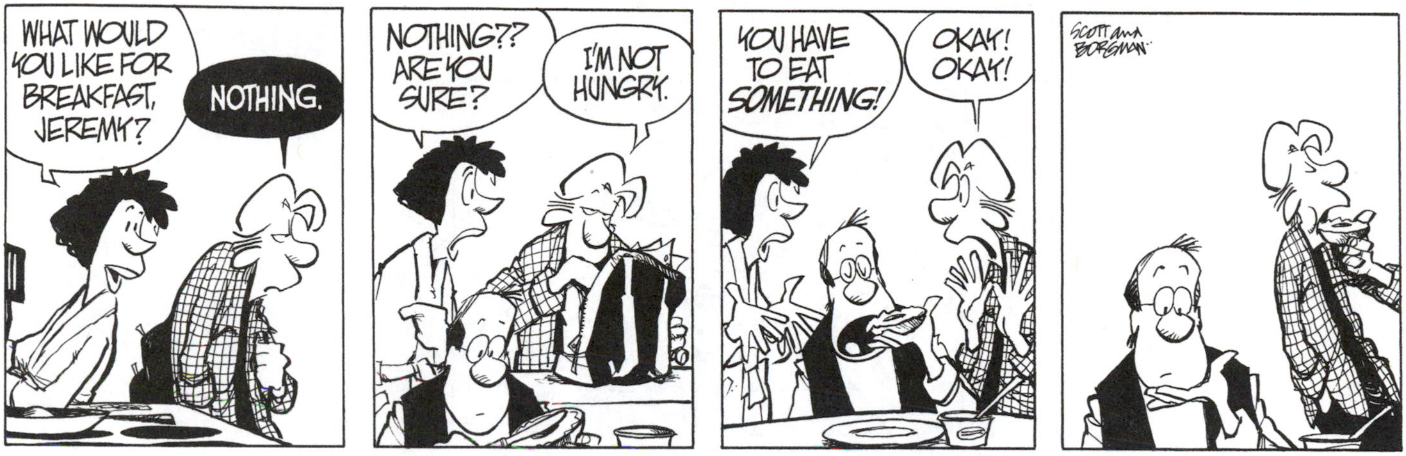
WHAT WOULD YOU LIKE FOR BREAKFAST, JEREMY?
NOTHING.
NOTHING?? ARE YOU SURE?
I'M NOT HUNGRY.
YOU HAVE TO EAT SOMETHING!
OKAY! OKAY!
SCOTT and BORGMAN

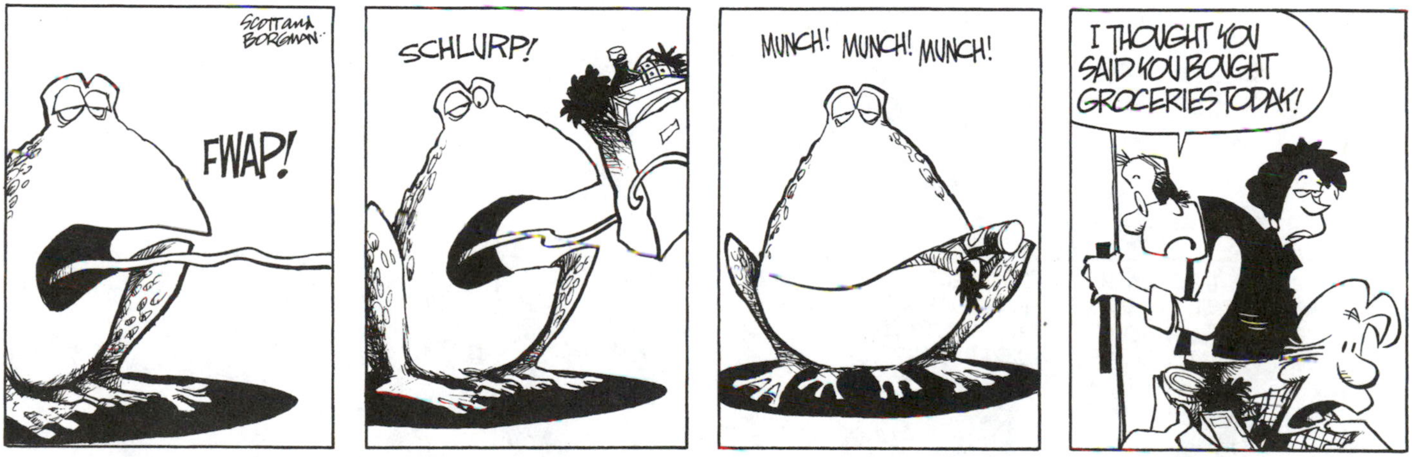
SCOTT and BORGMAN
FWAP!
SCHLURP!
MUNCH! MUNCH! MUNCH!
I THOUGHT YOU SAID YOU BOUGHT GROCERIES TODAY!

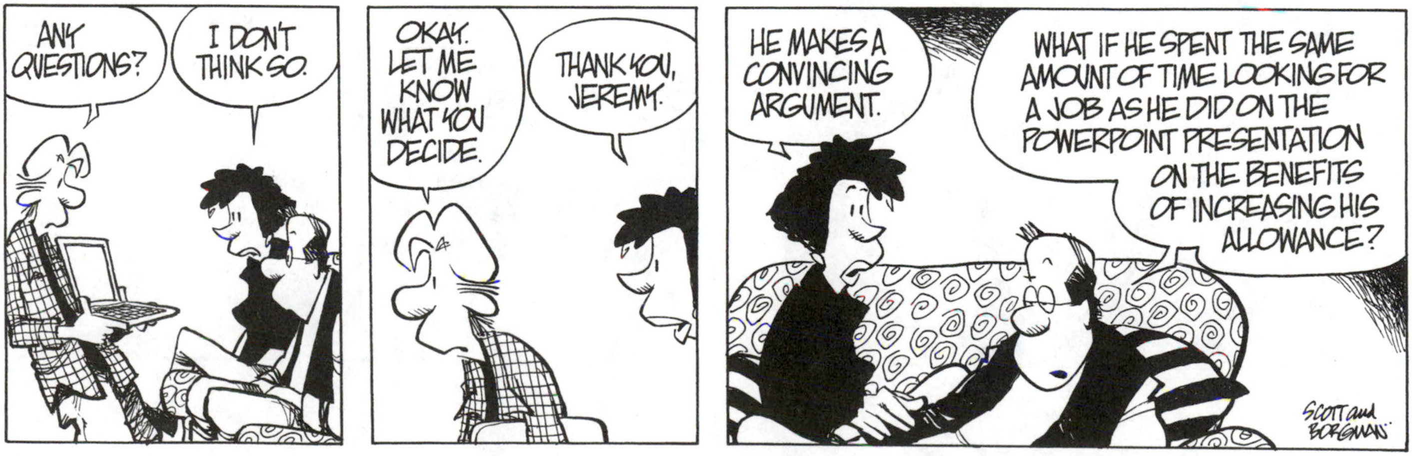
ANY QUESTIONS?
I DON'T THINK SO.
OKAY. LET ME KNOW WHAT YOU DECIDE.
THANK YOU, JEREMY.
HE MAKES A CONVINCING ARGUMENT.
WHAT IF HE SPENT THE SAME AMOUNT OF TIME LOOKING FOR A JOB AS HE DID ON THE POWERPOINT PRESENTATION ON THE BENEFITS OF INCREASING HIS ALLOWANCE?
SCOTT and BORGMAN

Zits
JERRY SCOTT and
JIM BORGMAN

Gender
A HANDY GUIDE TO THE SPECIES
SCOTT and BORGMAN
FEMALE
REMEMBER THAT GIRL WHO WALKED BY OUR ALGEBRA CLASS TWO WEEKS AGO?
THE ONE WITH THE STRAIGHT BROWN HAIR AND THE CUTE YELLOW SHOES? YEAH.
MALE
REMEMBER THE GUY WHO SITS BESIDE YOU IN HISTORY, ECON AND ENGLISH?
NO
FEMALE
YOU LOOK COLD! I'LL LET YOU WEAR MY SWEATSHIRT IF I CAN WEAR YOUR BOOTS.
OKAY!
MALE
YOU LOOK COLD.
FEMALE
THIS SANDWICH IS INCREDIBLE! WANT A BITE?
SURE!
MALE
THIS SANDWICH IS INCREDIBLE!
LOSER!
FEMALE
I'M BORED. CAN I BRUSH YOUR HAIR?
MALE
I'M BORED. CAN I SHAVE YOUR HEAD?

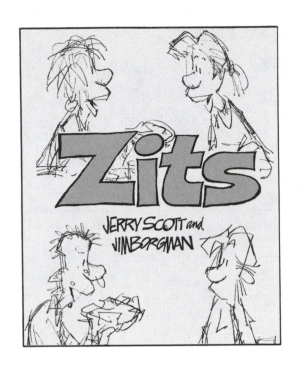

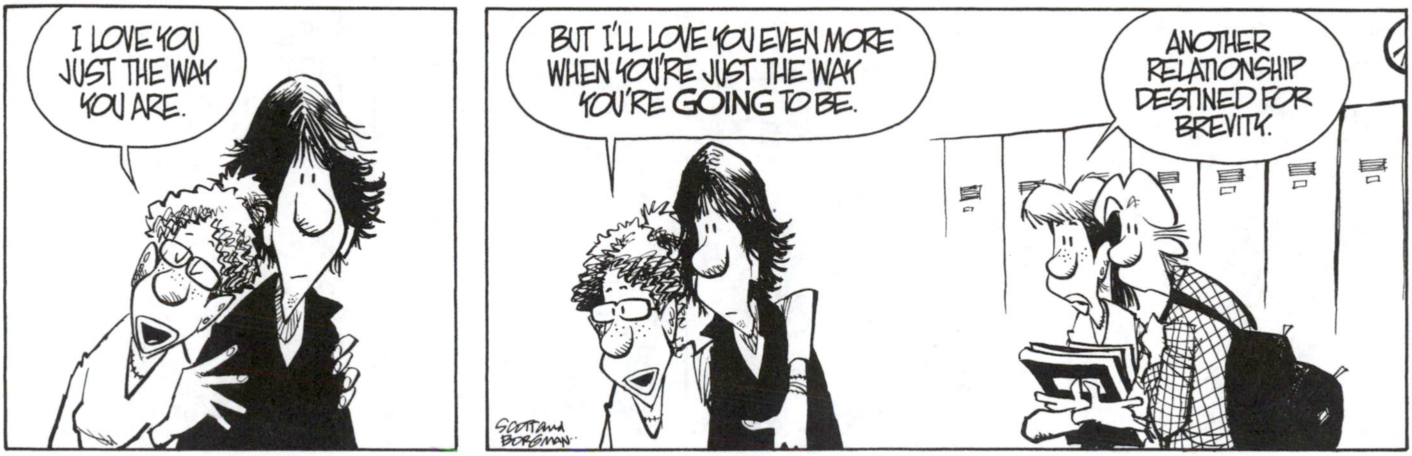
I LOVE YOU JUST THE WAY YOU ARE.
BUT I'LL LOVE YOU EVEN MORE WHEN YOU'RE JUST THE WAY YOU'RE **GOING** TO BE.
ANOTHER RELATIONSHIP DESTINED FOR BREVITY.

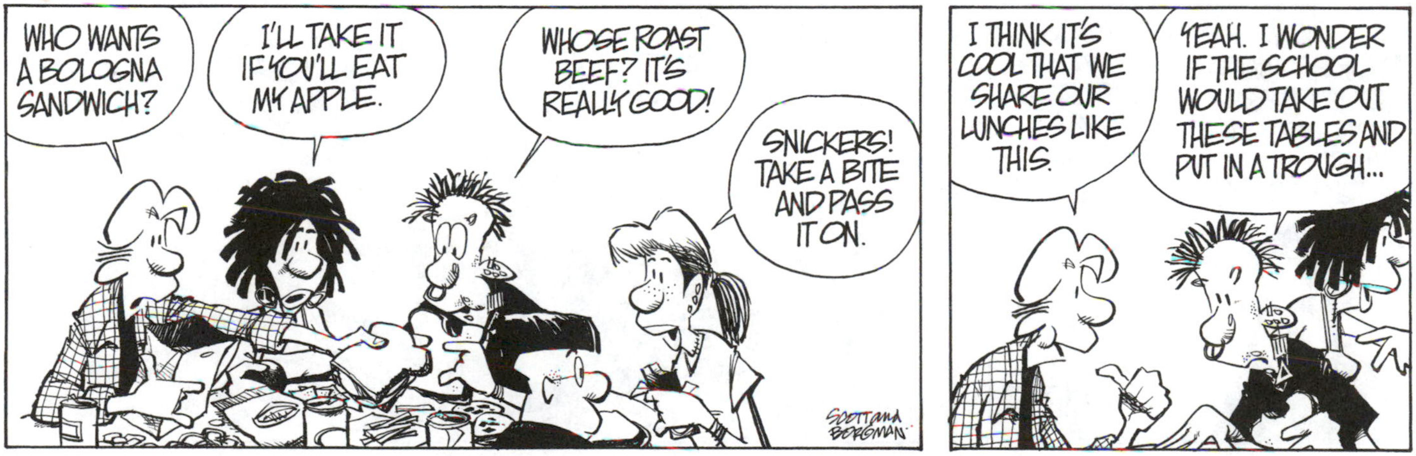
WHO WANTS A BOLOGNA SANDWICH?
I'LL TAKE IT IF YOU'LL EAT MY APPLE.
WHOSE ROAST BEEF? IT'S REALLY GOOD!
SNICKERS! TAKE A BITE AND PASS IT ON.
I THINK IT'S COOL THAT WE SHARE OUR LUNCHES LIKE THIS.
YEAH. I WONDER IF THE SCHOOL WOULD TAKE OUT THESE TABLES AND PUT IN A TROUGH...

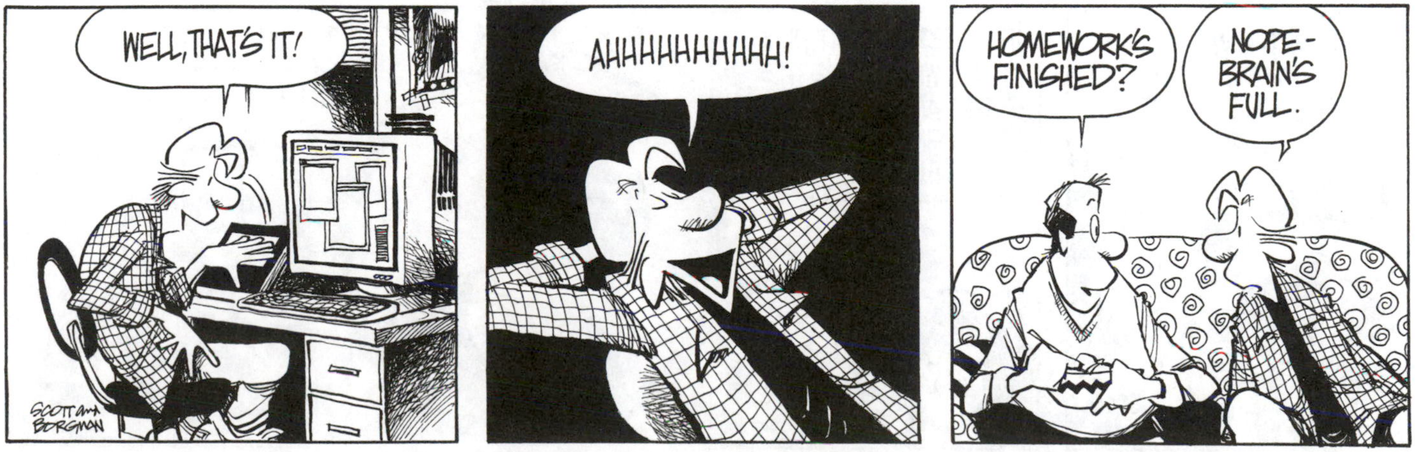
WELL, THAT'S IT!
AHHHHHHHHHH!
HOMEWORK'S FINISHED?
NOPE- BRAIN'S FULL.

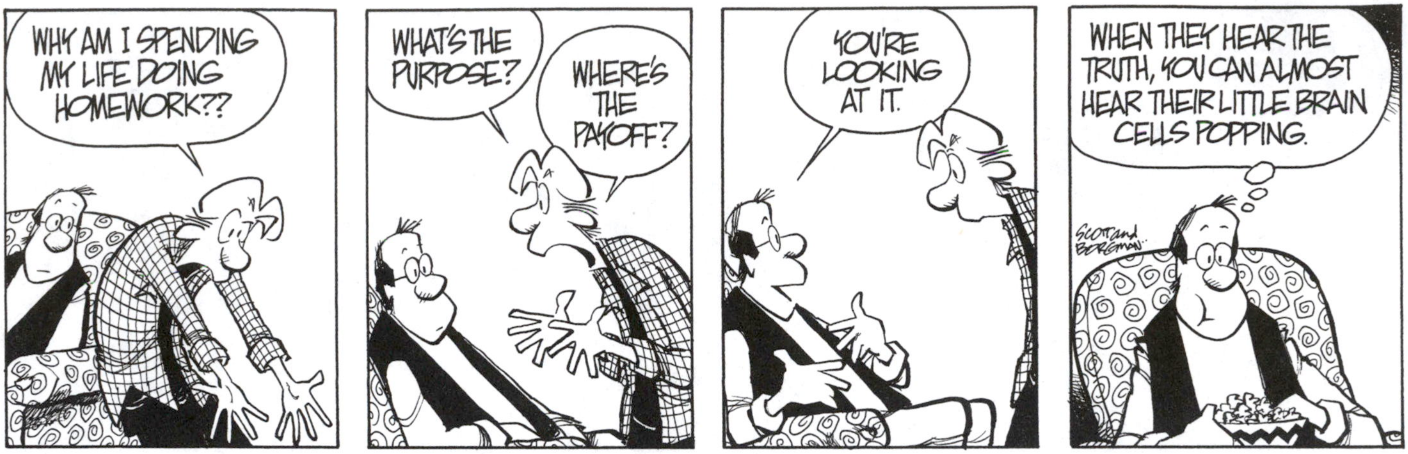
WHY AM I SPENDING MY LIFE DOING HOMEWORK??
WHAT'S THE PURPOSE?
WHERE'S THE PAYOFF?
YOU'RE LOOKING AT IT.
WHEN THEY HEAR THE TRUTH, YOU CAN ALMOST HEAR THEIR LITTLE BRAIN CELLS POPPING.

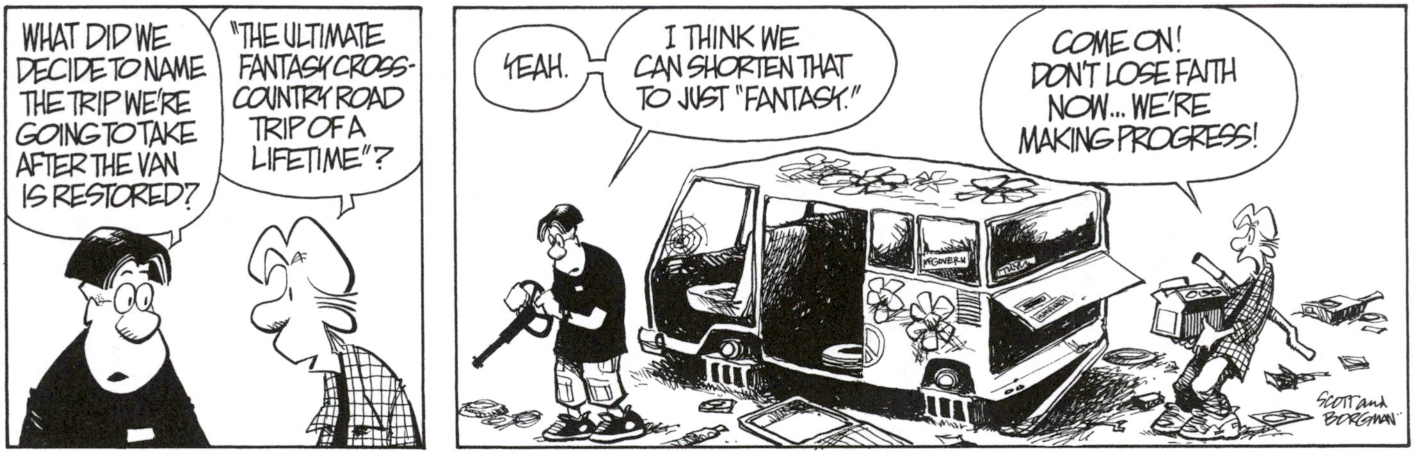
WHAT DID WE DECIDE TO NAME THE TRIP WE'RE GOING TO TAKE AFTER THE VAN IS RESTORED?
"THE ULTIMATE FANTASY CROSS-COUNTRY ROAD TRIP OF A LIFETIME"?
YEAH.
I THINK WE CAN SHORTEN THAT TO JUST "FANTASY."
COME ON! DON'T LOSE FAITH NOW... WE'RE MAKING PROGRESS!

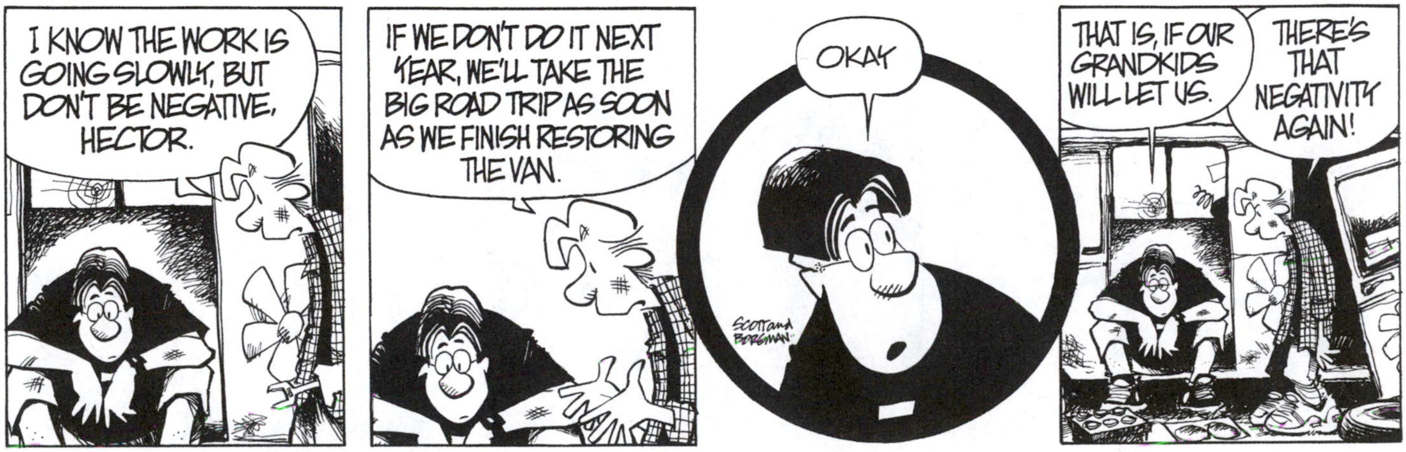
I KNOW THE WORK IS GOING SLOWLY, BUT DON'T BE NEGATIVE, HECTOR.
IF WE DON'T DO IT NEXT YEAR, WE'LL TAKE THE BIG ROAD TRIP AS SOON AS WE FINISH RESTORING THE VAN.
OKAY
THAT IS, IF OUR GRANDKIDS WILL LET US.
THERE'S THAT NEGATIVITY AGAIN!

Zits
by
JERRY SCOTT and
JIM BORGMAN

YOU LOOK EMOTIONALLY DRAINED.
WHEN YOU ONLY GET 4 MINUTES BETWEEN CLASSES YOU HAVE TO PACK IN A LOT.
SCOTT and BORGMAN

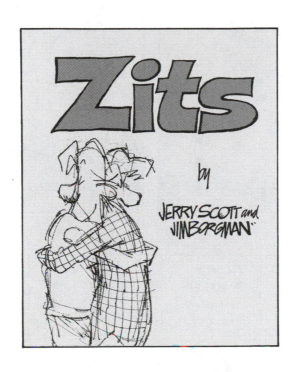

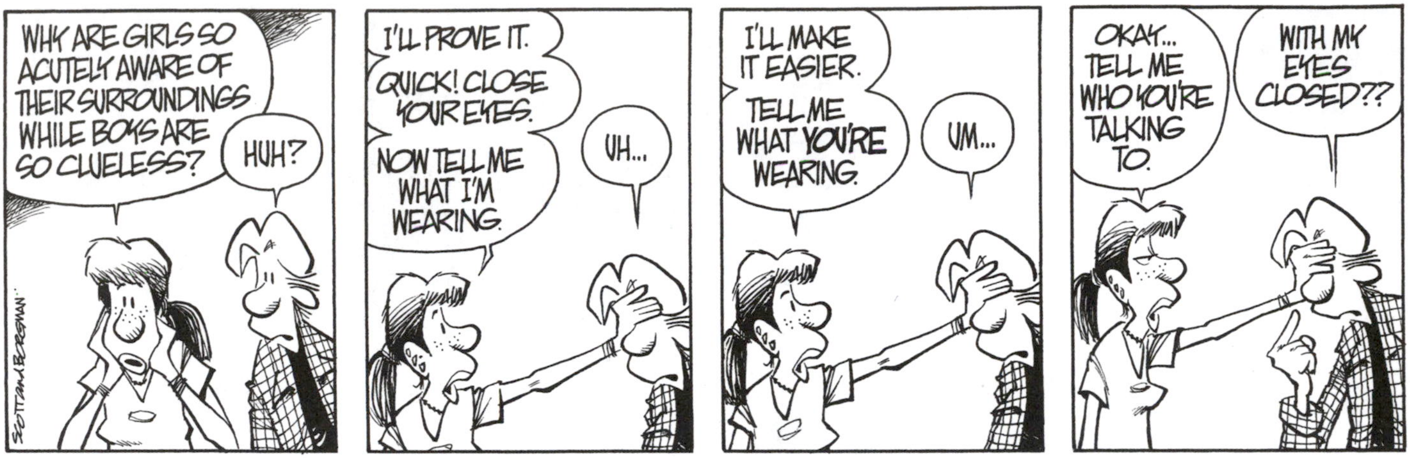
WHY ARE GIRLS SO ACUTELY AWARE OF THEIR SURROUNDINGS WHILE BOYS ARE SO CLUELESS?
HUH?
I'LL PROVE IT.
QUICK! CLOSE YOUR EYES.
NOW TELL ME WHAT I'M WEARING.
UH...
I'LL MAKE IT EASIER.
TELL ME WHAT YOU'RE WEARING.
UM...
OKAY... TELL ME WHO YOU'RE TALKING TO.
WITH MY EYES CLOSED??

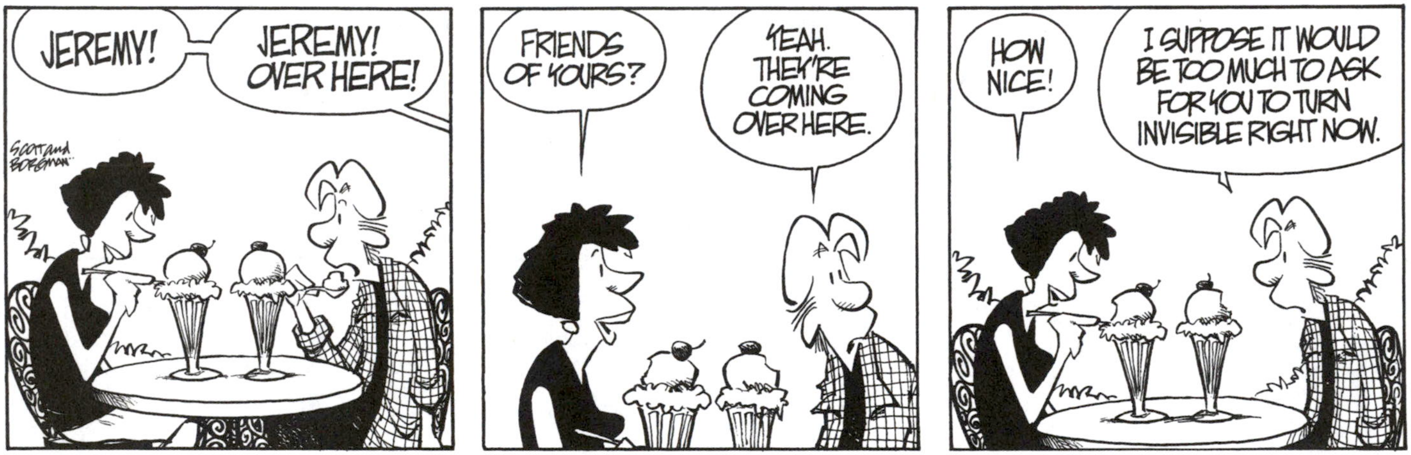
JEREMY!
JEREMY! OVER HERE!
FRIENDS OF YOURS?
YEAH. THEY'RE COMING OVER HERE.
HOW NICE!
I SUPPOSE IT WOULD BE TOO MUCH TO ASK FOR YOU TO TURN INVISIBLE RIGHT NOW.

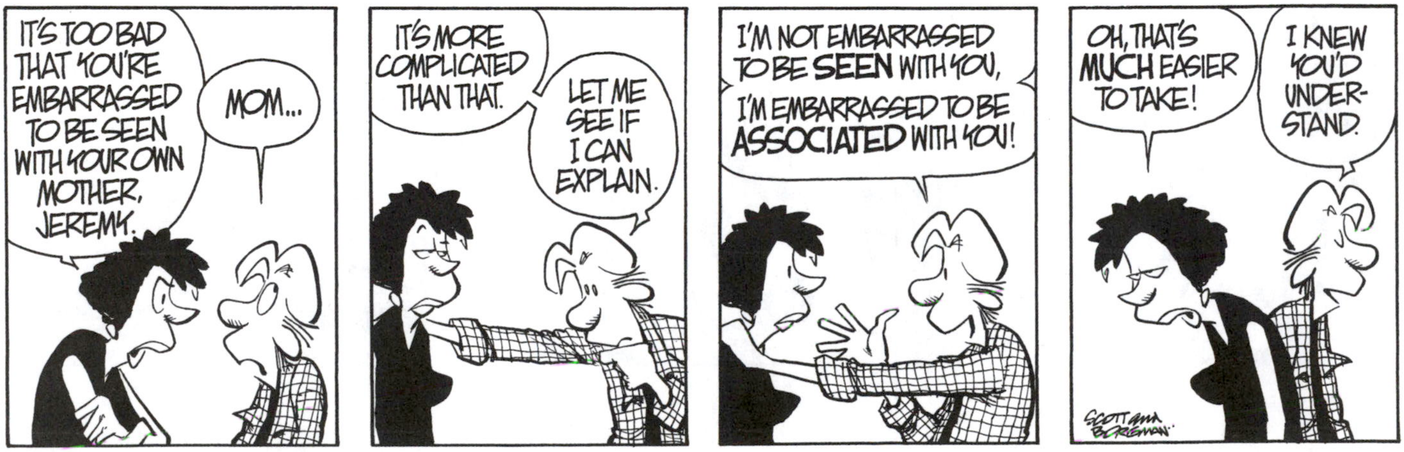
IT'S TOO BAD THAT YOU'RE EMBARRASSED TO BE SEEN WITH YOUR OWN MOTHER, JEREMY.
MOM...
IT'S MORE COMPLICATED THAN THAT.
LET ME SEE IF I CAN EXPLAIN.
I'M NOT EMBARRASSED TO BE SEEN WITH YOU,
I'M EMBARRASSED TO BE ASSOCIATED WITH YOU!
OH, THAT'S MUCH EASIER TO TAKE!
I KNEW YOU'D UNDERSTAND.

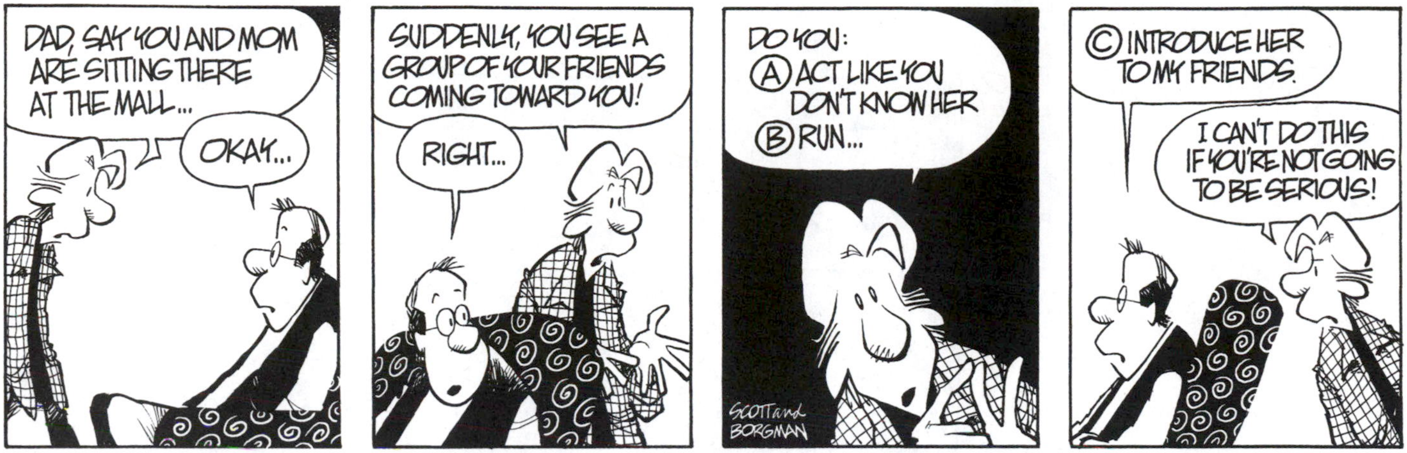
DAD, SAY YOU AND MOM ARE SITTING THERE AT THE MALL...
OKAY...
SUDDENLY, YOU SEE A GROUP OF YOUR FRIENDS COMING TOWARD YOU!
RIGHT...
DO YOU: (A) ACT LIKE YOU DON'T KNOW HER (B) RUN...
SCOTT and BORGMAN
(C) INTRODUCE HER TO MY FRIENDS.
I CAN'T DO THIS IF YOU'RE NOT GOING TO BE SERIOUS!

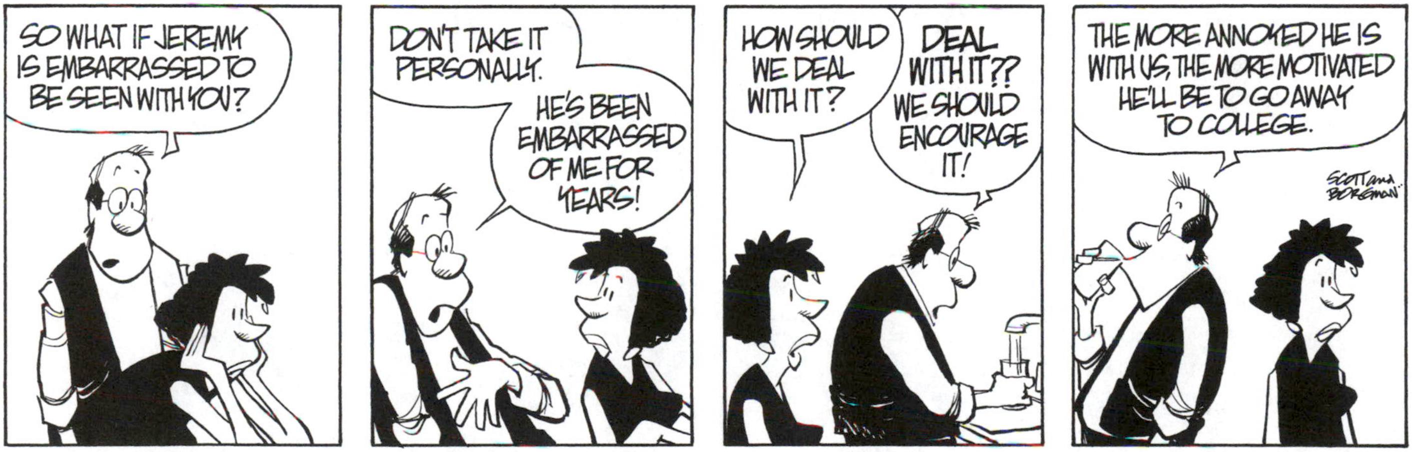
SO WHAT IF JEREMY IS EMBARRASSED TO BE SEEN WITH YOU?
DON'T TAKE IT PERSONALLY.
HE'S BEEN EMBARRASSED OF ME FOR YEARS!
HOW SHOULD WE DEAL WITH IT?
DEAL WITH IT?? WE SHOULD ENCOURAGE IT!
THE MORE ANNOYED HE IS WITH US, THE MORE MOTIVATED HE'LL BE TO GO AWAY TO COLLEGE.
SCOTT and BORGMAN

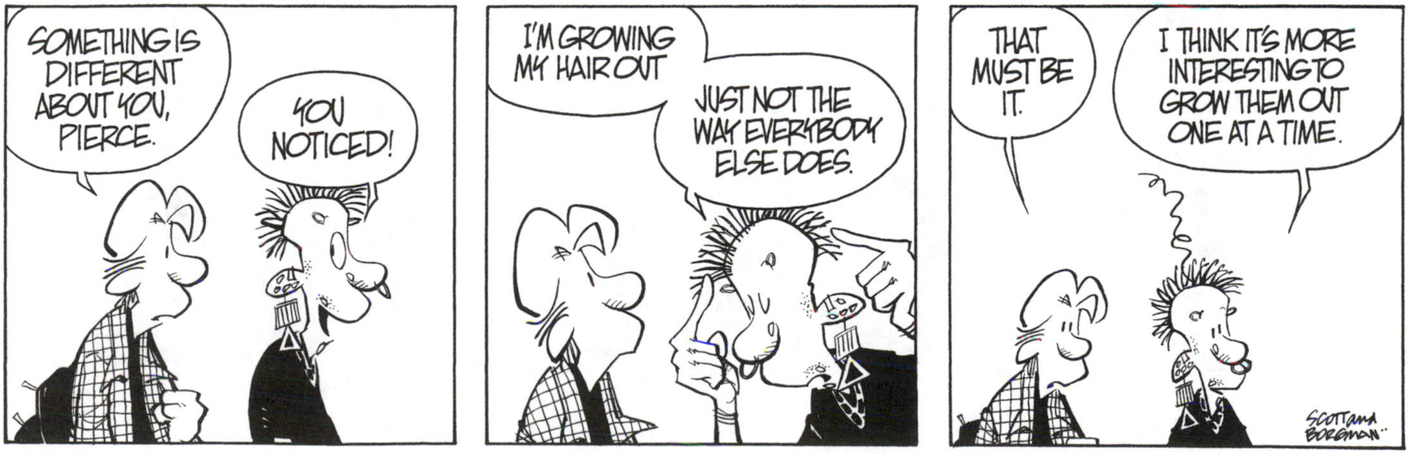
SOMETHING IS DIFFERENT ABOUT YOU, PIERCE.
YOU NOTICED!
I'M GROWING MY HAIR OUT
JUST NOT THE WAY EVERYBODY ELSE DOES.
THAT MUST BE IT.
I THINK IT'S MORE INTERESTING TO GROW THEM OUT ONE AT A TIME.
SCOTT and BORGMAN

Zits
by
JERRY SCOTT and
JIM BORGMAN
RING! RING!
H'LO?
HI MOM. IT'S ME.
JEREMY? WHERE ARE YOU?
ON MY WAY TO SCHOOL! WHERE DO YOU THINK?
SCH-- WAIT... WHAT TIME IS IT?
7:30
OH MY GOSH! WE OVERSLEPT!
NOBODY MADE YOUR BREAKFAST, OR FIXED YOUR LUNCH, OR GOT YOU OUT THE DOOR ON TIME, OR--
MOBY GRAPE
MOM! RELAX! I DID IT MYSELF.
I'M FINE.
SEE YOU LATER.
SCOTT and BORGMAN
ARE YOU OKAY?
WHAT'S THE WORD FOR FEELING GUILTY, RELIEVED, PROUD AND OBSOLETE ALL AT THE SAME TIME?

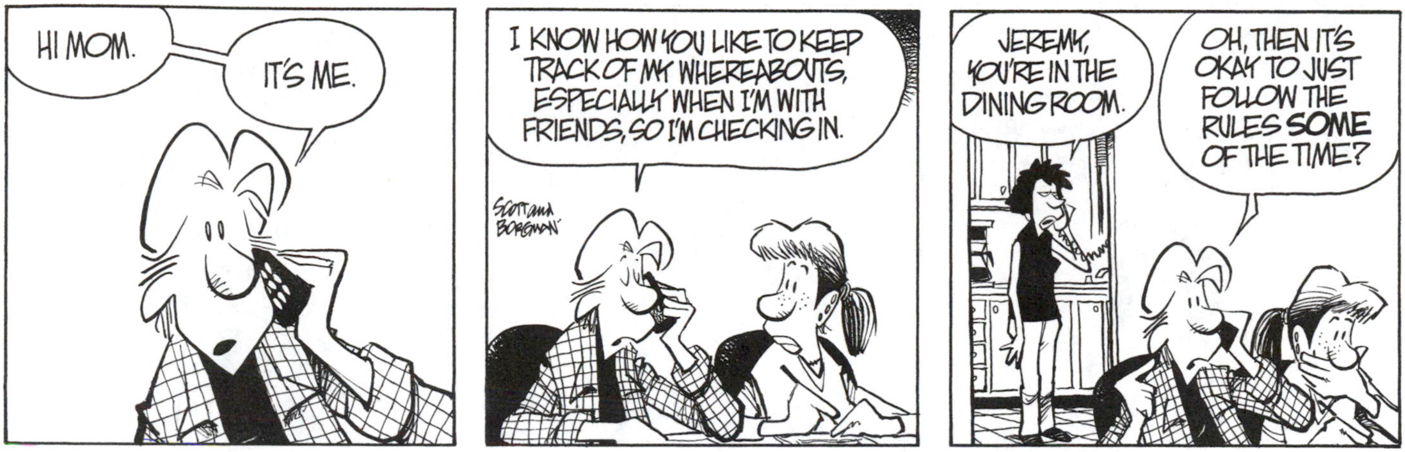
HI MOM.
IT'S ME.
I KNOW HOW YOU LIKE TO KEEP TRACK OF MY WHEREABOUTS, ESPECIALLY WHEN I'M WITH FRIENDS, SO I'M CHECKING IN.
SCOTT and BORGMAN
JEREMY, YOU'RE IN THE DINING ROOM.
OH, THEN IT'S OKAY TO JUST FOLLOW THE RULES **SOME** OF THE TIME?

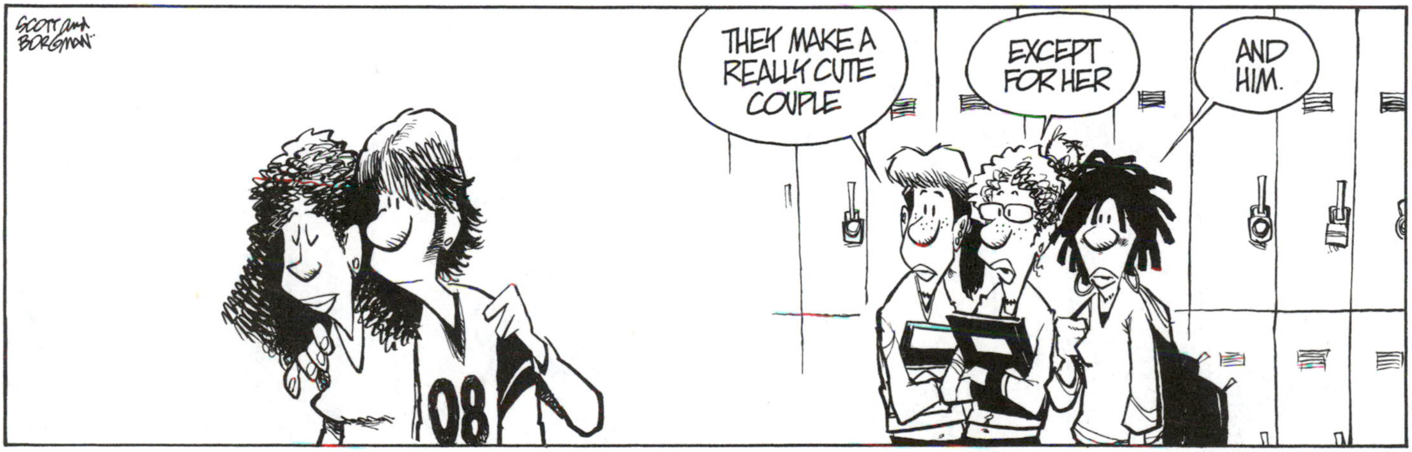
SCOTT and BORGMAN
THEY MAKE A REALLY CUTE COUPLE
EXCEPT FOR HER
AND HIM.
08

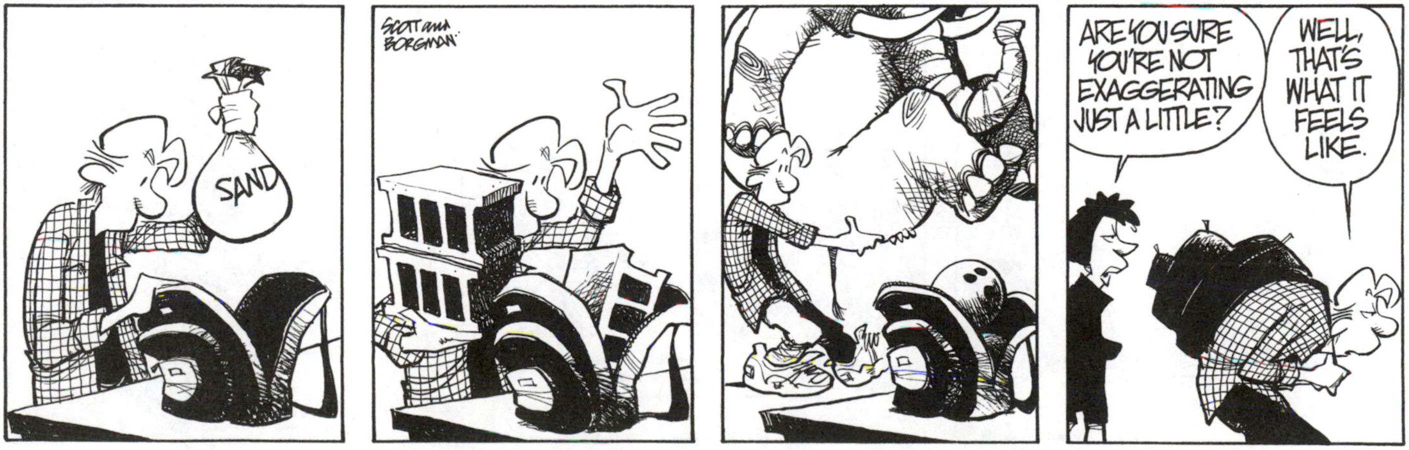
SAND
SCOTT and BORGMAN
ARE YOU SURE YOU'RE NOT EXAGGERATING JUST A LITTLE?
WELL, THAT'S WHAT IT FEELS LIKE.

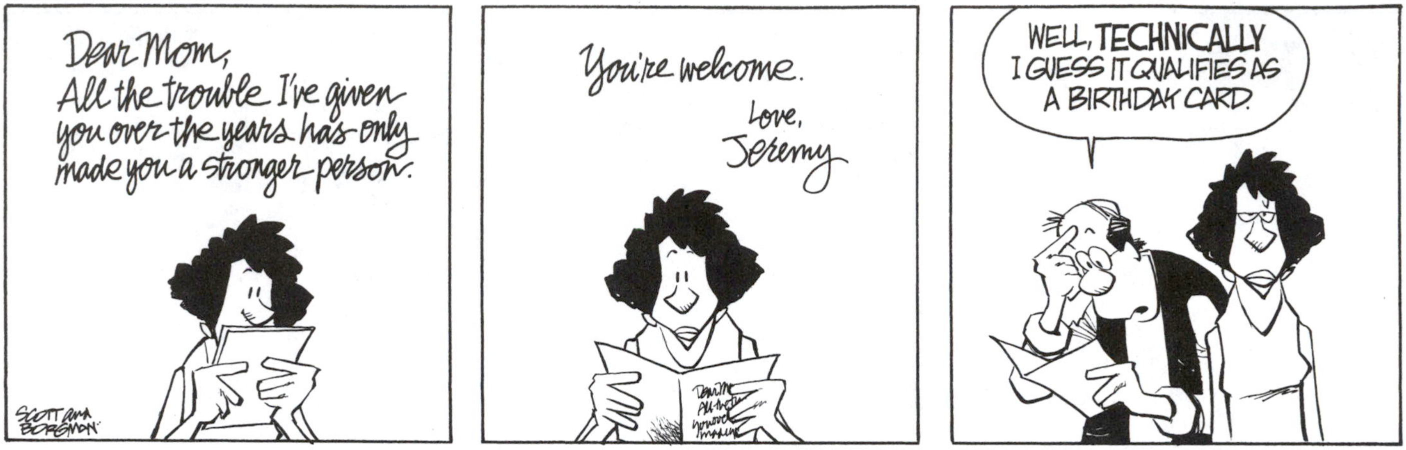
Dear Mom,
All the trouble I've given you over the years has only made you a stronger person.
SCOTT and BORGMAN
You're welcome.
Love,
Jeremy
WELL, TECHNICALLY I GUESS IT QUALIFIES AS A BIRTHDAY CARD.

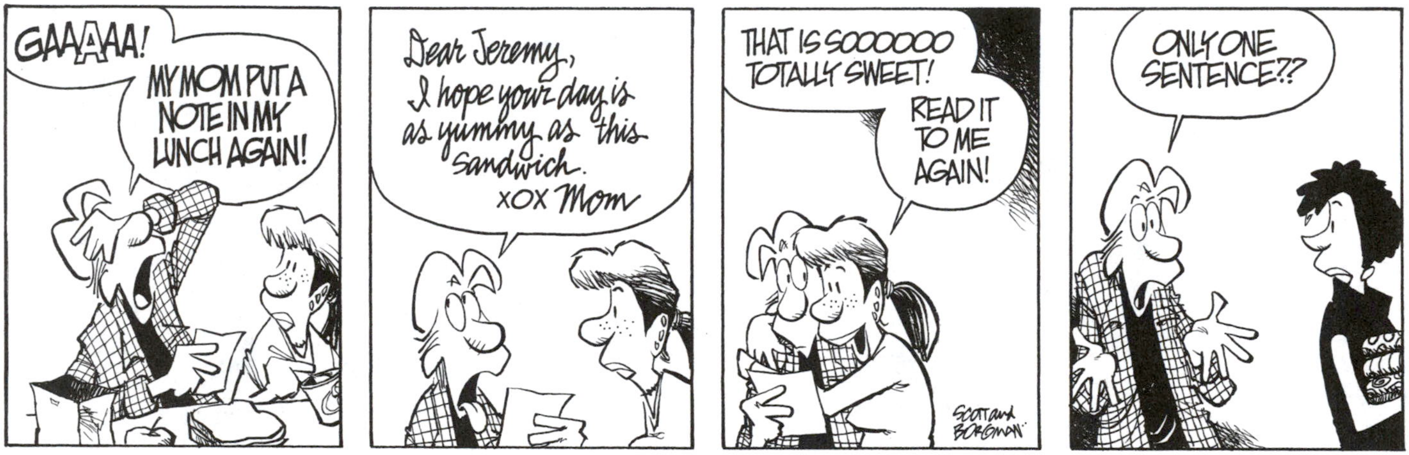
GAAAAA!
MY MOM PUT A NOTE IN MY LUNCH AGAIN!
Dear Jeremy,
I hope your day is as yummy as this sandwich.
xox Mom
THAT IS SOOOOOO TOTALLY SWEET!
READ IT TO ME AGAIN!
SCOTT and BORGMAN
ONLY ONE SENTENCE??

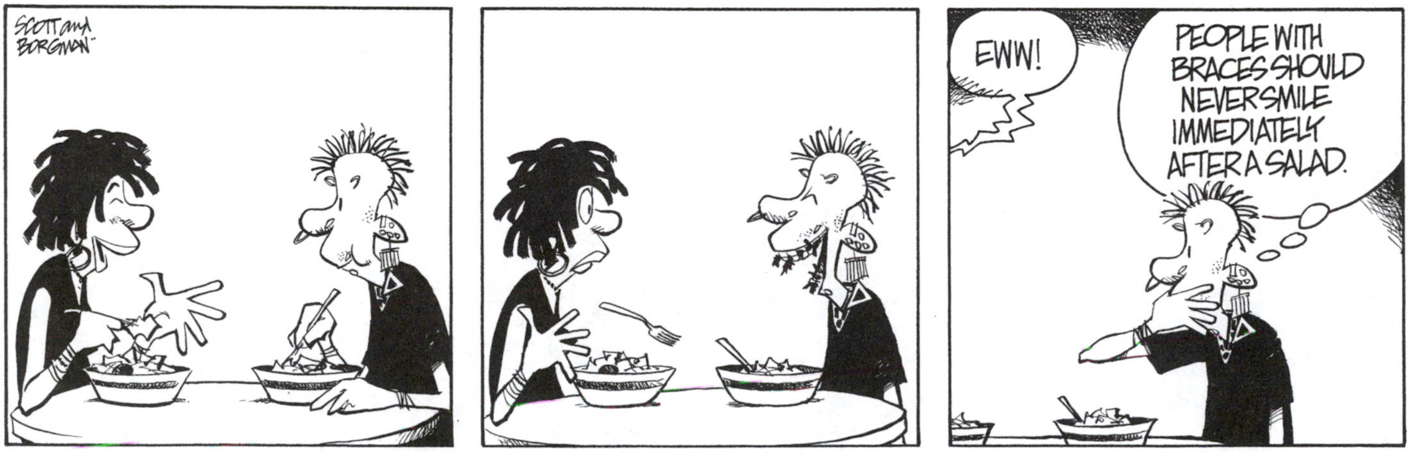
SCOTT and BORGMAN
EWW!
PEOPLE WITH BRACES SHOULD NEVER SMILE IMMEDIATELY AFTER A SALAD.

Zits
by
JERRY SCOTT and
JIM BORGMAN

6:00
6:12
6:29
6:43
6:57
I DID MY HAIR IN UNDER AN HOUR TODAY!
SOMETIMES WE ARE SO ALIKE, IT'S ALMOST SCARY.
SCOTT and BORGMAN

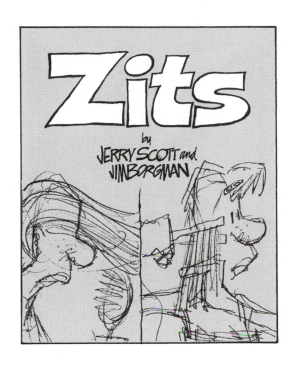